SILENT WITNESSES

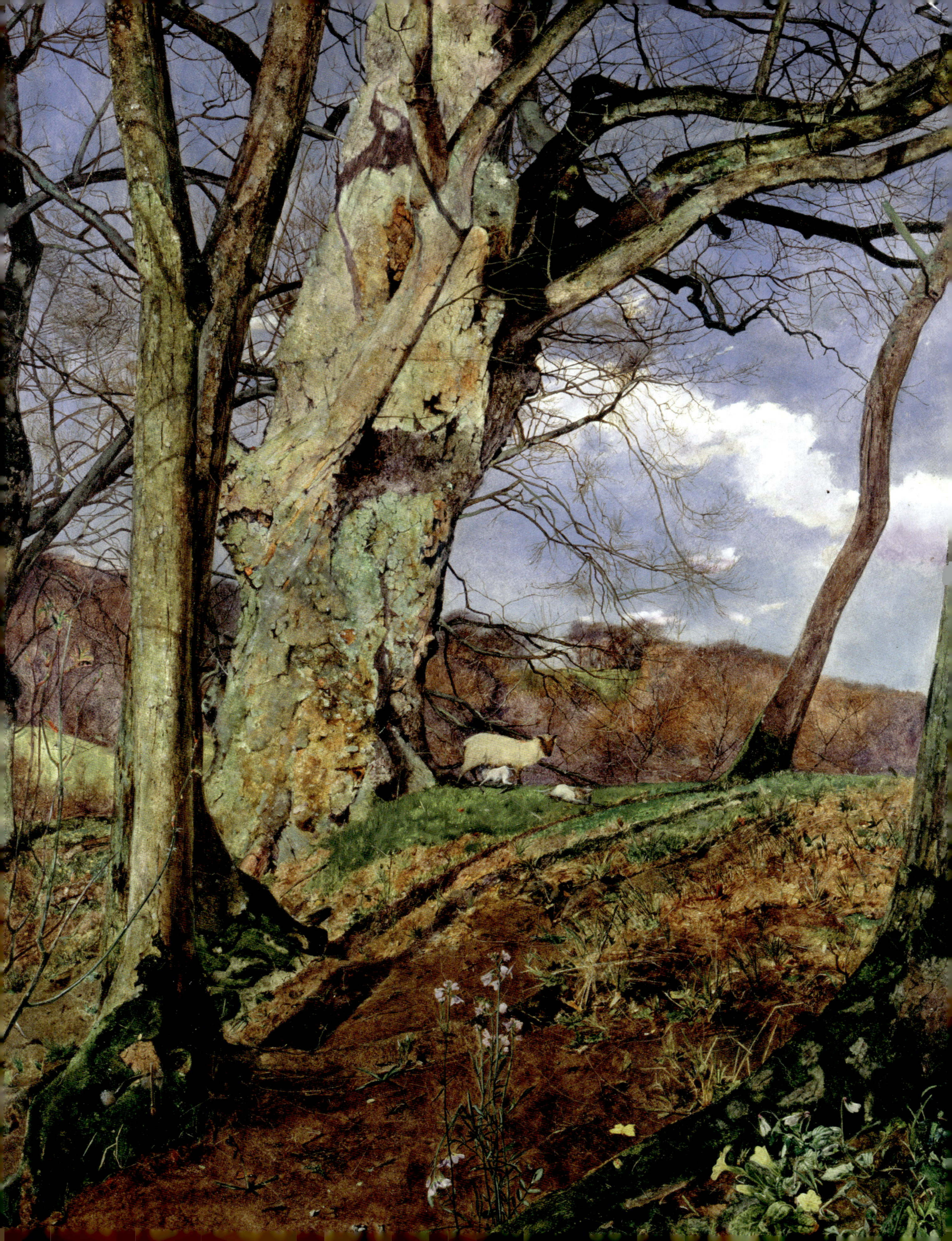

SILENT WITNESSES

Trees in British Art, 1760–1870

CHRISTIANA PAYNE

Sansom & Company

First published in 2017 by Sansom & Co
A publishing imprint of Redcliffe Press Ltd
81g Pembroke Road
Clifton
Bristol BS8 3EA

ISBN 978-1-911408-12-3

British Library Cataloguing in Publication Data
A catalogue record for this book is available
from the British Library.

Design and typesetting by Design Deluxe, Bath
Printed by Cambrian Press

Front cover: Samuel Palmer, *Pastoral with a Horse Chestnut Tree* (c.1830–1831). Watercolour, bodycolour and gum arabic, 33.4 x 26.8 cm. Image © Ashmolean Museum, University of Oxford (WA1929.37).

Frontispiece: John William Inchbold, *A Study, in March* (exhibited 1855) Oil on canvas, 53 x 35 cm. Image © Ashmolean Museum University of Oxford (WA1962.4.2)

Page 12: John Constable, *Study of trees made in the grounds of Charles Holford, Esq., at Hampstead* (c.1833). Graphite, 73.4 x 49.3 cm. Higgins Art Gallery and Museum, Bedford

Contents

Acknowledgements

Researching and writing this book has been one of the most interesting and pleasurable experiences of my life, and I have been well supported throughout. My colleagues at Oxford Brookes University have given generous financial help for illustrations and research trips, and well-timed sabbatical leave. The staff at the Yale Center for British Art were most welcoming when I went to see their paintings, watercolours and drawing manuals. I have also benefited greatly from the help and expertise of curators at the Ashmolean Museum and the Victoria and Albert Museum.

For advice, encouragement and various kinds of assistance, I am grateful to Abigail Armistead, Gary Browning, Francis Chester-Master, Colin Cruise, Elisabeth Fairman, Martin Groves, Carol Jacobi, Matt Larsen-Daw, Angela Lawson, Lavinia Lawson, Anne Lyles, Rupert Maas, Felicity Myrone, David Nash, Caroline Palmer, Victoria Partridge, Frances Rankine, Lisa Thornell, and Sarah Welcome. Many other people have helped along the way, and I hope that anyone I have omitted will see this as a failure of memory rather than of gratitude.

I am particularly grateful to Tom Wall, who took us on a fascinating walk through Payne Knight's Downton Vale, and to William Vaughan, who kindly read the manuscript and made invaluable suggestions for improvement. I also thank Beccy Speight, who has taken time out from a busy schedule to write a Foreword for the book.

My husband, Giles, has cheerfully driven me all over the country to look at woods and trees, and read through the entire text of the book three times. My daughter Charlotte has contributed many stimulating thoughts about trees and their place in the ecosystem, and even introduced me to a Druid.

John Sansom and Clara Hudson have been delightful to work with, as always, and I am grateful to Melinda Welch for designing such a beautiful book.

List of illustrations

Foreword

Beccy Speight, Chief Executive Officer, Woodland Trust

It is impossible to work in Grantham, Lincolnshire and avoid the A1 – or the Great North Road. And it is equally impossible (although not always the case in past decades) to now read the better known Romantic poets and avoid their 'odd' companion, John Clare. It may just be me, but as another articulated lorry thunders past, I always think I catch a glimpse out of the corner of my eye of a small, dusty but determined figure, trudging the verge, head down, heading north and home, always north and home. I was delighted to see mention of Clare's great poem *To a Fallen Elm* in this book. Surely his eventual madness was in part caused by the destruction of all he held dear in the countryside around his home in Northamptonshire – including the elm.

> Storms came and shook thee many a weary hour,
> Yet stedfast to thy home thy roots have been.[1]

Another place – Stourhead, the famous eighteenth-century landscape garden in Wiltshire. Working there at the turn of this century, it was not unusual for me to find the Head Gardener up a ladder in the house, peering with a magnifying glass at eighteenth and nineteenth-century paintings and engravings, trying to establish where trees should be shaped or replacements planted to hold true to the vision for the garden and its revelatory views, originally influenced by the paintings of Claude and Poussin amongst others. Painting with trees because of paintings, deriving visual and aesthetic spectacle in three dimensions – and then painting again the effect achieved.

The relationship between people and trees is multi-layered and whilst it has changed through time, its instinctive grounding has not. Inspired by the 800th anniversary of the 1217 Charter of the Forest, the Woodland Trust, the leading conservation charity for woods and trees, is leading a movement to set down how the modern-day relationship might be defined – and to explore its expression, particularly through the arts.

This book explores the relationship as expressed through fine art at a particularly fulsome time – when our relationship with trees was still very direct and immediate but also broadening. It is a fascinating exploration and having read it, you will see both our landscapes and paintings in a different and fuller way – 'the grass below – above the vaulted sky'.[2]

1 John Clare, *To a Fallen Elm*, c.1821.
2 John Clare, *I am*, c.1846.

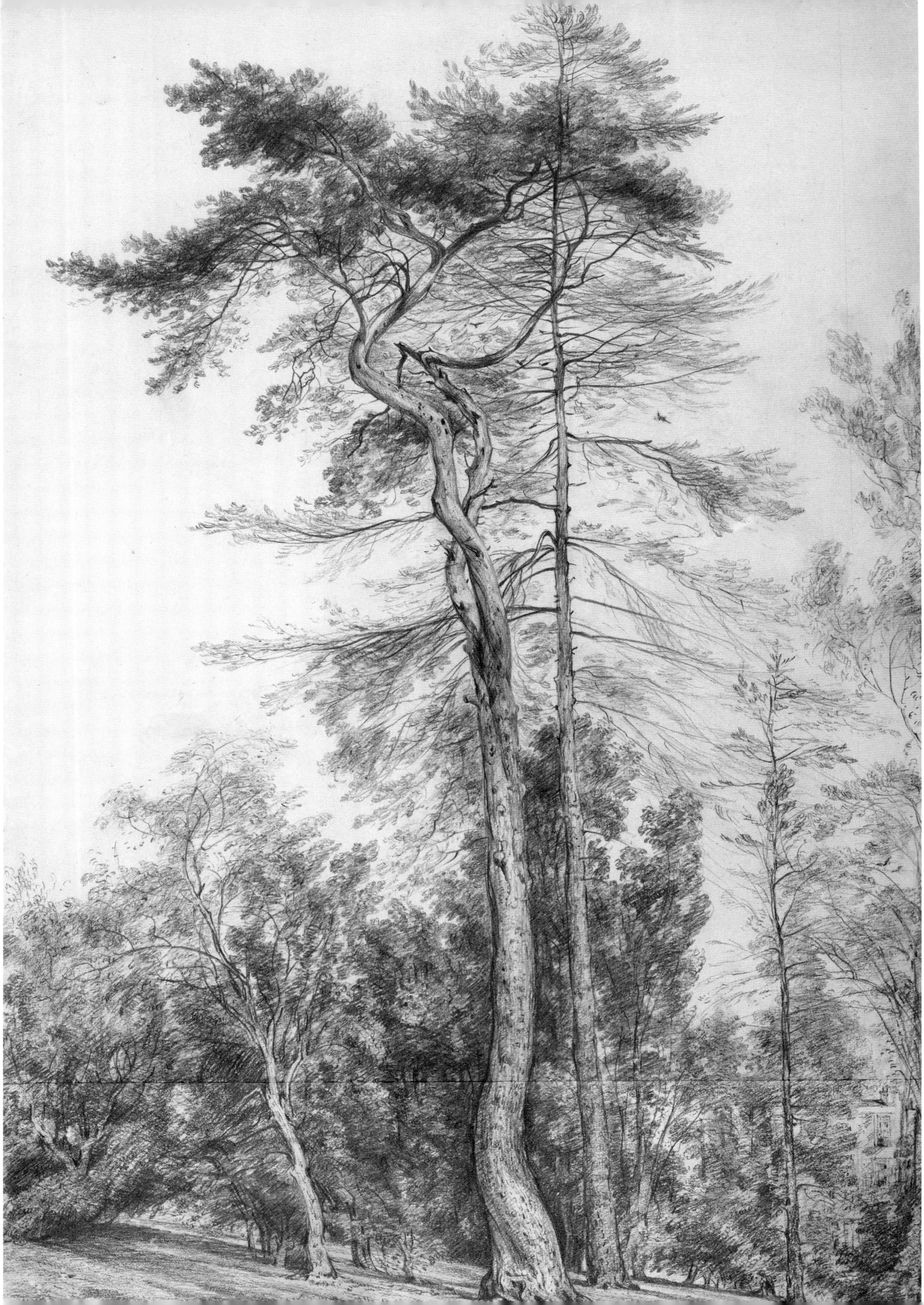

Introduction: Trees in Britain

> Among all the varied productions with which Nature has adorned the surface of the earth, none awakens our sympathies, or interests our imagination, so powerfully as those venerable trees which seem to have stood the lapse of ages, silent witnesses of the successive generations of men, to whose destiny they bear so touching a resemblance, alike in their budding, their prime, and their decay.
>
> (J. G. Strutt, *Sylva Britannica*, 1826)

Trees have been important in almost every culture in the world. They provide the practical advantages of food and shelter; they arouse wonder and delight. As huge living beings, with roots extending deep into the earth and branches seeming to touch the heavens, they have often been the focus for religious beliefs and cults. In many species their longevity far surpasses the length of a human life, or even the cumulative memory amassed over several generations. Hence they seem immortal: repositories of history.

A recent exhibition devoted to trees in German culture argued that the widespread forests were the reason why trees acquired such a significant role in painting, literature and music.[1] In Britain, the reverse seems to have been the case: Britons became attached to trees because they were relatively scarce. Britain has few native species, owing to the successive Ice Ages which cut the British Isles off from continental Europe. The usual estimate is of fewer than thirty broadleaved and five evergreens.[2] Shortages of timber caused concern from the sixteenth century onwards, and by the seventeenth century Britain was one of the least wooded countries in Europe, with woodland accounting for less than 5% of the land area.[3]

Yet Britain has more ancient trees, relative to its total woodland, than any other country in Europe, and individual trees have been much loved and protected. In the nineteenth century, 'portraits' of these trees treated them as if they were human subjects, and their 'character' and 'anatomy' were studied in a wide range of drawing manuals for amateur and professional artists. Many of Britain's most important landscape painters, including Paul Sandby, John Constable, Samuel Palmer, and Edward Lear, made themselves experts in the drawing and painting of trees.

The power of trees to amaze, delight and fascinate has been emphasized in several recent books and exhibitions. It was Roger Deakin's wonderful *Wildwood* that first led me to consider this area as a research topic. My understanding was deepened and expanded by *Under the Greenwood*, an exhibition at St Barbe Museum and Art Gallery, Lymington in 2013.[4] In the past year, Peter Wohlleben and Fiona Stafford have published inspiring books on trees, which have illuminated their social character, their role in English literature, and the strong bond that exists between human beings and these endlessly intriguing natural phenomena.[5]

This book covers a period of just over a century, when both the love of trees, and the inventiveness of British landscape painting, were at their height. The issues that preoccupied artists and writers then are still very relevant today. The world needs trees, both for aesthetic and practical reasons, and we particularly need them in this country. The Woodland Trust has been campaigning for more tree-planting and more access to woodlands in the United Kingdom since its foundation in 1972. In 2017 it launches the Charter for Trees, Woods and People, bringing together over seventy organisations to guide policy and practice. 2017 is, therefore, an opportune moment to reconsider the artistic response to the beauty and usefulness of the tree in Britain.

1 See the exhibition catalogue, *Unter Bäumen: Die Deutschen und der Wald* (Deutsche Historische Museum, 2012).

2 Paul A. Elliott, Charles Watkins and Stephen Daniels, *The British Arboretum: Trees, Science and Culture in the Nineteenth Century* (London: Pickering and Chatto, 2011), p. 11.

3 Ibid.

4 Roger Deakin, *Wildwood: A Journey through Trees* (London: Hamish Hamilton, 2007); Anne Anderson et al, *Under the Greenwood: Picturing the British Tree from Constable to Kurt Jackson* (Bristol: Sansom and Company, 2013).

5 Peter Wohlleben, *The Hidden Life of Trees: What they Feel, How they Communicate* (Vancouver: Greystone Books Ltd, 2016); Fiona Stafford, *The Long, Long Life of Trees* (New Haven and London: Yale University Press, 2016).

1 JOHN CONSTABLE

Flatford Mill

1816–17 | Oil on canvas | 101.6 x 127 cm

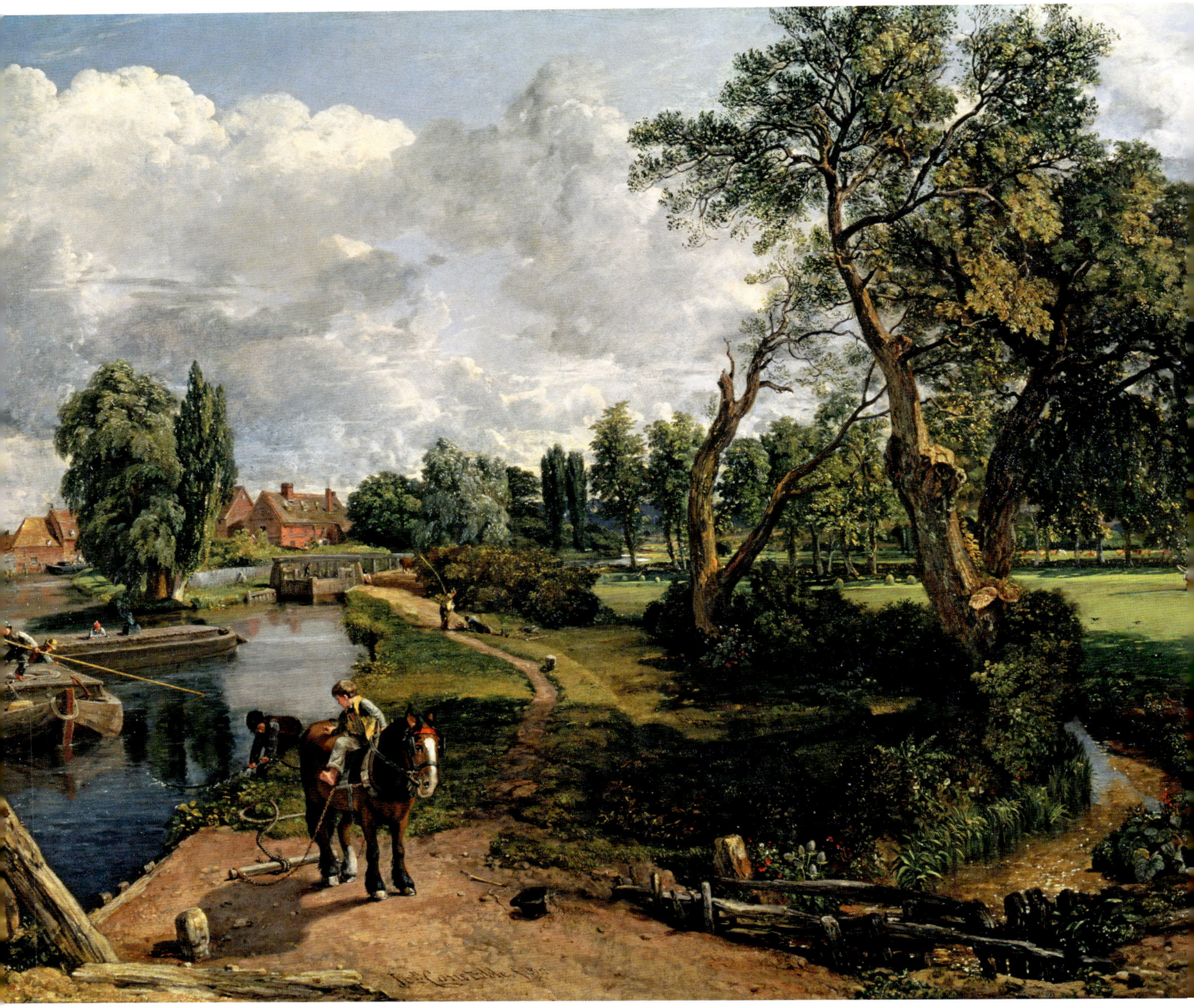

ONE

The Tree in the Landscape and in the Imagination: 1760-1870

JOHN CONSTABLE'S FAMOUS painting, *Flatford Mill* (fig. 1) is a powerful statement of his love of trees and his careful study of the different species: black poplars, elms and willows. The writers and artists discussed in this book were in no doubt about the importance of trees in the British landscape. Statesmen, naturalists and landscape gardeners also shared a passion for trees, which became particularly influential in the later decades of the eighteenth century. A new edition of John Evelyn's *Silva: or, a Discourse of Forest-Trees*, published in 1776, exhorted landowners to plant more trees in order to supply the navy. Fifteen years later, *Remarks on Forest Scenery*, by William Gilpin, encouraged artists and their patrons to find trees and woods picturesque.[1] Practical and aesthetic motives were combined in the appreciation of both native and exotic species.

Forests and woods were contested spaces, representing both authority and resistance from the earliest times. In Britain, 'forest' was an administrative term, referring to the areas where the monarchy, and some private individuals, retained hunting rights, and the forest law was in force: these included areas such as Exmoor, which actually had relatively few trees.[2] As Simon Schama has shown, the 'greenwood' was associated in Britain with freedom – the most famous of the royal forests was Sherwood Forest, the home of Robin Hood. Gilpin's *Forest Scenery* included a history of the New Forest, the royal forest founded by William I in about 1079. Gilpin complains about the trespassers who have built cottages in the Forest, and the indolent 'borderers' who steal deer and timber and become 'subtle, crafty, pilfering knaves.'[3] On the other hand, he admitted that these illegally-built cottages were sometimes 'the habitations of innocence, and industry; and the means of providing for a large family with ease, and comfort.'[4] In Gilpin's very influential writings, the forest had a dual character: the refuge of outlaws and gipsies on the one hand, a space for contemplation and aesthetic delight on the other.

In the nineteenth century, attempts to enclose the forests provoked controversy: putting up fences would protect the trees and increase the yields from timber, but such actions could lead to rural poverty and unrest, as people lost their homes and their livelihoods.[5] There were also disputes over fairs held in the forests, which were seen as magnets for lawlessness. Most of the royal forests contained ancient woodland, which was seen as rare and special even in the eighteenth and nineteenth centuries: Windsor and Epping Forests near London, or Wychwood Forest near Oxford, for example. Writers and artists were particularly inspired by the spectacle of the gnarled old oaks in Windsor Forest, on the edge of Windsor Great Park, which, even then, were many hundreds of years old. In the later nineteenth century key areas, such as Burnham Beeches to the west of London (fig. 2), were bought by city corporations to provide recreation for all. Artists found attractive subjects related to this general push for public access, from tumbledown cottages in the late eighteenth century to villagers collecting nuts or walking in the woods a hundred years later.

2 MYLES BIRKET FOSTER

Burnham Beeches

c.1861 | Watercolour with bodycolour | 21.0 x 33 cm

Location unknown. Photo courtesy of Bonhams

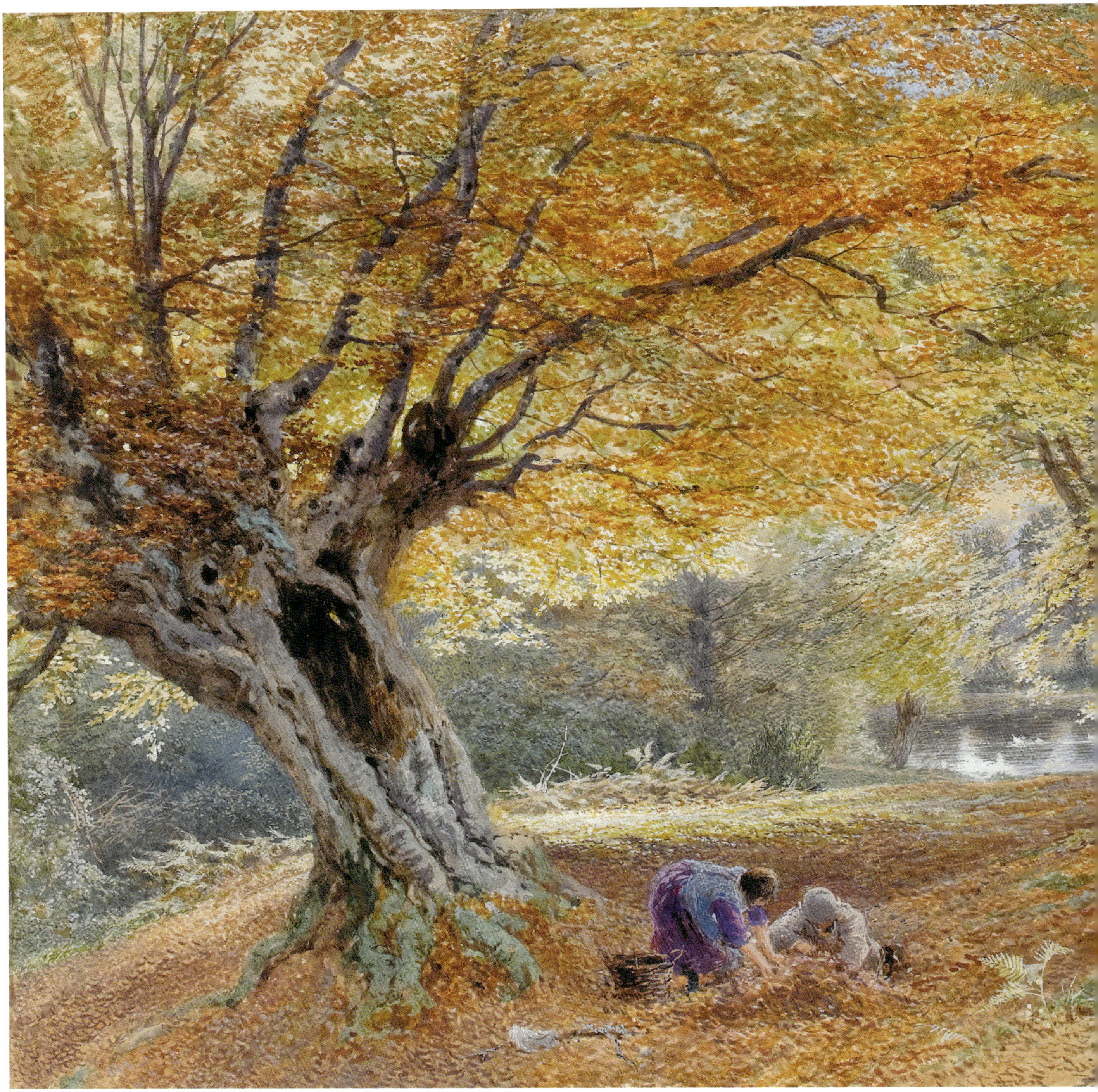

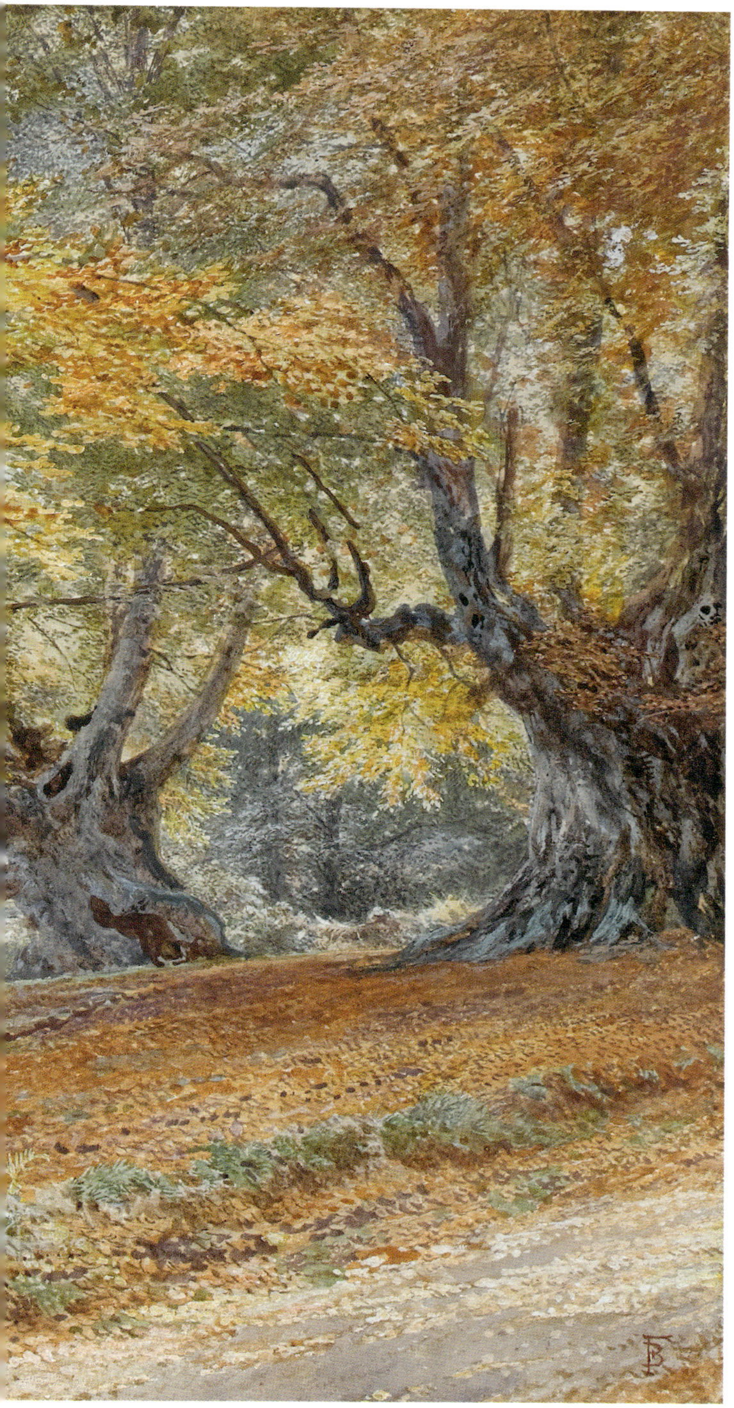

Outside the forests and woodlands, single trees, and small groups of trees, were striking features of the rural landscape. Trees in hedgerows, planted by farmers or self-seeded, provided shelter from the wind, to protect both arable land and grazing animals. According to Oliver Rackham, they were more plentiful in the mid-eighteenth century than before or since.[6] Often a village would have a large central tree, which became the focus for local patriotism and the continuation of semi-pagan customs. Typically, they would be adjacent to the village green and the village alehouse, a gathering point for open-air preaching or radical politics. One of the most famous examples is the sycamore tree at Tolpuddle in Dorset, under which the first trade union members met in 1834. Other ancient trees were boundary trees, which marked divisions between properties, parishes or counties, such as the Tortworth Chestnut in Gloucestershire (fig. 41) drawn by J. G. Strutt for his *Sylva Britannica* in 1824 and still standing today: it is recorded in the thirteenth century and may now be over a thousand years old.[7] Directly or indirectly, trees offered shelter and warmth. Trees on common land and waste would be available for the poor to use for firewood, while groups of trees next to farmhouses often indicated the availability of hospitality.[8] All these rural trees inspired great affection and offered plentiful subject matter for artists.

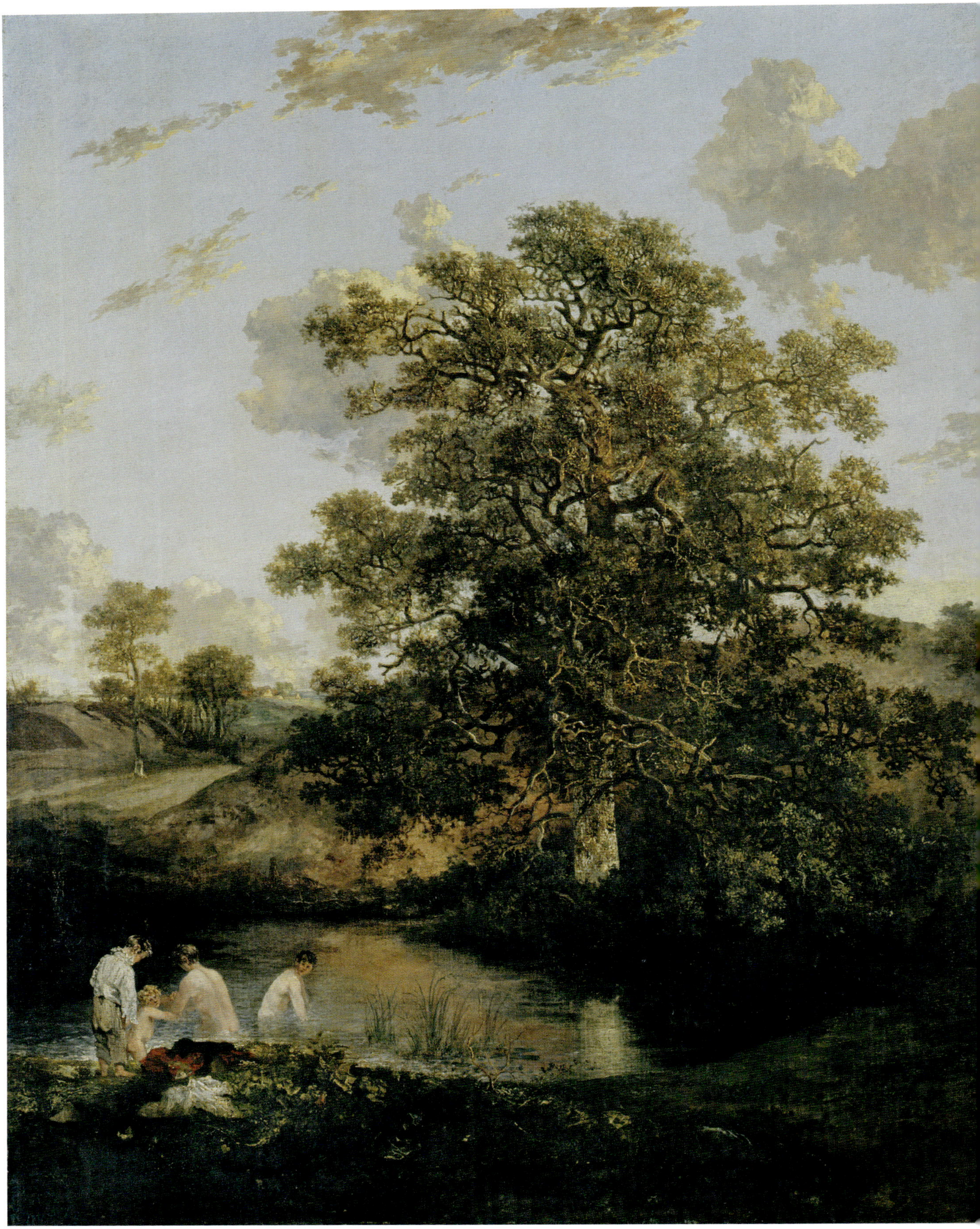

3 JOHN CROME
The Poringland Oak
c.1818–20 | Oil on canvas | 125.1 x 100.3 cm

More interesting to governments, however, were the many trees in the landscape on privately-owned land, planted for pleasure or profit, by large landowners, in timber plantations and landscaped parks and gardens. Two characteristics of Britain's historical development caused a big demand for timber: the substantial royal and merchant navies, which consisted until the later nineteenth century of wooden ships, and early industrialization. The slow-growing, dense timber of the oak (fig. 3), which conveniently grew in angular shapes or 'knee-timber', was the predominant wood used for warships. In 1796, William Marshall estimated that a 74-gun ship needed 2000 large well grown timber trees, of nearly 2 tons each, for its construction.[9] Most of these trees would be oaks. Elm was needed for keels, but only in the proportion of six or seven timber loads to every 100 loads of oak.[10] In 1812 the Commissioners of the Woods and Forests reported that 100,000 acres of trees would be sufficient to maintain the Royal Navy at its current size for ever, assuming that 1,000 acres would be felled each year and immediately replanted.[11] This calculation took into account the need for some of these oaks to grow for 100 years in order to produce the 'compass timber', that is, naturally curved pieces, that were used in the construction of a warship.

The problem was that the forests in the possession of the Crown were limited in extent – much more so than in other European countries. In 1812 they covered 115,000 acres, of which only 60 to 70 thousand acres were suitable for growing oak, which needs rich, well-drained soil. The total area of woodland in private hands in England, Scotland and Wales was calculated in 1887 to be just under 2½ million acres, so the Crown forests represented only a tiny proportion of the whole.[12] Instead, the state depended on private owners, aristocracy and landed gentry, to plant the trees that were needed, and it became a question of persuasion rather than government policy. Tree-planting was encouraged as a patriotic duty, and from 1757 to 1835 the Royal Society of Arts awarded prizes to those landowners who had planted the most trees. Between 1760 and 1835, private landowners are thought to have planted some 50 million timber trees, and some of the projects were huge, the biggest being Thomas Johnes's planting of almost five million trees, over thirty years, between 1786 and 1816, at Hafod, north Cardiganshire.[13] In contrast, landowners who cut down trees before they matured were stigmatized, especially in poetry, as spendthrifts, corrupt politicians, or money-grubbers.[14]

Industrialization also threatened the woodlands. John Evelyn's *Silva*, first published in 1664 to encourage tree-planting after the depredations of the English Civil War, was mainly focused on the needs of the navy, but he also noted that the multiplication of glass-works and iron-furnaces had diminished the supply of timber. He suggested that they should be moved to America, rather than depleting the woods at home.[15] By the late eighteenth century, timber was in great demand for charcoal (used in smelting iron), and for pit props in the coal mines, as well as for house-building and for all kinds of domestic uses in the rapidly expanding towns and cities, including fuel for cooking and heating. The use of oak bark for tanning leather was another major source of demand. This industry reached a peak in 1810, when it is estimated that it would have involved the annual felling of at least 500,000 tons of oak timber in a year, more than the number of oak trees consumed by the royal and merchant navies put together.[16] As a result of the high demand for wood, the price of trees rose sharply in the late eighteenth and early nineteenth centuries. In the late 1820s, oak trees sold for 2½ times their price, in real terms, in 1690. This cannot be attributed solely to ship-building or tanning, since the price of ash trees rose even faster in the same period.[17] Thus, trees acquired unprecedented cultural importance precisely at a time when their monetary value was also reaching a peak.

Evelyn's *Silva* was a major landmark in the history of British arboriculture. It is quoted by every subsequent writer on trees, and became even more widely known in a lavish edition with copious notes by the agriculturalist Dr Alexander Hunter and beautiful illustrations of leaves,

4 G. R. LEWIS

'The Cedar of Lebanon, full-grown tree at Syon'

Plate LXXXVI.A, p. 349, from J. C. Loudon, *Arboretum et Fructitem Britannicum, or, the Trees and Shrubs of Britain* (London: Longman, Orme, Brown, Green, and Longmans, 1838). 38.795 (v.8).

The Bodleian Libraries, The University of Oxford

flowers and fruit, published in 1776. Evelyn's express aim was to remedy the defect of the weakening of Britain's 'wooden walls'. In his conclusion, he wrote:

> ... our forests are undoubtedly the greatest magazines of the wealth and glory of this nation, and our Oaks the truest oracles of its perpetuity and happiness, as being the only support of that navigation which makes us feared abroad, and flourish at home.

Hunter endorsed these words and said they should 'constitute part of the Political Catechism of all Statesmen.'[18] In his Preface, Hunter points out that many of the oaks that were planted after the first publication of the work were used to construct the ships which took part in the Seven Years' War (1756-63):

> Soon after the publication of the Silva ... the Spirit for Planting increased to a high degree; and there is reason to believe that many of our Ships which, in the last war, gave laws to the whole world, were constructed from Oaks planted at that time. The present age must reflect upon this with gratitude; and it is to be hoped that we shall be ambitious to receive from posterity the same acknowledgments that we, at this moment, pay to the memory of our virtuous ancestors.[19]

Ironically, by the time the oaks stimulated by this edition grew big enough to be used by the naval dockyards, the navy was constructing ironclads. Nonetheless, the rhetoric of the 'wooden walls' lasted until the mid-nineteenth century at least, and continued to affect popular perceptions of oak trees.

Ships were needed for trade, exploration and the administration of the growing British empire, as well as for defence. Travellers brought back specimens of trees hitherto unknown in Britain – and because of the temperate climate, many could be planted out of doors. Collections of exotic trees, such as the important royal collection at Kew, grew rapidly in the later eighteenth century. In 1838, John Claudius Loudon published his eight-volume *Arboretum et Fructitem Britannicum* (fig. 4), 'in the hope of diffusing more generally, among gentlemen of landed property, a taste for introducing a greater variety of trees and shrubs in their plantations and pleasure-grounds.'[20] Hunter's edition of 1776 had already updated Evelyn's *Silva* with the addition of new varieties, but by 1838 the need was still more pressing. Loudon estimated that 89 new varieties of trees and shrubs had come into Britain in the sixteenth century, 131 in the seventeenth century, 445 in the eighteenth century, and 699 in the first 30 years of the nineteenth century.[21] This flood of new trees was doubly exciting because the number of native British trees was so small. There are, for example, only two indigenous varieties of oak in Britain, the English oak (*quercus robur*) and the Sessile oak (*quercus petraea*), but Hunter lists eighteen, including six from North America. Loudon describes 45 main types of oak, with many of these subdivided into different varieties, and adds several lists of oaks 'not yet introduced' from countries all around the world, including Asia Minor, China, Mexico and Africa.[22] The arrival of new varieties coincided with, and stimulated, an intense interest in classification and in natural history generally. Loudon was much more concerned than either Evelyn or Hunter had been with the beauty of trees, rather than with their utility, and he went to great lengths to obtain full-length portraits of individual specimens for his illustrations. He commissioned hundreds of these portraits: the *Arboretum Britannicum* was the first arboricultural publication to show entire trees, not just foliage, flowers and fruit. The portraits were of two types: the tree after ten to twelve years of growth, and when fully grown.

The shift, evident in Loudon's book, towards a more purely aesthetic appreciation of trees coincided with the fashion for landscape gardening, which had been gathering pace since the mid-eighteenth century. The formal style of the seventeenth century, with its straight lines and avenues, gave way to more 'natural' designs in the hands of William Kent, Lancelot 'Capability' Brown, and Humphrey Repton. Clumps and belts of trees served to frame vistas

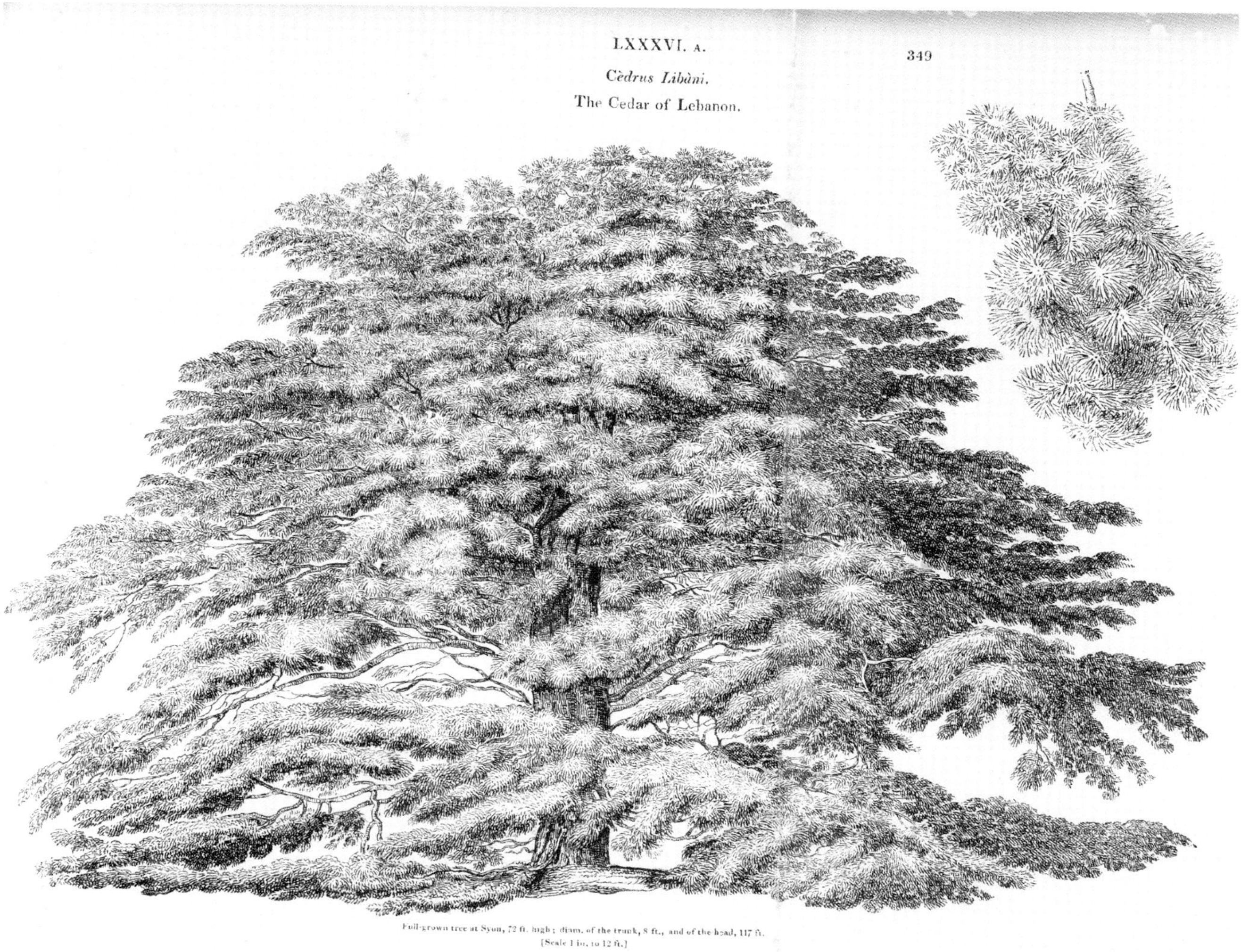

that were like the ideal landscapes of the seventeenth-century painter Claude Lorrain, and to obscure the relationship between an estate and its boundaries. In 1810, Uvedale Price emphasized the importance of trees in landscape gardening or 'improvement':

> It is in the arrangement and management of trees that the great art of improvement consists … In beauty, they not only far excel every thing of inanimate nature, but their beauty is complete and perfect in itself; while that of almost every other object requires their assistance.[23]

Price expressed his distaste for clumps and belts, a preference which brought him into a dispute with Humphrey Repton.[24] In general, he thought trees should be disposed in as natural a way as possible, to produce effects of intricacy and variety. However, like many authors, he had a lingering fondness for the avenue, a relic of a more formal taste, for its associations with Gothic churches and meditation:

> The avenue has a most striking effect … no other figure can give that image of a grand gothic aisle with its natural columns and vaulted roofs … The broad solemn shade adds a twilight calm to the whole, and makes it above all other places, more suited to meditation. To that also its straitness contributes; for when the mind is disposed to turn inwardly on itself, any serpentine line would distract the attention.[25]

By this time, straight avenues were unfashionable, and unlikely to be included in any new landscaping scheme. They came to be associated, then, with the well-established gentry and nobility rather than the nouveaux riches – as did old trees.

5 J. G. STRUTT

'The Great Oak at Fredville' (Majesty)

from J. G. Strutt, *Sylva Britannica; or, Portraits of Forest Trees, distinguished for their antiquity, magnitude, or beauty. Drawn from nature and etched by Jacob George Strutt*, (London: J. G. Strutt and Colnaghi and Co, 1822). 19182 a.6.

The Bodleian Libraries, The University of Oxford

Landscape gardens often incorporated old deer parks or monastic sites, and this meant that they had ancient trees in them, some standing alone so that they could reach the fullest possible development in their circumference and height. These became a focus of particular scrutiny in the late eighteenth century as part of a general interest in British antiquities. Ancient trees were associated with old families and also with paternalism and benevolence; those who cut them down were seen as vandals and upstarts. Strutt's *Sylva Britannica* consists of portraits of trees 'distinguished for their antiquity, magnitude, or beauty', with a commentary that evokes the historical associations of each tree, 'silent witnesses of the successive generations of men.'[26] Most of his examples are in gentlemen's parks, such as the three oaks known as Majesty (fig. 5), Stately and Beauty, in front of the family mansion of John Plumptre, Esq., Fredville in Nonnington, Kent.[27] Strutt expresses a hope that, as 'they are still likely to stand for many centuries' they will 'as long continue to delight the descendants of the family by whom they are at present so highly valued, and so carefully preserved.'[28] Strutt's was only one of many publications which celebrated these ancient trees. Loudon's decision to include portraits of young trees in his *Arboretum Britannicum* sprang from more radical political views. He provocatively stated that, if he had just one tree in his garden, it would be a young rather than an old one:

> With the latter tree the mind is carried back to times which, though interesting in some respects, it is desirable should never recur; with the former, it is carried forward along with all the improvements which are now contemplated, or in progress, in civilized society throughout the world.[29]

The cult of the ancient tree was associated with nostalgia, that of the young tree with social and political reform: Loudon produced an abridged edition of his book and hoped that the interest in trees would spread to all social classes. He was also internationalist in outlook, believing that the newly-introduced species should be disseminated through all the other countries of the world.[30]

However, Loudon was battling against the influential discourse of the Picturesque, generated by landscape gardening and tourism, in which ancient trees played a major role. William Gilpin and Uvedale Price, the two most influential authors of the movement, both had much to say about trees. Gilpin begins his *Forest Scenery* (1791) with the bold statement: 'It is no exaggerated praise to call a tree the *grandest*, and most *beautiful* of all the productions of the earth.'[31] His observations of the beauties of trees are extraordinarily perceptive and detailed, and include the forms of dead and dying trees, the variety of mosses on their trunks, and the roots that are visible above the ground.[32] He finds the felling of timber beautiful, as well as the timber-wain, 'an object of the most picturesque kind, especially when drawn by oxen.'[33] Both these subjects were taken up by artists, including Paul Sandby and John Linnell. Gilpin's book works systematically through the varieties of tree from the oak to the hawthorn, assessing each one for its picturesqueness. This is followed by what might be termed biographies of individual trees, the 'celebrated characters' who have 'distinguished themselves in the world.'[34] Price describes autumn as the painter's season, because of the varieties of colour to be found in the trees.[35] Both Price and Gilpin helped to foster the aesthetic appreciation of trees, the attention to the particular characteristics of each species, and the taste for woodland activities and habitations in art.

In this period in Britain, there was a particular tendency to see the tree as an individual, analogous to a human being. Rebecca Hey's popular book, *The Spirit of the Woods* (1837) regards trees as the most companionable of inanimate objects, which make music as they rustle in the wind, adapting their tones to the mood of the listener.[36] For her they are 'instinct with human feeling': the wintry music of the Scots pine is conducive to meditation, the alder stooping over a stream is an emblem of friendship, shading the stream in return for its nourishment.[37] Many quotations from the poets, and her own poems, reinforce these associations. William Cowper, William Wordsworth and

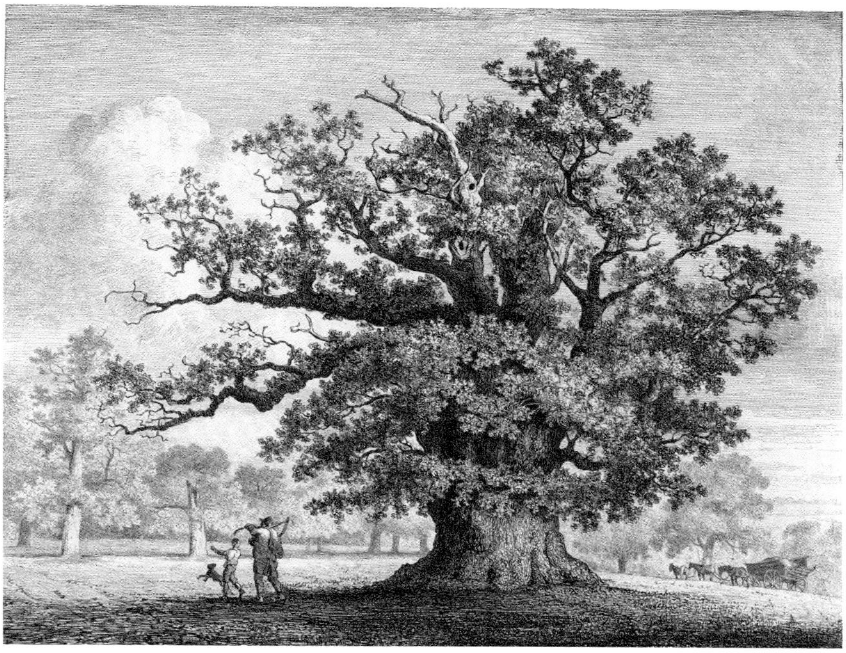

John Clare were all wounded by the destruction of particular trees, as if they had been old friends: Cowper's famous poem *The Yardley Oak* (c.1791), Wordsworth's *Yew-trees* (begun 1803-4, completed 1814) and Clare's *To a Fallen Elm* (c.1821) all address trees as if they were human beings. Artists had similar feelings. The best-known example of this is John Constable's description of an ash tree, a 'young lady' that had been 'disgraced' by having a signboard nailed to its trunk (fig. 51).[38] His biographer and friend, C. R. Leslie, said of Constable 'I have seen him admire a fine tree with an ecstasy of delight, like that with which he would catch up a beautiful child in his arms.'[39] In 1860 John Ruskin described the tree as a 'strange intermediate being', deserving of 'boundless affection and admiration' and even 'capable of a kind of sorrow.' In notes made for *Modern Painters*, he expressed the opinion that 'a good painter never introduces a passionless tree.'[40]

The attachment of writers and artists to trees echoes the reverence still paid to them in popular customs of pagan origin, which persisted in the eighteenth and nineteenth centuries despite attempts to stamp them out. Wordsworth was not alone in feeling, as he put it in his poem *Nutting*, that 'There is a spirit in the woods.'[41] May branches were brought inside to mark the onset of spring, and mistletoe and holly came indoors for Christmas, as they had done in midwinter long before the Christian era, to mark the winter solstice. Oak apple day was widely celebrated on the 29th of May, officially a day of thanksgiving for the restoration of the monarchy (because Charles II took refuge in an oak tree), but also a survival of a feast to mark the end of the birds-nesting season. In 1815 John Aikin deplored 'the mischief annually done to this noble tree (the oak) by the custom of cutting large branches for the celebration of the 29th of May.'[42] Writers repeatedly reminded their readers of the Druidic veneration for trees, and openly spoke of groves as 'temples'. Cowper's attitude to the ancient Yardley Oak was a particularly strong expression of a common sentiment:

> … Could a mind imbued
> With truth from heav'n created thing adore,
> I might with rev'rence kneel and worship Thee.
> It seems Idolatry with some excuse …[43]

A more secular kind of reverence is evident in Strutt's description of the Crawley Elm, an old tree which stood in the middle of the village, on the high road from London to Brighton, providing 'an inexhaustible source of pleasure to the train of village children who cluster like bees around it.' An old tree inspires veneration, he says, comparable to the feelings we have towards a monarch or a minister of religion (if in the dark recesses of a wood), or (in a hamlet or on a village green) towards a parent or an old friend. 'It would be impossible to see such a noble tree as the Crawley Elm felled without regret; – its aged head brought prostrate to the ground, its still green branches despoiled in the dust, its spreading roots left bare and desolate.'[44]

6 JOHN CONSTABLE
Salisbury Cathedral from the Bishop's Grounds
Oil on canvas | 87.6 x 111.8 cm
© Victoria and Albert Museum, London

Many writers dwell on the Christian symbolism of trees. Trees were a favourite analogy in religious writings, for example in those of the poet Samuel Taylor Coleridge and the churchman John Henry Newman.[45] It is hardly surprising that these ideas also affected art and literature. For Ruskin, a tree was 'a spire built downwards from the heaven' and the 'great forest aisle' was the best model for a cathedral.[46] The revival of Gothic architecture, thought to be derived from the observation of tree-growth, fostered an aesthetic appreciation of woods and forests, and the analogy between trees and Gothic arches is made explicit in Constable's painting, *Salisbury Cathedral from the Bishop's Grounds* of 1823 (fig. 6). William Gilpin, whose book contains relatively little evidence of his profession as a clergyman, nevertheless indicates, in a long footnote, the deeper meanings underlying his celebration of trees: the tree, he says, is like a community, presenting emblems of mortality, malady, famine, and depopulation. 'Nature is the great book of God.' The heathen moralist could only see that men, like trees, are subject to death. But Gilpin has a more positive message: 'Better instructed, learn thou a nobler lesson. Learn, that that God, who with the blast of winter shrivels the tree, and with the breezes of spring restores it, offers it to thee as an emblem of thy hopes … that power, which revives the tree, will revive thee also, like it, with increasing perfection.'[47] In contrast to Gilpin, Rebecca Hey weaves her insistence on Christian analogies throughout her book. For her, an ash grove in autumn (ash being one of the first trees to lose its leaves) is a welcome reminder that life is brief and uncertain, the aspen trembles because it provided the wood for Christ's cross, and cherry blossom is a foretaste of paradise.[48]

Christian symbolism and the older tradition of Platonic philosophy were combined in Samuel Palmer's account of the role played by a tree in a crucial childhood experience. When less than four years old, he claimed, he was watching with his nurse 'the shadows on the wall from branches of elm behind which the moon had risen.' As he said in later life, 'I never forgot those shadows, and am often trying to paint them.'[49] William Vaughan has shown how this account refers both to a consciousness of human mortality and to a sense of transcendence, of the unseen world lying behind natural appearances.[50] It is significant that it was a tree that produced the shadows: Palmer's Shoreham works, particularly his Indian ink drawings, often make use of dark tree silhouettes to invoke a magical and mysterious atmosphere.

Trees also offered plentiful political analogies. In an influential essay, Stephen Daniels has shown how woodland imagery was used, in the period between 1770 and 1830, to symbolize and naturalize conflicting political viewpoints.[51] Edmund Burke's comparison of the British aristocracy to oaks is well known. In his *Reflections on the Revolution in France* (1790) the British political system is presented as similar to mature parkland, in comparison to the levelling landscape of France. Young trees, on the other hand, were appropriated by radical thinkers as 'Liberty Trees', looking to an egalitarian future. Loudon's preference for young trees in his *British Arboretum* clearly stems from this progressive approach, while in Strutt's book, the interest in ancient trees is accompanied by a conservative political outlook, one that celebrates estates which remain in the same family for many generations. Trees could be used to suggest that paternalism and colonization were 'natural,' offering benefits to both sides, rich and poor, colonizer and colonized, alike. The elm, for example, is, according to Strutt, like a country gentleman: 'Loving society, yet averse from a crowd, delighting in fresh air, and room to expand its roots, and affording its aid to all the weaker plants in its vicinity that may seek its support.'[52] A colonial analogy was provided by the Moor Park lime tree, which has nineteen branches striking out at horizontal level, and bearing in their turn three or four upright limbs, like so many young trees, 'reminding the beholder of prosperous colonies, at once supported by, and adding to, the importance of their mother country.'[53]

Ruskin's writings also use trees as 'natural' arguments for a basically conservative political outlook. In one of his earliest publications, in 1837, he declares that woody

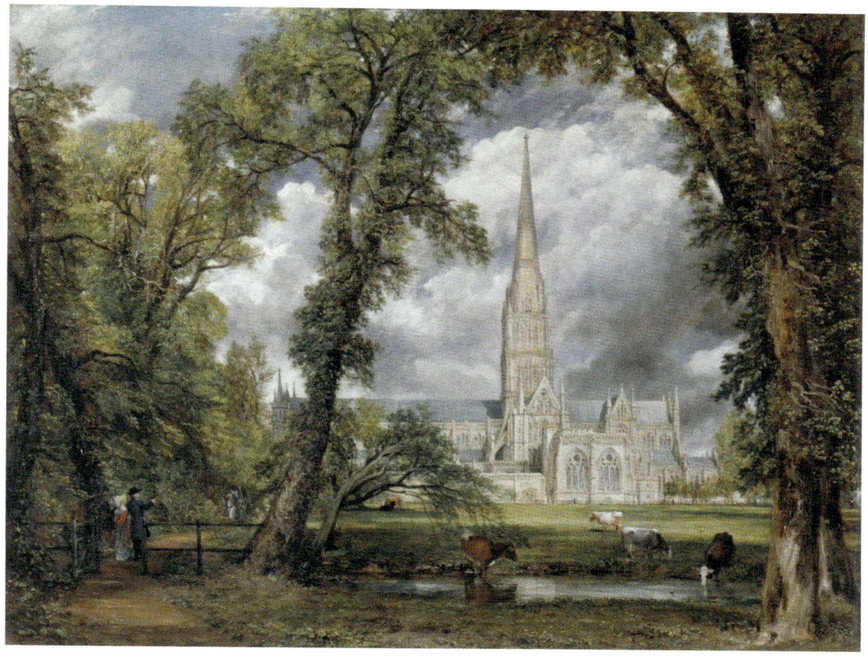

country inspires reverence for antiquity: 'The man who could remain a radical in a wood country is a disgrace to his species.'[54] He elaborates on this idea in *Modern Painters* Volume 5 (1860), where he writes that 'the power of every great people, as of every living tree, depends on it not effacing, but confirming and concluding, the labours of its ancestors.' The tree provides the model of a community in which each individual is like a single leaf, accepting its place in the whole, and in which a little family can grow into a great nation, which sends out branch colonies 'which enforce forms of law and life entirely different from those of the parent state.'[55] Ruskin's writings on trees are often seen as the cornerstone of modern environmentalism, with their consciousness of the interdependence of man and the natural world, but they have their origins in Burke's concept of an organic political system, which develops slowly, like the oak, over centuries, rather than being established anew on rational principles.

An awareness of empire played its part in the development of arboretums, which combined native with foreign trees in systems of planting which were at once aesthetic and botanical in motivation. From the late eighteenth century, it became fashionable to include an arboretum in the newly laid out grounds and garden around a private house. Humphrey Repton, for example, included an arboretum in his Red Book for Woburn in 1804. Arboretums were also established by botanical societies, becoming the foundations of public parks in the later nineteenth century. In the arboretum, it made sense to include many of the new varieties that had come in to Britain in the late eighteenth and early nineteenth centuries. Indeed, Loudon argued that it was a requirement of good taste that these foreign varieties, or at least improved versions of the native trees, should be included.[56] Loudon hoped that artists would learn to draw the new varieties of trees: 'as foreign trees become better known by the public generally, it will be necessary for artists to keep their art on a level with the state of knowledge of the times in which they live.'[57] However, the popular attachment to native trees, and the artists' preference for 'natural' and typically English rural landscapes, worked in the opposite direction. Artists continued to study the well-established round of oak, ash, elm and beech, generally taking an interest in foreign trees only when they wanted to depict foreign landscapes.

Between the undoubted natives such as the oak, ash, beech and elm, and the spectacular exotics such as the cedar of Lebanon and the banyan, there is a large number of trees which most people would accept as 'English' or 'British', yet they are not native to the British Isles. The horse chestnut, for example, is such a common feature of the landscape now that few would see it as exotic, yet it came into the country in the seventeenth century. Constable's painting of *Flatford Mill* (fig. 1), widely accepted as a quintessentially English landscape, depends for some of its most naturalistic effects on the contrasting shapes and colours of the native willow and the Lombardy poplar, first introduced in 1758.

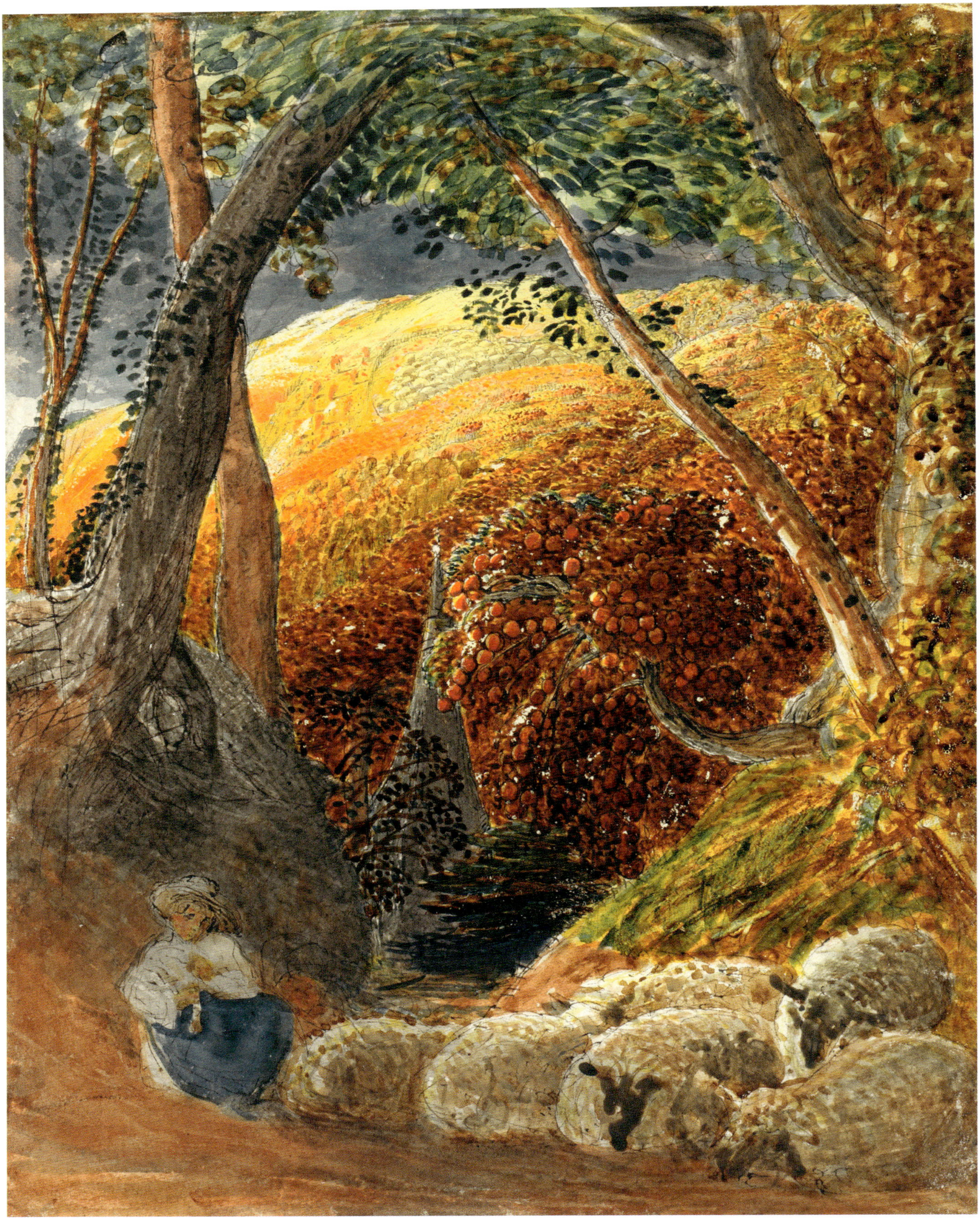

7 SAMUEL PALMER
The Magic Apple Tree
1830 | Pen, Indian ink and watercolour | 34.9 x 27.3 cm

Samuel Palmer's *Magic Apple Tree* (fig. 7), another icon of British landscape painting, also shows a tree that is technically foreign: the various varieties of orchard apples come from central Asia, and only the wild crab apple is a native. The weeping willow and the Spanish chestnut are two further trees that are not now regarded as exotic, though they have been fairly recent imports.

THE NATIVE TREES

Eighteenth- and nineteenth-century books on trees, whether on aesthetic theory or on arboriculture, invariably begin with the same four varieties, the native timber trees or forest trees: oak, elm, ash and beech.[58] These are (or, in the case of elm, were) common trees, all widespread in southern England, which can grow to a great size and are a source of useful wood. Artists' drawing manuals also start with these trees, carefully distinguishing the 'touch' that is appropriate for each one. The books then move on to other native varieties such as the willow, silver birch, black poplar, lime, Scots pine, yew, various kinds of fruit tree, and the naturalized imports, weeping willow, sweet chestnut and horse chestnut. For artists who travelled and painted foreign scenery, the olive, stone pine, and cypress were seen as characteristic of the Mediterranean, the palm and cedar of Lebanon and the Middle East, the banyan of India. Edward Lear, trying to choose between 'two extremes of affection for nature … English or Southern' instinctively thought first of the trees and associated vegetation: 'the former, oak, ash and beech … the latter olive – vine – flowers …'[59]

The oak begins Lear's list, as it does that of every other writer on trees. The oak was (and is) common throughout Britain, being seen both in woodland and in landscaped parks. It was regarded by Gilpin as the most picturesque tree, and the one that was most useful to the artist in forming a composition.[60] He gives a remarkably detailed description of the variety of colours of bark and mosses found on an oak tree – green velvet, brimstone, olive, white, dark brown, yellow and red.[61] Other writers comment on the variety of colour in the foliage of oak, especially at midsummer, when the new growth of the 'Midsummer shoot' provides a contrast with the darker foliage behind it.[62] The crooked and twisting growth pattern of the oak also provided a major attraction for artists. Oaks lived to a great age: in Strutt's collection of ancient trees for his *Sylva Britannica*, 21 out of 40 were oaks. The classic statement of the lengthy life-cycle of oak occurs in a poem by John Dryden, which is repeatedly quoted by subsequent writers:

> The monarch oak, the patriarch of trees
> Shoots, rises up, and spreads by slow degrees
> Three centuries he grows, and three he stays
> Supreme in state, and three more decays.[63]

As they age, oak trees acquire broad, irregular trunks with rounded projections. It is not surprising, then, that they were often compared to ageing men: writers use words like 'girth' and 'sinews' to describe their appearance. For Loudon, the oak was 'the most majestic of forest trees … the emblem of grandeur, strength and duration … the king of forest trees.'[64]

In addition to its aesthetic appeal, the oak was deeply symbolic. Charles II had hidden in an oak – hence the appropriation of oak apple day as a monarchist festival. More widely, the oak was celebrated as the source of the 'wooden walls' of the navy, and of ancient families. As Rebecca Hey claims, 'What the palm is to the tribes of the desert, and the banian to the inhabitants of the East, such is the oak to Britons. It is our citadel, the basis of our strength.'[65] She quotes William Shenstone, who saw oaks as symbols of the national (manly) character: 'As a brave man is not suddenly either elated by prosperity, or depressed by adversity, so the oak displays not its verdure on the sun's first approach, nor drops it on his first departure.'[66] Oaks were utilized by artists to provide a backdrop to portraits of owners of landed estates, like Gainsborough's *Mr and Mrs Andrews* (1748, National Gallery); but they could also be objects of portraiture themselves. John Crome's *Poringland Oak* (fig. 3) shows boys enjoying

8 JOHN CONSTABLE

Study of the Trunk of an Elm Tree

c.1821 | Oil on paper | 30.6 x 24.8 cm

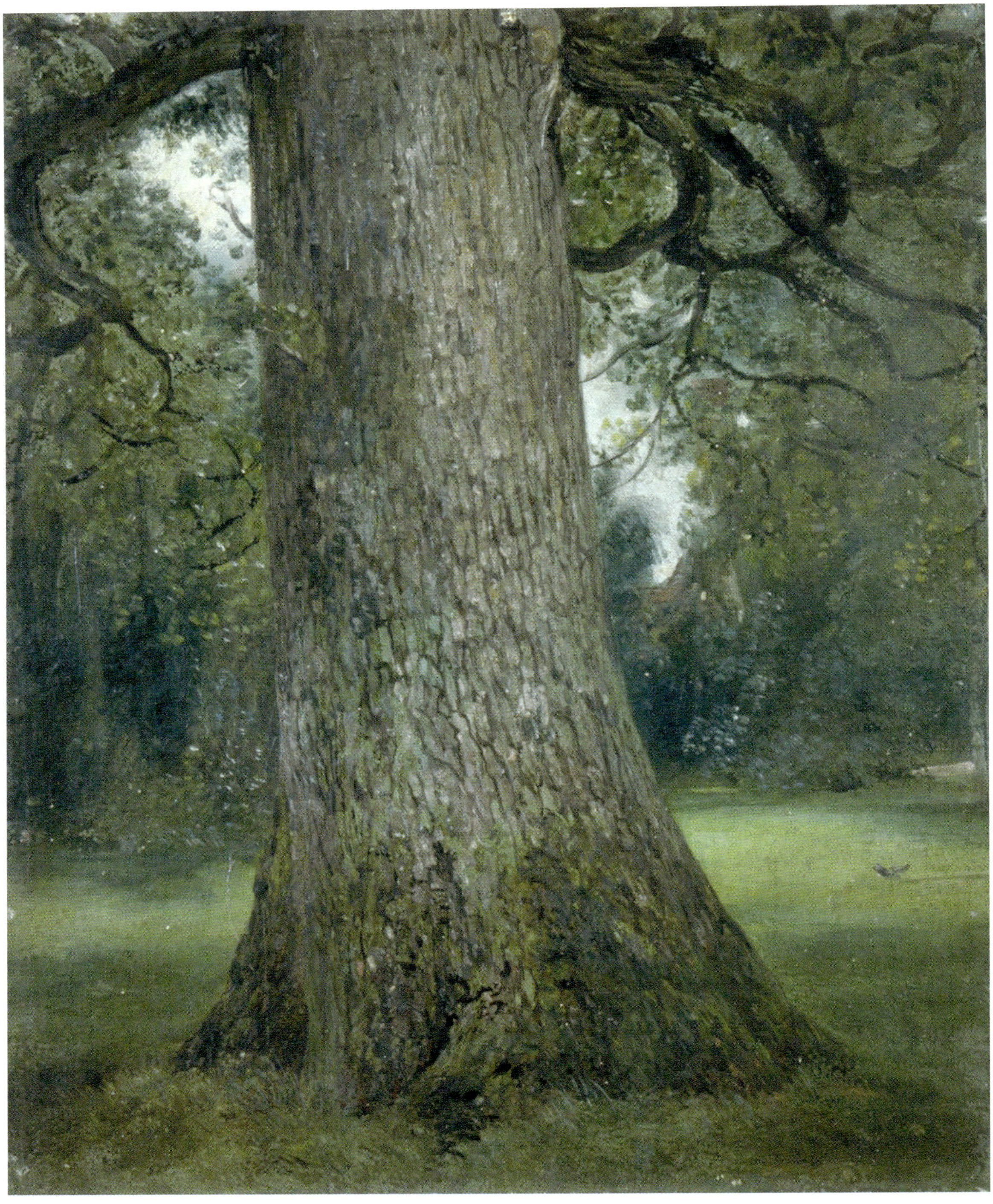

9 JOHN CONSTABLE
Study of Ash trees
1820 | Graphite | 32.8 x 23.8 cm

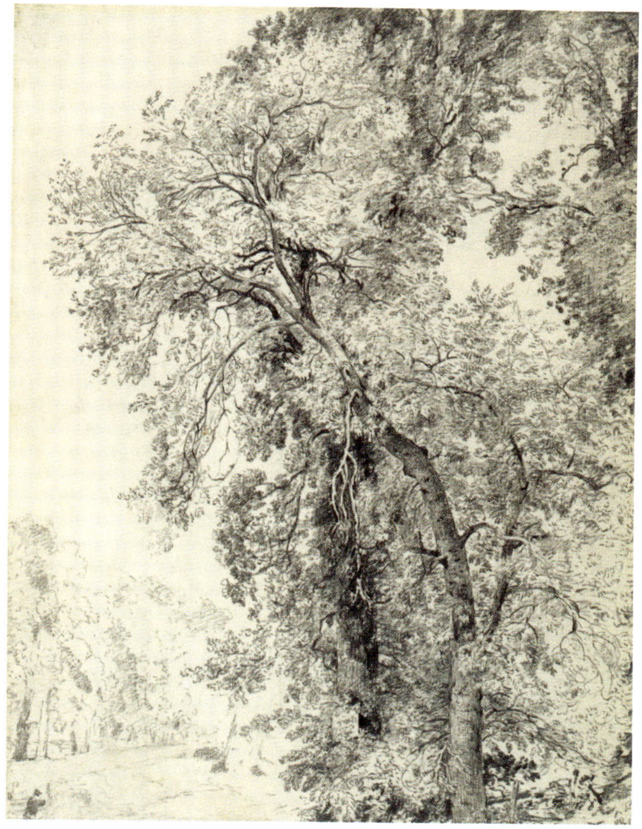

recreation in the shade of a much-loved village oak tree. Perhaps the largest tree-portrait of the nineteenth century was Mark Anthony's painting, *The Monarch Oak*, exhibited in 1853, which measured around sixteen by ten feet and seemed to reviewers to be life-size (fig. 90).

Elms were seen as a more workaday, less aristocratic tree than the oak: they were found in hedgerows, especially around London, on village greens, and next to cottages. Ruskin described the elm as a 'commonplace tree, rather prudent and practical than imaginative', whose leaf-structure reminds him of 'a merchant taking his occasional and restricted holiday.'[67] Constable's well-known study of the trunk of an elm tree (fig. 8) dwells lovingly on the texture and colours of its rugged bark. Today, mature elms are now extremely scarce in Britain as a result of Dutch elm disease, but in the eighteenth and nineteenth centuries they were very plentiful. According to John Aikin, writing in 1815, the elm was 'often planted singly or a few together in village-greens, where it affords both a majestic object and a pleasant summer shelter.' In 1748 a Swedish visitor noted that there were elms in nearly every square in London.[68] The artist Edward Kennion complained that his colleagues treated the elm as a pattern for all trees: 'The trees commonly used by painters and engravers, are nearest to character of Elm; this manner seems to be generally adapted for all trees, one reason of which may be, that the Elm is most in view of artists in the capital.'[69] The same author wrote that 'some of the finest parts of England owe much of their beauty to the "hedge-row Elms."'[70] Elms feature in Constable's rural landscapes, and in John Clare's poetry, as appropriate companions for cottages and arable fields. Gilpin declared that 'no tree is better adapted to receive great masses of light.'[71]

Both William Gilpin and Rebecca Hey begin their sections on the ash with Virgil's line 'fraxinus in sylvis pulcherrima', translated in Hey as 'the towering ash is fairest in the woods.'[72] Gilpin further declared, in a much quoted characterization, that the oak was the Hercules of the forest, the ash its Venus. Writers on trees often cited lines from the classical poets in praise of particular varieties. The first edition of Gilpin's *Forest Scenery* quotes such verses in the original Latin, with translations supplied separately. As a clergyman, Gilpin would have had a classical education, and he might presume that many of his readers, as members of the landed gentry and aristocracy, would have done the same. However, classical allusions are also plentiful, in translation, in later books, such as Rebecca Hey's *Spirit of the Woods*. Ash trees were valued for their lightness and delicacy. Useful as a timber tree, the ash was common in woods and forests but less often chosen as an ornamental tree because its season is relatively short: it is slow to produce leaves in the spring, and loses them earlier than other trees in the autumn. It is not always easy to distinguish ash trees in paintings, but the feathery foliage and graceful shapes of the trees in Gainsborough's landscapes from the 1760s onwards suggest a fondness for this species. Constable's biographer, C. R. Leslie, testifies that the ash was Constable's favourite tree, and says it is often introduced in his foregrounds.[73] Constable's drawings of ash trees were used as studies for these important foreground features (fig. 9).

10 SAMUEL PALMER
Pastoral with a Horse Chestnut Tree
c.1830–1831 | Watercolour, bodycolour and gum arabic | 33.4 x 26.8 cm

The beech was also celebrated in classical poetry, as Hunter noted in his commentary on Evelyn's *Silva*: Ovid and Virgil described shepherds resting in their spreading shade, and lovers carving their names on their smooth bark.[74] Beech trees were plentiful both in woodland and in parks. Strutt noted that 'In the spring its foliage, feathering almost to the ground, is exquisitely beautiful' and described how an old beech at Knole Park had a trunk which looked like 'a noble structure of clustering pillars … a fit residence for a sylvan deity.'[75] The beech has, perhaps, more poetical associations than any other tree. Writers frequently quoted Thomas Gray's description of the picturesque appearance of the roots of a beech tree emerging from the earth: '… yonder nodding beech,/ That wreathes its old fantastic roots so high.'[76] Thomas Campbell's poem, *The Beech Tree's Petition,* written in 1800, was illustrated by J. M. W. Turner in 1835 and quoted by Loudon in his *Arboretum Britannicum*: Campbell describes the tree as 'Love's own altar', because of the generations of couples who have made their vows in its shade.[77] In the 1860s and 1870s, the ancient trees of Burnham Beeches became a popular subject for artists such as Myles Birket Foster, who shows children gathering beech nuts, presumably to be fed to animals (fig. 2).

The sweet and horse chestnut (or chesnut) trees are not native to Britain, but were naturalized at an early stage, so by the eighteenth century they were a familiar sight, usually in parks rather than in woods, where they grew to a great size, both in width and in height. The (horse) chestnut avenue in Bushy Park, next to Hampton Court Palace, planted in 1699, became the site for popular festivities from 1838, when the park was opened to the public. 'Chesnut Sunday', the Sunday when the flowers on the trees were considered to be at their peak, provided a North European equivalent to the Japanese custom of picnicking under cherry blossom.[78] The popularity of the chestnut was further established through the idea of a 'spreading chestnut tree' at the heart of a village, which appears to originate in Henry Wadsworth Longfellow's poem, *The Village Blacksmith*, published in 1842.[79] Before this time, opinions had differed on the painterly value of the horse chestnut. Gilpin thought the tree as a whole 'totally unharmonious, and unpicturesque' and was followed by Kennion and Strutt, Kennion calling it 'lumpish', and Strutt complaining of the 'exceeding regularity of its form'.[80] But Hunter was most enthusiastic about it, 'a tree of singular beauty and use' which should be untrimmed and 'left to Nature to form their beautiful parabolic heads.'[81] Ideologically, the chestnut may have suffered because of its associations with grand houses and parkland. Loudon thought that it was an 'emblem of ostentation' because of the comparative uselessness of its fruit and timber, and the manner in which it scatters its flowers on the ground.[82] Nevertheless, it became a popular tree, perhaps partly because it was easily recognizable. The horse chestnut was a favourite tree of Samuel Palmer (fig. 10) and provides the natural symbols of resurrection in Henry Bowler's painting *The Doubt: 'Can these Dry Bones Live?'* (fig. 91). Ruskin, considering its leaf structure, thought it 'one of the crowned and lovely trees of the earth.'[83]

Artists had a particular fondness for those trees which grew in low-lying, marshy areas and along rivers, notably willows, poplars, and alders. The pollarded willow was a common sight in the countryside, and artists appreciated it for its slanting growth patterns and picturesque, knobbly shape. Some writers, including Strutt and Ruskin, found pollarded willows disagreeable because they were 'unnatural': Strutt wrote that 'they begin to be polled in the third year of their growth, and their decapitated trunks then present an unsightly spectacle, not much improved when they again sprout forth.'[84] Ruskin took a similar view, calling for artists to paint 'nature in all her liberty… not … cicatrized to the pollard.'[85] Nevertheless, pollarded willows were amongst the first trees to be selected for detailed delineation by the Pre-Raphaelites in the early 1850s, in Millais's *Ophelia* (Tate Britain) and Hunt's *Hireling Shepherd* (Manchester Art Gallery). They also appear frequently in Constable's landscapes.[86] Equally distinctive were the weeping willow, hallowed by its biblical associations as it was a reminder of the Jews weeping by the waters of Babylon,

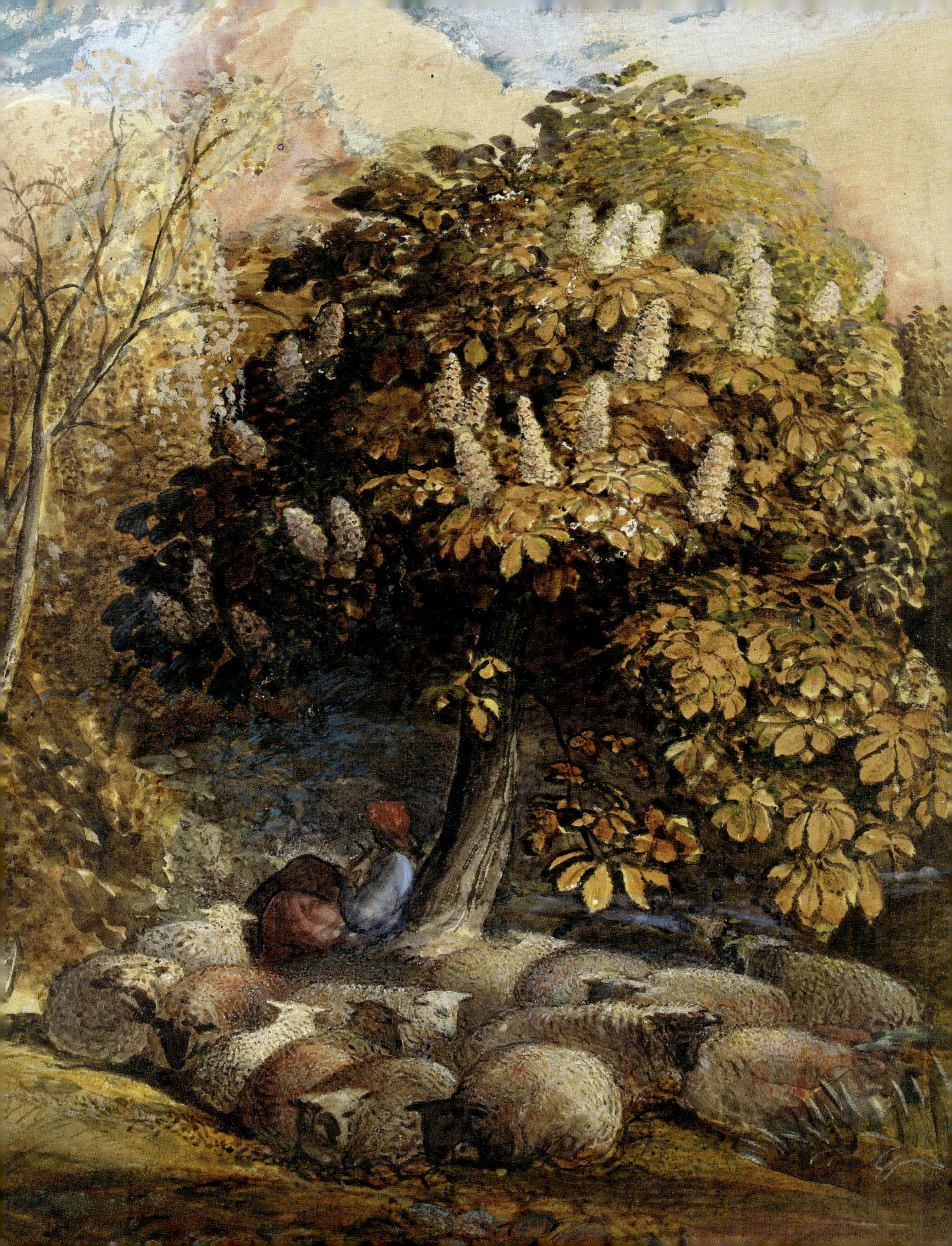

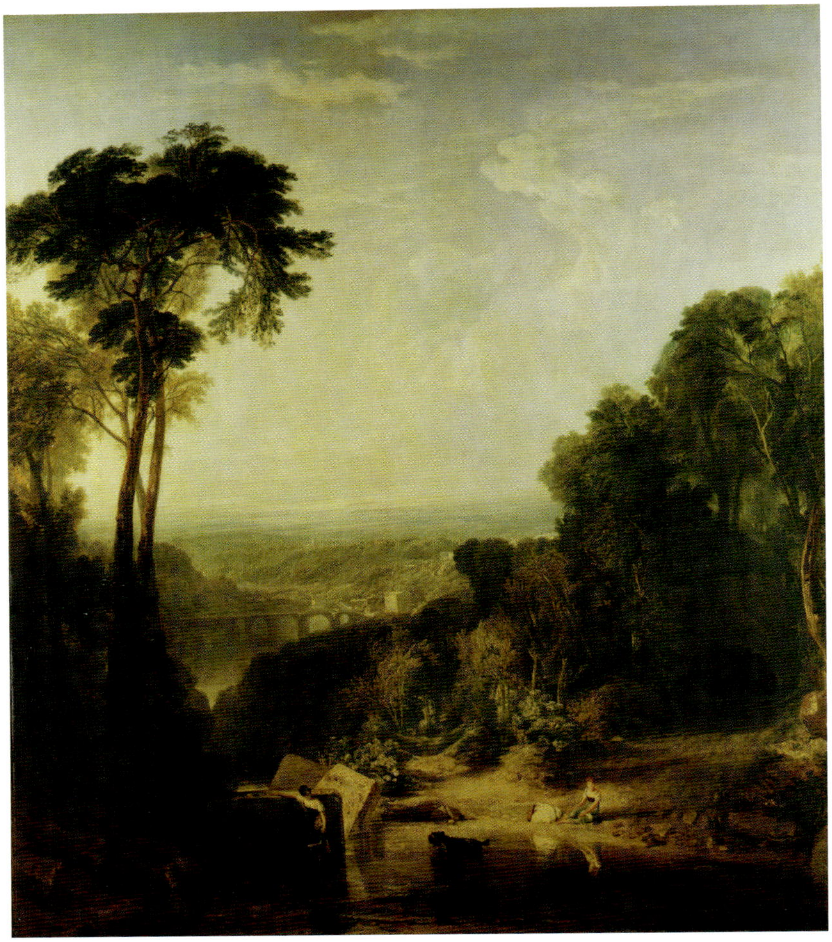

and the Lombardy poplar.[87] These trees offered pleasing varieties in shape and colour, useful both for the landscape gardener and the painter who wished to produce variety. Constable, for example, often introduces Lombardy poplars as vertical notes in his compositions. It has only recently been recognized that he also had a liking for the black poplar: the two trees closest to us on the bank of the river in *Flatford Mill* (fig. 1), long thought to be elm trees, are actually black poplars.[88] Strutt describes the black poplar as a classical tree, held by the ancients as sacred to Hercules. Constable, however, would have been more impressed by its ability to retain moisture and sparkle in the sunlight: Strutt says that in calm weather 'drops of water … hang upon its leaves, with the refreshing coolness of a summer shower.'[89]

Other trees favoured by writers and artists include the silver birch, sycamore, lime and Scots pine. The silver birch was praised as a slender, graceful tree, second only to the ash as the 'lady of the woods', in Coleridge's often-repeated phrase.[90] It was often associated with Scotland, but it also appears elsewhere in the work of artists such as Gainsborough, who used its pale trunk as a contrast to the dark undergrowth of woodland. A sycamore, its leaves not yet budded, provides the main motif in John William Inchbold's *A Study, in March* (fig. 92). Lime trees were seen by Hunter as proper for avenues and 'places designed for relaxation of mind', while Rebecca Hey's account stresses the sweet perfume of the flowers and the tree's association with the recreations of childhood and youth, of summer evenings lying in its shade and listening to the hum of bees collecting nectar from the flowers.[91] Britain has few native evergreens, but the Scots pine was a favourite of writers and artists, with its distinctive shape and the contrast between its pinkish trunk and grey-green foliage. The tall trees on the left of Turner's *Crossing the Brook* of 1815 (fig. 11) are Scots pines, often called Scotch fir in this period.

In eighteenth-century landscape gardening, and in traditional European landscape painting flowers rarely appear, so it is hardly surprising that flowering fruit trees only became popular in British art in the nineteenth century. Uvedale Price thought that blossom, on a large scale, was

11 J. M. W. TURNER
Crossing the Brook
1815 | Oil on canvas | 193 x 165.1 cm
© Tate, London 2017

discordant and and unpicturesque; but he conceded that 'fruit-trees ... in every situation give the chearfullest ideas' [sic] as they 'exhibit both in spring and autumn a striking image of fertility', and looked good in a village, near houses of a light colour.[92] Samuel Palmer's watercolours of pear and apple trees in blossom conform to this aesthetic, and *The Magic Apple Tree* (fig. 7) matches Price's description of the pleasure we experience when 'viewing a tree in its untouched luxuriant state, bending with the weight of its fruit.'[93] In Palmer's paintings blossoming fruit trees are a foretaste of paradise, as they are for Rebecca Hey. In John Everett Millais's *Spring (Apple Blossoms)* (1856-9, Walker Art Gallery, Liverpool), however, the trees act, as they do in Japanese art, as a reminder of the fragility of human life, a gloss on the youthful beauty of the girls in the foreground, emphasized (in case we miss the allusion) by the scythe on the extreme right.

The symbolism of trees often juxtaposes mortality with the Christian faith in an afterlife. This is particularly true of churchyards, where yew trees were (and still are) a common sight. Richard Mabey estimates that at least 500 churchyards in England and Wales alone contain yew trees which are as old as the church itself, and quite likely to be much older, suggesting that churches were built in locations already hallowed by pre-Christian tree worship.[94] Yews were planted in churchyards so that they would not poison cattle, but also, it seems, because their evergreen foliage symbolised eternal life. Gilpin points out that the yew was formerly what the oak is now, the basis of Britain's national strength, because longbows were made from its wood.[95] Wordsworth takes up this idea in his famous poem, *Yew-trees*, published in 1815: yew trees are a reminder of an earlier British history, before the 'wooden walls', when they provided the wood for the longbows of English archers, which helped them to defeat the French at Crecy, Agincourt and Poitiers. Wordsworth seems to assume that the tree is immortal: 'Produced too slowly ever to decay ... a natural temple scatter'd o'er/ With altars undisturbed of mossy stone.'[96] In 1822 the Ankerwycke Yew (figs. 42, 43), near Runnymede, was celebrated by Strutt as being over a thousand years old, a witness to Magna Carta: today the National Trust reckons that it is 2,500 years old, which would mean that it is older than any religious buildings on the site and even predates the Christian era itself.[97]

FOREIGN TREES

When they were at home, artists of this period were not much interested in painting the new species introduced and naturalized in Britain as a result of the activities of travellers. Their aim was to paint the characteristic features of the rural landscape: Constable spoke for many artists when he said a gentleman's park was his aversion – it is not beauty because it is not nature.[98] However, when artists travelled abroad, they were quick to familiarize themselves with trees which would instantly indicate to their viewers the country they were representing: the olive, stone pine and cypress for Italy and Greece, firs and larches in Switzerland, the palm and the cedar for the Middle East, the banyan for India.

From J. R. Cozens and Francis Towne in the eighteenth century, to Turner and Edward Lear in the nineteenth, the characteristic shapes and colours of olive groves, stone pines and cypresses defined the Mediterranean landscape. Gilpin mentions some stone pines in England, but maintains that they only develop their character in Italy: 'The soft clime of Italy alone gives birth to the true picturesque pine. There it always suggests ideas of broken porticos, Ionic pillars, triumphal arches, fragments of old temples ...'[99] In Lear's landscapes, the bluish tones and meandering trunks of olive contrast with the vertical punctuation of tall, dark cypresses. The Villa d'Este in Tivoli had some particularly famous ancient examples of the latter, which were captured in beautiful drawings by Samuel Palmer in 1838 (fig. 78). A slightly later generation of artists was captivated by the orange and

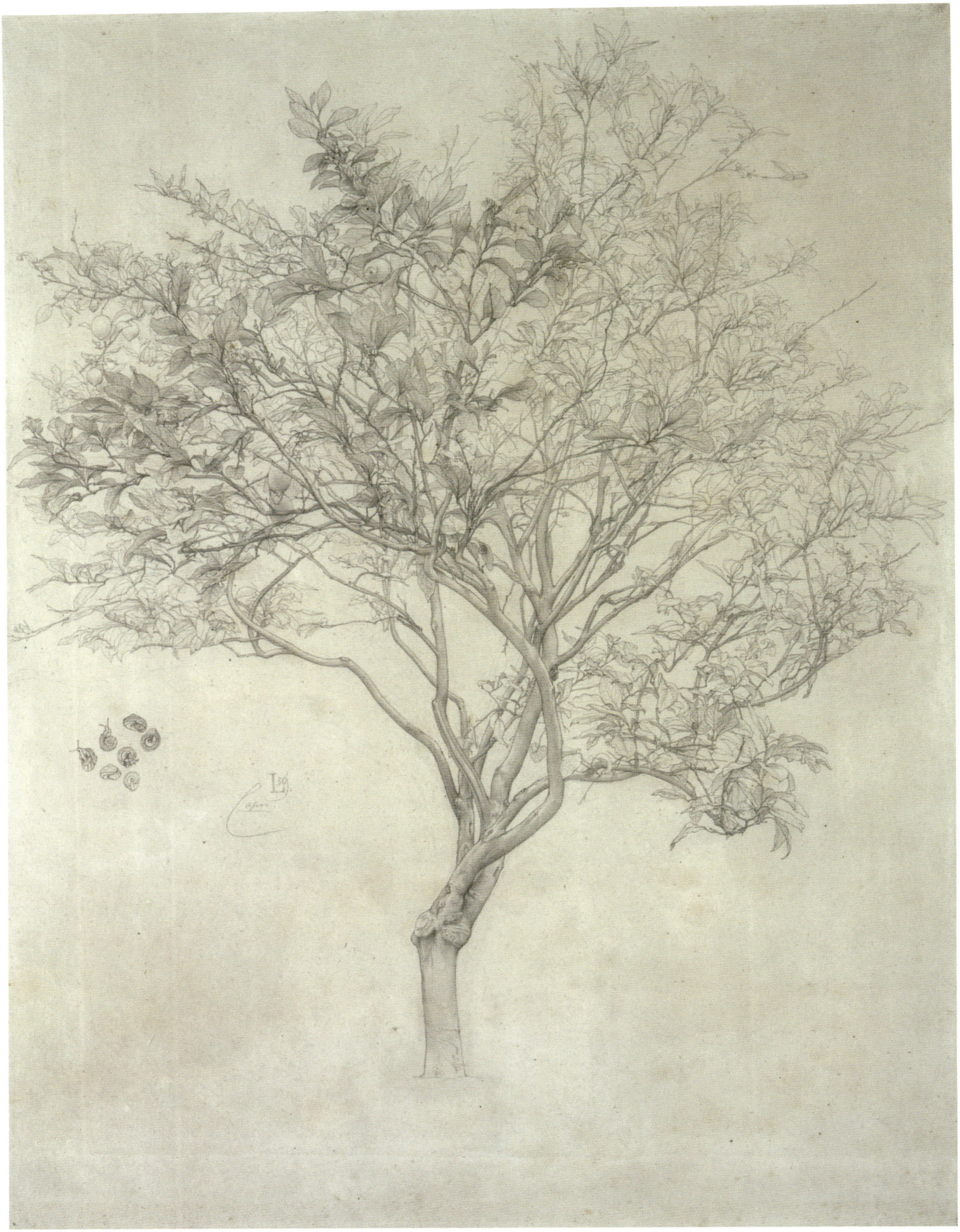

12 FREDERIC LEIGHTON
A Lemon Tree
1859 | Graphite | 53.4 x 39.4 cm
Private Collection

lemon trees of the Mediterranean coasts. Frederic Leighton, on Capri in 1859, made a meticulously detailed drawing of a lemon tree, a *tour de force* of draughtsmanship, produced in deliberate rivalry with the Pre-Raphaelites (fig. 12).[100]

In Switzerland, artists were more likely to look for trees that stood up to extremes of weather, rather than those which flourished in a gentle climate. The shattered pine, or larch was contrasted with the whiteness of snow or the barrenness of rock in sublime Swiss landscapes. Gilpin writes that the larch thrives in the Alps and the Appenines: 'Often it is felled by the alpine peasant, and thrown athwart some yawning chasm, where it affords a tremendous passage from cliff to cliff; while the cataract roaring away many fathoms below, is seen only in surges of rising vapour.'[101] In 1869, Edward Lear was thrilled by the forest of Bavella, in Corsica, where 'a changeful golden haze illumes the tops of the mighty peaks, a vast gloom below, resulting from the masses of black solemn pines standing out in deepest shadow from pale granite cliffs dazzling in the sunlight … no frenzy of the wildest dreams of a landscape painter could shape out ideal scenes of more magnificence and wonder.'[102]

The palm and the cedar of Lebanon both had strong biblical associations. With some exaggeration, Hey claimed that 'we meet with [the cedar of Lebanon] in almost every page of the Bible!'[103] Most palms could only be grown in Britain in hothouses, or on the south coast, but the cedar of Lebanon, one of the grandest trees of all, was often planted next to mansions (fig. 4). Several writers lamented that there were few trees left in Lebanon itself, but Lear made them the subject of a large painting, nine feet wide, in the winter of 1860-1, working partly from sketches he had made on the spot, but also from imported specimens in the garden of a hotel in Walton-on-Thames (fig. 71). A cedar of Lebanon provided the pinnacle of a landscape improvement scheme at Welbeck, the seat of the Dukes of Portland, where it was placed on the highest hill, amid more than 2000 acres of trees of different species, so that its noble and beautiful appearance would be seen all around the county.[104]

The banyan tree was fascinating for a different reason: it could not be grown in Britain, although, as Hey wrote, there were so many descriptions of it, in prose and verse, that the mind felt almost familiar with it. From her Christian standpoint, however, it stirred up associations with the polluted shrines of 'idolatry.'[105] Thomas Daniell and Edward Lear were more sympathetic, studying its proliferating trunks carefully to give an authentic flavour to their Indian landscapes (figs. 68, 84). Finally, there was the semi-mythical upas tree, a tree with no positive associations at all which was supposed to exist on the island of Java. Erasmus Darwin's description of it was followed by a long passage in Gilpin's *Forest Scenery*, which in turn inspired Francis Danby to produce a large painting of the tree in its desolate surroundings: it was reputed to be so poisonous that no living thing could survive near it. Danby's painting (now in the Victoria and Albert Museum) made a great impact at the British Institution in 1820: like Lear's *Cedars of Lebanon* and Mark Anthony's *The Monarch Oak* it was monumental in size, measuring 8 by 9 feet.

Danby's *Upas Tree* is exceptional: most of the paintings and written accounts of trees in this period treat them with reverence, emphasizing their beauty, their didactic value as illustrations of religious principles or analogies with human life, and their great value for mankind. Both writers and artists were very sensitive to the different characteristics of each type of tree, and well-known lines from the poets, both classical and modern, helped to encourage such discrimination. The needs of the navy, the vogue for landscape gardening, and the growth of the empire all encouraged a lively interest in, and appreciation of, trees in this period.

ENDNOTES

1 John Evelyn, *Silva: or a Discourse of Forest-Trees and the Propagation of Timber in his Majesty's Dominions … with notes by A. Hunter* (York: J. Dodsley et al., 1776); William Gilpin, *Remarks on Forest Scenery, and other Woodland Views (relative chiefly to picturesque beauty) illustrated by the scenes of New-Forest in Hampshire* (London: R. Blamire, 1791). The early editions of Evelyn's book had the title as *Sylva*; from the 4th edition, 1706, this was changed to *Silva*.

2 Charles Watkins, ed., *European Woods and Forests: Studies in Cultural History* (Wallingford and New York: CAB International, 1998), p. 2.

3 Gilpin, *Remarks on Forest Scenery, and other Woodland Views (relative chiefly to picturesque beauty) illustrated by the scenes of New-Forest in Hampshire* (London, 1791), Vol. II, Book III (from 3rd ed., 1808), pp. 40-42.

4 Gilpin, *Forest Scenery*, Bk. III, 1808, p. 47.

5 On the association of the 'greenwood' with freedom, see Simon Schama, *Landscape and Memory* (London: Fontana Press, 1996), pp. 140-1.

6 Oliver Rackham, *Trees and Woodland in the British Landscape: The Complete History of Britain's Trees, Woodlands and Hedgerows* (first published 1976; London: Phoenix Press, 4th impression, 2004), p. 190.

7 J. G. Strutt, *Sylva Britannica; or, Portraits of Forest Trees, distinguished for their Antiquity, Magnitude, or Beauty. Drawn from nature and etched by Jacob George Strutt* (London: J. G. Strutt and Colnaghi and Co, 1822), pp. 29-30.

8 Richard Mabey, *Flora Britannica* (London: Sinclair-Stevenson, 1996), p. 23.

9 N. D. G. James, *A History of English Forestry* (Oxford: Basil Blackwell, 1981, 1990), p. 147.

10 Ibid, p. 149.

11 Ibid, p. 150.

12 Ibid, pp. 181 and 191.

13 Keith Thomas, *Man and the Natural World. Changing Attitudes in England, 1500-1800* (London: Allen Lane, 1983), p. 210.

14 Tim Fulford, 'Cowper, Wordsworth, Clare: The Politics of Trees', *John Clare Journal*, no 14, July 1995, pp. 48-9, 53.

15 Evelyn, *Silva*, 1776, pp. 1, 577-8.

16 Oliver Rackham, *Ancient Woodland: Its History, Vegetation and Use in England* (London: Edward Arnold Ltd, 1980), p. 154.

17 Ibid, p. 165.

18 Evelyn, *Silva*, 1776, p. 573.

19 Ibid, Preface, no page numbers.

20 John Claudius Loudon, *Arboretum et Fructitem Britannicum, or, the Trees and Shrubs of Britain* (London: Longman, Orme, Brown, Green, and Longmans, 1838), Vol. I, p. v.

21 Ibid, Vol. I, p. 126.

22 Ibid, Vol I pp. cxxiv-cxxix, Vol III, pp. 1715-1948.

23 Uvedale Price, *Essays on the Picturesque* (London: J. Mawman, 1810), Vol I, pp. 259-60.

24 Ibid, pp. 245, 247.

25 Ibid, pp. 247-8.

26 Strutt, *Sylva Britannica*, title page and Introduction.

27 Ibid, pp. 4, 12, 36.

28 Ibid, p. 36. So far Strutt's wish has been fulfilled: 'Majesty' still survives and is currently estimated to be around 800 years old, and the Plumptre family still own the park.

29 Loudon, *Arboretum Britannicum*, Vol. I, p. 201.

30 Paul A. Elliott, Charles Watkins and Stephen Daniels, *The British Arboretum: Trees, Science and Culture in the Nineteenth Century* (London: Pickering and Chatto, 2011), p. 7.

31 Gilpin, *Forest Scenery*, Vol. I, p. 1.

32 Ibid, Vol. I, pp. 8, 10, 12, 19.

33 Ibid, Vol. I, p. 267.

34 Ibid, Vol. I, pp. 115-70.

35 Price, *Essays*, Vol I, pp. 171, 179.

36 Rebecca Hey, *The Spirit of the Woods, illustrated by coloured engravings* (London: Longmans, Rees, Orme, Green and Longman, 1837), p. vi.

37 Ibid, pp. xii, 44, 82-5.

38 R. B. Beckett, ed., *John Constable's Discourses* (Ipswich: Suffolk Records Society, 1970), p. 71.

39 C. R. Leslie, *Memoirs of the Life of John Constable, Esq., R. A., composed chiefly of his letters* (London: Longman, Brown, Green, and Longmans, 2nd ed., 1845), p. 310.

40 John Ruskin, *Modern Painters* Vol. 5, E. T. Cook and A. Wedderburn, eds. *The Works of John Ruskin* (London: George Allen, 1903-12), Vol. 7, pp. 14, 16, 18; MS of Modern Painters, fragment headed 'Vegetation', Cook and Wedderburn, eds., *Works*, Vol. 7, p. 479.

41 Wordsworth *Nutting*, l. 56. Written in 1798.

42 John Aikin, *The Woodland Companion, or, a brief Description of British Trees, with some account of their uses* (London: Baldwin, Cradock and Joy, 1815), p. 2. Esmond Harris, Jeanette Harris and N. D. G. James, *Oak: A British History* (Macclesfield: Windgather Press Ltd, 2003), p.142.

43 William Cowper, *The Yardley Oak*, ll. 6-9.

44 Strutt, *Sylva Britannica*, p. 33.

45 Michael Wheeler, *Heaven, Hell and the Victorians* (London: Cambridge University Press, 1994), p. 62.

46 Ruskin, *Modern Painters* Vol. 5, Cook and Wedderburn, eds., *Works*, Vol. 7, p. 62; *Stones of Venice*, Cook and Wedderburn, eds., *Works*, Vol. 9, p. 358.

47 Gilpin, *Forest Scenery*, p. 105.

48 Hey, *Spirit of the Woods*, pp. 26-7, 68-70, 105-7.

49 Raymond Lister, ed., *The Letters of Samuel Palmer* (Oxford: Clarendon Press), p. 823.

50 William Vaughan, *Samuel Palmer*.

Shadows on the Wall (New Haven and London: Yale University Press, 2015), pp. 5-8.

51 Stephen Daniels, 'The political iconography of woodland in later Georgian England', in Denis Cosgrove and Stephen Daniels, eds., *The Iconography of Landscape. Essays on the symbolic representation, design and use of past environments* (Cambridge: Cambridge University Press, 1988), pp. 43-82.

52 Strutt, *Sylva Britannica*, p. 5.

53 Ibid, pp. 15-16.

54 John Ruskin, *The Poetry of Architecture*, 1837-8, Cook and Wedderburn, eds., *Works*, Vol. 1, p. 69.

55 John Ruskin, *Modern Painters* Vol. 5, Cook and Wedderburn, eds., *Works*, Vol. 7, pp. 100, 49, 73.

56 Elliott, Watkins and Daniels, eds., *The British Arboretum*, pp. 17-21.

57 Loudon, *Arboretum Britannicum*, Vol. I, p. 14.

58 The English Oak (*Quercus robur*), the Field Elm (*Ulmus minor*), the Common Ash (*Fraxinus excelsior*) and the Beech (*Fagus sylvatica*).

59 Lear's diary for May 1863, quoted in Peter Levi, *Edward Lear: A Biography* (London: Macmillan, 1995), p. 192.

60 Gilpin, *Forest Scenery*, p. 31.

61 Ibid, p. 11-12.

62 Price, *Essays*, Vol. I, p. 179.

63 John Dryden, 'Palamon and Arcite', *Fables Ancient and Modern* (1700), book III l. 1058.

64 Loudon, *British Arboretum*, Vol. III, p. 1717.

65 Hey, *Spirit of the Woods*, p. 3.

66 Ibid. p. 4.

67 John Ruskin, *Modern Painters* Vol. 3 (1856), Cook and Wedderburn, eds., *Works*, Vol. 5, p. 265.

68 Aikin, *Woodland Companion*, pp. 16-17; Thomas, *Man and the Natural World*, p. 205.

69 Edward Kennion, *An Essay on Trees in Landscape; or, an attempt to shew the propriety and importance of characteristic expression in this art, and the means of producing it: with examples* (London: T. Bensley, 1815), p. 31.

70 Ibid, p. 42.

71 Gilpin, *Forest Scenery*, pp. 39-40.

72 Gilpin, *Forest Scenery*, p. 32, Hey, *Spirit of the Woods*, p. 22.

73 Leslie, *Memoirs*, p. 310.

74 Evelyn, *Silva*, p. 138.

75 Strutt, *Sylva Britannica*, p. 14.

76 Thomas Gray, *Elegy written in a Country Churchyard* (London: R. Dodsley, 1751), ll. 101-2.

77 Loudon, *Arboretum Britannicum*, p. 1959. Turner's illustration was in Campbell's *Poetical Works*, 1837. The original watercolour (c.1835) is in the National Gallery of Scotland.

78 See Ernest Law, *The Chesnut Avenue, Bushy Park, Hampton Court, historically described and illustrated* (London: G. Bell and Sons Ltd, 1919).

79 Henry Wadsworth Longfellow, *The Village Blacksmith*, l.1. Published in *Ballads and Other Poems*, 1842.

80 Gilpin, *Forest Scenery*, p. 61, Kennion, *Essay on Trees*, p. 36, Strutt, *Sylva Britannica*, p. 37.

81 Evelyn, *Silva*, pp. 166-7.

82 Loudon, *Arboretum Britannicum*, p. 465.

83 John Ruskin, *Modern Painters* Vol. 3 (1856), Cook and Wedderburn, eds., *Works*, Vol. 5, p. 265.

84 Strutt, *Sylva Britannica*, p. 23.

85 Ruskin, *Modern Painters* Vol I, 3rd ed. (1846), footnote to Conclusion. Cook and Wedderburn, eds., *Works*, Vol. 3, p. 627.

86 On pollards, see Elise Smith's illuminating article, '"The Aged Pollard's Shade": Gainsborough's *Landscape with Woodcutter and Milkmaid*', *Eighteenth-century Studies*, Vol 41, no 1 (2007), pp. 17-39.

87 For the biblical associations of the weeping willow, see Hey, *Spirit of the Woods*, p. 86.

88 Anne Lyles, ed., *Constable: The Great Landscapes* (London: Tate Publishing, 2006), p. 37.

89 Strutt, *Sylva Britannica*, p. 24.

90 Samuel Taylor Coleridge, *The Picture, or The Lover's Resolution* (1802), ll. 136-7 (these lines actually refer to a weeping birch).

91 Evelyn, *Silva*, p. 201; Hey, *Spirit of the Woods*, pp. 38-42.

92 Price, *Essays*, Vol. I, p.p. 174-5; Vol. II, p. 357.

93 Ibid, Vol. II, p. 358.

94 Richard Mabey, *Flora Britannica* (London: Sinclair-Stevenson, 1996), p.28.

95 Gilpin, *Forest Scenery*, p. 92.

96 Wordsworth, *Yew-trees* (1803), ll. 11, 29-30.

97 Strutt, *Sylva Britannica*, p. 8. For the current estimate of the tree's age, see https://www.nationaltrust.org.uk/runnymede/features/ankerwycke, retrieved 8th August 2016.

98 Letter to John Fisher, 7 October 1822. R. B. Beckett, ed., *John Constable's Correspondence* (Ipswich: Suffolk Records Society, 1962-69), Vol VI, p. 98.

99 Gilpin, *Forest Scenery*, p. 78.

100 On this drawing, see Allen Staley and Christopher Newall, *Pre-Raphaelite Vision: Truth to Nature* (London: Tate Publishing, 2004), p.48.

101 Gilpin, *Forest Scenery*, p. 71.

102 *Edward Lear in Corsica: The Journal of a Landscape Painter* (London: William Kimber & Co Ltd, 1966, first published in 1870 as *Journal of a Landscape Painter in Corsica*), p. 104.

103 Hey, *Spirit of the Woods*, p. 192.

104 Stephen Daniels, *Humphrey Repton: Landscape Gardening and the Geography of Georgian England* (New Haven and London: Yale University Press, 1999), p. 156.

105 Hey, *Spirit of the Woods*, pp. 183, 189.

13 JOHANN ZOFFANY

The Three Daughters of John, 3rd Earl of Bute

c.1763–4 | Oil on canvas | 101.2 x 126.5 cm

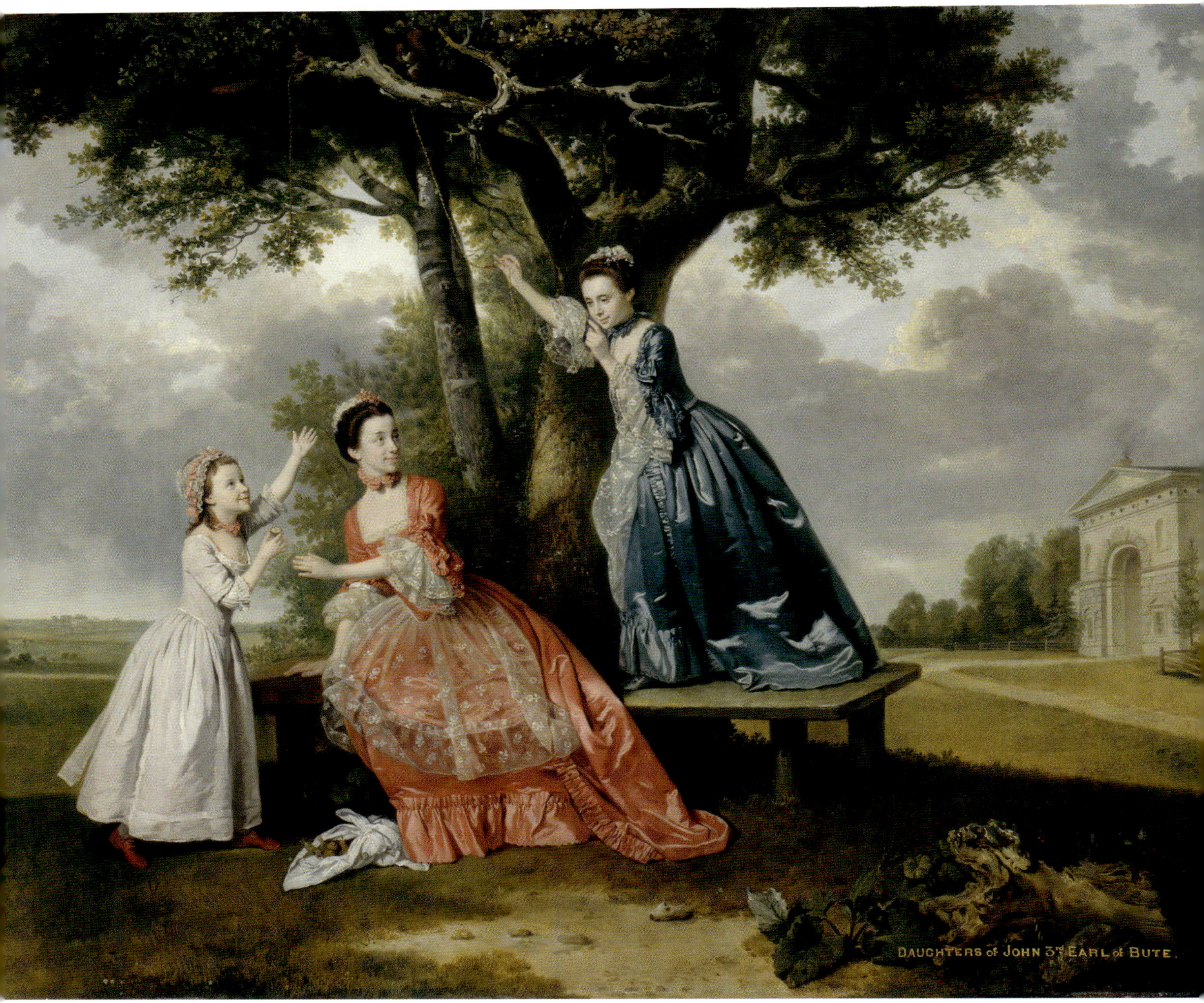

TWO

The Tree in Patrician Culture: 1760-1800

TREES WERE A focus of artistic interest across Europe in the later eighteenth century. New varieties came in as a result of colonization, exploration and international trade, while the work of Carl Linnaeus (1707-1778) led to frenetic activity in the classification of natural history specimens of all kinds. In France and Germany, as in Britain, the importance of planting for maritime trade and naval power was widely recognised. In Britain, and especially England, however, this development had a particular emphasis on trees as individual specimens. To this day, England has less tree cover than other European countries, yet it has the largest number of ancient trees. The reasons for this are to be found in country-house culture: the peculiar combination of landscape gardening, paternalism, and the pursuit of drawing as a polite accomplishment which characterized eighteenth-century England. There was a particular focus on the oak and the beech, trees which were celebrated in old woodland and recently remodelled parks, recognised as useful for their timber but also suited to the role of ornamental trees.

In this period, landscape painters were working predominantly for patrons with landed estates. These people owned landscapes by the seventeenth-century Old Masters, particularly Claude, they spent money remodelling their landscape parks with the help of Capability Brown and later Humphrey Repton, they read the poetry of Thomas Gray, William Cowper, and William Mason. Thomas Hearne and Paul Sandby painted trees in the landscaped parks of these patrons. Thomas Gainsborough refused to paint 'real views from nature' but his woodland scenes express the ideology of the patrician class in a different way, through their encouragement of sympathy for the poor. His paintings illustrate the view from the park, so to speak: the view of a landed rider travelling through the countryside, observing the poor at rest or on the move. They show the dependence of the poor on free firewood and on areas of ancient woodland where they could build their cottages. His 'cottage door' pictures repeatedly show cottages in symbiotic relationship with ancient trees, with troops of rosy-cheeked children tumbling out, a theme that was also taken up in the 1790s and the early nineteenth century by George Morland.

In an age when tree-planting was encouraged as a patriotic duty, and men (and women) of sensibility were supposed to take woodland walks as an aid to meditation, portrait sitters often chose to be depicted next to trees. In 1748 Gainsborough's Suffolk couple, in his painting *Mr and Mrs Andrews* (National Gallery), are shown in front of a mature oak, one which might have provided useful timber for the navy.[1] Further, younger oaks are seen in the middle distance on the right, indicating that this is an estate with an ongoing programme of planting to provide for the future, just as the Andrews' marriage will produce a new generation of children to continue the family line. Johann Zoffany produced a series of group portraits in the 1760s which all depict family members interacting against the backdrop of an ancient oak tree. The first of these are the two portraits of the children of Lord Bute, probably done in 1763: the backgrounds show his newly-bought estate at Luton Hoo, but the trees were probably based on specimens studied in London, perhaps at Kew Gardens, where Bute occupied a crucial role.[2] Bute's three sons are shown engaged in archery and birdsnesting, while the girls in *Three Daughters of John, 3rd Earl of Bute* (fig. 13) are playing with their pet squirrels. The tree in the portrait of the sons (Tate Britain) looks too far advanced in years to have any practical purpose as raw material for a warship. It refers rather to the idea of the family tree and to the sense of British history as stretching back through many centuries without foreign invasion, an idea that had particular appeal at the end of the Seven Years War. Some ten years later (and perhaps encouraged by visual expressions of this idea) Edmund Burke wrote of the aristocracy as 'the great oaks that shade a nation.'[3] Oak trees also feature in Joseph Wright of Derby's portrait of Jean-Jacques Rousseau's friend and translator, Sir Brooke Boothby, of 1781 (Tate Britain). Boothby is shown reclining in a grove, possibly the very grove that Rousseau retreated to in order to write his *Confessions*. This was called the Twenty Oaks Wood: although the trunks of the trees look more like birch, there are shadows of oak leaves on Boothby's clothes.[4]

In the same year that Lord Bute commissioned the portraits of his children, 1763, Roger Fisher, a shipwright of Liverpool, published a book entitled *Heart of Oak* to draw attention to a nationwide shortage of oak timber, which was particularly worrying after seven years of war with France. It was upon oaks, he argued, that 'the welfare of our king and country, our religion, laws and liberty depend ... for, without the art of shipbuilding, and proper materials wherewith to construct ships, we shall soon become a prey to the next aspiring invader.'[5] He blamed the new style of landscape gardening for this shortage, claiming that it had its foundation in 'French policy', which he contrasted with the previous arrangement of avenues around great houses:

> Formerly the grandeur of our noblemens and gentlemens seats was much increased by the vast quantity of woods, parks, and groves of timber growing all around them. ... [They] had the pleasure of viewing from every apartment the progress of their labours; still keeping in view the grand design, the naval power of Britain.
>
> When a little cloyed with enjoyment, or to retire from business, or for the sake of meditation, a walk for the space of a furlong, or little more, leads the wealthy inhabitant into a spacious wood. The variety of the scene revives his drooping spirits. On the branch of a full topt oak, at a small distance, the blackbird and thrush warble forth their notes, and, as it were, bless their benefactor. ... Variety of changes draw on the pleasing hour amongst the massy bodies of the full-grown oaks and thriving plants. The prospect of his country's good warms his heart. He returns and beholds his little offspring round his board, satiated with the views of the provision made for their defence in the thriving nurseries all around. He enjoys it a little while, and in a good old age lies down and dies in peace.[6]

By contrast, Fisher argues that his contemporaries have been duped by 'frenchified doctors' into believing that it is unhealthy to live in the midst of a wood, and so they cut down oak trees without considering the need for their replacement. Fisher's book stresses the utilitarian argument for planting trees, but his account of the landowner walking in his woods underlines the strong element of sentiment that was also involved.

An extraordinary amount of money was spent on remodelling landscaped parks in the eighteenth and early nineteenth centuries, in line with the 'natural' approach which replaced the formal gardens of the seventeenth century. The rigidly straight avenues, clipped hedges and topiary work, and geometrical planting schemes of the previous fashion were dismantled. By 1770 Horace Walpole could write with approval that 'We have given the true model of gardening to the world.' With the innovations of William Kent and then Brown, he wrote

> The living landscape was chastened or polished, not transformed. Freedom was given to the forms of trees: they extended their branches unrestricted, and where any eminent oak or master beech had escaped maiming and survived the forest, bush and bramble was removed, and all its honours were restored to distinguish and shade the plain.[7]

Walpole explicitly linked this new form of gardening with the political system. It was, he argued, suited to a free country, 'where emulation reigns among many independent particulars.' In France, by contrast, 'it is a curiosity to see an old tree' because, when they reach a certain bulk, they are marked by the crown surveyors as royal timber.[8]

While the detractors of Capability Brown claimed that he was despoiling the landscape of its trees, in actual fact it seems that he was not only planting vast quantities of trees, many of them in a half-mature state, but also ensuring that fine old specimens were displayed to their best advantage. It is true that his schemes led to the destruction of many straight avenues, but the modern consensus is that new plantations more than compensated for these losses. At Castle Ashby, Northamptonshire, for example, Brown removed three of the four avenues which radiated out to the four points of the compass, but developed extensive plantations around the ponds, making use of existing trees, especially old oaks. Beeches and chestnuts were added for variety, along with the occasional cedar.[9] At Caversham Park, Reading, he thinned the thickets so that the 'most noble' trees were left conspicuous.[10] In a rare statement of his principles, Brown stressed the need for 'infinite delicacy in the planting etc., so much Beauty depending on the size of the Trees and the colour of their leaves to produce the effect of light and shade so very essential to the perfecting of a good plan; as also the hideing what is disagreeable and shewing what is beautifull, getting shade from the large trees and sweets from the smaller sorts of shrubs etc. [sic].'[11] Brown thought of trees in utilitarian terms – they hid disagreeable objects and provided shelter from the sun – but also, evidently, as parts of a composition, where they would provide beauty, light and shade. Clumps of mature trees framed vistas as if in a painting, while dark foliage would set off the paler colours of cascades and delicate garden buildings.[12]

William Mason, who laid out Earl Harcourt's garden at Nuneham Courtney, wrote a long poem, *The English Garden* (1772), which includes a careful defence of the need to break up old avenues. Mixing pagan and Christian imagery, he asks:

> … where shall the Dryads fly
> That haunt yon ancient vista? Pity, sure,
> Will spare the long cathedral isle of shade
> In which they sojourn; Taste were sacrilege,
> If, lifting there the axe, it dar'd invade
> Those spreading oaks that in fraternal files
> Have pair'd for centuries …[13]

Mason stressed that he was reluctant to use the axe 'for my soul/ Holds dear an antient oak, nothing more dear;/ It is an antient friend', yet this was necessary. Some of these 'old protectors of the plain' could be saved, either by moving the trees ('A work of difficulty and danger try'd/ Nor oft successful found') or by adding saplings to break up the line and create groups of trees.[14] The felling of ancient trees was an emotive issue, and landowners took pride in preserving and celebrating those specimens which were several centuries old. In 1790 Hayman Rooke published an illustrated account of the 'Remarkable Oaks' in the park at Welbeck, an estate belonging to the Duke of Portland which incorporated parts of Sherwood Forest. He makes no mention of the use of oak for shipbuilding (despite commenting on the durability of its timber under water), but he does refer to the ancient Britons holding the oak sacred, and the Druids consecrating groves of oak as temples.[15]

Humphrey Repton criticized the 'Despotic fashion' for cutting down old trees, yet in his third Red Book for Welbeck (1803), he planned to move the house away from the ancient trees. He justified this move very carefully, aware of the Duke's fondness for the old trees and the general attitude of veneration towards them:

> Those venerable Oaks which no axe had dared approach, have gradually fallen under the Scythe of Time … However the mind may be gratified with contemplating the rude and decayed trunks of trees which have outlived the common period of vegetation, they excite a degree of melancholy incompatible with the cheerful enjoyment of modern life …

He flattered the family's sense of its role as guardian of the countryside, and likened the continuity of the ancestral line to the survival of the forest: the new house would stand in a place

> Where different generations of the same Family, may live among generations of Trees that the Family has judiciously provided to succeed those whose existence can no longer be prolonged.[16]

However, the plan remained unexecuted, presumably because the Duke was unwilling to give up his view of these ancient oaks.

14 PAUL SANDBY
Gentlemen conversing on a drive at Luton
c.1765 | Watercolour | 61 x 96.5 cm
Private Collection, © 1996 Christie's Images Limited

In eighteenth-century poetry, trees and woodland were explicitly linked to meditation and creativity. Thomas Gray, in his influential *Elegy written in a country churchyard* (1751) gives his obscure young poet a 'favourite tree', a beech:

> There at the foot of yonder nodding beech
> That wreathes its old fantastic roots so high,
> His listless length at noontide would he stretch,
> And pore upon the brook that babbles by.[17]

These lines became extremely well known. The attention they give to the exposed roots of beech trees may have encouraged Sandby to focus on this feature in his Luton Hoo watercolours (figs. 14, 15), while the image of the poet stretched out and poring over the brook has its visual counterpart in Wright's portrait of Brooke Boothby. William Cowper also writes about the noontide reverie in *The Task* (1785), book one:

> Our groves were planted to console at noon
> The pensive wanderer in their shades. …[18]

Cowper had a favourite walk through a particular wood near Olney, where he went to pray, and felt it had been 'desecrated' when the landowners felled some of the trees and reorganized it as an orderly plantation.[19] He attacked the landscape gardening of Capability Brown, with particular reference to his destruction of avenues:

> Ye fallen avenues! Once more I mourn
> Your fate unmerited, once more rejoice
> That yet a remnant of your race survives.
> How airy and how light the graceful arch,
> Yet awful as the consecrated roof
> Re-echoing pious anthems! …[20]

Like other writers of this period, Cowper thought of the arches made by an avenue of trees as equivalent to the aisles of a cathedral, strengthening the association with meditation.

The poets of this time also made clear distinctions between different varieties of trees, characterizing their different qualities and putting particular emphasis on those that were native to Britain. Cowper describes the ash, lime, beech, willow, poplar, elm, oak, maple and sycamore in a passage in book one of *The Task*, commenting on such details as their changing foliage, the smoothness of their trunks, the glossiness or otherwise of their leaves, and even their scents.[21] Richard Payne Knight, in his poem *The Landscape* (1794) shows a similar discrimination between species, and like other writers of the time, he writes at particular length about the beech and the oak. Echoing Cowper's complaints about Brown, Knight writes that Brown has reduced the opportunities for meditation in the landscape garden, banishing the 'thickets of high-bow'ring wood' which hung over rivers, providing shade for repose at noon.[22] He deplored the fashion for mixing native and foreign species, and planting larches and firs, calling on landowners to invoke, instead, 'Britain's genius' and

> … spread around the rich, high-clustering oak:
> King of the woods! Whose tow'ring branches trace
> Each form of majesty, and line of grace;
> Whose giant arms, and high-imbower'd head,
> Deep masses round of clust'ring foliage spread[23]

Knight wrote appreciatively of the varied tints of its foliage and of the individuality of each oak tree. He also praised the beech, for soils which were not rich enough for oak:

> No tree more elegant its branches spreads …
> No foliage shines with more reflected lights;
> No stem more vary'd forms and tints unites:
> Now smooth, in even bark, aloft it shoots;
> Now bulging swells, fantastic as its roots …[24]

Knight wrote in a footnote that the beech 'was a favourite tree of Claude.'[25] Horace Walpole, similarly, had described the lawns at Stanstead, the seat of the Earl of Halifax, 'richly enclosed by venerable beech woods, and chequered by single beeches of vast size' as recalling exact pictures by Claude.[26]

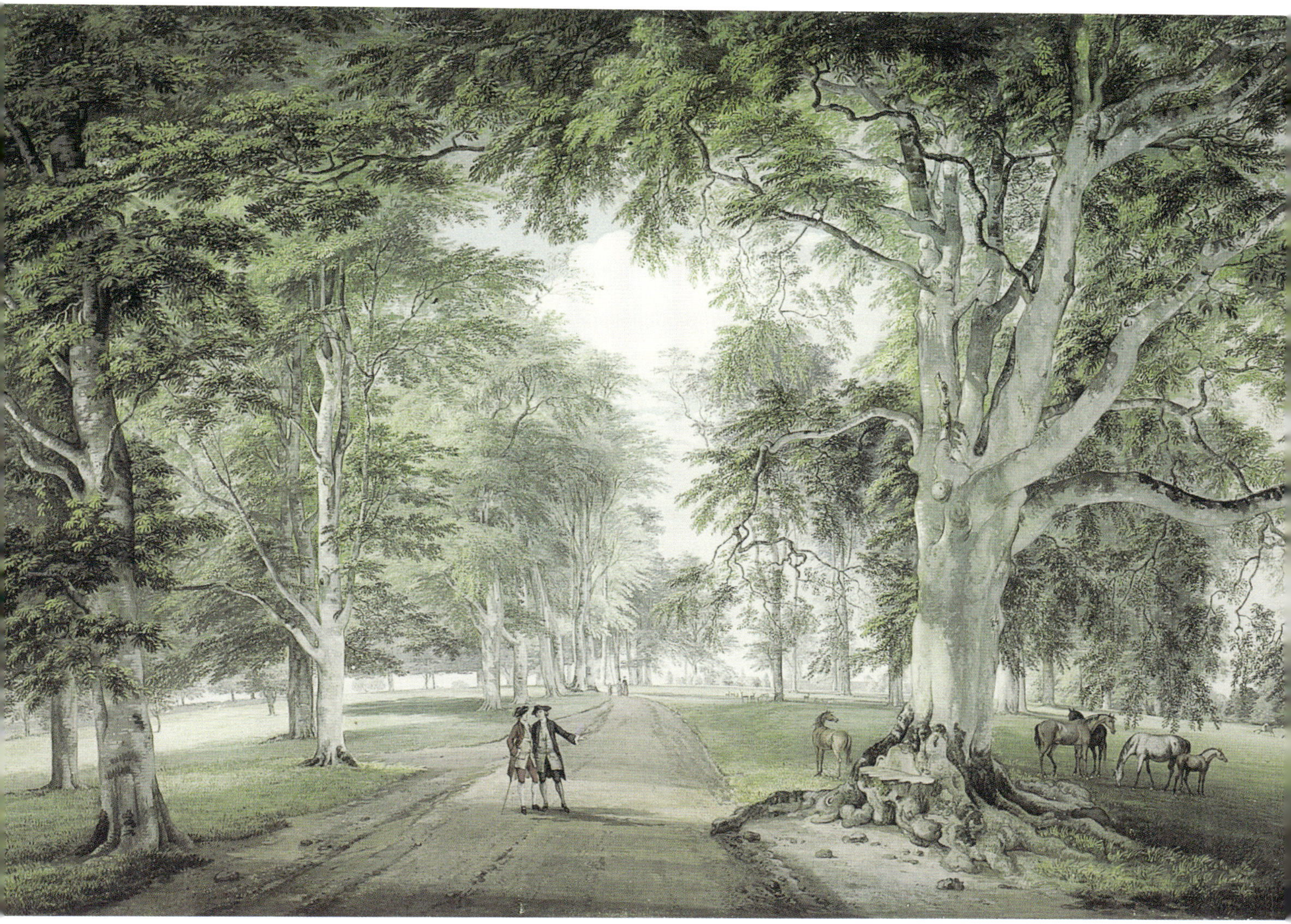

15 PAUL SANDBY

View in Luton Park

1765 | Watercolour | 51 x 74 cm

The Bute Collection at Mount Stewart

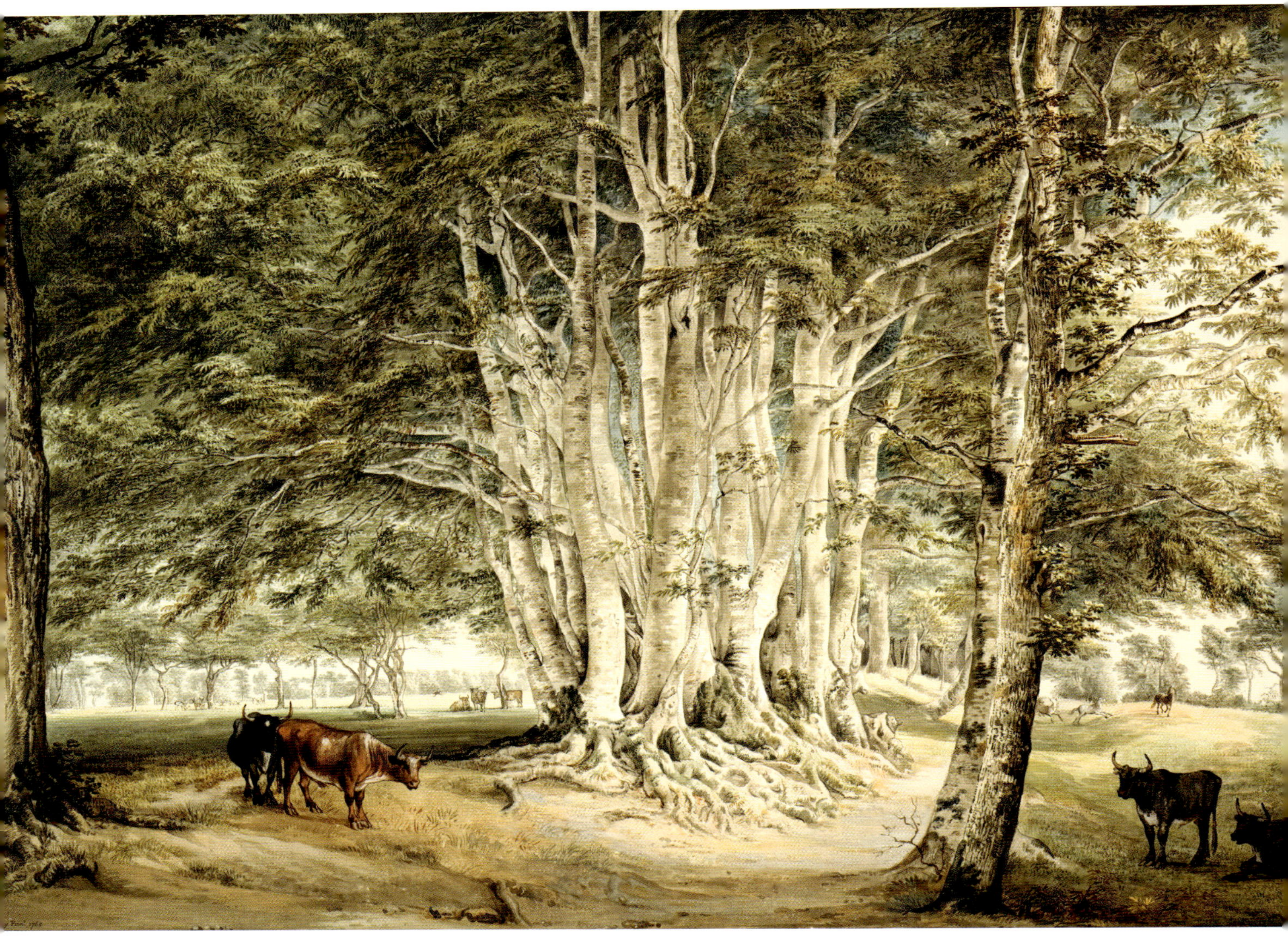

THE PARK: PAUL SANDBY AND THOMAS HEARNE

Trees figured prominently in the eighteenth-century debates over landscape gardening and the picturesque, and it is highly likely that the artist's patrons would have had decided views on the merits of avenues, the respect to be paid to ancient trees, and the propriety of planting particular species. Two patrons who commissioned substantial series of estate views featuring trees are known to have had a special interest in trees themselves. One was Lord Bute, who helped develop the gardens at Kew: in the early to mid-1760s he commissioned a series of some twenty views of his new estate, Luton Hoo in Bedfordshire, from Paul Sandby (figs. 14, 15). The other was Richard Payne Knight, who wrote knowledgeably about trees in *The Landscape*, published in 1794: in the mid-1780s he commissioned twelve views of the gorge on his estate at Downton in Shropshire, from Thomas Hearne (figs. 17, 18). These two commissions were of crucial importance for the development of the depiction of the tree in British art. Both artists went on to become famous for their skill in tree-drawing. Sandby became particularly well-known for his paintings of beech trees, while Hearne's speciality was, rather, the oak. Significantly, the beech and oak were the main trees featured in these two sets of views.

Both these commissions were for watercolours. Although some of the Downton series were exhibited at the Royal Academy, watercolour was a more private art than oil painting in this period. Watercolours were kept in portfolios, to be brought out and shown to visitors, or studied in moments of relaxation. Patrons and their visitors usually had some training as watercolourists themselves, and both Hearne and Sandby often went on sketching tours with those who bought their paintings. It was also common for the artists to act as drawing masters, if not to the buyers themselves then to their friends or relations. Paul Sandby, for example, taught Earl Harcourt, owner of Nuneham Courtney, and the two men can reasonably be described as friends. It has been suggested that it was Earl Harcourt who introduced Sandby to Bute. Sandby was also a friend of the poet and gardener William Mason, and of the poet Thomas Gray.[27] Poets, landscape gardeners, landowners and artists were all part of a shared culture, therefore, in which trees were probably a frequent object of discussion, and both Sandby and Hearne must have spent long periods staying with their patrons in order to paint so many views of their grounds. However, their depictions of trees were not simply confined to a circle of country-house owners and visitors. Exhibited works and prints spread the resulting interest in trees to a wider market in the 1780s and 1790s.

Paul Sandby was recently recognized as one of the first British artists to take an interest in the individual species and growth patterns of trees.[28] This can be traced initially to his connection with the Windsor Great Park, where his elder brother Thomas was Deputy Ranger. Thomas Sandby entered the service of the Duke of Cumberland, younger son of George II, in 1746, the year in which the Duke was made Ranger of the Forest. In 1754 Thomas Sandby produced eight views of Windsor Great Park, which were engraved, with help from Paul. Watercolours by Thomas from the early 1750s show an interest in contrasting shapes and sizes of trees, with some differentiation of the species. It is possible that Thomas initially taught Paul to draw trees, although Paul took the interest much further.

An important impetus must have been provided by the commission from Lord Bute for around twenty views of Luton Park in Bedfordshire.[29] This commission is rather mysterious. There is no contemporary documentation linking Sandby with Luton, or even with Lord Bute, apart from one exhibited watercolour of Someries Farm.[30] Two different dates appear on individual watercolours in the series – 1765 and 1767 – yet we know that Sandby worked quickly. The dates do not correspond to the numbers that appear on some of the watercolours: number 6 is dated 1767, but number 9 is dated 1765.[31] Number I must predate Zoffany's portraits, if (as seems very likely) it was used by Zoffany for the background to his painting of Lord Bute's daughters,

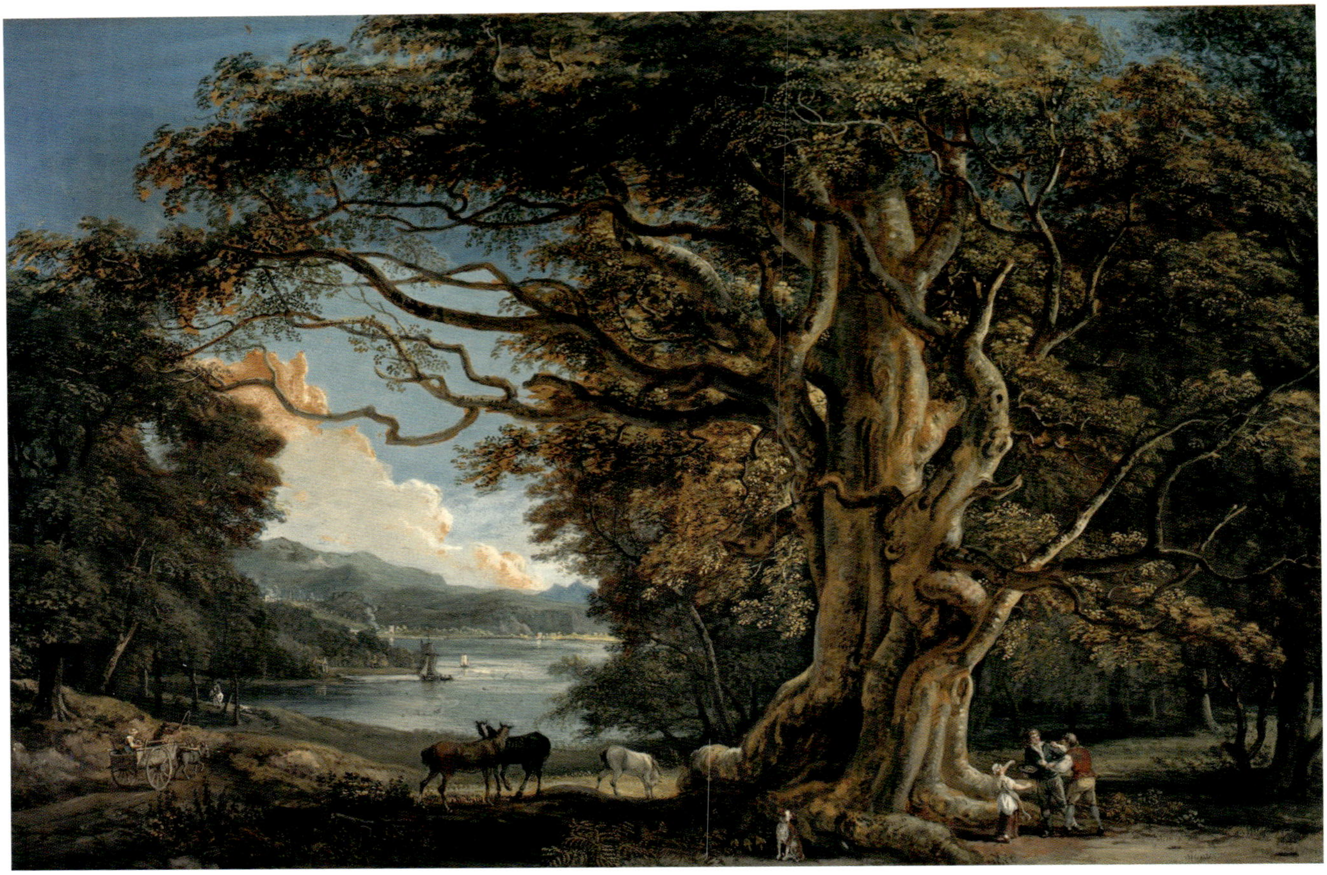

and this portrait must itself date from 1763-4.[32] If Sandby was working on this series for some four years, it is extraordinary that no independent documentary evidence of the commission survives. The watercolours were rediscovered in the Bute collection only in 1996, in an album. One reason for their neglect – which has had the happy result that they are in excellent condition – is that the Butes did not stay at the estate for long. Also, Lord Bute himself seems to have tired of the estate, and of the country life in general, quite quickly: his magnificent mansion, designed by Robert Adam, was never finished.

The watercolours are remarkably individual and delicate in execution: Sandby avoided conventional formulae, rising to the challenge of depicting unfamiliar compositions and basing them on his own detailed observation. We do not know whether it was Sandby or Bute who chose the subjects of the watercolours, but it is more likely to have been the patron. There is an unusual preponderance of detailed depictions of trees: eight of the views could reasonably be described as portraits of individual trees, or groups of trees. These comprise two studies of a set of massively gnarled beeches, which have evidently grown from ancient coppicing, three views of a ride between large beech trees (fig. 14), a view of a more elegant beech coppice (fig. 15) and two single studies dominated by a birch and an ash respectively. Surprisingly, there are few oaks, suggesting that it was Bute's scientific interests, rather than any patriotic fervour, that lay behind this series. Bute made up for the scarcity of oaks in the watercolours, however, in his commission for the family portraits by Zoffany, in which ancient oaks provide the backdrop for his playful children.

Brown's improvements would most likely have used these spectacular trees as eye-catching elements in the landscape design. Visiting the estate in 1768, Arthur Young noted its 'many fine beeches' and a history of Luton, published in 1855, commented that 'the openings or breaks through the woods, the hollow dales, and groups of fine beech trees present an agreeable variety to the landscape painter.'[33] In Sandby's watercolours, cattle, deer and horses wander freely through the estate, and figures suggest paternalism on the one hand and gentlemanly aesthetic appreciation on the other. A woman gathers faggots in one of the views of the gnarled beeches, while in one of the views of the rides two well-dressed men stand in conversation, one gesturing

16 PAUL SANDBY

Ancient Beech Tree

1794 | Bodycolour | 69 x 103 cm

towards a seat which has been carved out of the protruding roots of the nearest beech tree (fig. 14). The beeches are shown from a low and close viewpoint, so that their lofty scale impresses the viewer. The ash and birch, however, are shown as complete trees, displaying their fine, elegant shapes. In all the watercolours in the series, the attention to detail in such features as the bark of the trees, the root systems, and the distribution and fall of the foliage, leave one in no doubt as to the species that are represented. The attention devoted to this series would have given Sandby a mastery of tree drawing which was to underpin his later work.

In subsequent estate views, Paul Sandby shows a sensitivity to the contrasting shapes and textures of different kinds of tree. This was continued in a delightful series of views he produced of his own and his brother Thomas's gardens in the 1790s and early 1800s. At the same period he was producing scenes of activities in the woodyard at Windsor Great Park. The greatest impact of his depiction of trees came, however, in the monumental paintings he exhibited of ancient beech trees in the years after 1790, such as *Morning* (now known as *Ancient Beech Tree*, fig. 16), which was shown at the Royal Academy in 1795. The tree, with its muscular trunk and spreading branches, dominates the composition. Its exposed roots give it the appearance of an animal rather than an inert object, and this impression is strengthened by the curving intricacies of its branches. Thick bodycolour has been applied for the foliage, in a spotting technique which has later echoes in the work of Samuel Palmer. The impression of sunlight behind the tree and shining through its branches and foliage is skilfully evoked.

Paul Sandby's depictions of trees were widely celebrated, both in his lifetime and subsequently. A biographical notice published in 1801 (appropriately quoting his old friend Thomas Gray) praised the range of his art 'from the shrub that blossoms in the hedge-row to the poplar that glitters in the glade, from the nodding beech, *that wreathes its old fantastic roots so high*, to the majestic oak, that towers on the summit of the mountain.'[34] In 1833, an article stated that Sandby's 'studies from nature in Windsor Great Park and the adjacent forest … were much and deservedly admired by all the painters in oil.'[35] As founder members of the Royal Academy with royal connections, the Sandby brothers were highly respected and very influential. Paul Sandby's pupils included the father of James Duffield Harding, who was later to write one of the most influential drawing manuals on trees, and Sir John Leicester, future patron of Turner. We catch a glimpse of his views on the iconography of trees from one of his last letters, written in 1808 to his friend Gandon, an architect in Ireland:

> … while French slaves are planting the tree of liberty in various parts of the world, you with more utility are raising and fostering young plants, to give you shade, pleasure and profit – let the majestic oak, king of the future forests, be found with a numerous offspring to augment in future time the British navy ... the majestic forests of Windsor have long bowed their heads to the adze of keen necessity and lust of lucre … I really am delighted with your planting; it is the best hobby a reasonable man can mount. In the juvenile part of my life I put a few acorns in my brother's gardens at Windsor, and found great pleasure in viewing the opening buds.[36]

Sandby's reference to French 'slaves' implies that for him the oak was, as it had been for Fisher in 1763, a guarantor of British liberty. He stresses the patriotic significance of planting and cultivating trees, in order to provide material for the navy in years to come.

Like Sandby's, Thomas Hearne's career suggests a close association between the values of the artist and those of his landed patrons. He had a friendship, which lasted for many years, with Sir George Beaumont: the two men met in 1771 and went on sketching tours together, to the Lakes in 1777, to Scotland in 1778. Hearne painted several sets of estate views, including views of Beaumont's own estate at Coleorton. Some of these paintings were conventional views of grand new houses seen across parkland designed according to the principles of Capability Brown, with broad

17 THOMAS HEARNE
View from below Pool's Farm
1785 | Watercolour over graphite | 34.6 x 49.8 cm
Private Collection

sweeps of grass and water in the foreground. In many others, however, Hearne depicted a more natural-looking landscape, one in which trees predominated.

Hearne's first exhibits at the Royal Academy, in 1781, were three views of Heveningham Hall, Suffolk, the seat of Sir George Vanneck. These celebrated the completion of a smart new mansion and a Brown landscaped park. Two of them were views of the house, one of which was engraved in 1782. It shows Sir George and his lady riding in a carriage, with a further carriage nearer the house. Mature oaks (suitable for the navy) frame the view on the left. The letterpress to the engraving points out that the house is 'backed by large Trees, with extended Plantations of Oak, Beech, Fir and other Timber.'[37] A later commission from the Earl of Ashburnham, similarly, resulted in views of trees and woodland.[38]

Sir George Vanneck also commissioned Hearne to make a drawing of the famous oak tree on his estate known as Queen Elizabeth's Oak, so called because Elizabeth is reputed to have shot a deer from this tree when staying with her cousin Lord Hunsdon. The drawing is lost (though the tree is still standing), but Hearne's friend, Charles Davy, described measuring it with Hearne, in an account which was partly quoted in Gilpin's *Forest Scenery*:

> As I measured it with that ingenious artist in a rough way, to settle, in some degree, the proportions of its bulk, it was found to be nearly eleven yards in circumference … I am persuaded this cannot be less than five or six hundred years old.[39]

Hearne's interest in trees intersected with his interest in old buildings, which he recorded in his series of engraved views, *The Antiquities of Great Britain*. He began working on this series in 1778 and published it in 1786. Davy recounts how the principal arm of the tree reminded them of 'the winding staircase in a lofty Gothic tower.' The great hall in the old mansion nearby, which Davy, and perhaps Hearne as well, saw before it was demolished by Joshua Vanneck, was apparently 'built round six straight massy oaks, which originally upheld the roof, as they grew.'[40] Thus, old buildings and old trees were interchangeable as emblems of British antiquity.[41]

Hearne's two most important commissions were for sets of estate views at two locations on the Welsh Borders – Downton Vale (now known as Downton Gorge), near Ludlow, and Moccas Park, near Hereford. The twelve Downton views were for Richard Payne Knight, who had cut a path along both sides of the gorge adjoining his park. Apart from the occasional figure, the paths, and the bridges, most of Hearne's watercolours suggest a 'natural' landscape, one in which the trees have propagated themselves, and in which the walker can immerse him or herself in the grandeur of rocks and water. In several of the compositions, a large tree in the foreground spreads its branches over the top of the picture. Knight wrote later on, in his poem *The Landscape*, that

> Large stems of trees, and branches spreading wide,
> May oft adorn the scenes which they divide;
> For pond'rous masses, and deep shadows near,
> Will shew the distant scene more bright and clear[42]

Payne Knight was an admirer and collector of Claude's landscape paintings, and to some extent he is simply stating one of the principles of Claudian landscape composition, but Hearne's trees really spread across open space in a way that Claude's more compact trees do not, filling the sky with their foliage. Hearne's foreground trees have aesthetic, practical and ideological implications: they frame the view and shade the path for the traveller, but they also indicate the new freedom which had come in with the natural style of gardening, and, by implication, the freedom of the political system itself. Knight, like Walpole, equated unrestricted growth with political freedom: elsewhere in his poem he had written of the ancient forest, 'Where ev'ry shaggy shrub and spreading tree/ Proclaimed the seat of ancient liberty.'[43]

Three of the watercolours indicate the artifice which has gone into the construction of the Vale as an aesthetic experience. In *View from below Pool's Farm* (fig. 17), the

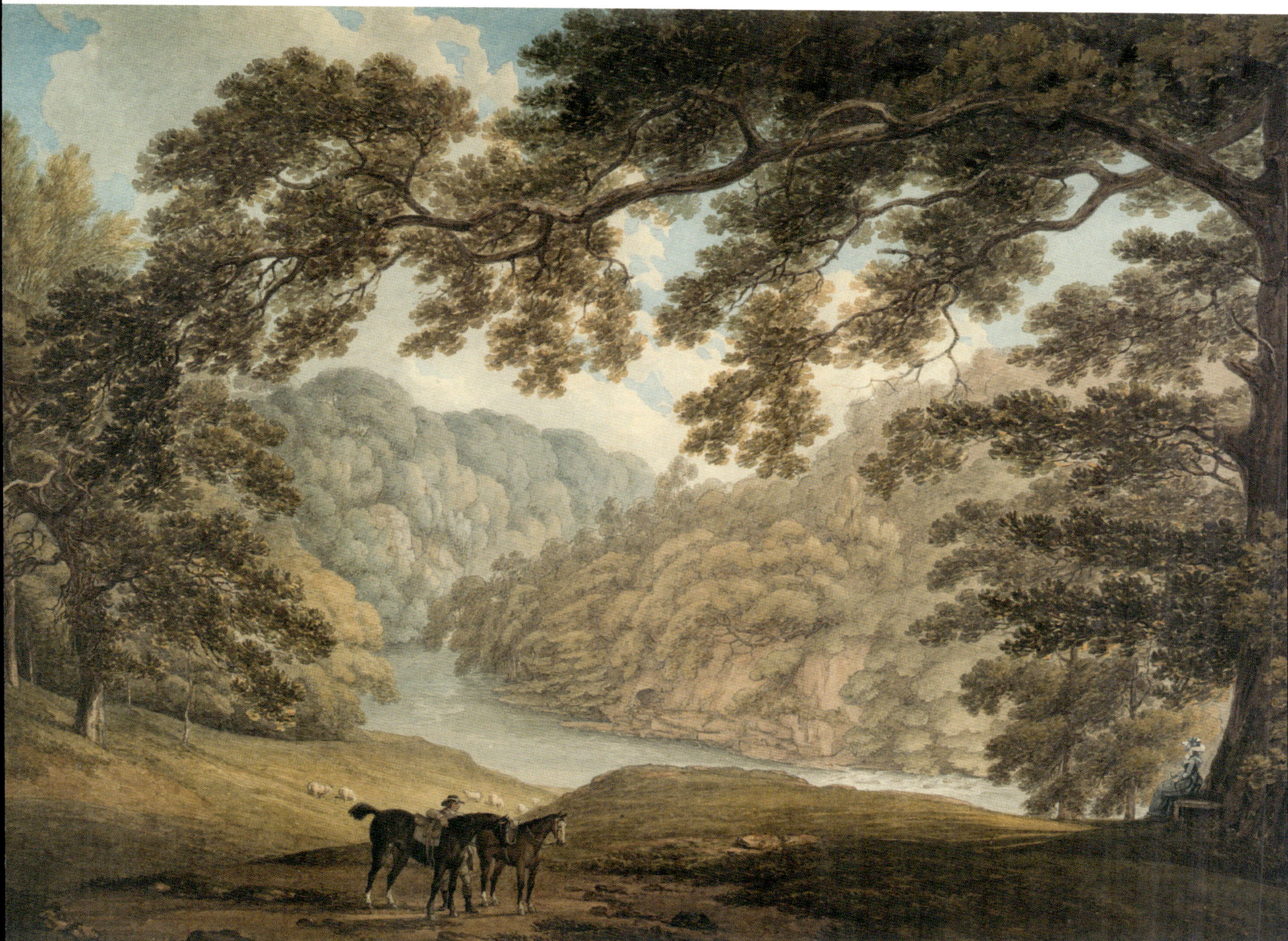

18 THOMAS HEARNE
Castle Bridge viewed from Downstream
1785 | Watercolour over graphite | 33.7 x 49.3 cm
Private Collection

foreground consists of smooth grass and a groom holds two horses, one of which has been fitted up with a sidesaddle. On the right we see the rider of the second horse, a lady in a long dress and broad-brimmed hat, sitting on a bench on front of a tree and enjoying the view. But the real star of this scene is the tree, a mature oak, which extends its branches 'unrestricted', in Horace Walpole's phrase, out over the entire landscape.[44] Nearly all the watercolours in the series have mature oaks in their foregrounds. Downton Vale really does have many mature oaks at the level of the paths, and their branches do indeed stretch out across the river, seeking the light. Two further scenes show a previously existing building, the Haymill, a working water mill on the river, before and after an extension has been added. This extension looks as if it has been added to cater for the refreshment needs of Payne Knight's visitors: potted plants are arranged around the outside, and through the open window we catch a glimpse of a lady in a hat, perhaps the same one who gazes out upon the landscape in *View from below Pool's Farm*. Once again, however, the composition is dominated by a mature tree.

Hearne's watercolours are remarkably true to the character of the scenery he depicts, and in some cases the trees he uses for his foregrounds can still be identified. The oak tree in *Castle Bridge viewed from Downstream* (fig. 18) was still standing in 2012, and the tree clinging to the rock and growing out at an almost vertical angle in *The View Upstream* (private collection) could also be identified: in recent years Natural England had cut off some of its branches as they feared its weight might pull down part of the bank. Hearne seems to have enjoyed contrasting the rugged branching of his foreground oaks with the fluffier ashes on the opposite bank, where, indeed, ashes still stand, presumably the descendants of the trees of the 1780s.[45] As David Morris has remarked, 'Hearne's drawings of trees matured rapidly through this series. He had always been alert to their structure and linear patterns, but he now concentrated on variegated foliage at different distances from the eye, while taking an almost architectural approach in the arranging of trees in his compositions.'[46]

Four of the Downton views were exhibited at the Royal Academy, in 1785 and 1786, each one being described as 'View upon the river Teme at Downton in Herefordshire, the seat of Richard Payne Knight Esq.' The titles point to the dual nature of the landscape – a natural river rather than an artificial lake, but nevertheless part of a gentleman's estate. Hearne went on to produce a similar set of watercolours for Payne Knight's friend, Sir George Cornewall of Moccas in Herefordshire. Cornewall, like Knight, had come to live on his estate as an adult: Knight inherited Downton from a childless uncle, while Cornewall married an heiress, and changed his name in 1771 to that of her family. Cornewall was a vigorous planter of trees. In 1836, John Claudius Loudon met Mr J. Webster, who reported that, as 'gardener and forester' at Moccas since 1793, he had superintended the planting of 'nearly 300,000 oaks, besides other trees.'[47] Cornewall also had an estate in Grenada, so he would have been very aware of the importance of oak trees in supplying timber for the royal and merchant navies. His timber was shipped down the Wye and Severn to Bristol, where slave ships and merchant ships were built and sailed to the West Indies.[48]

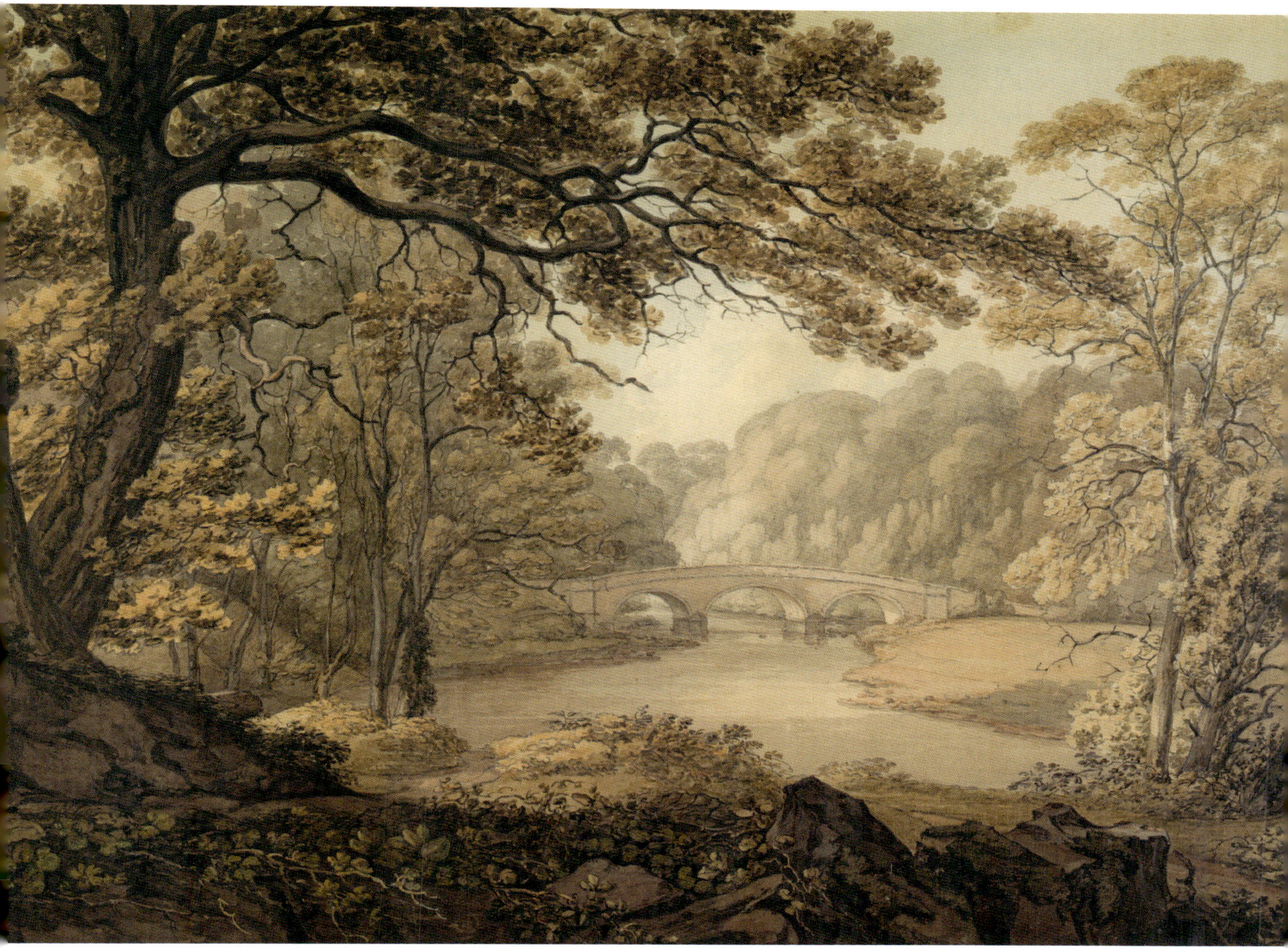

19 BENJAMIN T. POUNCY *after* THOMAS HEARNE
View of an Oak Tree in Moccas Park, Herefordshire
1798 | Engraving | 27.7 x 36.3 cm
British Library

At Moccas, Sir George Cornewall inherited an old deer park, noted for its ancient oak trees, beech trees and Spanish chestnuts. *View of an Oak Tree in Moccas Park* (fig. 19) is a portrait of one of the most famous of these trees, based on a drawing by Hearne. It was also depicted in Strutt's *Sylva Britannica* in 1822 (no. XIX). The young man sitting on the fallen part of the trunk may be intended to represent the son and heir, young George, born in 1774 and thus around 14 or 15 when the drawing was made. The oak tree no longer survives: it was recently estimated to date from c.1064.[49] Another watercolour from the series shows a fine beech tree, although, curiously, Hearne does not appear to have taken any interest in the Spanish chestnuts at Moccas. The letterpress to the print follows a quotation from Gilpin's *Forest Scenery* with a patriotic declaration:

> The oak is the first in the class of deciduous trees; and it is a happiness to the lovers of the picturesque that it is as useful as it is beautiful. … surely, no one who is a lover of his country, but, in addition to the pleasure which he has in contemplating this noble plant, must feel his heart glow on reflecting, that from its produce springs the British Navy, which gives our Island so honourable a distinction among surrounding nations.[50]

As David Morris has pointed out, the inclusion of the heir stresses the continuity of past and present, and it also acts as a reminder of the young men who manned the country's warships.[51] In addition, it suggests, like Zoffany's portraits of the Bute children, the idea of a family tree. This idea was particularly appealing to those who could not trace their

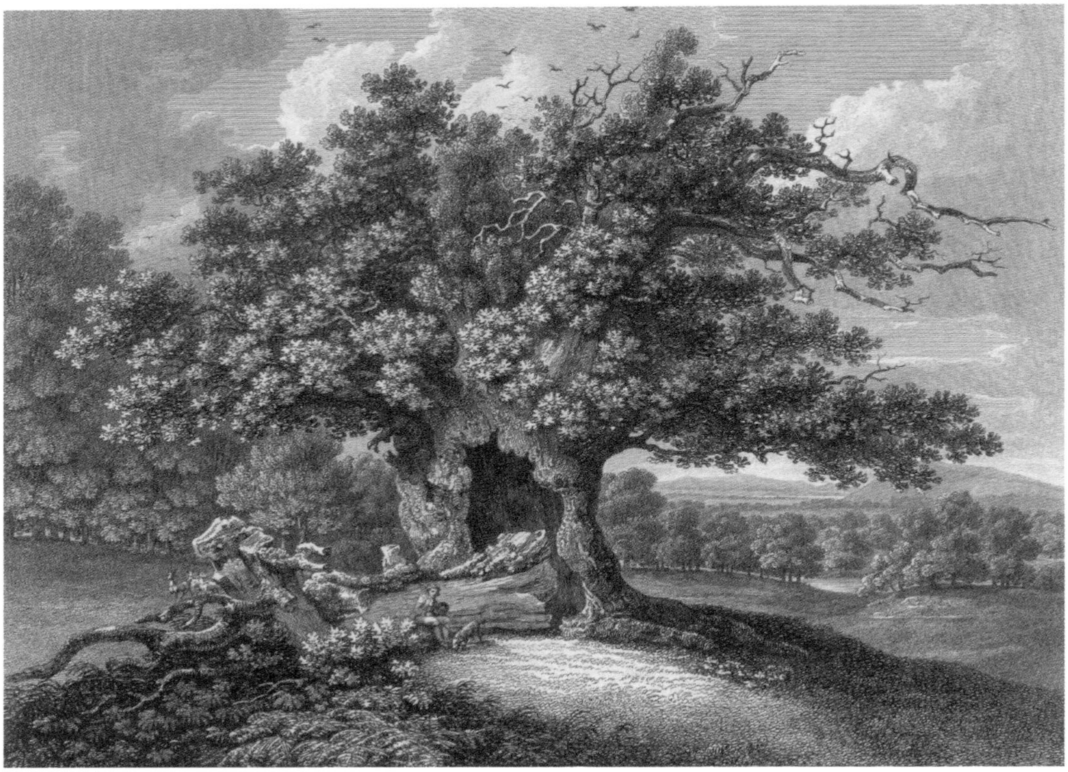

ownership of an estate back through several generations. Old trees were usually regarded as the sign of continuous family occupation over several centuries, but when Sandby and Hearne recorded their venerable oaks and beeches for Bute, Vanneck and Cornewall, the landowners were relative newcomers. Vanneck's family had been at Heveningham for some twenty years; Cornewall had been at Moccas for seventeen; Bute had bought the Luton Hoo estate only a year or two earlier. Knight, similarly, had been at Downton for some twelve years when Hearne produced his series of watercolours.

Like Paul Sandby, Hearne had an influence on the next generation of artists, through the dissemination of prints and through personal connections. The oak tree with its 'branches spreading wide' was a device he used frequently in his later series of prints, *Rural Sports*.[52] Hearne's friendships with Sir George Beaumont and Dr Thomas Monro meant that his watercolours were available to Constable and Turner. Constable, in particular, would have appreciated some of his later watercolours of river scenes in Essex, in which old cottages are shown in a flattish landscape next to willows, elms and poplars, very much the kind of scenery he would study in the Stour Valley.[53]

THE FOREST: THOMAS GAINSBOROUGH, BENJAMIN WEST AND GEORGE MORLAND

The counterpart of the landscaped park was the forest or woodland – areas of the countryside where nature looked comparatively wild, and where peasants might be encountered, still living in a relative state of independence. Thomas Gainsborough's landscapes often show this kind of terrain, and in the 1770s and 1780s he developed a new motif, the 'cottage door' which showed cottages against a backdrop of ancient trees, usually oaks (figs. 21, 22). In these settings labourers were shown in an idyllic state of nature, which combined simple living with domestic happiness. The theme was also taken up by Benjamin West, and was given a more modern and historically specific dimension in the 1790s and early 1800s by George Morland, whose cottagers wear contemporary clothing. Gainsborough's cottage door paintings were bought by wealthy individuals, but became well known through exhibitions. Morland's, on the other hand, were widely disseminated in the form of prints, and thus penetrated further down the social scale. Gainsborough's versions of the cottage door theme have puzzled modern observers, who have suggested that the figures illustrate the practice of wet-nursing, or the poverty caused by enclosure.[54] Less attention has been paid to the role of the trees in these works. They shelter the cottages so effectively that they seem, to modern eyes, to swamp them: their trunks obstruct doorways, and precariously placed dead branches threaten to flatten cottages and their inhabitants alike. To contemporaries, however, these old trees were the equivalent of the trees around a mansion, ensuring that the poor, like the rich, could enjoy the benefits of contemplation and peace that woods and forests offered.

Gainsborough was very fond of trees, both in reality and as subjects for painting. In a well-known letter he writes of how figures in a landscape painting simply 'create a little business for the Eye to be drawn from the Trees in order to return to them with more glee.'[55] Whether his trees are predominantly derived from reality or from imagination is a matter of some dispute. Scholars have noted how many of the crisply-detailed trees in his earlier paintings are lifted directly from the work of seventeenth-century Dutch painters such as Jacob van Ruisdael, Adam Pynacker and Jan Wijnants.[56] In later life he is supposed to have painted from model landscapes in which broccoli served for clumps of trees. However, this anecdote appears to be derived from only one unreliable source, and other accounts mention him bringing in stumps and branches to his painting-room.[57] There are also drawings of trees which were clearly done from nature, including a study of a beech tree on the estate of Uvedale Price.[58] Silver birches and oaks predominate in his earlier work, but in the 1760s he seems

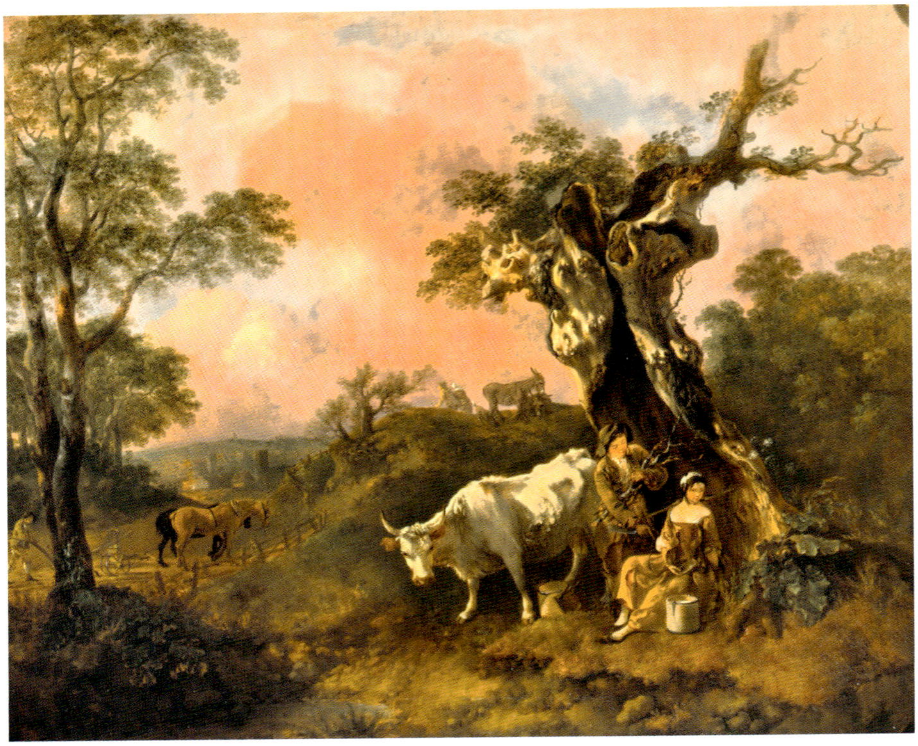

20 THOMAS GAINSBOROUGH | *Landscape with Woodcutter and Milkmaid*
1755 | Oil on canvas | 106.7 x 128.2 cm | From the Woburn Abbey Collection

to have preferred softer, feathery trees, beech and ash, going back to oaks in his landscapes and fancy pictures of the 1770s and 1780s. The meaning of the trees in his landscapes is also open to varying interpretations. Elise Smith has pointed out the significance in his landscapes of pollards, which she sees primarily as metaphors for productivity and connectedness in the rural economy: the oak pollard in his *Landscape with Woodcutter and Milkmaid* of 1755 (fig. 20) would have provided new shoots which could be cut for firewood, fencing and other uses.[59] However, this painting had a decorative function as a chimneypiece, and Gainsborough's later inclusion of a pollard in his painting of fashionable London life, *The Mall* (1783; Frick Art Gallery, New York), indicates that he also appreciated the curving lines of an old pollard for purely aesthetic reasons, as earlier scholars such as John Hayes have argued.[60] In the *Landscape with Woodcutter and Milkmaid*, the hollow oak provides a dark background for the figure group against which the milkmaid's white cap stands out dramatically, and its light-catching, irregular excrescences and diagonal placement are echoed and balanced by similar characteristics in the white cow which stands alongside it.

The cottage door pictures pose similar questions about the balance between aesthetics, meaning and verisimilitude. Did eighteenth-century peasants really live in cottages that were so closely overhung by ancient trees? Or was this just a fantasy of simple life as Gainsborough and his patrons thought it should be lived? The artist's friend, Uvedale Price, wrote in his *Essays on the Picturesque* of the symbiotic relationship between cottages and old trees, as if of two living beings:

> Cottages appear to repose under their shade, to be protected, sometimes supported by them; and they, on the other hand, hang over and embrace the cottage with their branches: it seems as if they could never have been separated from each other; and there would be a sort of cruelty in dividing them.[61]

This relationship between old trees and cottages is shown in all five of Gainsborough's cottage door paintings, including *The Woodcutter's Return* (fig. 21) and *The Cottage Door with Children Playing* (fig. 22).[62] In each case, the cottage is a one or two-room thatched hovel, with few or even no windows and a central doorway.

21 THOMAS GAINSBOROUGH
The Woodcutter's Return
c.1780 | Oil on canvas | 147.3 x 123.2 cm
Belvoir Castle, Leicestershire, UK/Bridgeman Images

22 THOMAS GAINSBOROUGH
The Cottage Door with Children Playing
c.1777–8 | Oil on canvas | 122.5 x 149.2 cm
Cincinnati Art Museum, Ohio, USA, given in honour of Mr and Mrs Charles F. Williams by their children, Bridgeman Images

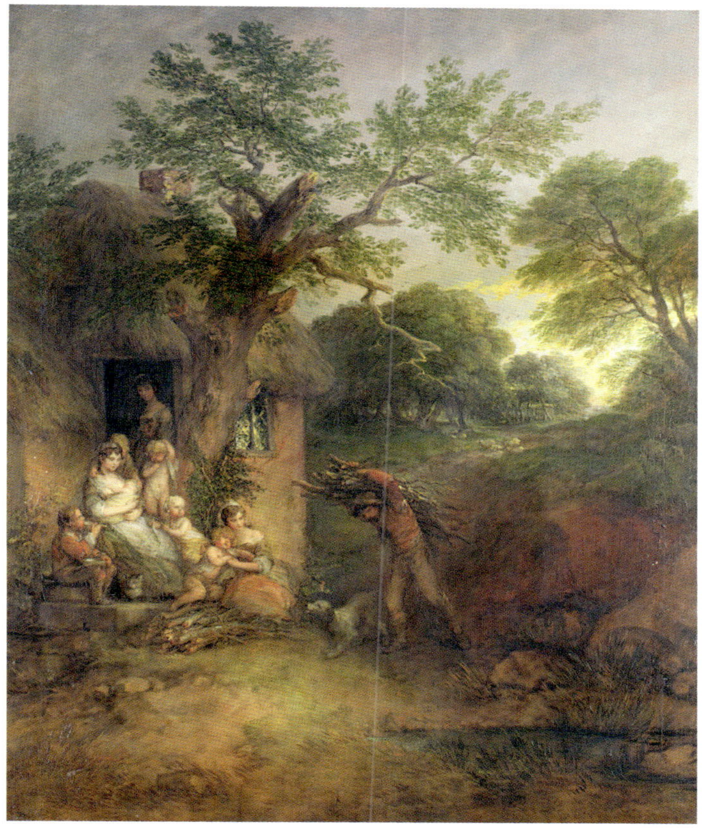

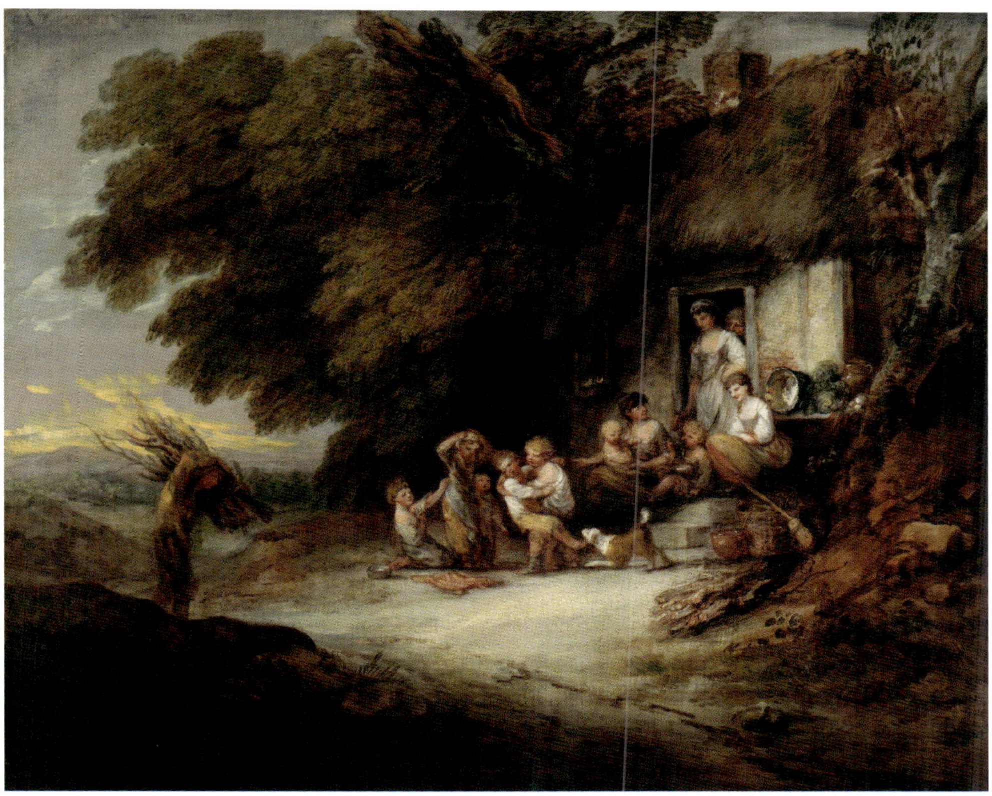

23 BENJAMIN WEST
A View in Windsor Great Park
c.1783–5 | Oil on canvas | 153.1 x 215.5 cm | Royal Collection Trust

Contemporary reactions to these pictures are unanimous in seeing them as depictions of health, innocence and domestic bliss. *The Woodcutter's Return* was a 'scene of beauty and domestic love', *The Cottage Door* was 'a scene of happiness that may truly be called Adam's paradise.'[63] The *Cottage Door with Children Playing* was described in a review as taken from Shenstone's *Schoolmistress*: this is now seen as an error, since the painting clearly does not show a school, but the actual extract quoted by the critic is a good match, since it describes the children rushing out into the sunshine to play. The poem makes a connection between the children's games and political liberty, asking Heaven to shield their pastimes, 'For well may Freedom, erst so dearly won,/ Appear to British elf more gladsome than the sun.'[64] In his cottage door paintings, Gainsborough reverts to his former preference for oak trees. An anonymous poem published in the month of his death claims that this was his favourite tree, and stresses its patriotic resonance:

> But most the Druid oak with towering head,
> His genius suited, and his fancy fed;
> The Briton's boast, the source of Gaul's despair,
> The Painter's idol, and the Prince's care.[65]

If Gainsborough's painted oaks suggested warships and naval victories over France to this writer, then it could be argued that, in a cottage door scene, the oak shelters the peasant family, just as it shelters the children of Lord Bute, both practically and metaphorically as a symbol of the British navy that protects the coasts from invasion.

Some indication of how contemporaries would have viewed paintings like *The Woodcutter's Return* is provided by a passage in William Mason's poem, *The English Garden* (1772). As night falls, he writes,

> …the plodding hind,
> That homeward hies, kens not the cheering site
> Of his calm cabbin, which, a moment past,
> Stream'd from its roof an azure curl of smoke,
> Beneath the sheltering coppice, and gave sign
> Of warm domestic welcome from his toil.
> Nor is that Cot, of which fond Fancy draws
> This casual picture, alien from our theme.
> Revisit it at morn; its opening latch,
> Tho' Penury and Toil within reside,
> Shall pour thee forth a youthful progeny
> Glowing with health and beauty: (such the dower
> Of equal heav'n) see how the ruddy tribe
> Throng round the threshold, and, with vacant gaze,
> Salute thee; …[66]

The 'sheltering coppice' of trees encloses a scene of calm, warmth, domesticity, health and beauty, despite its admitted drawbacks of labour and poverty. Mason's 'plodding hind' returns home, like the fathers in Gainsborough's cottage door paintings, while the 'youthful progeny' that pour forth from the cottage are like the children in *The Cottage Door with Children Playing*. The amateur painter Mary Hartley, writing to William Gilpin in 1789, makes a similar association between domesticity, health, and a thatched cottage propped up by an ancient tree, when she imagines a scene 'where a little straw-roofed cottage shou'd peep out from behind an old hollow oak, with fantastical branches elbowing over it – a little blue smoke coming out of a small chimney, backed by the dark shade of a high and deep wood behind – a young woman at the door, with an innocent unaffected countenance the rose of health on her cheek, and an infant in her arms …'[67] In an explicit reference to Gainsborough's paintings, she goes on to enumerate the children playing on the steps and the father coming home, stooping to embrace two little boys who run to meet him.[68] In all these accounts, the deep woodland setting is seen as appropriate to the depiction of happy, healthy families.

There was some logic in this association of woodlands with peasant happiness. In unenclosed woodland, squatters could build cottages from rubble, mud and other materials and thatch them with straw: it was widely believed that

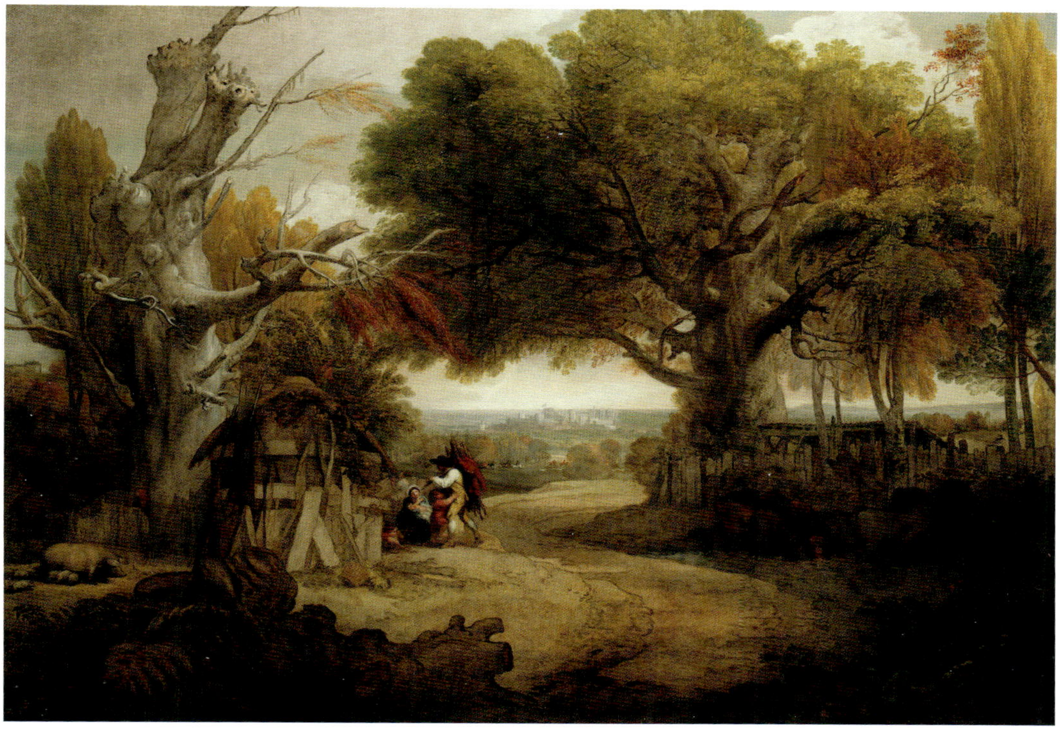

if you could raise a cottage overnight, and have the roof on and smoke issuing from a chimney by morning, you obtained a legal right to live in it.[69] There was plenty of fuel close at hand for open fires, and pigs could be fed on acorns, beechnuts and ash seeds from the trees. Such self-sufficiency could be supplemented by the employment of fathers and sons as woodmen, supplying fuel to the houses of the wealthy at a time when wood fires were the norm. It is likely that these hovels were built against tree trunks to provide a source of stability, as well as additional shelter to make up for any deficiencies in roofing. Sometimes they actually incorporated old hollow trees as part of the cottage accommodation. John Thomas Smith gives an account of a beech tree near Sand-pit Gate, in Windsor Forest, a drawing of which he exhibited at the Royal Academy in 1787:

> This grey and silver beech was the loftiest in the forest … his capacious and hollow trunk, with a small additional hut, afforded accommodation for a woodman, his wife, four children, a sow and a numerous litter of pigs.[70]

In Smith's account, this 'happy family retreat' was the object of benevolent attention from King George III, who had a snug brick cottage built for the family when their tree home became dangerous and had to be cut down.

The original tree-cum-cottage was depicted in a large oil painting by Benjamin West, exhibited at the Royal Academy in 1785 as *Landscape representing the Country near Windsor* (fig. 23). This shows the hollow tree and the 'small additional hut', complete with the rustic family, its pigs, and George III riding to hounds in the middle distance. Behind the family, a boy is picking fruit – apples or pears – from a laden tree, reminding viewers of another practical benefit of life in the woods. The old beech tree is balanced by a mature oak which dominates the composition, and in between them, lit up by the evening sun, we see Windsor Castle. The ramshackle hut looks as if it might, indeed, have been built overnight. The contrast with the sturdier cottages depicted by Gainsborough and Morland suggests that we are meant to read the latter as homes which have been improved over several generations, as squatters' cottages often were, with the original lath and plaster infill being replaced by bricks. It seems likely that West hoped George III would buy the painting, but it remained in his possession until his death. When it was sold in 1829 it was described as a 'graphic allegory' in which the peaceful home of the woodman was linked with the 'domestic peace' of the castle, 'the example of which dispensed moral good to every grade of the subjects of this virtuous king and queen.'[71]

24 GEORGE MORLAND
The Happy Cottagers
1793 | Mezzotint | 50.7 x 60.7 cm

George Morland took up the cottage door theme and gave it a more contemporary character, dressing his rural figures in modern clothes and giving them more credible occupations that help to suggest how they support themselves. His cottages also look like one or two-room, single-storey hovels leaning against ancient trees and located in the depths, or on the edge of the forest. In *The Happy Cottagers* (fig. 24), the mother knits, there is a fat pig in a pigsty and ducks on a pond. She wears a straw hat and her children are clothed in breeches and jackets. However, as in Gainsborough's paintings, the oak tree (or trees) dominates the composition, filling the entire width of the sky. His contemporaries said that Morland was particularly good at painting the oak tree.[72] He makes the implicitly patriotic symbolism of the oak explicit here, by placing a sprig of leaves on the hat worn by the older boy, suggesting that he is celebrating oak apple day in honour of the restoration of Charles II. The title (presumably given when the painting was engraved and issued as a print) also makes explicit the theme of the earlier cottage doors. John Barrell has shown how the cottage door was used as an instrument of political propaganda in the 1790s, when similar prints were distributed by the Association for the Preservation of Liberty and Property against Republicans and Levellers.[73] They were used to convey the message that Britain, with its ancient liberties, like its ancient trees, could offer a good life even to its poorest inhabitants, who would not benefit from the new political ideas being introduced from France.

In *Rustic Ease* (British Museum), Morland depicted a labourer stretched out on the ground in front of his cottage next to an old beech tree, looking fondly at his wife and child. J. Hassell, one of Morland's biographers, describes the engraving in terms that are reminiscent of Roger Fisher's description of the wealthy landowner walking in his plantations, even mentioning the birdsong that would accompany such scenes in real life:

> The deepest recess of a forest is here introduced, with a cottage in one corner: the repose of this scene is what every mind, harassed amidst the hurry and bustle of the metropolis, must naturally sigh for. … The solitude which pervades the scene before us, with the notes supposed to be issuing from the minstrels of the forest, all contributing to repose, have a grand and pleasing effect.[74]

Hassell compares this picture to the treasures of repose in the simple life of Rousseau. It was the writings of Rousseau, of course, which were the inspiration for Wright's portrait of Brooke Boothby, who is also shown reclining in a woodland setting. To modern observers such comparisons may seem absurd: the life of a peasant or labourer was completely different from that of a landowner. However, the portraits, landscapes and cottage-door pictures discussed in this chapter all share a common theme. Trees are used to convey the concept of England as a place of established customs, old families, paternalism and liberty. Both in the park and in the forest, the emphasis is on ancient trees, especially oak and beech, symbols of liberty and poetic inspiration.

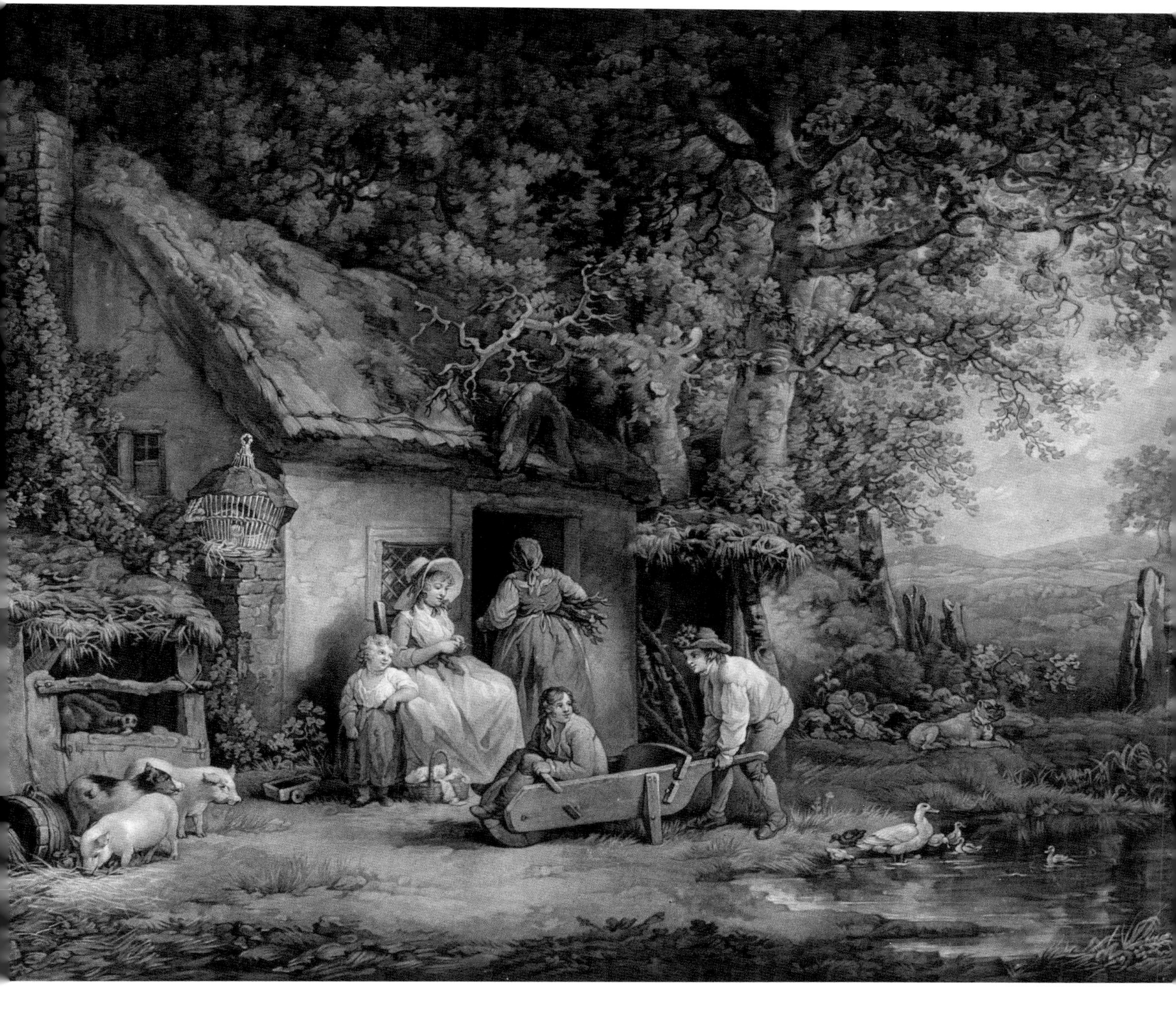

ENDNOTES

1 This particular oak was, however, left to grow old and survived into the twenty-first century on the Auberies Estate Farm.

2 Martin Postle, ed., *Johann Zoffany, RA: Society Observed* (New Haven and London: Yale University Press, 2011), pp. 244-5. For Zoffany's other portraits of sitters with trees, see Kate Retford, '"Peculiarly happy at taking likenesses": Zoffany and British Portraiture', ibid., p. 108.

3 Edmund Burke, letter to the Duke of Richmond, November 17th 1772.

4 See Stephen Leach, 'Good Melancholy Monsieur: Joseph Wright's Portrait of Sir Brooke Boothby', *British Art Journal*, Vol. 15, issue 1 (Autumn 2014), pp. 110-112.

5 Roger Fisher, *Heart of Oak, the British Bulwark* (London: J. Johnson, 1763), p. 7.

6 Ibid., p. 37.

7 Horace Walpole, *On Modern Gardening* (London: Brentham Press, 1975), pp. 29, 23.

8 Ibid, p. 31.

9 Dorothy Stroud, *Capability Brown* (London: Faber & Faber, 1975), p. 108.

10 Stroud, *Capability Brown*, p. 132.

11 From the draft of a letter to Revd. Thomas Dyer, who had made enquiries on behalf of a French friend, in 1775. Pakenham correspondence, quoted in Stroud, *Capability Brown*, p. 157.

12 Stroud gives the examples of the Great Cascade at Blenheim and the summerhouse at Burghley: ibid, pp. 130, 77.

13 William Mason, *The English Garden* (London: R. Horsfield, 1772, ll. 318-324.

14 Ibid, ll. 334-336, 341, 330-331, 337-339.

15 Hayman Rooke, Esq., F.S.A., *Descriptions and Sketches of some Remarkable Oaks in the Park at Welbeck, in the County of Nottingham, a Seat of His Grace the Duke of Portland* (London: J. Nichols, 1790), pp. 5-6, 18.

16 Quoted in Stephen Daniels, *Humphrey Repton: Landscape Gardening and the Geography of Georgian England* (New Haven and London: Yale University Press, 1999), p. 166.

17 Thomas Gray, *Elegy written in a Country Churchyard* (London: R. Dodsley, 1751, ll. 101-104.

18 William Cowper, *The Task*, 1785, book 1, ll. 760-761.

19 Tim Fulford, *Landscape, Liberty and Authority: Poetry, Criticism and Politics from Thomson to Wordsworth* (Cambridge University Press, 1996), pp. 55-6.

20 Cowper, *The Task*, book I, ll. 338-343.

21 Ibid, ll. 300-320.

22 Richard Payne Knight, *The Landscape, a didactic poem* (London: W. Bulmer & Co, 1794), Book I, ll. 293-8.

23 Ibid, Book III, ll. 62-66.

24 Ibid, Book III, ll. 83, 85-8.

25 Ibid, p. 5

26 Walpole, *Modern Gardening*, p. 26.

27 In 1760 letters from Mason and Gray, to Lord Nuneham, praise Sandby's paintings and refer to him as 'Mason's friend'. Johnson Ball, *Paul and Thomas Sandby, Royal Academicians: An Anglo-Danish saga of Art, Love and War in Georgian England.* (Cheddar, Somerset: Charles Skilton Ltd, 1985), p. 195.

28 John Bonehill and Stephen Daniels, eds., *Paul Sandby: Picturing Britain* (London: Royal Academy, 2009), p. 191.

29 12 of these views were sold at Christie's, London, in the sale 'British Watercolours from the Bute Collection', 3 July 1996, lots 103-14. A further three are illustrated in Bonehill and Daniels, eds., *Picturing Britain*, cat. Nos. 89-91. Lot 103 in the Christie's sale is numbered '19'.

30 *Someries Farm near Luton, Bedfordshire*, exhibited at Society of Artists, 1768, now in Birmingham Museum and Art Gallery.

31 Christie's Sale, 1996, lots 104, 113.

32 Postle, ed., *Johann Zoffany*, pp. 244-5.

33 Bonehill and Daniels, eds., *Picturing Britain*, p. 212; Frederick Davis, *History of Luton, with its hamlets, etc* (printed for the author, 1855), p. 20.

34 Anon, *Public Characters of 1800-1* (Dublin, 1801), p. 462, quoted in Bonehill and Daniels, eds., *Picturing Britain*, p. 13.

35 Cited in William Sandby, *Thomas and Paul Sandby, Royal Academicians* (London: Seeley & Co Ltd, 1892), p. 116.

36 Ibid, p. 268.

37 Photograph of engraving in Witt Library.

38 *A Drive in Ashburnham Park* (Rhode Island School of Design) and *In Ashburnham Park* (Fitzwilliam Museum). These are undated, but may have been done towards the end of Hearne's life: the family sale in 1953 included another drawing by Hearne, *The Vale of Ashburnham*, dated 1814. (Sotheby's, 15 July 1953, The Ashburnham Collection).

39 Charles Davy, *Letters addressed chiefly to a young Gentleman upon subjects of Literature*, Letter XXVII, 1787, pp. 235-6.

40 Ibid, p. 237. Sir Joshua Vanneck died in 1777.

41 The Vannecks themselves were not, however, an ancient British family: Sir Joshua was a Dutch merchant, born Van Neck, who had emigrated from The Hague in 1722. He bought the Heveningham estate in 1759.

42 Knight, *The Landscape*, p. 35, ll. 240-3.

43 Ibid, p. 40, ll.39-40.

44 This part of the Vale has now been planted with conifers, so it is impossible to say whether the tree really existed. On the evidence of the other watercolours in the series, however, it is very likely that it did.
45 However, he seems to have ignored two features which are very obvious in the landscape today: the yews, for which Payne Knight seems to have a particular predilection, and the coppiced broad-leaved limes. Some of the yews were planted by Payne Knight, so they would have been mere saplings in the 1780s.
46 David Morris, *Thomas Hearne and his Landscape* (London: Reaktion Books, 1989), p. 93.
47 Susanne Seymour, Charles Watkins and Stephen Daniels, 'Sir George Cornewall: management, improvement and landscaping, 1771-1819', in Paul T. Harding and Tom Wall, eds., *Moccas: An English Deer Park. The history, wild-life and management of the first parkland National Nature Reserve* (Peterborough: English Nature, 2000), p. 56.
48 Ibid, p. 58.
49 Tom Wall, 'A landscape of remarkable trees', in Harding and Wall, *Moccas*, p. 83.
50 Morris, *Thomas Hearne*, p. 98.
51 Ibid, p. 98.
52 See, for example, *Ploughing* and *Coursing* from this series of 12 prints.
53 For example, *At Much Easton, Essex* (c. 1790) and *Near Witham, Essex* (1793), both in the British Museum.
54 For these interpretations, see Susan Sloman, '"Innocence and Health": Nursing Women in Gainsborough's Cottage-door Paintings', and Michael Rosenthal, 'Gainsborough's Cottage Doors: A Matter of Modernity', in Ann Bermingham, ed., *Sensation and Sensibility. Viewing Gainsborough's Cottage Door* (New Haven and London: Yale University Press, 2005), pp. 37-51 and 77-95.
55 Letter to William Jackson, August 23 1767. Mary Woodall, ed., *The Letters of Thomas Gainsborough*, rev. ed. (Bradford: Cupid Press, 1963), p. 99.
56 John Hayes, *The Landscape Paintings of Thomas Gainsborough* (London: Philip Wilson, 1982), pp. 74, 77.
57 The broccoli is mentioned in an account by an unidentified 'Amateur of Painting' who claimed to have known Gainsborough at Bath, published in the *Somerset House Gazette*, 6 March 1824, Vol. 1, p. 348 (Hayes, *Landscape Paintings*, p. 95). Gainsborough left Bath in 1774 and died in 1788, so this was published long after the event.
58 Whitworth Gallery, University of Manchester.
59 Elise L. Smith, '"The Aged Pollard's Shade": Gainsborough's Landscape with Woodcutter and Milkmaid', *Eighteenth-Century Studies*, Vol. 41, no. 1 (2007), pp. 17-39.
60 See, for example, Hayes, *Landscape Paintings*, Vol. I, pp. 77, 155.
61 Uvedale Price, *Essays on the Picturesque*, Vol. II (London: J. Mawman, 1810), p. 351.
62 The other three are *Cottage Door* (1780, Huntington Art Gallery, San Marino), *Cottage Door with Girl and Pigs* (1786, Ipswich Museum and Art Gallery) and *Peasant Smoking at a Cottage Door* (1788, University of California, Los Angeles).
63 Poem, cited in Michael Rosenthal and Martin Myrone, eds., *Gainsborough* (London: Tate Publishing, 2002), p. 219; and *Morning Chronicle*, cited in Bermingham, ed., *Sensation and Sensibility*, p. 2.
64 Quoted in *The General Advertiser*, 30 April 1778.
65 Poem by W. de W., published in Wiltshire periodical, *The County Magazine*, August 1788, II, no. 32, p. 123, cited in Susan Sloman, *Gainsborough in Bath* (New Haven and London: Yale University Press, 2002), p. 170.
66 Mason, *English Garden*, ll. 400-414.
67 Mary Hartley to William Gilpin, 23 October 1789, quoted in Carl Paul Barbier, *William Gilpin: His Drawings, Teaching, and Theory of the Picturesque* (Oxford: Clarendon Press, 1963), p. 114.
68 Ibid. This last detail seems to be her own invention, however: she was probably thinking of Gray's *Elegy*: 'No children run to lisp their sire's return,/Or climb his knees the envied kiss to share.' (ll. 23-4).
69 See Colin Ward, *Cotters and Squatters: Housing's Hidden History* (Nottingham: Five Leaves, 2002).
70 John Thomas Smith, *A Book for a Rainy Day, or, Recollections of the events of the last sixty-six years* (London: Richard Bentley, 1845), pp. 111-12.
71 Robins catalogue, 22-25 May 1829, quoted in Helmut von Erffa and Allen Staley, *The Paintings of Benjamin West* (New Haven and London: Yale University Press, 1986), p. 430.
72 George Dawe, *The Life of George Morland, with Remarks on his Works* (London: Vernor, Hood and Sharpe, 1807), p. 194; J. Hassell, *Memoirs of the life of George Morland* (London: James Cundee, 1806), p. vi; J. T. Smith, *Nollekens and his Times* (London: Henry Colburn, 1828), p. 339.
73 John Barrell, 'Spectacles for Republicans', in Bermingham, ed., *Sensation and Sensibility*, pp. 53-73.
74 Hassell, *Memoirs of the life of George Morland*, p. 130.

25 MISS S. A. YOUNG

'Elm at the Beginning of March'

Plate 7 from *Studies of Trees, with and without Foliage*, 1834. Yale Center for British Art, Paul Mellon Collection (Folio B Q 3)

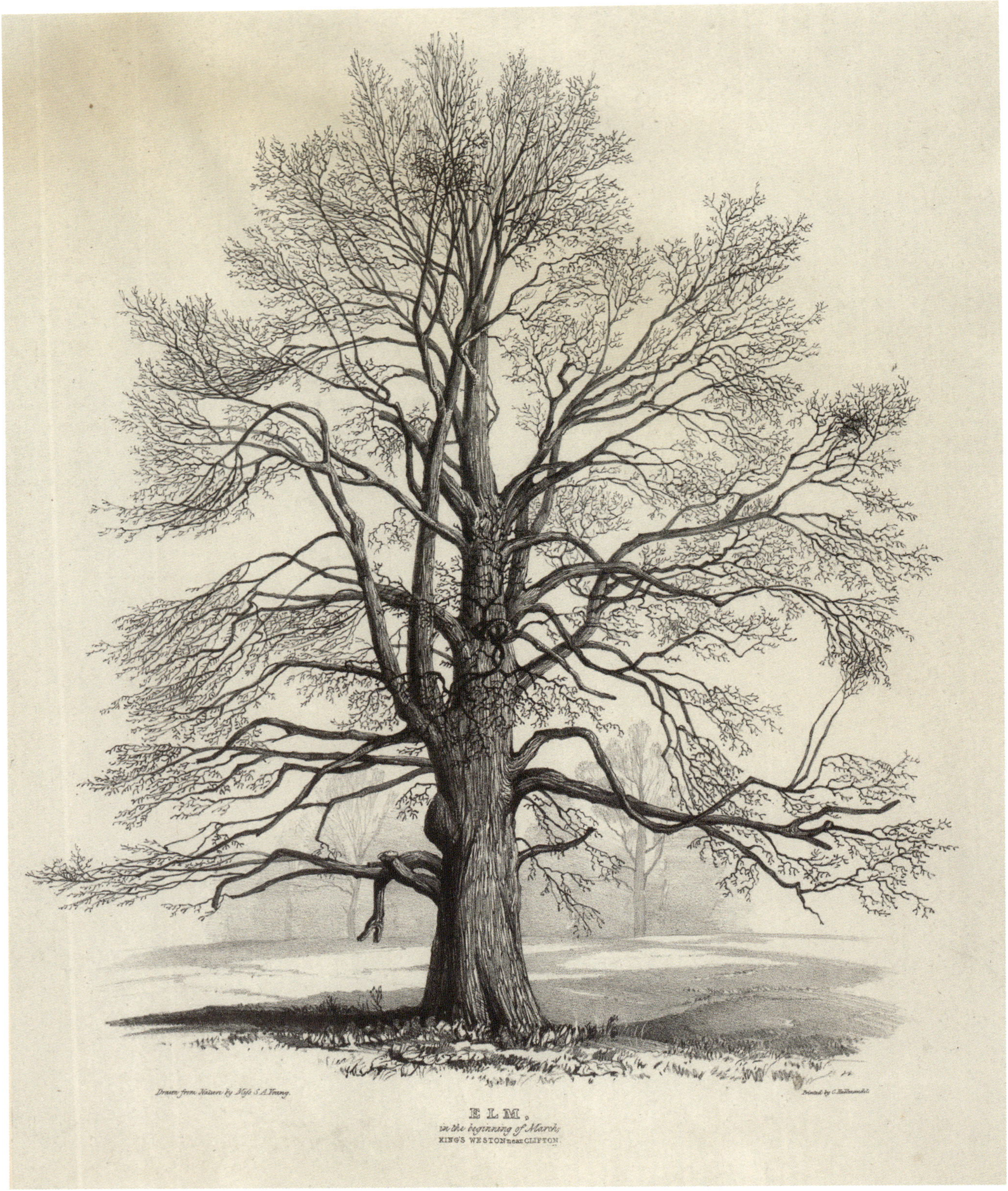

THREE

Woodland Anatomy: The Drawing of Trees

THE FIRST HALF of the nineteenth century saw a massive explosion of interest in the drawing of trees. Amateurs spent many happy hours engaged in the careful delineation of specimens in their parks or gardens, and landscape gardeners and naturalists used draughtsmanship as an essential aid to their recording of new species. Accordingly, drawing masters produced a wide range of manuals which offered models and formulae to assist in these activities. Professional landscape painters, too, devoted much effort to acquiring facility in tree drawing as a fundamental artistic skill, the equivalent of figure drawing for the historical or genre painter. The emphasis in the drawing manuals was, firstly, on distinguishing the 'character' of the different species of trees; and secondly, on developing methods of drawing that would facilitate a more naturalistic, a more scientific way of drawing an entire tree. Professional artists used these manuals, but also developed their own methods of achieving a closer approximation to what they could see when they sat down to draw, or paint, from nature. This period witnessed, in the productions of John Constable and Samuel Palmer, some of the best tree drawings ever produced; their work emerges from a generation of artists whose watercolours, etchings, engravings and lithographs of trees achieve a high degree of naturalism and expressive power.

Given the interest in trees in country-house culture, and the emphasis laid on the acquisition of the 'polite art' of drawing, it is hardly surprising that many of the most enthusiastic tree sketchers in this period were landowners and their families. Joshua Bryant's *Progressive Lessons on the Art of Drawing Landscapes* (1807), which opens with a substantial section on trees, begins by praising the productions of a whole series of aristocrats. Many of his readers, he asserts, must have seen the delineations of the Princess Elizabeth, Lady Diana Beauclerc, Lady Lucan, and the Countesses Spencer, Harrington, and Warwick, whose productions do honour to the age, while 'the Earls of Harcourt, Warwick, and Aylesbury [sic], Sir George Beaumont, &c &c, are as much distinguished by their taste in the arts as by the rank they hold in society.'[1] This was obviously intended to flatter his readers, as most of those mentioned did not exhibit in public, but there was also an element of truth in his assertion. Lord Harcourt was a pupil and friend of Paul Sandby, whose watercolours have sometimes been attributed to the artist, and drawings of trees by Beaumont have survived which suggest that Constable could have learned from him. One of the most impressive of the illustrated books on trees, *Studies of Trees, with and without Foliage* (1834, fig. 25) was produced by Miss S. A. Young, a modest lady amateur, who claimed that the sketches were done from Nature 'during a short residence near Clifton, chiefly to beguile the tediousness of a lingering indisposition' and that if she has failed in her adherence to truth she 'trusts it will not be attributed to personal presumption or vanity.'[2] John Claudius Loudon may have been thinking of Miss Young when he wrote in his *Arboretum Britannicum* that 'it will always be found that ladies who reside in the country, and have studied botany ... will imitate the touch of trees better than professional landscape painters.'[3] The 600 tree portraits included in his eight-volume work included, amongst those by professional landscape painters, many attributed to 'Miss M. L.' and 'Miss F. L.', his own sisters.

26 ALEXANDER COZENS

'Oak, Pollard Oak, Palm and Italian Pine'

from *The Shape, Skeleton and Foliage of 32 Species of Trees*, 1771.

Beinecke Rare Book and Manuscript Library, Yale University

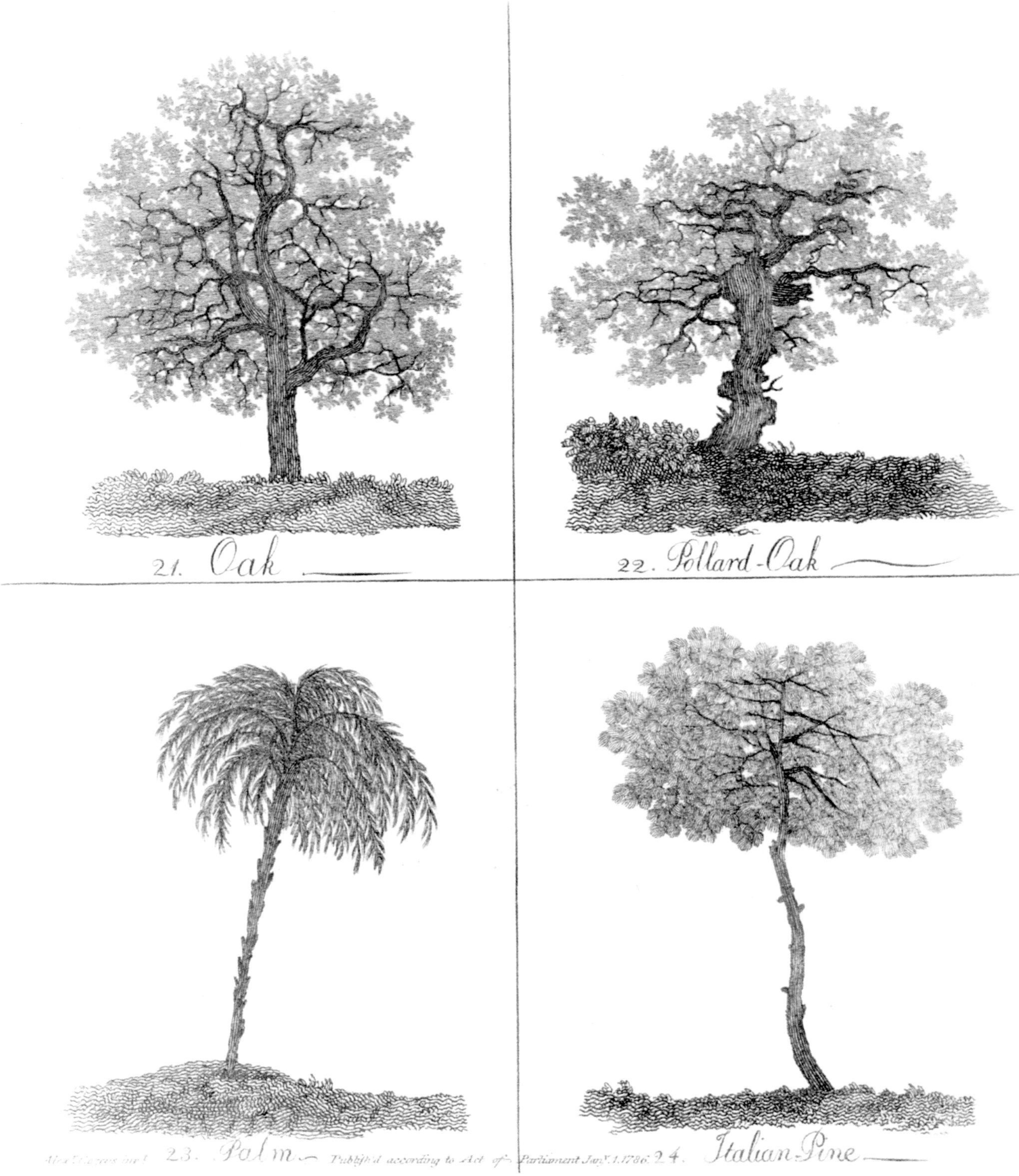

27 J. D. HARDING

'Oak and Ash, outline and shadow'

Plate XII from J. D. Harding, *Elementary Art, or, the Use of the Lead Pencil, advocated and explained* (London: Charles Tilt, 1834). 1701 c. 32. The Bodleian Libraries, The University of Oxford

CHARACTERS OF TREES: THE DRAWING MANUALS

Undoubtedly, one reason for the plethora of drawing manuals devoted to trees was the market provided by these amateur sketchers. From Alexander Cozens's set of etchings, entitled *The Shape, Skeleton and Foliage of 32 Species of Trees* (1771; fig. 26) to George Barnard's *Trees from Nature* (1868), a succession of books and collections of illustrations set out to assist the amateur or student in the drawing of trees.[4] Several drawing manuals set exercises of increasing difficulty: Joshua Bryant's *Progressive Lessons* (1807) began with the strokes to be used, and then went on to stumps and sprays before giving illustrations of whole (though rather small) trees.[5] James Duffield Harding's *Elementary Art* (1834, fig. 27), similarly, has a long section on foliage which builds up from the basic strokes, through the pattern of shadow, to shadows combined with outline, before going on to stems (trunks) and branches, and eventually to whole trees.[6] Barnard's *Handbook of Foliage and Foreground Drawing* (1853) also starts, like Bryant, with the basic strokes to be used in tree drawing. Other publications consisted of sets of prints without letter-press, intended either as models for students to copy,

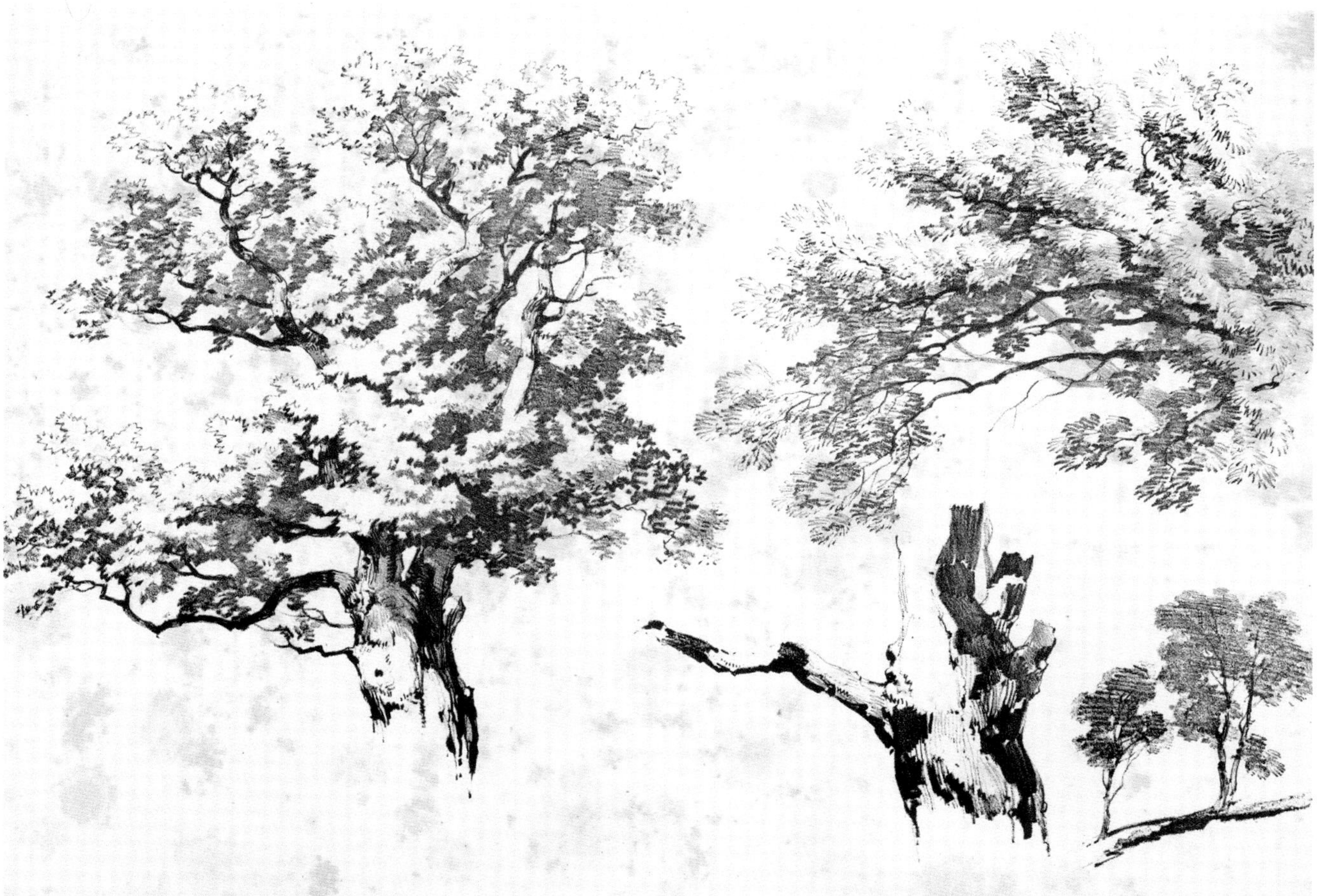

28 JOHN MARTIN

'Lime'

Plate 1 from *Characters of Tree, in a Series of Seven Plates*, (London: R. Ackermann, 1817). Etching.

Yale Center for British Art, Paul Mellon Fund (Folio A Q 6)

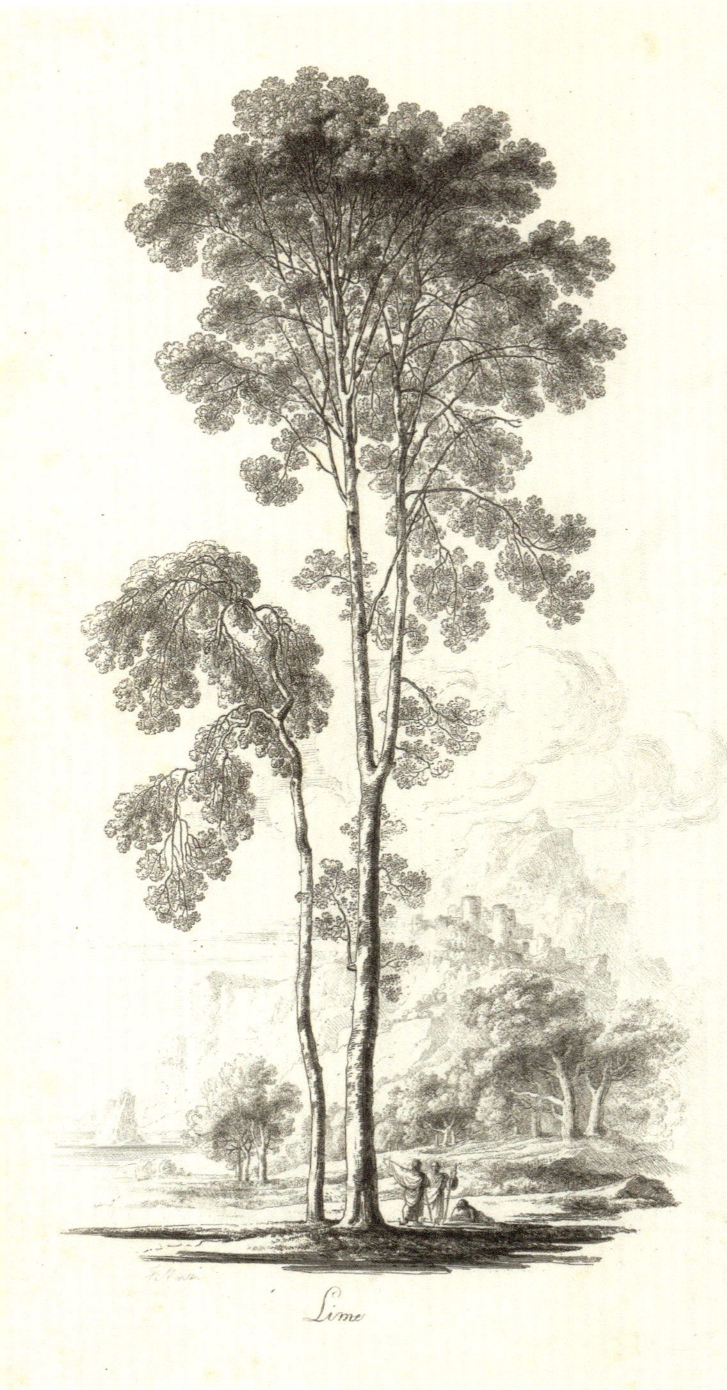

such as Laporte's *Characters of Trees* (1800) or else works of art in their own right, like John Martin's *Characters of Trees* (1817, fig. 28).[7] Lavishly-produced illustrated books on trees, the most important of which were Jacob George Strutt's *Sylva Britannica* and H. W. Burgess's *Eidodendron*, published by subscription within a few years of each other in the 1820s, provided further models for artists.[8] With the exception of important studies by Beryl Hartley and Ann Bermingham, these books on trees have been little studied, and they have largely been overlooked in histories of this crucial period in the development of British landscape painting, and yet their influence was enormous.[9]

Many of the manuals were printed using the new art of lithography, which preserved the character of the artist's drawing (although in reverse) including soft shading. Harding praised lithography in *Elementary Art* as 'the Art which alone could enable me to do the work.'[10] With lithography, the drawing-master could recreate the experience of a private lesson for a wider public. The standard practice in such lessons was that the master would provide drawings for the student to copy. By buying one of the manuals, the amateur or artist could teach themselves, for a fraction of the price of employing a drawing-master. One of the cheaper manuals, for example, George Harley's *Lessons on Drawing Trees* (1829) cost only 2s 6d.[11] Those collections which were etched or engraved, such as Martin's *Characters of Trees* and Strutt's *Sylva Britannica*, have a much more highly detailed and more linear style than the lithographs, and their complexity would have made them difficult to copy. Alexander Cozens's *Shape, Skeleton and Foliage* is unique in its use of superimposed silhouettes, which recall the techniques of eighteenth-century portrait silhouettes. Most of the others focus less on line than on the contrasts of masses of light and shade to give a sense of volume. The majority of the manuals are solely concerned with drawing, but a few include colour, including Louis Francia's *Progressive Lessons tending to elucidate the characters of trees* (1813) and David Hall M'Kewan's *Lessons on Trees, in Water Colours* (1860).[12] The nature of the drawing manual made it imperative to produce relatively simple drawings, patterns and rules, which could be copied and learned by those who might never become professional artists: hence there is a tendency to formulae and schemata, at times reminiscent of the *Mustard Seed Garden Manual* used by Chinese artists from the seventeenth century, especially in the prescription of precise types of notation for different species.[13]

In 1846, Henry Twining considered the degree of detail which should be shown in a painting of a tree, and concluded that both art and the general interest in trees had changed since the time of the 'old masters':

> For our guidance, we have the examples of the old masters; but a change in the style of painting, as well as a more general taste for the culture of trees, and, consequently, a better knowledge of their characters, often render necessary a considerable deviation from the course which they have pursued. The landscape portrait is now in general the most acceptable production in this branch, and it requires that the various kinds of trees and plants should be indicated with much more precision than in the composition, or classical landscape.[14]

It was no longer possible, Twining implies, for artists to fob the public off with a representation of 'general nature' or of a 'generic tree' which could be an oak, an ash, a beech or an elm – increasingly, their viewers (who might well be amateur artists themselves) knew the difference. He acknowledges the influence of landscape gardening in the connection he makes between 'a more general taste for the culture of trees' and 'a better knowledge of their characters', and distinguishes between the 'composition' – a landscape devised in the imagination – and the 'portrait' – a depiction of a particular place, a particular tree, studied from nature.

Artists of this period strove to grasp the 'character' of particular types of tree. Sir Joshua Reynolds advocated that artists should aim at general effect rather than minute particulars, but in his Eleventh Discourse, delivered in December 1782, he acknowledged that they should look at the 'general character of the species, the order of the branches, and the masses of the foliage' when depicting a tree.[15] Joseph Holden Pott's *Essay on Landscape Painting*, published in the same year, noted that 'The English park and forest, afford an infinite variety of character in its trees, and endless choice of foliage', and claimed (not entirely accurately) that this gave English painters an advantage over the Dutch, who had to make do with willow, poplar and elm.[16] He went on to devote a substantial section of his *Essay* to the 'characters of trees most beautiful in landscape.'[17] The word 'character' crops up repeatedly in the titles of many of the publications, both drawing manuals and sets of etchings, that followed. J. R. Cozens's *Delineations of the General Character, Ramifications and Foliage of Forest Trees* of 1789 was followed by J. Laporte's *Characters of Trees* in 1800. Then came François Hüet-Villiers's *Rudiments and Characters of Trees* in 1806, Louis Francia's *Progressive Lessons tending to elucidate the Characters of Trees* in 1813, and John Martin's *Characters of Trees* in 1817.[18] Each of these publications consisted of separate drawings of examples from the individual species, often a remarkable number: Hüet-Villiers's lithographs, for example, were issued in seven parts, each of which showed five different types.

The manuals insist that different species of trees should be recognizable in paintings. Edward Kennion, the author of a comprehensive book on the drawing of trees, published in 1815 but probably written in the early years of the century, comments that 'even in works of superior merit it is but seldom that we see more than a representation of trees in general, without the pleasure of being able to name the particular kind of each … We think it necessary in painting to make the clearest distinction between a Cow and a Horse, while an Ash and an Elm are depicted under the same general scrawl called a tree' – but trees, he reminds us, are more important in landscape than animals.[19] And Louis Francia, in 1813, says that his object is to elucidate the distinct character of trees, 'that distinguishing stamp, or mark, which, however slightly hinted at, still conveys to the beholder a full representation of the object intended; for instance, as

29 EDWARD KENNION

'Character of Tufting: Ash'

Plate XVI from E. Kennion, *An Essay on Trees in Landscape; or, an attempt to shew the propriety and importance of characteristic expression in this art, and the means of producing it: with examples* (London: T. Bensley, 1815). 1705 c. 1. The Bodleian Libraries, The University of Oxford

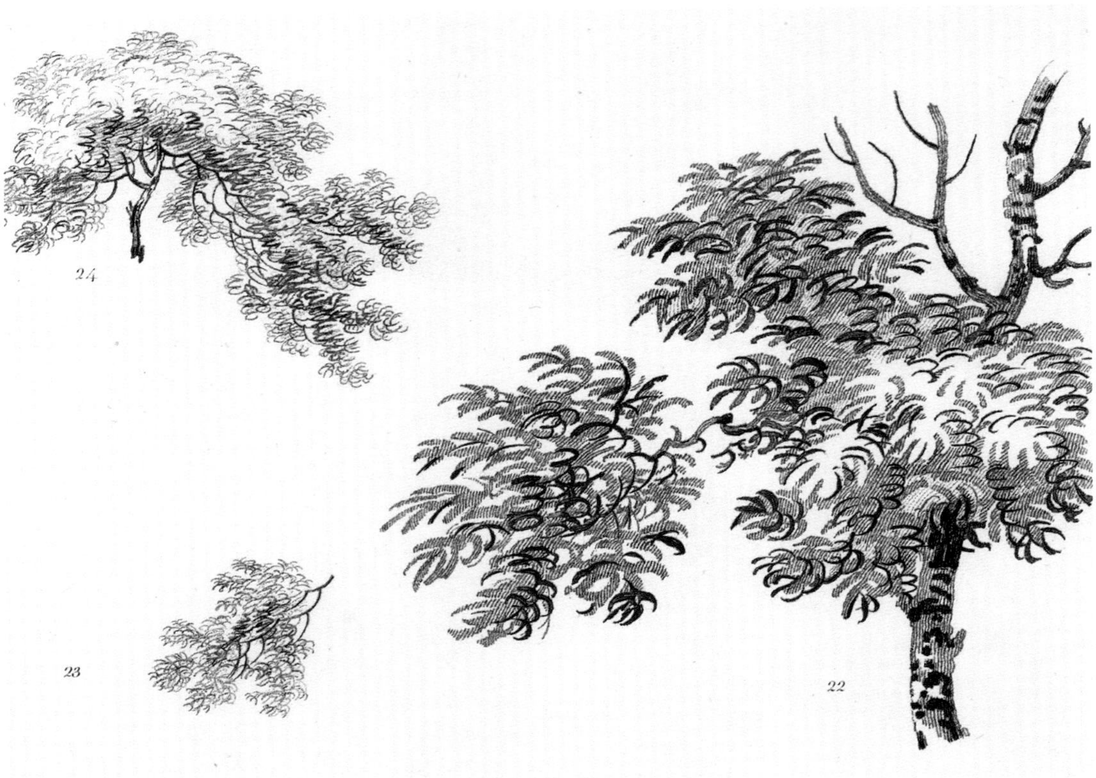

the leaves of the Oak are widely different from those of the Poplar, so should they be expressed as to prevent the possibility of doubt or mistake.'[20] Character was not just a question of different leaf shapes: Frank Howard in his *Science of Drawing* (1839) divides trees into three classes, those in which the branches are lost in the uniform mass of the whole, such as the oak, elm, or horse chestnut; those in which the simplicity of outline is affected by the projection of the branches, such as the beech, ash or willow; and those in which the ramifications are slightly covered with foliage, and the general form of the tree is divided into detached masses, such as the sycamore, white poplar or Scotch pine.[21] However, Harding, in *Elementary Art*, tried to avoid the obsession with differentiating the species and return to a more Reynoldsian concern with general nature, saying that the student would waste his time 'in prosecuting a study more within the province of the Botanist or the Gardener, than the Painter.'[22] Harding, accordingly, starts with exercises to enable the student to draw any tree before going on to the character of different species.

Most of the manuals, however, illustrate a range of different species. They usually start with the four timber trees – oak, ash, beech, elm – although a few leave out the beech. This may have been because the beech was difficult to draw: many of the illustrations of beeches are excessively feathery, and artists had the most success with it when they concentrated on the massive trunks of old beech trees rather than the foliage.[23] In 1834, Sir Thomas Dick Lauder agreed with Gilpin that the beech was 'unpicturesque, or, in other words ... an unmanageable subject of art', and yet, he argued, the very circumstances which made it so made it very beautiful to look at.[24] Other popular trees include the birch, horse chestnut, Lombardy poplar, and willows. Pollarded trees are unusual in the manuals: Alexander Cozens includes the pollard oak and the lopped elm (fig. 26), but later writers seem to have ignored examples of trees whose growth has been affected by human intervention, apart from the pollard willow, which was so common in the British countryside that it could hardly be left out. Non-native trees appear rarely: the emphasis is on drawing the native varieties, and occasionally those that have been naturalized in Britain such as the cedar of Lebanon and the acacia, while the chestnuts and sycamore, long naturalized, were treated as native trees.

The manuals generally pay lip service to Gilpin's claim that the oak is the most picturesque of the native trees, though many of the examples of oaks in their manuals are rather more venerable than their representations of other trees, as if the oak was a survivor from an earlier age. Many writers spring, like Lauder, to the defence of the beech, and several show a distinct preference for the ash. Pott, in 1782, praised the ash and the elm as particularly valuable to the artist:

> The ash is the most elegant of all trees, affording to the painter an opportunity of displaying the neatness and precision of his pencil more than any other … its slender and graceful branches admit the light through all parts … and, when well handled upon canvas, affords [sic] a sharpness and delicacy not to be equalled … The elm is a fine rich tree, and often grows to a most gigantic size, in which state it is wonderfully majestic … which, with its sober hues and the crispness of its foliage, renders it a noble object for the painter.[25]

Francia agreed with Pott's preference for the ash, describing it as 'the most playful and buoyant of all Trees … for beauty of form and elegance of distribution in its branches, as well as character, we know of no tree surpassing the ash.'[26] Writing in the 1850s, George Barnard notes that the foliage of elm is excellent for its breadth of light and shade, 'forming rounded masses which are more easily imitated than those of most other trees' while the chief beauty of the ash consists in the lightness of its appearance.[27] By this time the discussion of the relative artistic merits of different species had filtered down to the schoolroom, so that his pupils at Rugby School were apparently able to answer such exam questions as 'What is considered the noblest English tree?' and 'Is the Horse Chestnut formal or picturesque?'[28]

The manuals concentrate on two particular ways of representing a tree: large masses of light and shade to suggest volume, and a characteristic 'touch' for the outlines made by the 'tufts' or groups of leaves peculiar to each species. As Beryl Hartley and Ann Bermingham have shown, the idea of the 'touch' was of crucial importance in the development of drawing techniques in the manuals. Hartley has argued that artists were behaving like field naturalists, making discoveries as a result of their observation of nature which enabled them to depict trees more accurately than before. Bermingham, however, has pointed out that the concern with touch put a new emphasis on copying.[29] William Marshall Craig, in 1793, argued against a generalizing treatment of nature, stating that 'Every different subject or material should be expressed by a different line or touch, which Nature will always point out, if attended to': he criticized artists for using conventional touches drawn from artistic precedent rather than from nature itself.[30] The idea of the touch was elaborated more fully in Kennion's *Essay on Trees in Landscape* (1815), where the 'leading characters' of oak, elm and ash are distinguished: a starry 'Elliptic Asterisk' for oak, wavy lines and flattened ovals for elm, and 'a figure consisting of five curved lines united at one point' for ash (fig. 29).[31] The touch is therefore produced by a combination of the actual shape of the leaf and its manner of growth on the spray. Charles Kennion, Edward's son, who edited the book, claimed that George Barrett had invented the appropriate touch for elm and ash, and that Kennion himself invented the touch for the oak, but that 'the merit of a consistent application of the system belongs to Kennion.'[32] Once these shapes had been mastered, Kennion argued, they could be adapted for all the other species.[33]

30 J. G. STRUTT
'Horse Chestnut at Burleigh'
Plate XXXVII from J. G. Strutt, *Sylva Britannica; or, Portraits of Forest Trees, distinguished for their antiquity, magnitude, or beauty. Drawn from nature and etched by Jacob George Strutt* (London: J. G. Strutt and Colnaghi and Co, 1822). 19182 a.6.
The Bodleian Libraries, The University of Oxford

Kennion's 'system' may have been derived from observation, but the results do not look particularly naturalistic. The later refinements of it by J. G. Strutt and J. D. Harding were rather more successful. Strutt wrote an article on the oak, published in May 1828, for John Claudius Loudon's *Magazine of Natural History*, which illustrated the 'touch' formed by a spray of leaves.[34] Loudon himself published a further article in 1835, which gave precise instructions for determining the correct touch, by drawing a leaf, and a cluster of leaves, firstly from close to and then from the same distance at which the tree itself will be drawn, before proceeding to draw the whole tree.[35] Meanwhile, Harding's manual, *Elementary Art*, had come out in 1834. While he claims to teach the student to paint trees in general rather than specific botanical detail, and also says that the character of a tree is expressed as much in the stem (trunk) and branches as in the forms of the foliage, he clearly follows Kennion and Strutt in prescribing particular shapes for the masses of light and shade, shapes that are angular for the oak and more rounded for the ash (fig. 27).[36] Harding does not use the word 'touch', nor does he mention Kennion, Strutt or Loudon in his text, but his manual is part of the same discourse, which encouraged artists and amateurs to look at trees in terms of broad masses of light and shade, with the forms made by these masses being the crucial indicator of the character of the tree and hence of its species. Loudon's essay of 1835 was intended to be used by those artists and amateurs providing drawings for his *Arboretum Britannicum*, so a correct indication of the species was of vital importance. In the *Arboretum Britannicum* itself, he says at first that the only works which have noticed the subject of the touch of trees are Gilpin's *Forest Scenery* and Kennion's *Essay on Trees*; later in the first volume, however, he recommends Harding's *Elementary Art* as 'a work at once artistical and philosophic.'[37]

Loudon notes that one of the difficulties of his project in collecting the 600 tree portraits for the *Arboretum Britannicum* was that draughtsmen and engravers would insist on showing the distinct shape of individual leaves. Loudon thought this was as bad as giving the shape of the individual bricks when drawing a house.[38] In their texts, the manuals are almost unanimous in pointing out that leaf shapes cannot be seen from the distance at which the whole tree is visible, therefore they should not be shown in a drawing. Pott ridicules the 'bungler' who aims to show everything – 'every leaf of his tree is to be displayed.'[39] In the same year, 1782, Reynolds referred to a painter in Rome who had endeavoured to paint every leaf on a tree, as an example to avoid.[40] In his *Essay*, Kennion admonishes artists that 'all minute attention to the leafing of trees and drawing the shapes of leaves in the tufts is a capital error.'[41] Drawing every leaf of a tree was associated with botany, or else with the infancy of art. Kennion quotes Jean-Jacques Rousseau's approval of the flowers of the horse chestnut (which Kennion regards as wholly unpicturesque) to prove his point that the study of natural history is 'particularly unfavourable to picture … the person who could the most happily describe the parts and properties of a tree, would be the worst fitted of all others to represent it to the eye.'[42] Harding, similarly, states categorically that 'the student is never called upon to substitute botanical delineation for *pictorial effect* … he is not a painter of leaves in detail, but deals with the masses, the common forms, and the larger features.'[43]

The horse and Spanish chestnuts always presented a problem for those who said leaf shapes should not be shown, and Harding does his best to avoid them, excluding them altogether from *Elementary Art* (1834) and a further publication, *The Park and The Forest* (1841), and including the Spanish chestnut in his later *Lessons on Trees* only as an ancient tree with few leaves showing.[44] Of nine other books and sets of prints that include the horse chestnut, only four show the leaves separately outlined and none at all show it in flower.[45] John George Wood in 1815 provided a further reason for artists to avoid precise details of leaves: 'In the infancy of the Art, the first painters endeavoured to depict every leaf of the tree, and every hair of the head; but, as painting improved, this laborious and unprofitable style fell into disuse, and an attempt was made to represent, by more general means, the *effect* produced by the hair, and also that produced by the leaves of the tree.'[46] Despite all these strong statements, however, Craig outlines the leaves in the illustrations to his Essay in 1793, Hüet-Villiers starts his manual with finely-detailed drawings of leaves, and Strutt also tends to outline his leaves, both in his drawings for the *Sylva Britannica* and in the drawings he provided to Loudon.

Many of the trees in the drawing manuals look very much alike. However, John Martin's series of six trees, published in 1817, with a further plate of drawings of sprays and leaves, is very individual (fig. 28). His trees are enormously tall and slender, particularly the pine, ash and lime, and they are shown with diminutive figures at their base, mostly in Roman togas. Their elongated proportions may have been suggested to Martin by Turner's carefully detailed pine trees in his painting *Crossing the Brook* (fig. 11), exhibited two years earlier: this type of tree became a characteristic feature of Turner's landscapes in subsequent years. In Martin's etchings, the ramification is shown in great detail, so that some of the trees look as if they only have leaves on their far side. In this respect they are like Alexander Cozens's trees, but Martin has also shown the foliage in great detail in a largely linear style, with the leaves separately outlined in the case of the horse chestnut. These are trees fit for a grand historical composition rather than a naturalistic landscape, and they demonstrated the expressive power that was possible with the subject, while also responding to the demand by Craig and Hüet-Villiers for a more minutely-studied approach to foliage.

ILLUSTRATED BOOKS: STRUTT, BURGESS AND LOUDON

The expressive power of the tree is also a feature of two important later publications, Jacob George Strutt's *Sylva Britannica* (fig. 30) and Henry William Burgess's *Eidodendron* (fig. 31). Both were self-consciously patriotic, Strutt's work celebrating the traditions of liberty in

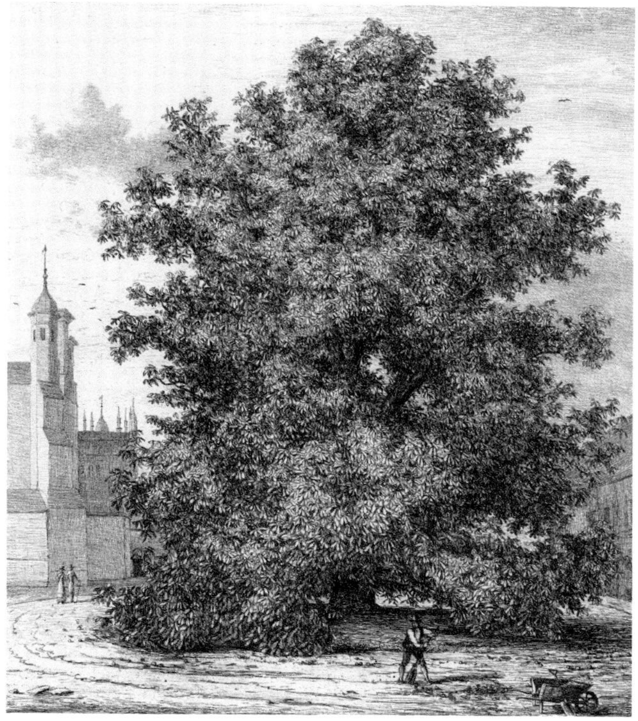

British history while Burgess took a more monarchical line. Indeed, the book version of the *Eidodendron* was dedicated to two Kings, George IV and William IV, and one of the trees featured is 'Queen Charlotte's tree' in Windsor Forest. In both publications the illustrations are portraits of particular trees, usually of great age and very often oaks. Burgess extracts the maximum drama from his venerable subjects, adopting low viewpoints and a loosely finished drawing style, while Strutt's technique is tighter and more detailed. Both works were favourably reviewed. Strutt was commended for 'giving perfectly the character of each species, without those botanical details which do not belong to the picturesque and grand.'[47] Burgess was criticized for including 'mutilated individuals' amongst his trees, but his work was regarded as performing a service in bringing 'the character of trees more into the notice of junior artists, to whom the work will give good examples for imitation, and a useful direction to their ideas in this branch of their profession.'[48] By 1833 Burgess's reputation had evidently grown, as 'the powerful author of the Eidodendron' was being mentioned in the same breath as David Wilkie and Daniel Maclise, as proof that British art was not in decline.[49]

By the time John Claudius Loudon published his *Arboretum Britannicum* (fig. 4) in 1838, the idea of the 'tree portrait' was well established. His 600 illustrations were meant to provide an objective, scientific way of comparing

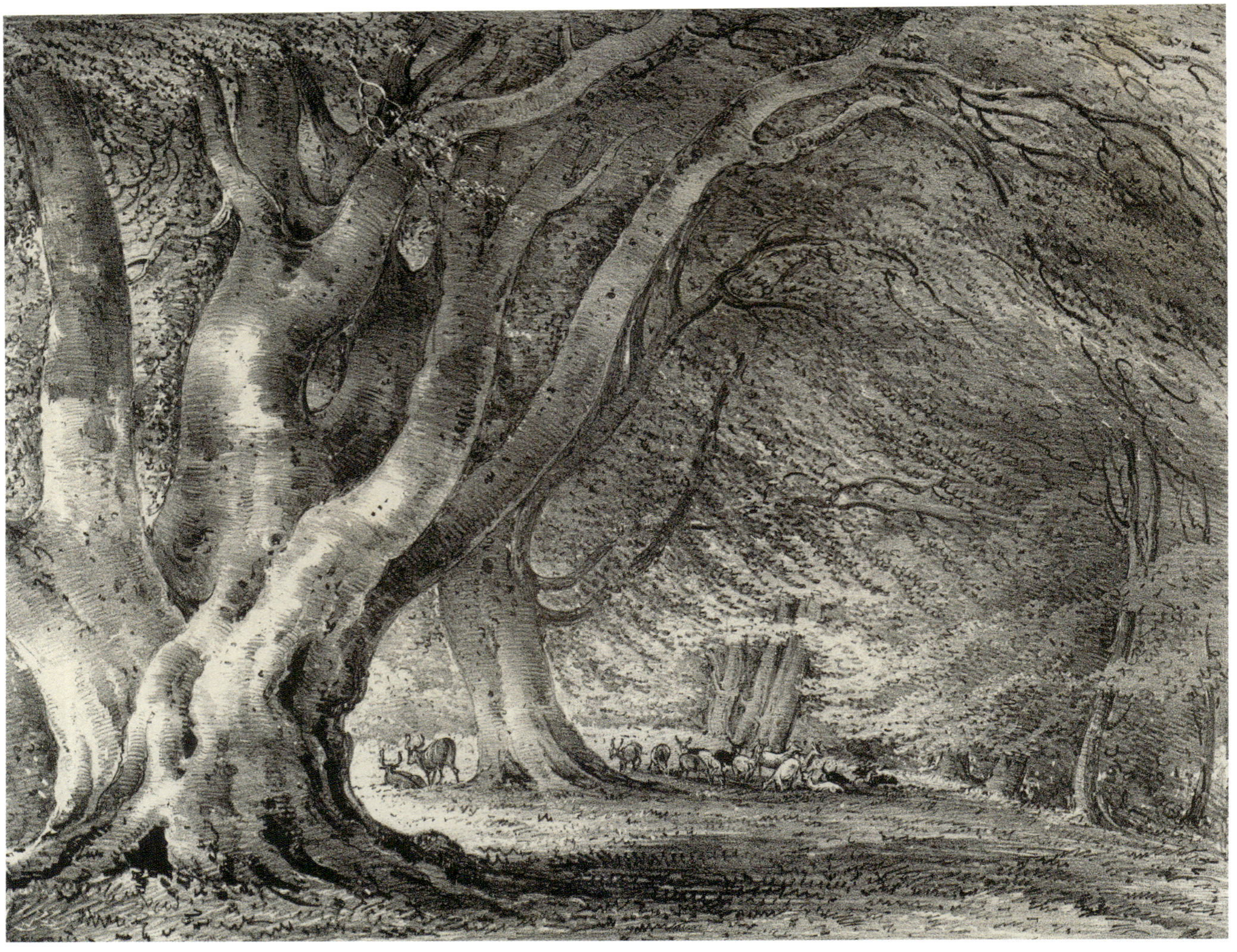

the different species. If artists followed the guidelines laid down in his essay of 1835, he thought, they could bring the different priorities of art and science together, enabling the landscape gardener 'to see trees with the eyes of both an artist and a botanist.' He wanted artists to show trees in their most characteristic and beautiful forms: the horse chestnut, for example, should be drawn in June, when it is in flower.[50] Beryl Hartley has pointed out that it was landscape painters, rather than botanical artists, who led the way in the representation of whole trees, because botanists were not interested in entire trees until the 1820s. The Linnaean classification system put the emphasis on the reproductive elements, the flower, the fruit and the seed. However, Loudon followed the natural system of classification, which took a holistic approach, considering the nutritional structure – the roots, trunk, branches and leaves – as well.[51] In 1824, the *Eclectic Review* complained that the Linnaean system had had an effect similar to that of revolutionary ideas about the social order: 'they [the botanists] have been so much occupied with the seed, and the blossom, and the phenomena of fructification, as to bring down the oak and the beech to the level of the nettle and the bull-rush, confounding all gradations of rank in a most radical equality.'[52] The shift of interest to the forest trees, led by 'the monarch oak' might, therefore, be seen as partly motivated by political conservatism. Certainly, the subscription lists for the volumes by Strutt and Burgess show that they had widespread support amongst the landed aristocracy, who also stood to suffer from 'radical equality'.

By the 1820s and 1830s, then, there was no longer such a conflict of interest between the botanical and the picturesque. However, it is noticeable that the tree portraits in the *Arboretum Britannicum* do not conform to a single pattern. The work of the individual artists is easily distinguished: the plates by 'Miss M. L.' have soft shading, irregular leaf shapes and little sense of structure;

31 H. W. BURGESS

'Beech Trees in Knowle Park, Kent'

Plate 24 from H. W. Burgess, *Eidodendron: Views of the general Character and Appearance of Trees Foreign & Indigenous as connected with picturesque Scenery* (London: J. Dickinson, 1827). Yale Center for British Art, Paul Mellon Fund (Folio AD 50)

John Martin's are in the same style as his etchings of 1817, with their tall proportions and emphasis on skeleton and outline; and H. W. Jukes adopts a characteristically 'dotty' treatment in the lighter parts of his foliage. In one case two full-grown specimens of the same tree, the Scots pine, follow one another and the results are totally different: H. Le Jeune's tree has tightly-compacted masses of foliage, like an elm, while W. A. Nesfield's is loose and feathery, its branches suspended from the trunk in broad sweeps. Even when allowance is made for the differences between individual trees, this contrast is surprising and reflects the very different styles of the two artists.[53] The plates by G. R. Lewis (fig. 4) probably come the closest to Loudon's prescriptions, with separate masses of foliage whose shapes correspond to the 'touch' appropriate to the species. Despite Loudon's strictures, most artists do show the leaves separately outlined, and when it comes to the horse chestnut they revert to picturesque prejudice: of the nine horse chestnuts illustrated in the main sequence of portraits, not one is shown in flower. The publication as a whole is, nevertheless, impressive. Trees are shown as young or old, in summer and in winter, so that those intending to plant them could see how they would look in different seasons and over time.

THE ANATOMY OF TREES

The emphasis on the overall structure of the tree – including its 'skeleton' of ramification – was partly a result of the change in botanical methods of classification. But it also had implications for artistic practice and the rising status of landscape painting. Artists were encouraged to see the drawing of trees as the equivalent, for the landscape painter, of the anatomical study and life drawing of the human body that constituted the main course of training for the figure painter. In his Eleventh Discourse, delivered in 1782, Sir Joshua Reynolds followed his assertion that an artist who looked at the 'general character of the species, the order of the branches and the masses of foliage' would be able to produce a true resemblance of a tree, by saying that 'a Landscape-painter certainly ought to study anatomically … all the objects which he paints.'[54] The first of the British publications on trees for artists, Alexander Cozens's book, clearly refers to this idea in its title: the trunk and branches are like the skeleton of the human body, the foliage like its drapery. His plates have been compared to biological charts illustrating the circulation of the blood in the human body.[55] In 1828, Strutt proudly proclaimed that his sketches of trees had been 'acquired by diligent study in the living academies of nature, – the groves and forest of our native country' (rather than, presumably, the moribund Life School of the Royal Academy).[56] In the following decade, Miss S. A. Young and G. R. Lewis published prints of trees with and without foliage: a review of the latter, published in 1838, criticizes the 'shapeless failures perpetrated by our landscape painters, from their ignorance of or inattention to what may be called "woodland anatomy".'[57] George Barnard, in *Trees from Nature* (1868), similarly urges students to observe the growth of the tree accurately 'for the faithful delineation of the tree skeleton is as important as the correct drawing of the bones in the human figure, and it is as great a mistake to cover a faulty stem and branches with heavy masses of foliage (believing in this way to hide defective articulation), as to load a figure with drapery, and then imagine that thorough knowledge of the limbs underneath is thus rendered unnecessary.'[58]

At the Royal Academy, the student began by drawing from sculpture before progressing to the Life School – in other words, copying art before copying nature – and the drawing manuals are based, implicitly or explicitly, on a similar process. Copying from the manuals was the essential first step: Harding in his *Lessons on Trees* (1850) says his drawings of the outlines of foliage should be copied over and over again, the ultimate aim being to make the pupil 'capable of observing nature truly for himself.'[59] Hüet-Villiers claims that Gainsborough began by borrowing drawing books, and 'made so rapid a proficiency that he was very soon qualified to copy from nature', by drawing sketches of the trees around his father's house. Such 'minute

32 JOHN CONSTABLE
Elm Trees in Old Hall Park, East Bergholt
1817 | Graphite | 59.2 x 49.4 cm

attention to individual nature' was the only foundation for excellence in art.[60] Writing in 1853, Barnard cited Turner as an example of an artist who began as 'an elaborate copyist of nature' in his earlier days.[61] Both writers seem to have exaggerated these artists' interest in studying trees from nature. Studies of actual trees by Gainsborough are rare; his drawings of trees are usually quite sketchy, with diagonal shading used to delineate the general shape of the tree rather than the details of its foliage. Turner's drawings of trees date, as Barnard says, from the start of his career. An early drawing of an oak tree uses conventional methods like those recommended in the drawing manuals, with large areas of light surrounded by a 'starry' outline.[62] Turner's trees in *Crossing the Brook* (fig. 11) demonstrate great skill in the delineation of branching and foliage, but in later life, he apparently told a follower that he wished he could do without trees in his paintings.[63] Curiously, Gainsborough and Turner are the only artists recommended by the drawing manuals, perhaps to overcome the objection that a great artist can manage with generalized, or few trees, rather than because of their positive virtues as tree draughtsmen.

There must have been many amateur and jobbing artists who used the conventions of the drawing manuals when drawing trees, even if they were studying them from nature. More ambitious artists, however, developed their own techniques for delineating trunks, branches and foliage, and if they did start with these conventions would have discarded the attempts based on them. A chance survival of a set of drawings by Edward Lear shows how this artist – who later became extremely proficient in tree drawing – began by applying drawing manual techniques. An oak tree at Parham was evidently studied from nature, but Lear divided the foliage into areas of light and shade bounded by zigzag lines – the characteristic 'touch' of oak. This drawing (dated 30 September 1834) is usually associated with Lear's study of Harding's *Elementary Art*, (fig. 27) which was published in the same year,[64] but it seems that Lear was also using techniques derived from earlier, cheaper manuals, such as George Harley's, with its lines of shading going in different directions. He may, in fact, have been trying to apply the lessons of Harding's book to cure himself of bad habits learned from other manuals. Lear's oak tree is one of a series of four tree drawings by him in the Yale Center for British Art. The other three all have dates in October, and show Lear gradually becoming more proficient: by 21 October a drawing of two oaks has sketchier, less laborious notation for the foliage and the trees look much more lively.[65] What is particularly interesting about this series is that by 1834 Lear was already a skilled draughtsman, who had produced many superb watercolours of parrots for his book, *Illustrations of the Family of the Psittacidae* (1832).[66] He evidently saw tree drawing as a specialist skill, for which he needed to go back to first principles.

JOHN CONSTABLE

In contrast to Lear, John Constable seems to have avoided the systems of the drawing manuals in his many drawings of trees. The best of these are in graphite, then known as lead pencil, which Kennion saw as particularly suitable for expressing the outlines of foliage:

> The black lead pencil will be found very useful in the delineation of trees. It is particularly advantageous in producing that doubtfulness of edge, so characteristic of thin and open foliage, without any raggedness, or the least indetermination of form; and which no other material has yet accomplished in an equal degree.[67]

In Ian Fleming-Williams's view, Constable was able to avoid systems of conventional notation because of his contact with John Thomas Smith, who, as we saw in Chapter Two, exhibited a drawing of a beech tree at the Royal Academy in 1787.[68] Other early influences included Gainsborough, George Frost, and John Malchair, who had taught Sir George Beaumont, Constable's friend and patron, at Oxford.[69] Fleming-Williams also considered that Constable had an innate dislike for repetitive movement, which was, of course, the essence of the drawing manual method for

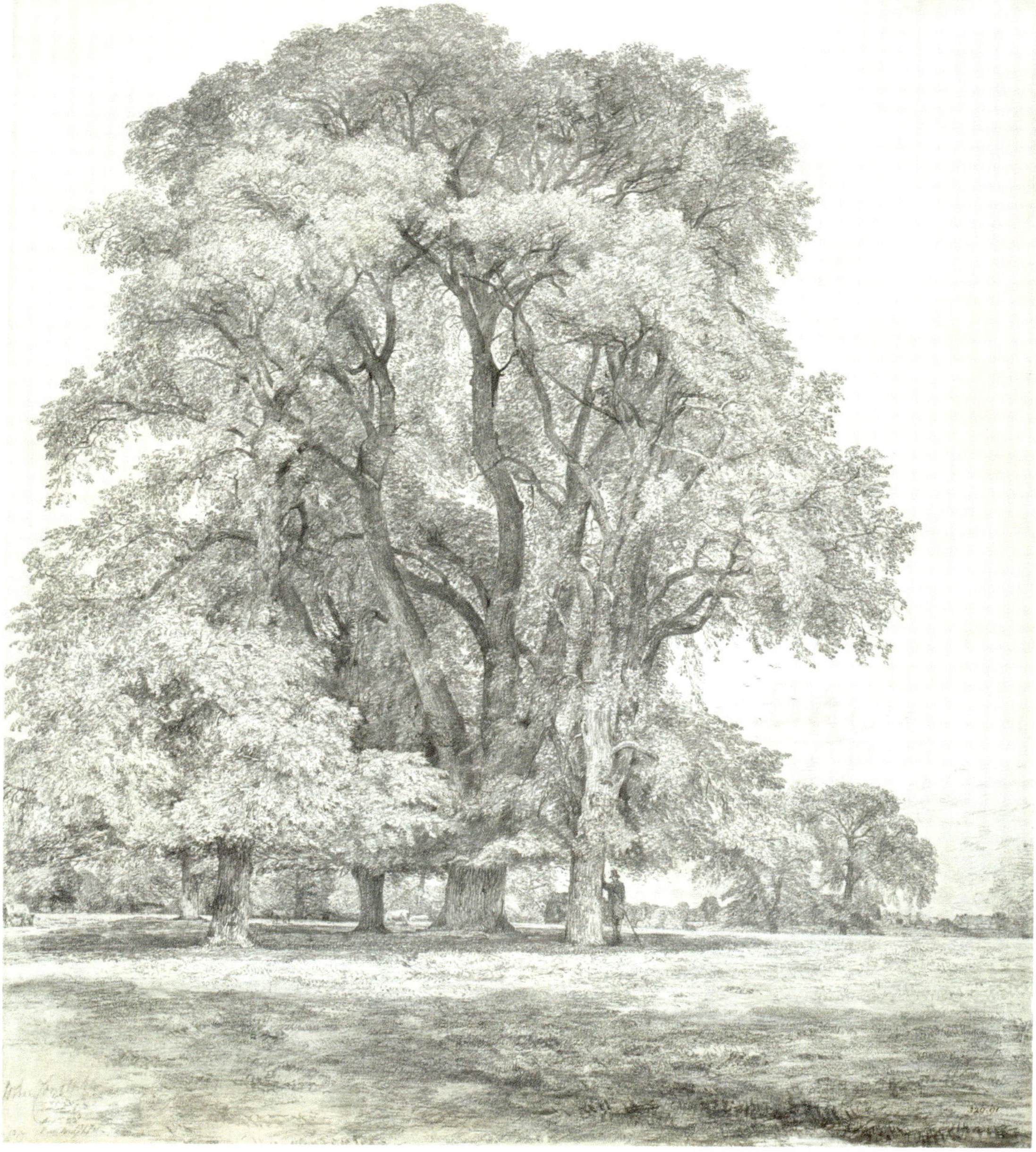

delineating trees. Instead, Constable instinctively wanted each touch or stroke to be different, if only fractionally, from the next.[70] In a drawing of oak trees made in 1813, Constable has used some of the standard 'starry' outlines, but only in limited areas.[71] His use of the pencil exploits its ability to suggest the soft edges of foliage, as Kennion advocated. The contrast between the dark lines of the trunk and branches and the lighter foliage may suggest that Constable had studied Alexander Cozens's etchings on trees, which he certainly would have known. Constable made tree drawings throughout his life: on several occasions he drew trees at twilight, when they appeared as silhouettes, another indication of the possible influence of Cozens.[72]

One reason why Constable devoted so much attention to trees was that he saw trees in landscape painting as the equivalent of human actors in history painting. In a lecture on landscape, given at Hampstead in the summer of 1833, he spoke at length about Titian's painting, *The Death of St Peter Martyr,* which he regarded as 'the foundation of all the styles of landscapes in every school in Europe in the following century … an admirable union of history and landscape.'[73] In this painting (which Constable knew only from a print) the expressive, twisting trunks of the trees shared in the human drama of the scene. These trees seem to have haunted Constable's imagination throughout his life. In 1800 he found a tree at Helmingham whose S-shaped trunk was similar to one of the trees in the Titian, and even had branches suggestive of outstretched arms: this was incorporated in a drawing, *Helmingham Dell,* to which he repeatedly returned in later years as the basis for finished

33 JOHN CONSTABLE
Fir Trees at Hampstead
1820 | [actually Scots pines] | Graphite | 23.3 x 16 cm
© Victoria and Albert Museum, London

oil paintings.[74] The twisting tree trunks in his later paintings, *Dedham Vale* (1828, National Gallery of Scotland) and *Salisbury Cathedral from the Meadows* (1831, Tate Britain) are also reminiscences of the trees in Titian's painting: they demonstrate Constable's long study of the anatomy of trees, much like a virtuoso twisting nude in the foreground of a history painting. Constable even made cartoons of his tree studies, as a history painter might do with a life drawing, squaring them up and transferring them to the canvases of his exhibition oil paintings. We know that he did this on at least two occasions, for *Boys Fishing* in 1813, and for *The Valley Farm* in 1835. In 1817, after *Flatford Mill* (fig. 1) came back from the Royal Academy, he made a careful drawing of the principal trees, the black poplars, and repainted this part of the picture, using his drawing as a guide.[75]

By 1817, when Constable made the large drawing, *Elm Trees in Old Hall Park, East Bergholt* (fig. 32), he had perfected his tree-drawing technique. Here he uses a system of squiggles that give the impression of the shapes of elm leaves without actually defining them. There are still some traces of the Gainsborough method of diagonal shading, but this is overshadowed by Constable's control of the tonal values, so that the masses of foliage have a real sense of volume. The drawing was exhibited at the Royal Academy in 1818, but remained in Constable's possession. The survival of a tracing for the drawing, scaled up for transfer, is evidence of the care Constable took to ensure that his depiction of the trees was absolutely accurate.[76] The main tree is the kind of ancient tree in parkland that Strutt was to include in his *Sylva Britannica* some five years later. The handling of the foliage in the lower left is quite similar to the method Strutt developed for his etchings, and it is also close to the treatment of foliage in the etchings of Jacob van Ruisdael, which Constable is known to have admired and copied.[77] Indeed, Constable's drawing would have translated well into etching itself. Constable and Strutt were quite close friends by the 1820s: they socialized with each other's families, Constable subscribed to the *Sylva Britannica* and lent Strutt money when the latter became hard up.[78]

Even more impressive is Constable's sketchbook drawing, known as *Fir Trees at Hampstead* of 1820 (fig. 33; the trees are actually Scots pines). Here the treatment is less linear and the graphite is used very strongly to create deep shadows, throwing the lighted parts of the foliage into relief. Light sparkles through the darkest shadows, where these represent foliage rather than trunks, as Constable has left tiny parts of the paper bare in these areas. In this drawing Constable is also very successful in suggesting textures – the stiffness of the pine needles, the roughness of the ridged bark – through his pencil marks. It seems highly likely that this drawing was the one mentioned by C. R. Leslie in an anecdote about William Blake in his *Life* of Constable:

> The amiable but eccentric Blake, looking through one of Constable's sketch books, said of a beautiful drawing of an avenue of fir trees on Hampstead Heath, 'Why, this is not drawing, but inspiration,' and he [Constable] replied, 'I never knew it before; I meant it for drawing.'[79]

Constable often showed his sketchbook drawings to friends and acquaintances, and he also exhibited another finished drawing of trees in 1834 (fig. 50) so his proficiency in drawing trees would have been quite widely known. Like Pott in his *Essay on Landscape Painting*, Constable showed a preference for the elm and the ash, as well as the black poplar along with the other poplars, willows and alders that grow in riverside locations: oaks are relatively rare in his work, and beeches and horse chestnuts never appear. As we have seen, Leslie claimed that his absolute favourite was the ash. In 1823, on a ride with Sir George Beaumont, Constable stopped to make a sketch of 'the finest ash I ever saw' while the baronet held his horse for him. This is quite a brief sketch, unfortunately, as Constable was presumably unwilling to take too much advantage of his patron's patience, but he had time to sketch in the surroundings, including buildings and a figure to establish the scale of the impressive mature tree.[80]

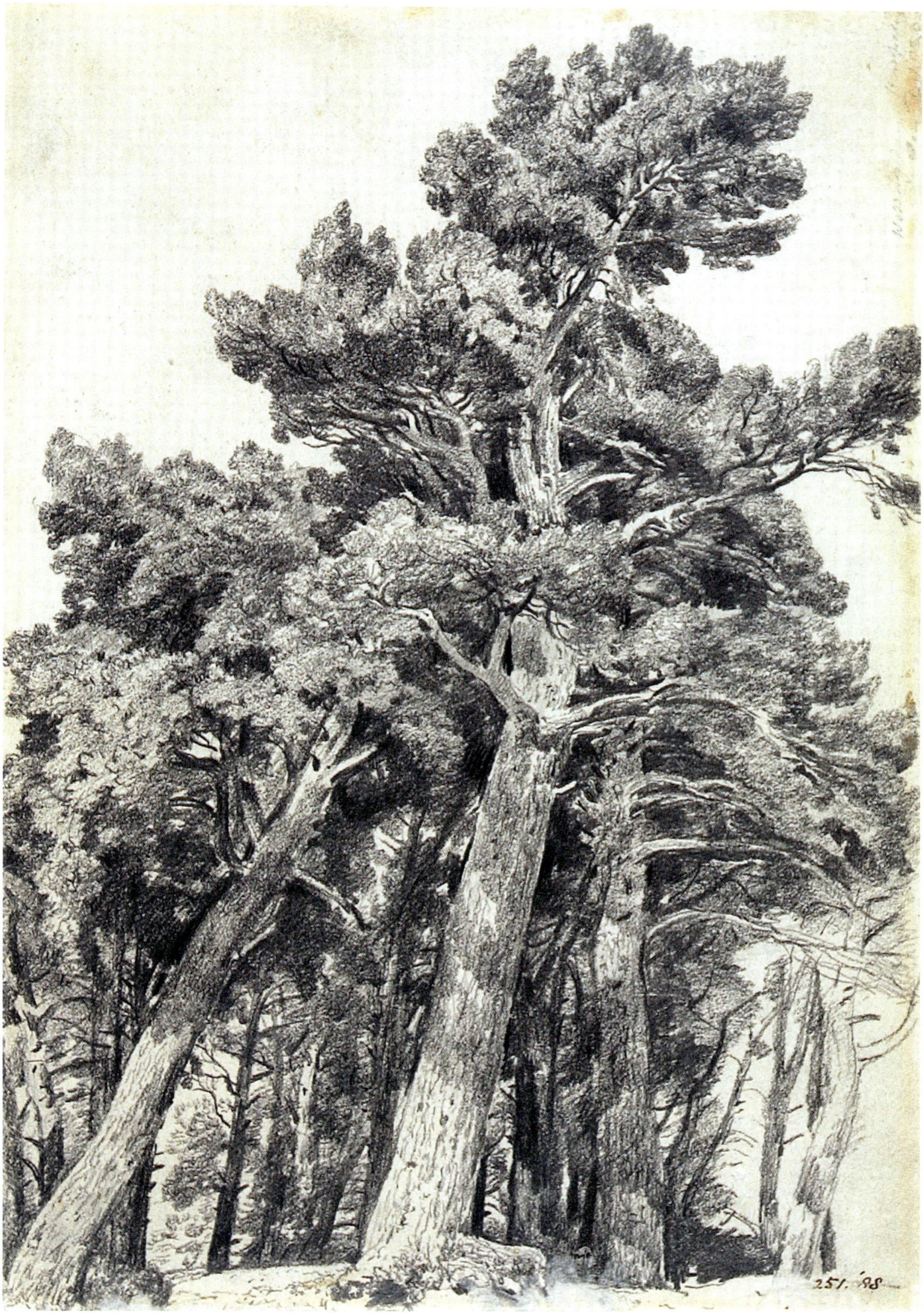
251. '88

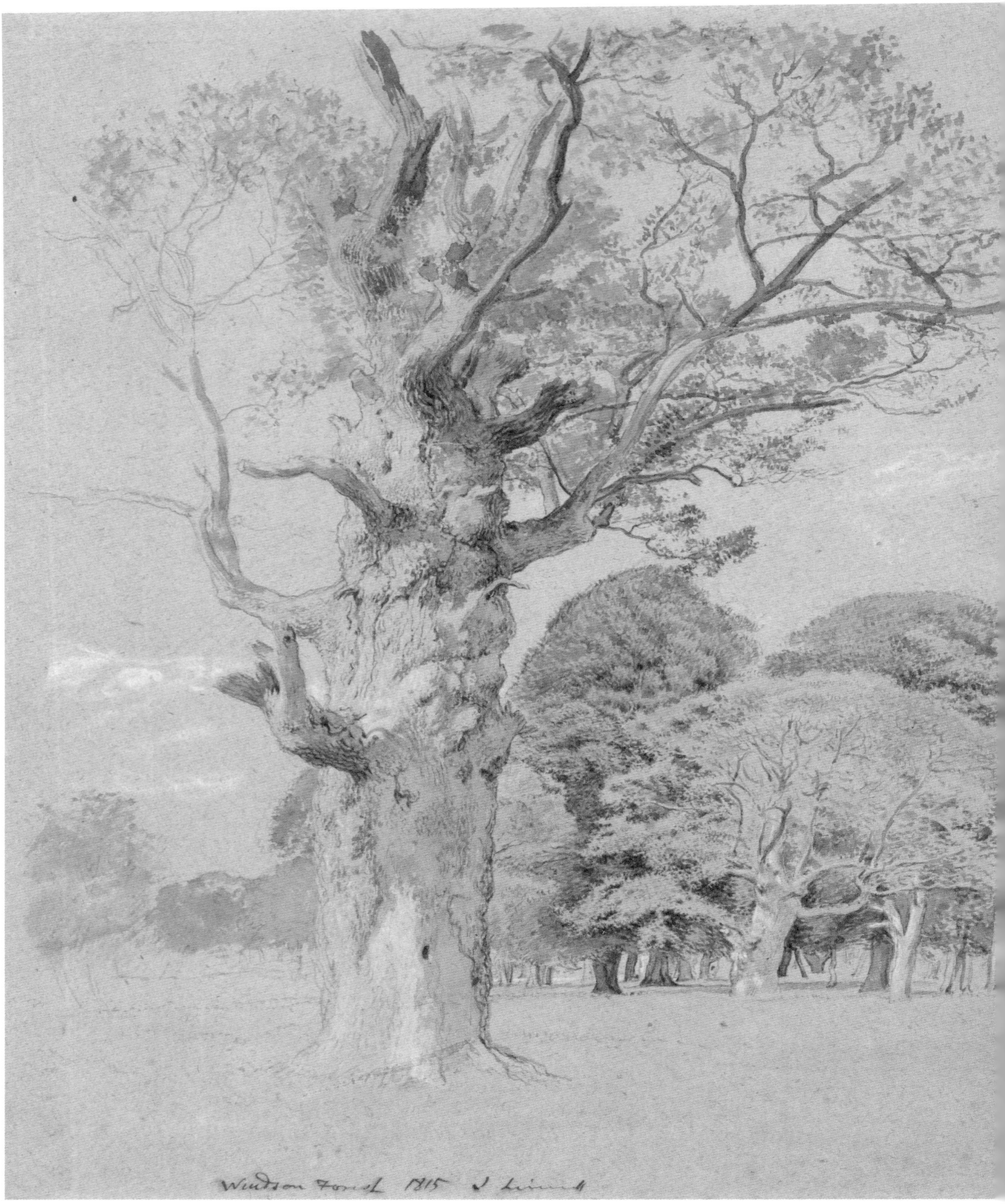
1815

34 JOHN LINNELL
Windsor Forest
1815 | Graphite and watercolour with touches of white on blue paper | 32.5 x 42.9 cm

LINNELL, WARD, HILLS AND PALMER

Amongst Constable's contemporaries there were several who were making careful studies of trees, directly from nature, in the decades of 1810-20 and 1820-30 – just at the time when so many books on trees, and sets of etchings of trees were being published. One was John Linnell, whom Constable knew as a neighbour at Hampstead and who may well have been present when Blake looked at Constable's sketchbook, since Blake came to Hampstead several times to visit Linnell. Linnell made two sketching trips to areas where there were ancient forests in 1815 and 1816. In May 1815 he spent about a month at Winkfield, near Windsor Forest to make studies of trees and woodcutters, and in May 1816 he stayed for about a week in Sevenoaks for the same purpose.[81] Windsor Forest had long been famous for its ancient oaks, and popular with artists at least since the time of Paul Sandby. Linnell was collecting material for genre paintings of woodcutters, a subject which had been successfully treated by Sandby in a number of watercolours in the 1790s.[82] Linnell's watercolour, *Windsor Forest* (fig. 34) dates from the first sketching trip in 1815: Linnell used it as the basis for an exhibition picture (fig. 55) in 1818. The textures on the trunk of the old tree, and, in the background, the contrasting light and shade and colours of the foliage, are all evidence of Linnell's careful study in the open air. Other studies from the same period, in pencil and black chalk, heightened with white, show the trunks of trees that have been cut down and debarked, or the complex ramification of old trees that have little foliage left.[83] These studies remained in Linnell's possession, and they would doubtless have been shown to the young Samuel Palmer when Linnell befriended him in 1822.

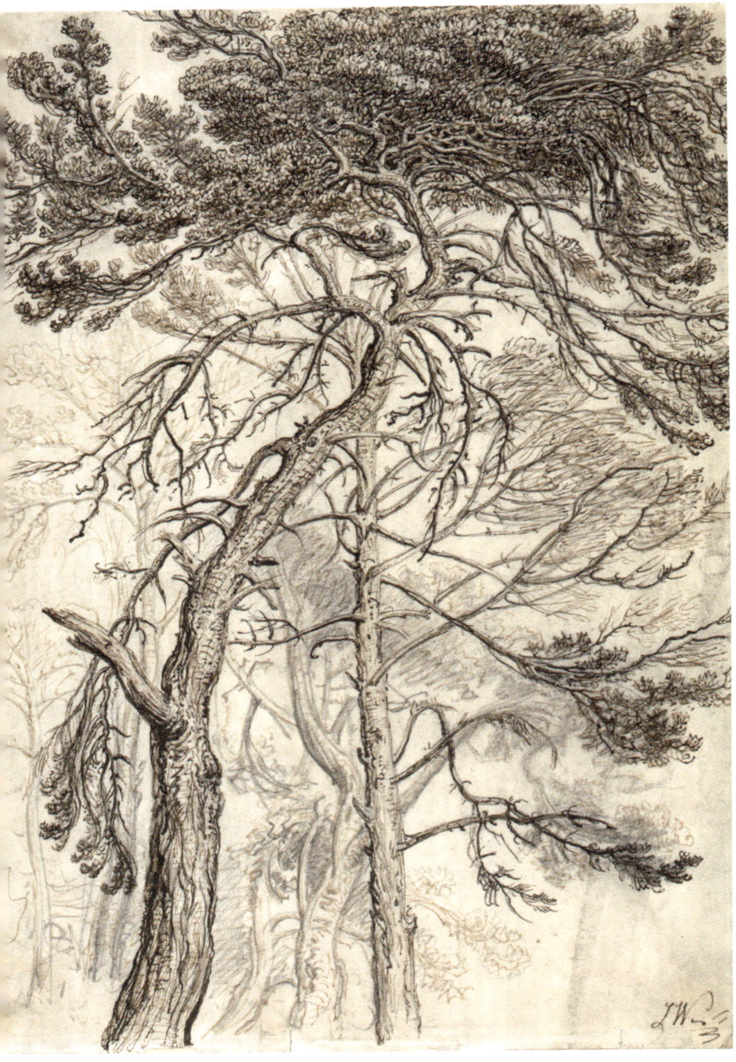

35 JAMES WARD
Study of Trees
Graphite, brown and black ink | 37.5 x 27 cm
Yale Center for British Art, Paul Mellon Collection

Another artist who was making detailed studies of trees at this time was James Ward. A series of pencil drawings, all dated August 1820, depict old oaks in the parks of Lord Bagot and 'Mr Howard'. These are similar in format to the tree portraits later published by Strutt in his *Sylva Britannica*, or those in Loudon's *Arboretum Britannicum*, but they are less detailed and somewhat experimental, as Ward tries out different forms of notation for the foliage in different parts of the drawing.[84] His *Study of Trees* (fig. 35) is undated, but is more assured than the 1820 series so it presumably was done later – perhaps when Ward had seen the sense of the rhythm and movement of tree growth that was achieved by Burgess in the *Eidodendron*. In this drawing, the addition of pen and ink emphasizes the outlines of the curving branches, which seem to writhe about like the tentacles of a sea creature. In contrast to Ward, the tree studies of his friend and sketching companion Robert Hills (fig. 36) are lyrical evocations of the effects of sunlight on woodland. Here he studies the intertwining roots of a group of beech trees, infusing them, like Ward, with a strong impression of growth and movement. Hills's studies of trees are generally undated, but they were probably made in the 1820s, when he may have been associated with Samuel Palmer and his circle.

This widespread interest in trees, and in studying them direct from nature, is the background to the work of Samuel Palmer, who took a very original approach to tree drawing. Palmer deliberately avoided the slick modern methods of representing features in landscape, to go back to more primitive techniques from the 'infancy of art', which John George Wood had castigated as producing a 'laborious and unprofitable style' which included depicting 'every leaf of a tree'.[85] Palmer's 1824 sketchbook demonstrates the evolution of his ideas. From the start, he regards trees as an active, living presence in the landscape, similar to humans: he writes on an early page: 'Sometimes trees are seen as men. I saw one a princess walking stately with a majestic train.' This was followed by a page, now lost, on which he drew no fewer than twenty-three kinds of trees, presumably copied from one of the drawing manuals.[86] Further pages of the sketchbook include many drawings of tree trunks and foliage, probably done from nature, but then on page 119 he switches to more stylized representations, strongly linear in style, based on a combination of imagination and earlier artistic sources. He seems to have been particularly affected by Albrecht Dürer's woodcut, *The Flight into Egypt* (c.1504), with its twisting and textured tree-trunks.[87] However, Palmer continues to study trees from life in the later pages of the book, and shows a particular fondness for the horse chestnut. In a remarkable piece of observation he makes notes on a drawing of young chestnuts in very early spring: their tightly-furled leaves looked 'peculiar at a little distance like horizontal pencil dashes.'[88]

36 ROBERT HILLS

Beech Trees

Watercolour and graphite | 21.3 x 28.3 cm

Yale Center for British Art, Paul Mellon Collection

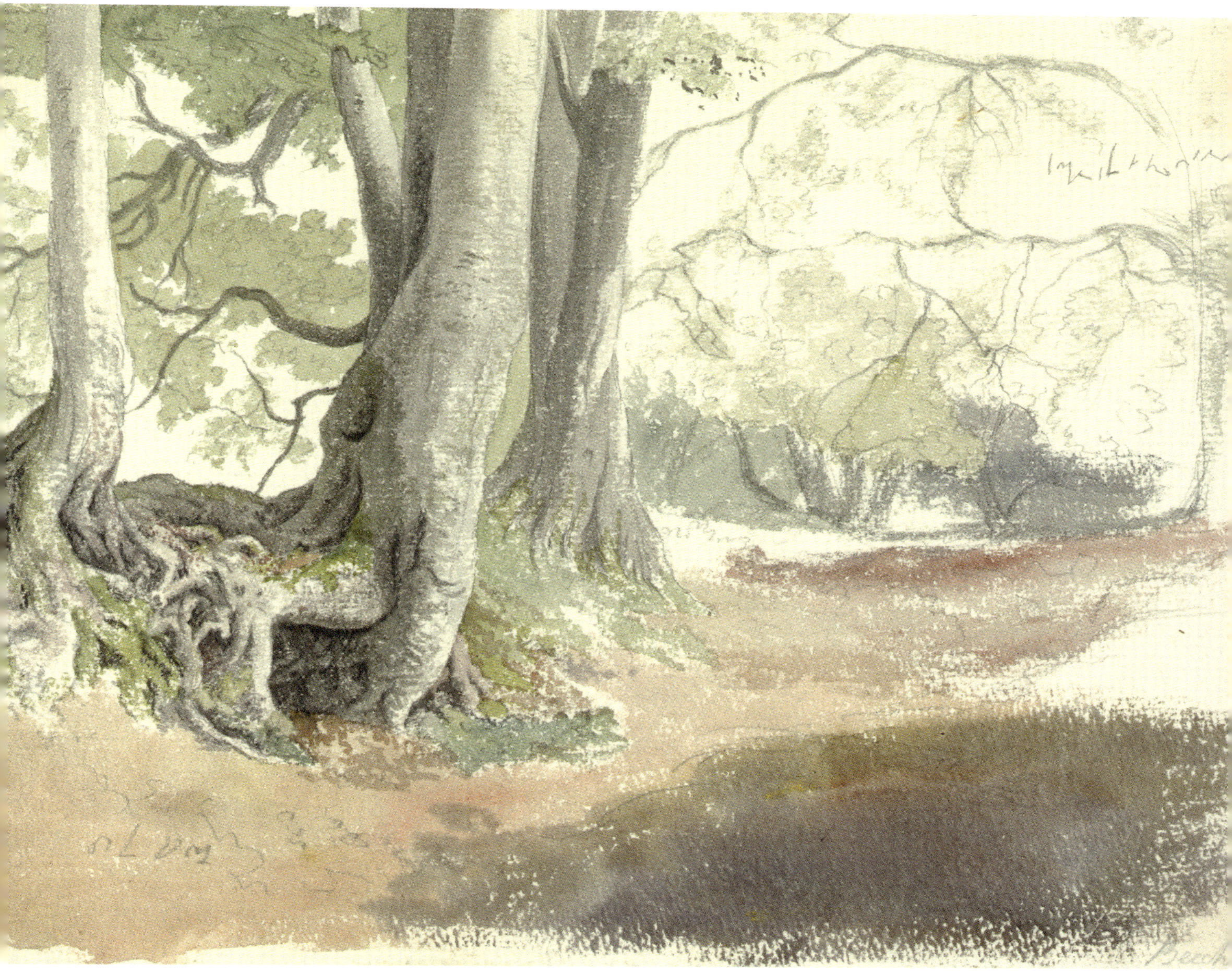

37 SAMUEL PALMER
Early Morning
1825 | Brown ink and sepia mixed with gum arabic | 18.8 x 23.2 cm
Image © Ashmolean Museum, University of Oxford (WA1941.107)

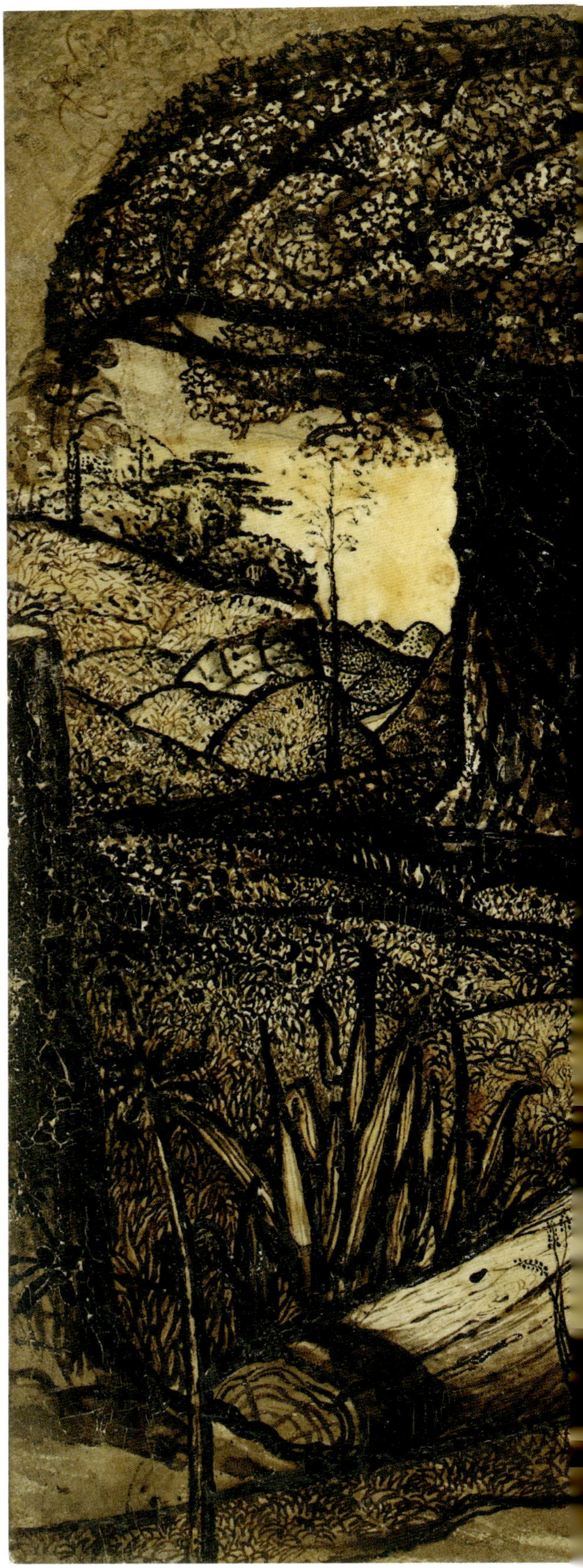

The sketchbook studies of tree trunks pay close attention to the contrasting shapes and textures of the bark, and this is a feature also of the trees in the set of six sepia drawings Palmer produced in 1825. In these he deliberately flouts the rules laid down in the drawing manuals. The leaves of each tree are separately outlined and the horse chestnut is given pride of place, in the drawing entitled *The Skirts of the Wood* where it is the central feature in the composition. On the other hand, Palmer follows the drawing manuals in distinguishing sharply between the characters of the different varieties of tree. It is not always absolutely clear what species his trees are meant to be, but there is no doubt of their difference from one another. The contrasting shapes are exaggerated to the point of caricature. In *Early Morning* (fig. 37) the mushroom-shaped oak tree must be imagined to be a pollarded oak, similar to the one Linnell includes in the background of his drawing in Windsor Forest (and conceivably suggested by this drawing). Its foliage is divided into masses, like the masses of light and shade visible in the trees in the manuals, but these are thickly outlined so that they appear, rather, like the leaded divisions in a stained-glass window. The trees in the foreground, with their contrasting trunks, might be ash, birch and elm, while in the background to the right there seems to be an ancient spreading oak, its masses of foliage again outlined like parts of a stained-glass window.

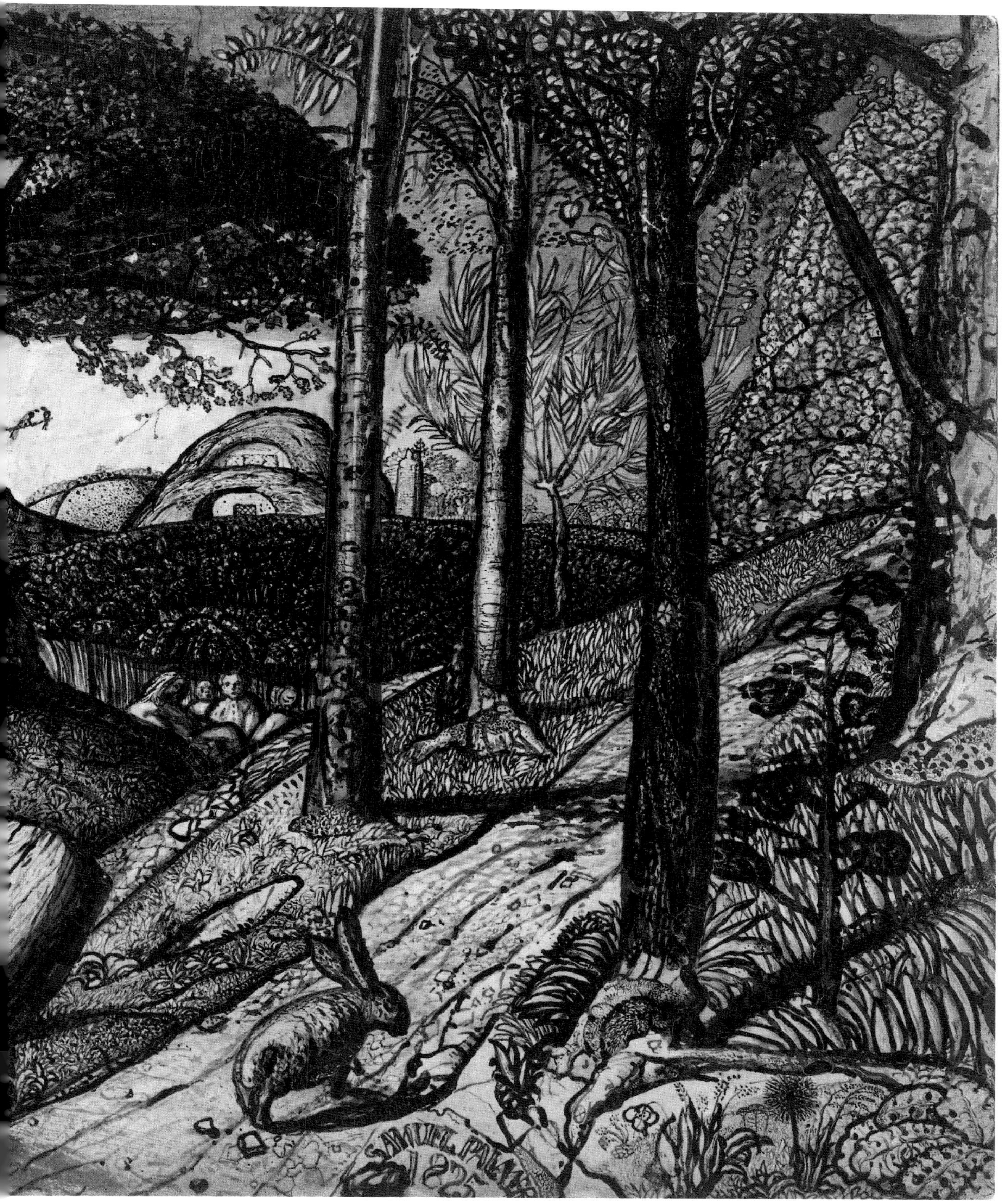

38 SAMUEL PALMER
Ancient Trees, Lullingstone Park
1828 | Graphite | 26.7 x 37.1 cm
Yale Center for British Art, Paul Mellon Collection

As is well known, John Linnell tried to persuade Palmer to make studies direct from nature, perhaps hoping that these would cause him to modify the excesses of his ultra-primitive style. As a result of a commission from Linnell, Palmer made studies of the ancient oaks and beeches in Lullingstone Park, the kind of trees that had recently been studied by Strutt and Burgess in their publications. Palmer, whose father was a bookseller, may well have seen Burgess's *Eidodendron* when it was published in 1827: his drawings at Lullingstone were made in the following year, and their dramatic, low viewpoints are similar to the one chosen by Burgess for his drawing of an ancient beech at Knole Park (fig. 31). Indeed, the pencil drawing, *Ancient Trees, Lullingstone Park* (fig. 38) is so close to Burgess's plate in its composition that it is difficult to believe the similarities are purely coincidental. Drawings of ancient beeches by Linnell and David Roberts also seem to be derived from Burgess's composition.[89] However, the comparison also brings home how closely Palmer studied the details of his trees, and how successful he was in giving them the appearance of vigorous growth and life. Palmer obviously considered the exercise to be analogous to figure drawing. He wrote to Linnell that he was distracted by the surface textures, but knew he should be trying to capture the 'anatomical' details – the 'grasp and grapple of the roots; the muscular belly and shoulders; the twisted sinews':

> Milton, by one epithet, draws an oak of the largest girth I ever saw; – 'Pine and Monumental Oak.' I have just been trying to draw a large one in Lullingstone; but the Poet's tree is huger than any in the park: there, the moss, and rifts, and barky furrows, and the mouldering grey, tho' that adds majesty to the lord of forests; mostly catch the eye before the grasp and grapple of the roots; the muscular belly and shoulders; the twisted sinews.[90]

His description makes the drawing sound like a figure by Michelangelo rather than the drawing of a tree.

Palmer modified his style in the late 1820s and early 1830s so that it was less 'outrageous', but he continued to be unorthodox in his depiction of trees. He produced vibrant, colourful watercolours of fruit trees in blossom, which had been neglected by the drawing manuals, and he continued to draw horse chestnut trees. The horse chestnut evidently appealed to Palmer for the very reason that Kennion and Harding disliked it – it could be drawn with separately outlined leaves, even in works that were otherwise relatively naturalistic. In *Pastoral with a Horse Chestnut Tree* (fig. 10) he even shows it in flower, something that none of the manuals, and none of Loudon's artists, had ventured to do. Trees play an important part in Palmer's vision of a bountiful, spiritual landscape at Shoreham. Their leaves, silhouetted against the sky, deepen the mysterious effect of moonlight, while their abundant fruits and blossoms convey the notion of an earth that has been designed by a benevolent God for mankind's sustenance and enjoyment. To get this effect he needed to combine imagination and a knowledge of 'primitive' art with sufficient study from nature to enable the viewer to believe this ecstatic vision is not entirely impossible. Palmer's trees are otherworldly, but they also have strong links with the more naturalistic studies being made in the same period by Linnell, Constable, Strutt and Burgess.

Palmer's trees bear the impress of an original artistic personality, a different kind of 'character' to the differentiation between species prioritized by the manuals. His ability to see trees 'as men' was, however, shared by many of his contemporaries. As well as considering the drawing of trees to be a kind of 'woodland anatomy', there was a tendency to use another anthropomorphic term in thinking of studies of individual trees as 'portraits'. There is an analogy here with the manuals that presented different 'types' of human figures, or provided guidelines for portraying the successive stages of human life. The next chapter will move from artistic techniques to the subject matter of these tree portraits, and to the interest in the biography and historical context of the individual tree, with a special emphasis on those artists, and poets, for whom particular trees were more than simply the representatives of a species.

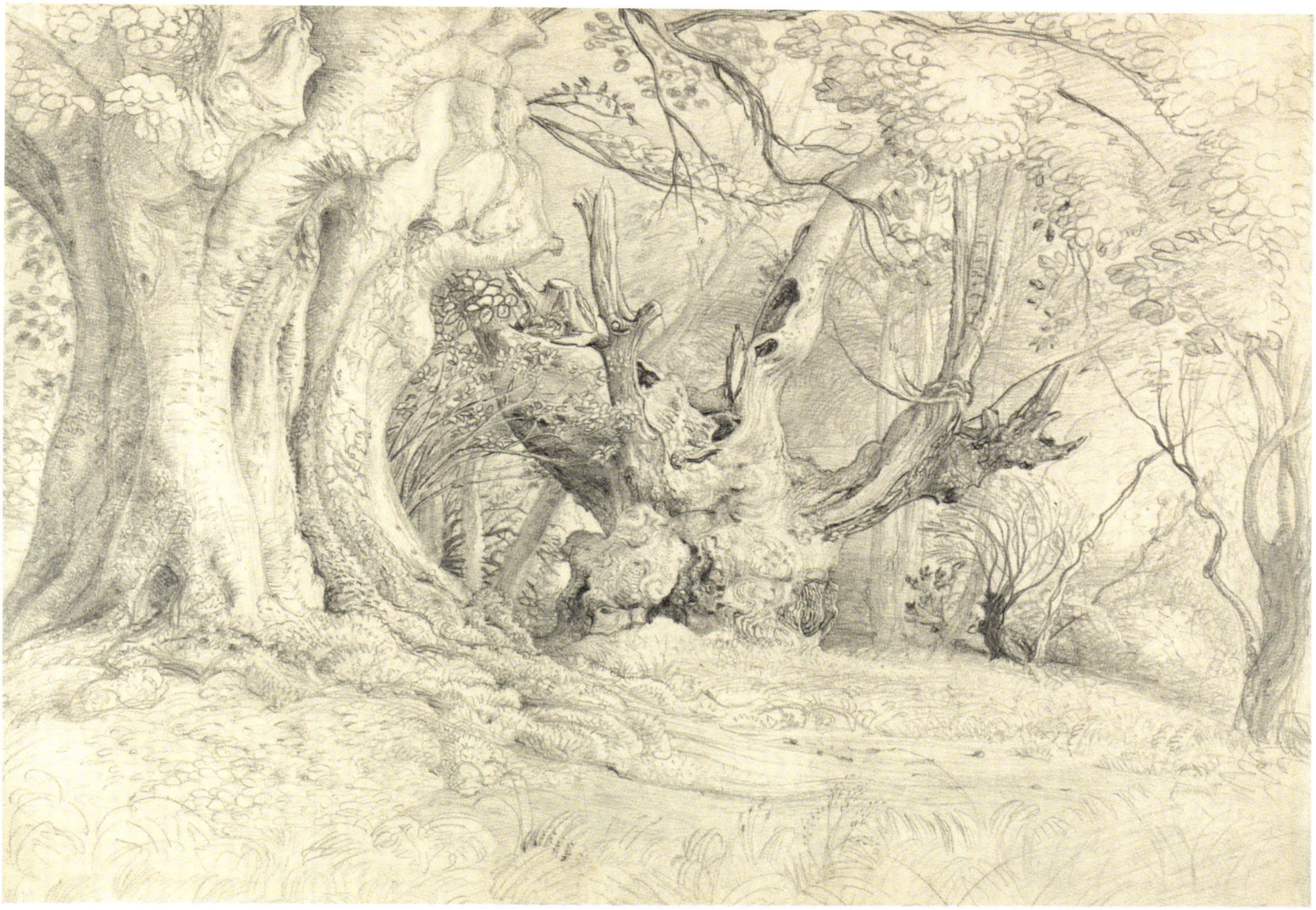

ENDNOTES

1 Joshua Bryant, *Progressive Lessons on the Art of Drawing Landscapes* (London: Rudolph Ackermann, 1807), p. 4. Sir George Beaumont, and the Earl of Aylesford, both exhibited at the Royal Academy, but the others did not.

2 Miss S. A. Young, *Studies of Trees, with and without Foliage* (Edinburgh: Abram Thomson; London: Longman & Co; Glasgow: John Reid & Co; Dublin: John Cumming, 1834), title page with list of subscribers.

3 J. C. Loudon, *Arboretum et Fruticetum Britannicum, or, the Trees and Shrubs of Britain* (London: Longman, Orme, Brown, Green, and Longmans, 1838), Vol. I p. 13.

4 Alexander Cozens, *The Shape, Skeleton and Foliage of 32 Species of Trees* (1786); George Barnard, *Trees from Nature* (London: Winsor and Newton, 1868). On the drawing manuals, see Ann Bermingham, *Learning to Draw. Studies in the Cultural History of a Polite and Useful Art* (New Haven and London: Yale University Press, 2000), pp. 108-17.

5 Bryant, *Progressive Lessons.*

6 J. D. Harding, *Elementary Art, or, the Use of the Lead Pencil, advocated and explained* (London: Charles Tilt, 1834).

7 J. Laporte, *Characters of Trees, drawn and engraved by J. Laporte* (London: John P. Thompson, 1800); *Characters of Trees, drawn and etched by F. Martin [sic], landscape painter to HRH the Princess Charlotte and HRH the Prince of Saxe-Coburg* (London: Ackermann, 1817).

8 H. W. Burgess, *Eidodendron: Views of the general Character and Appearance of Trees Foreign & Indigenous as connected with Picturesque Scenery* (London: J. Dickinson, 1827); J. G. Strutt, *Sylva Britannica; or, Portraits of Forest Trees, distinguished for their Antiquity, Magnitude, or Beauty, drawn from nature and etched by Jacob George Strutt* (London: J. G. Strutt and Colnaghi and Co, 1822).

9 See Beryl Hartley, 'The Living Academies of Nature: Scientific Experiments in Learning and Communicating the New Skills of Early Nineteenth-century Landscape Painting', *Studies in History and Philosophy of Science*, 27 (June 1996), pp. 149-80; and her thesis, 'The Artist as Naturalist and Experimenter: Landscape Painting and Science 1740-1850' (PhD thesis, Imperial College, University of London, 1995); also Bermingham, *Learning to Draw*; and Peter Bicknell and Jane Munro, *Gilpin to Ruskin: Drawing Masters and their Manuals, 1800-1860* (Cambridge: Fitzwilliam Museum, 1987).

10 Harding, *Elementary Art*, p. 79.

11 George Harley, *Lessons on Drawing Trees* (London: R. Ackermann, 1829). The price is printed on the title page.

12 Louis Francia, *Progressive Lessons*

tending to elucidate the characters of trees, with the process of sketching, and painting them in Water Colours (London: T. Clay, 1813) and [David Hall M'Kewan], *Lessons on Trees, in Water Colours, by M'Kewan* (Westminster: W. Dufour, 1860).

13 Mai-mai Sze, ed., *The Mustard Seed Garden Manual of Painting, Chieh Tzu Yuan hua chuan 1679-1701: a facsimile of the 1887-1888 Shanghai edition* (original author: Gai Wang) (Princeton: Princeton University Press, 1977).

14 Henry Twining, Esq., *On the Elements of Picturesque Scenery, considered with reference to landscape painting* (London: printed for private distribution by George Barclay, 1846), p. 88.

15 Sir Joshua Reynolds, *Discourses on Art*, ed. Robert R. Wark (New Haven and London: Yale University Press, 1975), p. 199.

16 [Joseph Holden Pott], *An Essay on Landscape Painting, with remarks general and critical, on the different schools and masters, ancient or modern* (London: J. Johnson, 1782), pp. 55-6.

17 Ibid, p. 83.

18 J. R. Cozens, *Delineations of the General Character, Ramifications and Foliage of Forest Trees*, 1789 (set of etchings, British Museum); François Hüet-Villiers, *Rudiments and Characters of Trees, Drawn and Engraved* (London: R. Ackermann, 1806). His name is also given in this publication as Villiers Huet. For full details of the others, see notes above.

19 Edward Kennion, *An Essay on Trees in Landscape; or, an attempt to show the propriety and importance of characteristic expression in this art, and the means of producing it: with examples* (London: C. J. Kennion, 1815), pp. 7-8.

20 Francia, *Progressive Lessons*, Advertisement.

21 Frank Howard, *Frank Howard's Science of Drawing, being a Progressive Series of the Characteristic Forms of Nature. Part One: Trees* (London: William Pickering, 1839).

22 Harding, *Elementary Art*, p. 34.

23 John Martin's *Characters of Trees* (1817) includes oak, elm and ash, but not beech, his other trees being pine, horse chestnut, and lime. George Harley's *Lessons on Drawing Trees* (1829) also leaves out the beech, including pollard willow and Spanish chestnut instead.

24 *Remarks on Forest Scenery, and other woodland views, by the late William Gilpin, A. M. edited by Sir Thomas Dick Lauder, Bart* (Edinburgh: Fraser & Co; London: Smith, Elder & Co; Dublin: W. Curry, Jun. & Co, 1834), Vol I, pp. 100-101. Lauder specified the way the leaves reflect the sun's rays as one of these circumstances.

25 Pott, *Essay on Landscape Painting*, pp. 87-8, 88-9.

26 Francia, *Progressive Lessons*, No. 8.

27 George Barnard, *Handbook of Foliage and Foreground Drawing* (London: Ingram, Cooke & Co, 1853), pp. 19, 15.

28 Answers: the oak, and formal. George Barnard, *Handbook of Foliage and Foreground Drawing*, 2nd ed., London: Griffith and Farran, 1870, p. 115. Barnard says that the questions are 'extremely simple … suited to the capacity of even the most juvenile pupil.'

29 Hartley, 'The Living Academies', p. 149; Bermingham, *Learning to Draw*, p. 116.

30 William Marshall Craig, *An Essay upon the Study of Nature in Drawing Landscape* (London, 1793) p. 21.

31 Kennion, *Essay on Trees*, pp. 28, 30, 32.

32 Ibid, p. iv.

33 Ibid, p. 33.

34 J. G. Strutt, 'The principal Forest Trees of Europe, considered as Elements of Landscape', *Magazine of Natural History*, Vol I (1829), Part II, September 1828, pp. 244-5.

35 J. C. Loudon, 'Directions for drawing Trees and Botanical Specimens from Nature, to any given scale, and more especially to the Scales adapted to the "Arboretum Britannicum"', *Gardener's Magazine*, XI, (1835), p. 401.

36 Harding, *Elementary Art*, pp. 34, 53.

37 Loudon, *Arboretum Britannicum*, Vol I, pp. 14, 203.

38 Ibid, Vol I, p. 207.

39 Pott, *Essay*, p. 98.

40 Reynolds, *Discourses*, p. 199.

41 Kennion, *Essay on Trees*, p. 17.

42 Ibid, p. 40.

43 Harding, *Elementary Art*, p. 34.

44 Harding, *Lessons on Trees*, Plate 19.

45 The nine are A. Cozens, Hüet-Villiers, Kennion, Martin, Strutt, Burgess, Childs, Barnard 1853, Barnard 1870. Hüet-Villiers, Martin, Strutt and Childs show the leaves separately outlined.

46 John George Wood, *The principles and Practice of Sketching Landscape Scenery from Nature* (London: Bentley and Son, 1815), Part III, p. 1.

47 *The Literary Gazette and Journal of Belles Lettres, Arts, Sciences &c*, Vol 10 (1826), p. 203.

48 'J. M. Chelsea', in *Magazine of Natural History*, vol 2, 1829, p. 52.

49 Review of Allan Cunningham *British Painters*, vol VI, *The Gentleman's Magazine*, Vol. 103, part one (1833), p. 614.

50 Loudon, 'Directions', pp. 410, 406. On Loudon and the *Arboretum Britannicum*, see Paul A. Elliott, Charles Watkins and Stephen Daniels, *The British Arboretum: Trees, Science and Culture in the Nineteenth Century* (London: Pickering and Chatto, 2011).

51 Hartley, 'The Artist as Naturalist', pp. 18-21, 107.

52 *Eclectic Review*, Feb 1824, pp. 174.

53 Loudon, *Arboretum Britannicum*, Vol. VIII, 312 and 313.

54 Reynolds, *Discourses*, p. 199.

55 A. P. Oppé, *Alexander and John Robert Cozens* (London: Adam and Charles Black, 1952), p. 47.

56 Strutt, 'The principal Forest Trees', p. 39.

57 *Athenaeum*, 14 July 1838, p. 499.

I have not been able to locate a copy of Lewis's publication.

58 Barnard, *Trees from Nature*, Preface.

59 Harding, *Lessons on Trees*, notes on Plate II, and first page (unpaginated).

60 Hüet-Villiers, *Rudiments and Characters of Trees*, introductory text (unpaginated).

61 Barnard, *Handbook of Foliage*, p. 3.

62 Turner, *Oak Tree, Hampton Court, Herefordshire*, c. 1796 (Whitworth Art Gallery, University of Manchester).

63 'Pyne told me that Turner said he wished he could do without trees.' Stillman cites this as a contrast to Théodore Rousseau, who 'worshipped' trees (W. J. Stillman, *The Autobiography of a Journalist*, (London: Grant Richards, 1901), Vol. I, pp. 141-2.)

64 Scott Wilcox, *Edward Lear and the Art of Travel* (New Haven: Yale Center for British Art, 2000), cats. 5, 6.

65 Edward Lear, *North Stoke, Oct 21 1834* (Yale Center for British Art, B1997.7.14).

66 See Vivien Noakes, *Edward Lear 1812–1888* (London: Royal Academy, 1985), pp. 79-91.

67 Kennion, *Essay on Trees*, p. 42.

68 Ian Fleming-Williams, *Constable and his Drawings* (London: Philip Wilson Publishers Ltd, 1990), p. 40.

69 Ian Fleming-Williams et al., *Constable: A Master Draughtsman* (London: Dulwich Picture Gallery, 1994), pp. 58-65; for Malchair, see Colin Harrison et al., *John Malchair of Oxford, Artist and Musician* (Oxford: Ashmolean Museum, 1998).

70 Fleming-Williams, *Constable and his Drawings*, p. 19.

71 Private collection. Graham Reynolds, *The Later Paintings and Drawings of John Constable* (New Haven and London: Yale University Press, 1984), cat. no. 13.16.

72 For silhouette drawings of trees by Constable, see, for example, Reynolds, *The Later Paintings and Drawings*, cat. nos. 23.11 and 23.12. Both these drawings were made at 9 o'clock on a summer evening. Constable probably heard about Cozens's treatises on landscape from Sir George Beaumont, who was taught by Cozens when he was a pupil at Eton. Constable made copies of Cozens's drawings of clouds.

73 R. B. Beckett, ed., *John Constable's Discourses* (Suffolk Records Society), p. 46. The painting was destroyed in a fire in 1867.

74 Graham Reynolds, *The Early Paintings and Drawings of John Constable* (New Haven and London: Yale University Press, 1996), cat. no 00.1; Reynolds, *The Later Paintings and Drawings*, cat. nos 26.21 and 30.1.

75 Reynolds, *The Early Paintings and Drawings*, cat. no 13.7; Reynolds, *The Later Paintings and Drawings*, cat. nos 35.4, 17.1, 17.20.

76 The tracing was sold at Christie's, London, on 3 July 2012.

77 For Constable and Ruisdael, see Seymour Slive, *Jacob van Ruisdael, Master of Landscape* (London: Royal Academy, 2005), pp. 29-35.

78 See R. B. Beckett, ed., *John Constable's Correspondence* (Ipswich: Suffolk Records Society, 1962-9), Vol. II, pp. 304, 317, 324, 357, 412, 420, 423, 429. The first mention of J. G. Strutt and his wife comes in November 1823, when Constable asks his wife if she has seen the Strutts; later on, the couples lend books to each other and the Strutts invite Constable to go to the theatre with them. A copy of *Sylva Britannica* was in Constable's library. The final evidence of contact between the two families is a letter from Strutt to Constable, dated January 25th 1830, apologising for not repaying a loan. It is evident from this letter that Strutt had got himself into serious financial difficulties, and these are the probable explanation for his departure from England to live abroad in 1830 or 1831 (R. B. Beckett et al, eds., *John Constable: Further Documents and Correspondence* (Tate Gallery and Suffolk Records Society, 1975), p. 301).

79 Leslie, *Memoirs*, p. 280.

80 Reynolds, *The Later Paintings and Drawings*, cat. no 23.26.

81 Linnell's MS. Autobiography, written in 1863, now in the Fitzwilliam Museum, Cambridge, pp. 49, 51.

82 Compare, for example, Sandby's *Tree Felling*, c. 1800 (Nottingham City Museums and Galleries).

83 See, for example, a set of eight drawings, 'Tree Studies at Windsor, Tythrop, Derbyshire, Rook's Hill and Underriver, Kent', Sotheby's, London, 30 November 1978, lot 8, and other drawings recorded at the Witt Library, Courtauld Institute.

84 Yale Center for British Art, New Haven, B1993.30.119, B1975.4.784, and B1986.29.264.

85 Wood, *The Principles and Practice*, Part III, p. I.

86 M. Butlin, *Samuel Palmer's Sketchbook, 1824* (Clairvaux: Trianon Press, 1962), p. 3 and commentary. The missing page 4 was in the 1926 exhibition of Palmer's work at the Victoria and Albert Museum: Martin Hardie and James Laver, with notes and introduction by A. H. Palmer, *Catalogue of an Exhibition of Drawings, Etchings and Woodcuts by Samuel Palmer and other Disciples of William Blake* (London: Victoria and Albert Museum, 1926), Cat 50, p. 33.

87 William Vaughan et al, *Samuel Palmer 1805-1881: Vision and Landscape* (London: British Museum, 2005), p. 102.

88 Butlin, *Palmer's Sketchbook*, p. 177.

89 John Linnell, *A Beech Tree* (private collection), illustrated in Katharine Crouan, *John Linnell: A Centennial Exhibition* (Cambridge: Fitzwilliam Museum, 1982), p. 80, here dated (p. 23) to 1828; David Roberts, *Trees in Northwick Park*, undated (Yale Center for British Art, B1981.25.2661).

90 Letter to John Linnell, 21 December 1828, R. Lister, ed., *The Letters of Samuel Palmer* (Oxford: Clarendon Press, 1974), pp. 47-8.

39 WILLIAM MONKHOUSE *after* GEORGE WILLIAM FOTHERGILL

'The Cowthorpe Oak'

Frontispiece from Charles Empson, *The Cowthorpe Oak*, 1842. G. A. fol. A. 173

The Bodleian Libraries, The University of Oxford

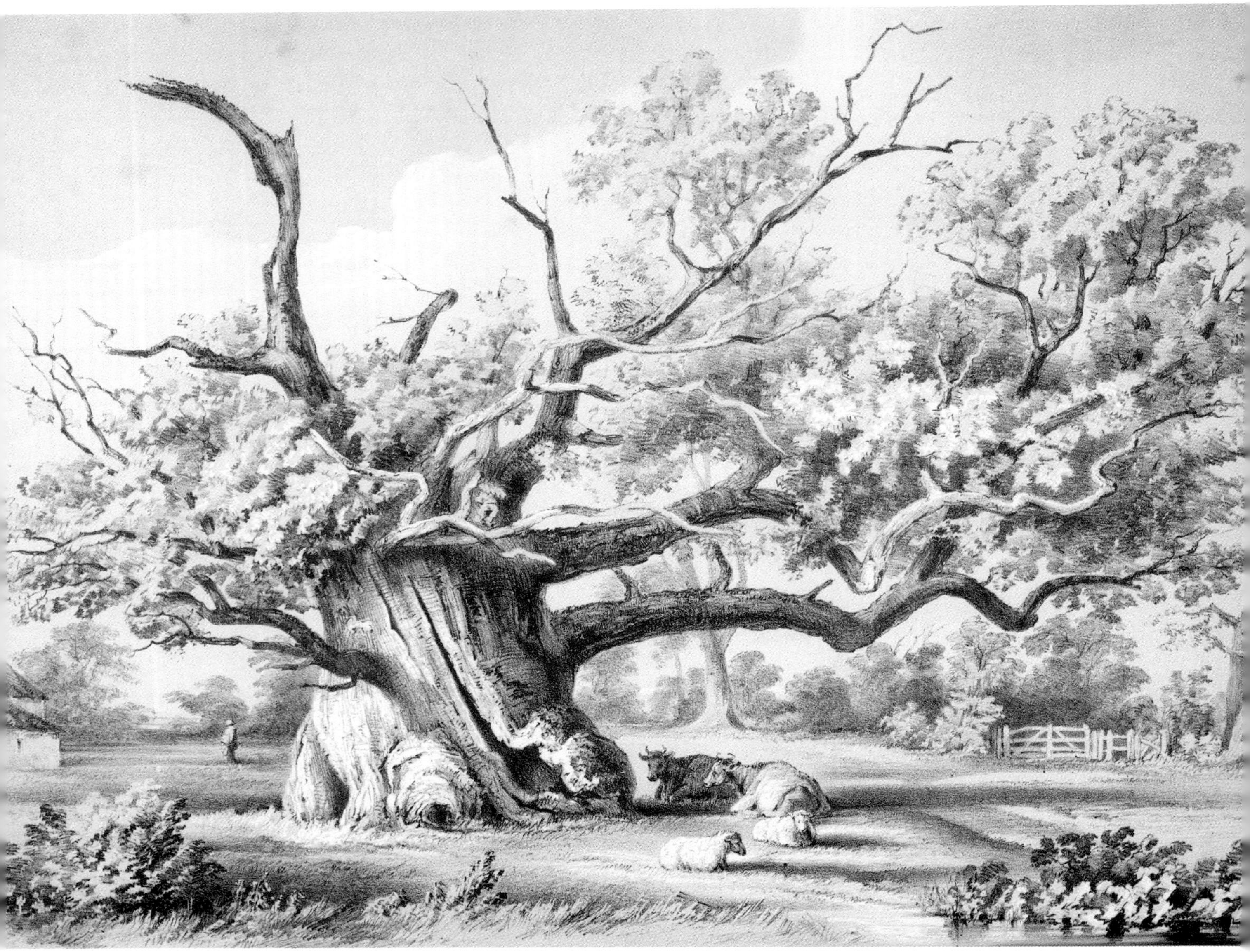

FOUR

'Idolatry with Some Excuse': Portraits of Remarkable Trees

If trees were like human actors in the landscape, then it followed logically that they could be the subject of another artistic genre, that of portraiture. Writers on trees produced what they called 'biographies' of individual trees, and the illustrations to Loudon's *Arboretum Britannicum* were explicitly described as 'portraits.' Artists took care to be accurate, not just in distinguishing the species, but in showing how an individual tree had grown over the years. The events it had witnessed, the role it had played in its surroundings, the stories associated with it, all of these were woven into the accounts of particular trees. The great age, and correspondingly large dimensions, of old trees became a special object of fascination. Biographies of named trees are provided in Evelyn's *Silva*, Gilpin's *Forest Scenery* and Loudon's *Arboretum Britannicum*; large-scale portraits of them were collected in Strutt's *Sylva Britannica* and Burgess's *Eidodendron*.[1] The fashion for tree portraiture encompassed prints, drawings and oil paintings by a substantial number of artists. As with portraits of people or animals, the trees were subject to varying degrees of idealization, and their surroundings and accompanying figures helped to indicate their character or history.

As we have seen, Britain today has more ancient trees than other European countries, despite the fact that its tree cover in general is relatively sparse. One reason for this is the veneration accorded in the eighteenth and nineteenth centuries to individual specimens, unashamedly described by the poet William Cowper as 'idolatry' and summed up by Keith Thomas in the title of one of the chapters in his classic work, *Man and the Natural World*, as 'The worship of trees.'[2] Old trees were associated with the Druids, much admired in this period as the original 'ancient Britons' who had supposedly worshipped the true God in woods and groves before knowing of Christianity. These trees were regarded as the sites of important gatherings and of other key moments in the history of democracy. In landscaped parks, they stood for the benevolent rule of the aristocracy and landed gentry, with their correspondingly long-lived family trees. In villages and on common land, they stood for community and resistance to oppression. Ancient trees were the focus for fairs and preaching, excursions and entertainments, popular customs and superstitions. If they were hollow, they could be enclosing refuges, where people and animals were able to hide from their pursuers; or simply novel places for tea and dinner parties. They could harbour unmarried mothers in childbirth, sellers of ale, or even entire families. Individual trees could, therefore, appeal to a wide range of social and political views and suggest many layers of significance.

The connection of old trees with the Druids is made in many publications in this period. Ronald Hutton, in his comprehensive study of the history of the Druids, has argued that there was a 'Druidic century' in British culture from 1740 to 1860, and that the underlying reason for this was the 'need for a common past to the new British superstate that had been constructed by the early eighteenth century.'[3] Following the publications of William Stukeley in the 1740s, it was widely believed that the Druids had built the megalithic monuments such as Stonehenge, and that they had preached the immortality of the soul. Furthermore, they became embodiments of British patriotism because of their presumed resistance to the Romans, and this was underlined by their devotion to the oak, which was, of course, also a patriotic symbol because of its role in providing wood for warships.[4] By the late eighteenth century, modern societies of Druids began to be formed, often with radical political leanings.[5] Writers of books on trees, from Evelyn onwards, link the Druids to the practices of the Biblical patriarchs, including Abraham, who used trees and groves for their religious rites before the building of tabernacles and temples. Eighteenth and nineteenth-century ideas about the Druids were based on a small number of more or less questionable sources, only one of which, Pliny, mentions their reverence for the oak. As Gilbert Burnett commented, in his essay on oak trees which was published in the book edition of Burgess's *Eidodendron*: 'Much has been said, because little has been truly known concerning the ancient reverence in which trees were held.'[6] Nevertheless, he goes on to describe Britain as the headquarters of the Druidic faith, and the Druids as priests and philosophers, characterized by an undying love of freedom, who followed three basic principles: to worship God, do no evil and be valiant in battle.[7] A later, anonymous book on *English Forests and Forest Trees* associates the Druids with early Parliaments and with Christianity:

> Under the oak-trees from which the old Druid cut the mistletoe, Saxon Parliaments, or Witangemots, have doubtless been held, and in all likelihood many a Christian church now occupies the site of one of those old oak-groves.[8]

Ancient trees could, therefore, evoke this common heritage which embodied the supposed (or desirable) virtues of the modern British nation: religious faith, virtuous behaviour, democratic principles, love of liberty and resistance to foreign invasion.

SOME FAMOUS TREES

Trees were given names, which in most cases simply indicated their location, but nevertheless suggested an individual personality, sometimes according with their physical characteristics. The Cowthorpe Oak (fig. 39), for example, was next to a farmhouse, and spread its huge branches in a somewhat ungainly manner: Strutt described it as being 'like some aged peasant, whose toil-worn limbs still give evidence of the strength which enabled him to acquit himself of the labors of his youth.'[9] The Ankerwycke Yew (figs. 42, 43), by contrast, has a name which suggests medieval religious practices, their mysterious nature emphasized by its thick, dark branches. Some trees were associated with particular people: Sir Philip Sidney's oak was supposed to have been planted to mark the birth of the poet, while Queen Charlotte's Oak was a tree in Windsor Forest which the Queen had asked to be spared from the axe because it commanded such a wonderful view.[10] The names of others reminded people of important historical events, such as the Abbot's Oak at Woburn, where the abbot who refused to give up his monastery was hanged in 1537.[11] The Parliament Oak in Clipston Park, in Sherwood Forest, was supposed to have been the site of a Parliament held by Edward I in 1290.[12] There were also several Gospel Oaks, whose name indicated the practice of beating the bounds of the parish, reading verses from the Bible at strategic points. A further group of trees acquired their names directly from their physical characteristics. A trio in the park at Fredville, Kent, were named Majesty, Stately and Beauty in recognition of their contrasting characters. Another pair of trees, the property of the Marquess of Northampton in Yardley Forest, were called Gog and Magog, presumably because of their short, squat and rather monstrous appearance.[13] The Beggar's Oak at Bagot Park, meanwhile, acquired its name because beggars were able to sit on its exposed roots (fig. 40).

Old trees exercised a particular fascination when they were hollow, as was often the case with ancient oaks and yews. There are many references to lunches, teas and dinner inside these trunks, such as Gilbert Burnett's account of the King's Oak in Windsor Forest:

> We lunched in it September 22nd, 1829: it would accommodate at least twenty persons with standing room, and ten or a dozen might sit down comfortably to dinner. I think at Willis's and in Guildhall I have danced a quadrille on a smaller space.[14]

The Bowthorpe Oak, in Lincolnshire, was provided with a floor, benches and a door in 1768, since when 'frequently twelve persons have dined in it with ease;' prior to this it was used as a feeding place for calves and a pigeon house, according to the letterpress accompanying J. C. Nattes' engraving of it in 1800.[15] When John Clare wrote a sonnet on it in the 1820s it seemed a 'melancholy tree,/Age-rent,

40 JOHN GLOVER

The Beggar's Oak

c.1820s | Oil on canvas | 76.2 x 114.3 cm

Private Collection, © Christie's Images Limited 2017

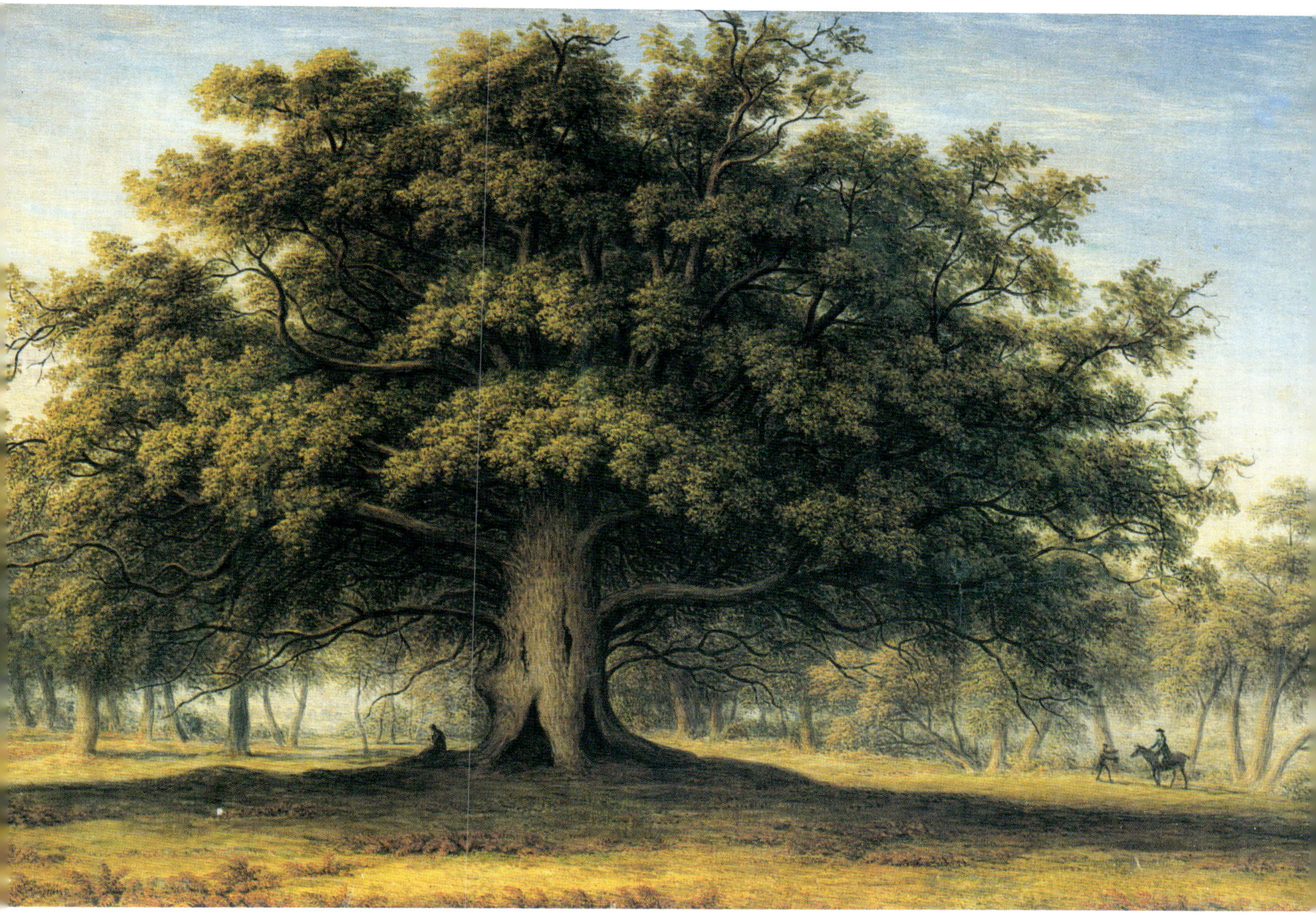

41 J. G. STRUTT

'The Tortworth Chestnut'

1824 | Plate XXIX from J. G. Strutt, *Sylva Britannica; or, Portraits of Forest Trees, distinguished for their antiquity, magnitude, or beauty. Drawn from nature and etched by Jacob George Strutt* (London: J. G. Strutt and Colnaghi and Co, 1822). 19182 a.6

The Bodleian Libraries, The University of Oxford

and shattered to a stump,' yet it was still surviving in 2015 and looking extremely healthy.[16] Hollow trees could also provide shelter and refuge. The story of Charles II hiding in an oak tree after his defeat at the Battle of Worcester was well known; another Royalist, Sir John Rous, apparently hid in a hollow oak tree for two or three days while Roundheads occupied his mansion, his wife creeping out at night to bring him food and water.[17]

In the later eighteenth century, these individual trees became the object of increased interest, both aesthetic and sentimental. The picturesque theorists, particularly Gilpin, celebrated the beauty of ancient trees; the poets gave them a voice and a character, and spoke out against indiscriminate felling. Francis Mundy's poem, *Needwood Forest*, first published anonymously in 1776, was a very influential polemic against the enclosure of Needwood Forest in Staffordshire and the destruction of its oak trees. The hero of the poem is the huge, 600-year-old Swilcar Oak, which makes an impassioned speech:

> High in the midst with many a frown
> Huge SWILCAR shakes his tresses brown,
> Out-spreads his bare arms to the skies,
> The ruins of six centuries,
> Deep Groans pervade his rifted rind–
> –He speaks his bitterness of mind.[18]

He calls on the 'impious … barbarians' to stop, or at least to fell him instead of the young oak trees around him, but he fears that instead

> … ye will leave me with disdain
> A mould'ring land-mark on the plain.[19]

Mundy addresses the oak, in turn, as 'Thrice venerable Druid'.[20] The poem was published with responses from four other poets, Erasmus Darwin and his son, Anna Seward and Brooke Boothby. Darwin, too, addresses the Swilcar Oak directly: 'Hail, stately oak, whose wrinkled trunk hath stood/ Age after age, the sov'reign of this wood.'[21] As a result of these poems, the Swilcar Oak became a very famous tree, and Strutt begins his *Sylva Britannica* with it. An engraving of it had previously been published in John Britton's *The Beauties of England and Wales*, where it was one of 14 illustrations in the section on Staffordshire, the others all being buildings – castles, old churches, ruined abbeys and mansions.[22] The tree seems to have decayed visibly between 1807, the date of the engraving, and the 1820s when Strutt studied it. In Strutt's etching, it is accompanied by fallen branches and woodmen, perhaps suggesting that the tree itself is now in danger of being cut down. In 1857, however, it was still healthy enough to be the site of a picnic for the children of 'the National and Infants' Schools' in nearby Uttoxeter, who were 'conveyed in waggons, gaily decorated, accompanied by their teachers and friends.'[23]

The Yardley Oak of William Cowper's eponymous poem was even more famous, but in this case the identification of the tree was uncertain, and Cowper's name for it was not the generally accepted one. Written in 1791 or 1792 but unpublished in Cowper's lifetime, the poem first appeared in the third volume of William Hayley's *Life* of the poet in 1804.[24] It rapidly became famous, and is quoted repeatedly, and at length, in many of the books on trees published in the first half of the nineteenth century. Cowper speaks at first of the 'reverence' with which he approaches the tree, and says that to worship it would be 'Idolatry with some excuse' since our forefathers the Druids found sanctity in oak trees.[25] The poem then becomes a meditation on the passage of time and the inevitability of decay, a metaphor for life in general and human life in particular:

> … as century rolled
> Slow after century, a giant bulk
> Of girth enormous with moss-cushion'd root
> Upheav'd above the soil, and sides imboss'd
> With prominent webs globose, till at the last
> The rottenness which Time is charged to inflict
> On other mighty Ones found also thee – [26]

Cowper dwells on the physical characteristics of the ancient tree, which inspire sympathy as if it were an aged human

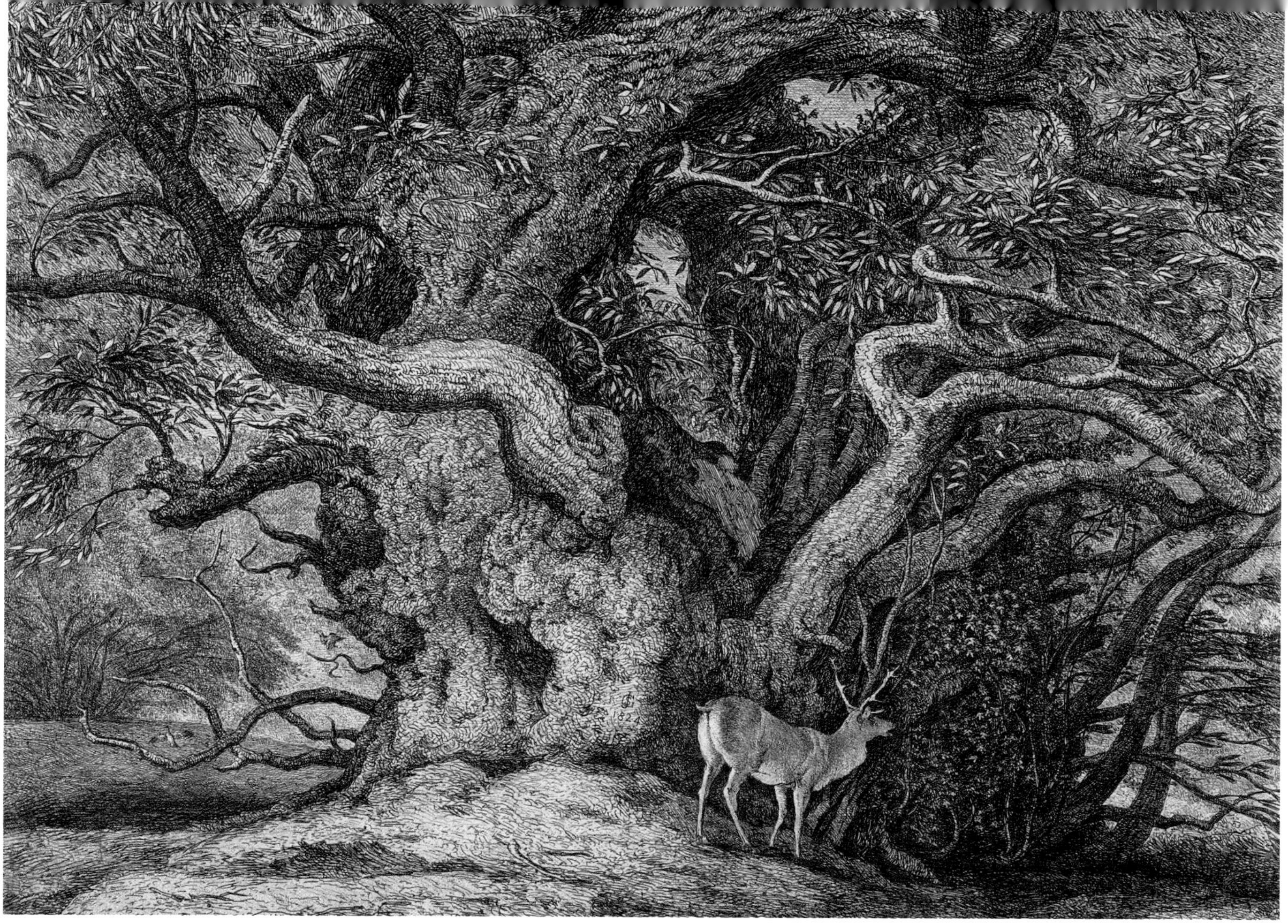

being. The modern opinion is that the Yardley Oak was a tree called Judith, said to have been planted by William the Conqueror's niece,[27] but in the early nineteenth century it was identified with the tree known as Magog, which consequently became the target of souvenir hunters. According to Gilbert Burnett, writing in 1829, 'it has been attacked both with the saw and hatchet, and large fragments were continually being borne off in triumph, to be converted into snuff-boxes and other utensils, until the Marquis of Northampton, whose property it is, caused large nails and spikes to be driven into it' in an attempt to preserve it.[28] Such indignities – which would surely have horrified Cowper – were inflicted on many of these ancient trees, an unfortunate by-product of the interest they aroused.

Mundy and Cowper dwelt on the aspects of old trees that had human parallels: their suffering, the infirmities of age and the sadness of death. Other writers were obsessed by their measurements. Evelyn's *Silva* includes a list of prodigious British trees, following the example set by Pliny in his *Natural History*. He gives their height, their circumference at a particular height from the ground, and the number of people, or cattle, that could stand under their shade. Since his explicit purpose was to encourage landowners to plant trees for the navy, he also gives figures for the volume of timber they contain, and the value of that timber. Evelyn seems to assume that these large old trees will be felled, but he makes an exception for boundary trees, such as the Tortworth Chestnut (fig. 41): 'such venerable trees … should be spared for the most noble and natural boundaries to great parishes, and gentlemen's estates.'[29] Throughout the eighteenth century, local historians noted trees of exceptional size, and measuring these trees (and squeezing numbers of people into hollow trunks, sometimes, apparently, cheating by having children standing on adults' shoulders) became a popular pastime. The original *Sylva* was not illustrated, but Hunter's 1776 edition of *Silva* includes illustrations of two celebrated examples, the Cowthorpe Oak and the Greendale Oak. The Cowthorpe Oak is not mentioned by Evelyn, but Hunter claims that it is larger than any of the trees he discusses. In his illustration (a large fold-out plate, based on a drawing by William Burgh) the tree is shown in winter, its leafless branches stretching out wide, especially on the left-hand side, from a truncated stem which ends in a jagged edge.

Hunter included no fewer than four illustrations of his other example, the Greendale Oak, which is mentioned in Evelyn's text: Evelyn says it has eight very large branches remaining, and reckoned that 225 cattle could stand in its shade. By 1776 it had only one of these branches left and looked bizarre: the first Duke of Portland had had a large arch cut in it, to prove his claim that he could drive his carriage through it.[30] Two of Hunter's plates are dedicated to the tree's measurements. The remaining branch puts forth luxuriant foliage, providing proof of the tree's vitality and its ability to survive such vandalism. In 1790 Hayman Rooke produced a booklet with illustrations of the Greendale Oak, along with other trees on the estate of the Duke of Portland 'taken under favour of his repeated hospitality at Welbeck'. The text praises the appearance of a four hundred-acre plantation of new trees, 'all planted by the present Duke of Portland.'[31] Landowners were evidently pleased to have their ancient trees recorded and their philanthropic efforts publicized. The Duke of Portland was particularly fond of his ancient trees, and made a collection of images and descriptions of famous examples.[32]

The appearance of Gilpin's *Forest Scenery* in 1791 gave further impetus to the sympathetic interest in individual trees. Gilpin writes that 'as many trees, as well as men, have distinguished themselves in the world, it seemed proper to devote a few pages to the particular mention of such celebrated characters.'[33] In contrast to Evelyn, he laments the fact that old trees are cut down before they reach the height of their beauty:

> Wherever trees can be turned to profit, they are commonly cut down long before they attain picturesque perfection. The beauty of almost every species of tree increases after its prime; and unless it have the good fortune to stand in some place of difficult access, or under the protection of some patron whose mansion it adorns, we rarely see it in that grandeur and dignity which it would acquire by age.[34]

Gilpin says that he could produce a long list of celebrated trees, 'but I reject all such trees as have either been only casually mentioned [in other publications], or have had their value merely ascertained by a timber merchant's rule.'[35] Instead, Gilpin gives extended accounts of a few trees, including the Tortworth Chestnut (fig. 41). 'Traditional accounts', writes Gilpin, 'suppose it to have been a boundary-tree in the time of King John; and I have met with other accounts, which place it in the same honourable station in the reign of King Stephen … This tree is at present in hands, which justly value, and protect its age.'[36] Gilpin also gives 'biographies' of the Fairlop Oak in Hainault Forest in Essex (fig. 44), famous for the annual fair that was held beneath its spreading branches, and the Cadenham Oak in the New Forest, which was reputed to produce buds on the old Christmas Day, January 5th. The latter is an interesting example because Gilpin himself (despite being a clergyman) is clearly sceptical about the beliefs of what he calls 'the philosophers of the forest,' and is inclined to attribute the tree's early budding to purely natural, rather than miraculous causes.[37] While he gives measurements occasionally, these never include cubic feet of timber or monetary value, except in the case of Damory's Oak in Dorset (which in the seventeenth century was inhabited by an old man who sold ale in it), sold for fourteen pounds in 1755 'when it was fit for nothing but firewood.'[38]

Gilpin's plea that old trees should not be cut down was important, because even very aged trees could be of great value as timber. A famous case was that of the Golynos Oak, which grew on an estate within four miles of Newport, Monmouthshire, close enough to the coast to be transported to the naval dockyards. A printed sheet about it is included in a collection of images of famous trees made in the early nineteenth century by Sir Joseph Banks, the well-known naturalist and President of the Royal Society. This sheet records that Thomas Harrison (His Majesty's Purveyor of Plymouth Dockyard and Dean Forest) bought it for 100 guineas, spent £82 on felling and sawing it, and sold the 2426 feet of timber that it produced for nearly £600. The tree was not only valuable in monetary terms, it was also extremely useful because of the curved and angled pieces it contained which could be used in the construction of warships. The same publication includes a list of the uses to which the timber was put, including 'one upper piece stem for a hundred gun ship', 'three lower futtocks each one hundred guns' and 'about twenty knees, all of which were large enough for the Navy'.[39] The case of the Golynos oak showed how profitable an old tree could be; this was in 1810, at the height of the Napoleonic Wars, when there was a strong demand for oak wood and prices were correspondingly high.

THE SYLVA BRITANNICA

The progression from descriptive written 'biographies' to images of remarkable trees reached a peak in the 1820s, when Jacob George Strutt and Henry William Burgess produced their sets of prints. Both the *Sylva Britannica* of Strutt and the *Eidodendron* of Burgess were originally issued in instalments, and their dated title pages were completed some years prior to publication, leading to some confusion over their publication dates. In 1826 Strutt published his etchings in a lavish folio edition, with historical and poetic notes on each of his named trees, written by himself. Burgess's lithographs appeared in a similarly grand folio edition in 1830 or 1831, accompanied by a lengthy essay on oaks (the author's name is not given in the volume, but it is known to be by Gilbert Burnett, the botanist).[40] Both books were published by subscription, and in each case the list reads like a roll-call of the hereditary aristocracy and landed gentry of the country, starting with the King. Burnett's book is dedicated to the King, while Strutt's book is dedicated to the Duke of Bedford, and his subscription list includes John Constable, his personal friend.

The subtitles of the works indicate their differing emphasis. Strutt's is subtitled 'Portraits of Forest Trees, distinguished for their Antiquity, Magnitude or Beauty'. Burgess's suggests a more generalized, less portrait-oriented approach: 'Views of the general Character and Appearance of Trees, Foreign and Indigenous as connected with Picturesque Scenery.' Only a minority of Burgess's illustrations are of named trees, while nearly all of Strutt's are. Even when they illustrate the same tree, Strutt's emphasis is more towards the particular, and his drawing style more descriptive.[41] When Strutt's plates can be compared with trees still surviving today, such as the Tortworth Chestnut, he does seem to have been remarkably true to the character of the tree, in this case giving a convincing idea of the profusion of growth around the trunk and the springing curves of the branches (fig. 41). Strutt appears to have travelled around the country, seeking out remarkable trees in order to record them for posterity. He was a well-educated artist, with a wide knowledge of the literature on trees, both historical and poetic. He was also a keen collector of, and dealer in Old Master prints, particularly those of Waterloo.[42] Burgess, in contrast, was a drawing master, and his plates provide a variety of images of trees that his pupils would be able to copy.

Strutt followed up his folio edition of 1826 with a reduced edition, in 1830. In the latter, he omitted some of the trees from gentlemen's estates and added others that would have a wider popular appeal, such as Burnham Beeches and the Gospel Oak at Stoneleigh. In the commentary on the Gospel Oak, he takes the opportunity to discuss the custom of 'beating the bounds', that is, marking the boundaries of a parish by going round it once a year, and stopping at remarkable spots and trees, led by the clergy, to recite passages from the Bible. Strutt claims that it is still common in various parts of the kingdom, but his description of it is in the past tense, implying that it has more or less died out:

> … it must have been a soothing sight to witness the devotional feelings of the multitude, thus called forth in the simplicity of patriarchal worship in the open air, and surrounded by the works of God.[43]

Strutt adds that the old oak was especially suitable as an altar, since 'in times of yore the worshippers of God were wont to do [this], in their solemn groves, before temples made by hands were built to Him, and the place of His holy tabernacle fixed by His own divine revelation.'[44] Strutt enlarged the text for the octavo edition, generally adding quotations and anecdotes to his previous descriptions and comments. In one instance, the commentary on the Wych Elm at Bagot's Mill, the changes he made suggest that he felt he had taken too radical a stance in the folio edition. In the folio edition of *Sylva Britannica*, Strutt claimed that the pleasure felt by a poor cottager in looking at a fine tree was purer than that of the 'owner of large domains, who sees the woods that were planted by his ancestors prostrated beneath the axe, to satisfy the demands of some scheme of luxury or ambition.'[45] In the 1830 edition he took out this provocative passage, replacing it with a long quotation from Washington Irving's *Bracebridge Hall*, published in 1822, praising the generosity of the English nobility, and including Irving's appreciation of their aesthetic approach to their trees:

> I have heard a noble earl descant on park and forest scenery with the science and feeling of a painter: he dwelt on the shape and beauty of particular trees on his estate, with as much pride and technical precision as though he had been discussing the merits of statues in his collection.[46]

This passage may well have struck a chord with Strutt because it corresponded to his own experiences in the company of people who loved their trees, but it also appears to provide a justification for the wealth and power that went with the ownership of large estates.

Strutt follows his etching of the Swilcar Oak in *Sylva Britannica* with one of the Beggar's Oak. The two trees stood only three miles apart, the latter being on the estate of the 2nd Lord Bagot. Two other trees from Lord Bagot's estate, the Squitch Bank Oak and the Wych Elm at Bagot's Mill, are also included in the book, and Strutt declares that it was in Lord Bagot's park that he first made sketches for the book, encouraged by the owner.[47] In his text Strutt notes that the Beggar's Oak 'is supposed to have received its name … from the accommodation it is so well calculated to afford in its ample canopy, "star-proof", and its moss-grown roots, to the weary mendicant who may have been tempted to seek the shade of its branches, for repose or shelter.'[48] However, his etching shows no beggars, only the famous Bagot goats, and in his 1830 edition he adds the words 'in former times', as if he wishes to stress that Lord Bagot is a benevolent landowner whose property is now free from poverty.[49] The emphasis given to this tree, nevertheless, is a reminder of another way in which landed wealth could be justified, through paternalism and charity.

It seems that Lord Bagot was encouraging other artists besides Strutt to think of producing a series of portraits of famous trees in the early 1820s. In 1820, James Ward made drawings of 'Mr Howard's Large Oak' at Wichnor on August 5th, an 'Oak in Lord Bagot's Park' on August 8th, and 'The Beggar's Oak' on August 12th.[50] The last of these is inscribed: 'A Celebrated Ancient Tree on Lord Bagot's Blithfield Hall Estate in Staffordshire.' John Glover produced two oil paintings, one of the Beggar's Oak and the other of 'The Swilker Oak' [sic], most probably in the 1820s, before he left England for Tasmania in 1831. In Glover's painting of *The Beggar's Oak* (fig. 40), a woman is seen sitting on the 'moss-grown roots', while a man appears to be soliciting alms from a man on horseback in the middle distance. This painting is not known to have been exhibited and may have been a commission from Lord Bagot. Glover's depiction of the Swilcar oak shows it growing luxuriantly and surrounded by saplings, which may indicate that both paintings were meant to refer to former times, as 'historical' portraits of the trees.[51] Lord Bagot himself had a keen interest in the history of his estate. He transformed Bagot Hall by giving it a Gothic remodelling, and he collected and transcribed many of the historical documents he found in the house, producing a book about it in 1824. In this book he writes of his 'noble patriarchal oaks' and shows pride in his 'stately timber, (certainly not surpassed, if in any degree equalled, in the United Kingdoms).'[52] The book includes the dimensions and values of three trees: the Beggar's Oak, the Squitch Oak, and the Cliff or King Oak.[53]

Strutt is full of praise for Lord Bagot. He notes that the timber of the Beggar's Oak was valued at £202.14s.9d in 1812, but, in contrast to Evelyn's encouragement for owners to fell their trees, Strutt extols those who resist the temptation:

> … this noble tree, as well as many other of the 'giants of the forest', with which Bagot's Park abounds, are secure from the axe, under the protection of their present munificent proprietor; who best shows his sense of the value of the woody domains received from his ancestor, by endeavouring to secure the same gratification to his posterity; annually planting a large portion of his estates, with a taste and zeal which well deserve to be imitated, by all such landed proprietors as may be actuated by a laudable ambition to make their private possessions a source of public ornament, and of national wealth.[54]

Strutt's prose is pompous and convoluted, but the message is clear: a good landowner treats his ancient trees with respect and will not be tempted to fell them for profit; at the same time, he plants new trees for the benefit of posterity. The value of timber had fallen since the end of the Napoleonic Wars, and Lord Bagot's book includes the 1823 valuation of the Beggar's Oak, which had dropped to £195.1s.4d.[55] Even the latter was a huge sum, however.

THE SYMBOLISM OF ANCIENT TREES

Ancient trees took on various different meanings. Keith Thomas has argued that they were cherished for 'what they symbolized to the community in terms of continuity and association' and that 'as social change accelerated, the desire to preserve such visible symbols of continuity grew stronger.'[56] Strutt's *Sylva Britannica*, with its repeated compliments to members of the landed gentry and aristocracy, would seem to bear this out. On the other hand, Strutt shows a consistent sympathy for rebels, including John Hampden, the barons who forced King John to sign Magna Carta, and the abbot hanged by Henry VIII.[57] The 1820s was a decade in which the movement to reform Parliament was gathering strength, and these examples of resistance to authority could be accommodated within a Whig view of British history, according to which the growth of Parliament and respect for the law ensured liberty for all. Strutt dedicated the book version of *Sylva Britannica* to the 6th Duke of Bedford, another aristocrat who, like the Duke of Portland, collected pictures of famous trees. His dedication pays tribute to the longevity of the family (which is like that of the oak tree) but also to their championship of 'well-regulated liberty':

> When I first entreated Your Grace's permission to dedicate to the Representative of the House of Russell the following PORTRAITS OF FOREST TREES, I was influenced by an irresistible association in my own mind between the stedfastness [sic] and independence universally attributed to the 'Lord of the Woods, the long-surviving Oak', and the same characteristics which have for ages past distinguished the noble family of Bedford; a family whose name will be always venerated in the annals of English History, as the champions of lawful right and well-regulated liberty.

The 6th Duke, and his son, Lord John Russell, supported gradual, legal reform, which would preserve the existence of the aristocracy and gentry, rather than the radical change which would be brought about by revolution. Indeed, Lord John Russell had been trying, all through the 1820s, to get the Parliamentary seats of rotten boroughs transferred to the industrial cities, an aim he eventually achieved with the Great Reform Act of 1832.

Old trees were widely seen as symbols of Britain's tradition of Parliamentary democracy and gradual reform. They were associated with early Parliaments and moots held by the Anglo-Saxons. Horace Walpole, as we saw in Chapter Two, regarded an old tree as a symbol of liberty, which in France would be appropriated by the King. In 1831, it was proposed that the freedom of the city of York be presented to Lord Brougham, the city's MP and prominent reformer, in recognition of his advocacy for the rights and liberties of his fellow-subjects, in a box of heart of oak. The Lord Mayor, the Hon Edward Petrie, said he would have great

42 H. W. BURGESS
'An Old Yew, Ankerwycke near Staines'
Plate 43 from H. W. Burgess, *Eidodendron: Views of the general Character and Appearance of Trees Foreign & Indigenous as connected with picturesque Scenery* (London: J. Dickinson, 1827).
Yale Center for British Art, Paul Mellon Fund (Folio AD 50)

pleasure in doing so. 'He would supply the wood requisite from the celebrated Cowthorpe oak on his estate, beneath which, he believed, a Parliament was once held.'[58] This must have seemed particularly appropriate because the Cowthorpe Oak was renowned as the largest, and one of the oldest, oaks in England. Hunter, in his notes on Evelyn's *Silva*, said it was larger than any of the oaks described by Evelyn: 'When compared to this, all other trees are but *Children* of the Forest.'[59] At this time it was said to measure 16 yards in circumference at a height of 3 feet from the ground. Today, it is regarded as the largest girthed English oak ever recorded in Britain.[60] In 1857 it was reckoned to be 1600 years old.[61]

The Cowthorpe Oak was depicted many times. As we have seen, the large fold-out page in Hunter's edition of *Silva* shows it in winter, from the north. A print by J. Laporte, preserved in the Joseph Banks collection and dated 1806, takes exactly the same viewpoint but shows the tree in summer, with the local church in the background. In August 1816, J. M. W. Turner made two detailed drawings of the tree, from both north and south, presumably intending to make a finished watercolour of it.[62] Strutt's plate shows it from the south, without the church, and he gives it suitably rustic accompaniments to convey his idea of it being like an 'aged peasant': cattle, pigs and a farm waggon. The drawing reproduced in Charles Empson's book on the tree, published in 1842 (fig. 39), is very similar to Strutt's.[63] None of these sources, however, makes any mention of a Parliament being held under the tree, and it is likely that Edward Petrie was mixing it up with other old oak trees, such as the Parliament Oak in Sherwood Forest. Early twentieth-century photographs show the Cowthorpe Oak with a large number of supports, and it appears to have died in the 1950s.[64]

A tree which had more credible associations with the development of Parliamentary democracy was the Ankerwycke Yew. This still flourishes today, on an island in the Thames between Wraysbury and Runnymede, on land now owned by the National Trust. Both Strutt and Burgess

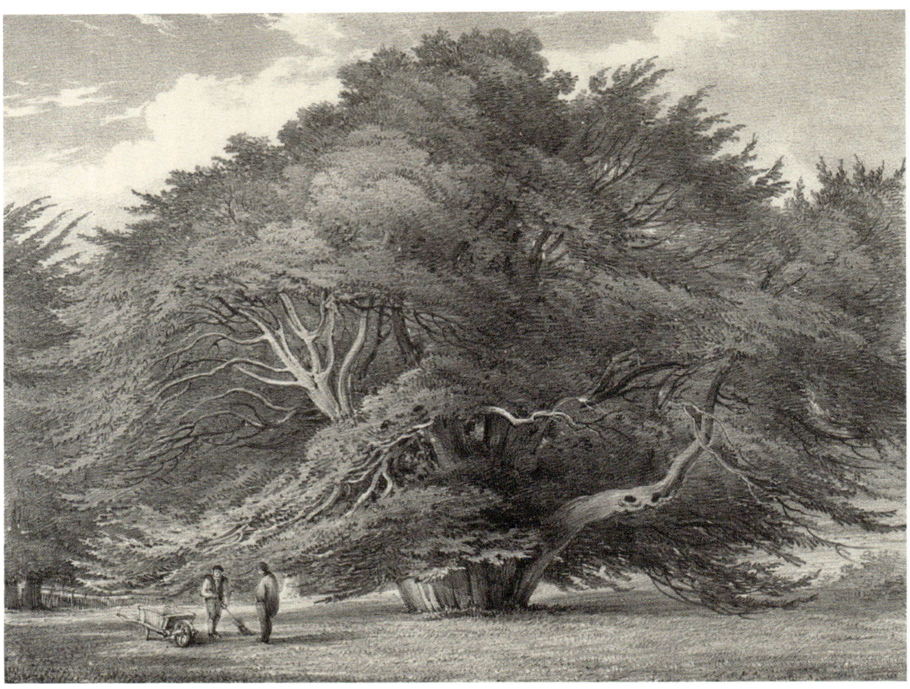

43 J. G. STRUTT

'The Yew Tree at Ankerwyke'

Plate VIII from J. G. Strutt, *Sylva Britannica; or, Portraits of Forest Trees, distinguished for their antiquity, magnitude, or beauty. Drawn from nature and etched by Jacob George Strutt* (London: J. G. Strutt and Colnaghi and Co, 1822). 19182 a.6.

The Bodleian Libraries, The University of Oxford

include it in their plates, but their depictions of it are very different (figs. 42, 43). Strutt, who describes it as being in the grounds of John Blagrove, Esq, shows it neatly trimmed around its trunk. In Burgess's view, however, its foliage grows in great sweeps towards the ground, and its owner is given as G. S. Harcourt, Esq. Both artists show it accompanied by gardeners, indicating its current role as a decorative object in a gentleman's pleasure grounds. Even allowing for Burgess's generally more romantic approach, the contrast is dramatic. Strutt's drawing was made in 1822 or earlier, Burgess's probably in 1829, the year when Harcourt repurchased the land from the estate of John Blagrove, who had died in 1824.[65] Tastes were changing, and the yews which had formerly been clipped into topiary shapes were now being allowed to grow naturally. Strutt's depiction of the furrowed trunk conforms more closely than Burgess's plate to the tree's appearance today, but both show it in an open, parkland setting, very different from its current situation in dense undergrowth.

Recently, it has been proposed that the Ankerwycke Yew was the site of the signing of Magna Carta. Allen Meredith argues that it would have been seen as neutral territory between King John's camp and the barons at Runnymede, and an appropriate spot to take oaths, protected by the old priory.[66] Strutt, too, was keen to associate this old tree with an event widely seen as the foundation of democracy and liberty, not just in Britain but in America and around the world. Strutt notes that Henry VIII is supposed to have courted Anne Boleyn beneath its branches, but it was better to remember it as 'the silent witness of the conferences of those brave barons who afterwards compelled King John to sign Magna Charta.'[67] George Simon Harcourt believed that Magna Carta was signed on the adjacent island, close to the tree, then, but not actually underneath it. In 1834, he rebuilt and enlarged the fisherman's cottage on Magna Carta Island, installing the so-called 'Charter Stone' that had been preserved in old Ankerwycke House.[68]

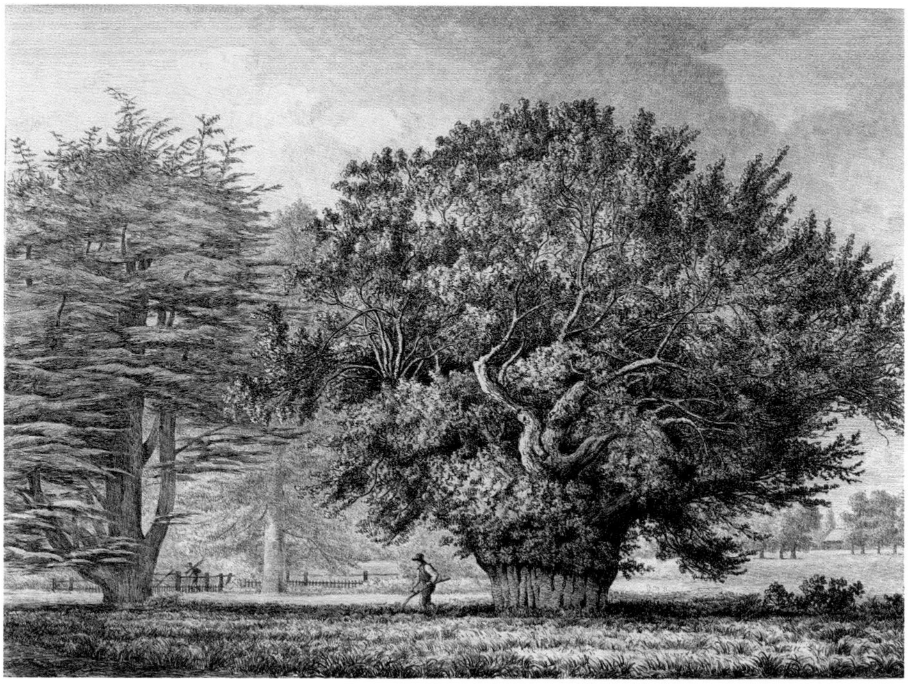

The Fairlop Oak in Hainault Forest, near the East End of London, was another famous tree celebrated for its role in bringing a community together, even long after the tree itself had died. Gilpin describes it in his *Forest Scenery*:

> About a yard from the ground, where it's [sic] rough fluted stem is thirty-six feet in circumference, it divides into eleven vast arms; yet not in the horizontal manner of an oak, but rather in that of a beech. Beneath it's shade, which overspreads an area of three hundred feet in circuit, an annual fair has long been held, on the 2d of July; and no booth is suffered to be erected beyond the extent of it's [sic] branches.[69]

The annual fair was founded around 1720 by Daniel Day, an eccentric philanthropist. In 1775 Samuel Hieronymus Grimm exhibited a watercolour of the fair (fig. 44), in which the tree accords with Gilpin's description and the fairgoers look well-to-do and decorously behaved. In the changed circumstances of the 1790s, when public gatherings raised fears of sedition, attempts were made to curb the fair: in 1793 no stalls or booths were permitted to be erected, though in the following and subsequent years it was held as usual.[70] Trees had the potential to become the focus for activities which could be seen as dangerous by the authorities. John Wesley preached many sermons under trees, the liberty tree was a symbol of revolution, and the Tolpuddle Martyrs, whose attempts to found a trade union in 1834 led to their transportation, also met under a tree, in their case a sycamore.

In 1805, a fire, lit by picnickers, accidentally destroyed much of the Fairlop Oak, and it was finally blown down in a gale in 1820. At the fair held in 1813, only one leaf appeared at the end of a bough, and a man paid a boy half a crown to climb the tree and bring it back to him – like a holy relic.[71] The fair continued, however, on the open space left by the tree and in the surrounding forest: by 1843 thousands were attending from the poor, and newly populous districts of the East End, and the Essex magistrates, nervous of popular disturbances, limited it strictly to one day rather than a whole weekend. It only ceased when the area was enclosed and the trees pulled down.[72] The wood of the Fairlop Oak itself found a new role: it was used for the pulpits of a new church at St Pancras. *The Times* commented:

> This tree was the contemporary of the Druids, and from its noble size probably was itself once the object of worship, having the parasite mistletoe removed from its branches by the golden sickle. That it should now be in the centre of Christian worship must excite reflection in all who are acquainted with its 'strange history', nor can the Church be regarded as unworthy a visit by the most superficial.[73]

The idea that old oak trees might once have been sacred trees, worshipped by the Druids, was very common; it was thought fitting, then, that their wood should be incorporated in Christian churches.

TREE PORTRAITS ON CANVAS AND ON PAPER

The widespread interest in ancient trees produced a demand for images of them, long before Strutt and Burgess produced their prints. At first, these were often drawn by amateurs, like Hayman Rooke, but then professional artists began to be involved, sometimes being required to copy a drawing by an amateur. The depiction of these trees became part of the fashion for recording and illustrating British antiquities, which reached a peak in the years of the Napoleonic Wars. Engraved portraits of old trees were popular, both to stand alone and as plates in topographical collections of the beauty spots and antiquities of the counties. Thomas Hearne produced portraits of famous trees, the Moccas Park Oak (fig. 19) and the Wymondley Chestnut, which were reproduced as engravings. The Swilcar Oak, as we have seen, was included in *The Beauties of England and Wales*, and the Bowthorpe Oak in Howlett's *Views in the County of Lincoln*, published in 1800. Another example of this was the

44 SAMUEL HIERONYMOUS GRIMM
Fairlop Oak and Fairlop Fair
1774–5 | Watercolour | 40.3 x 53.6 cm

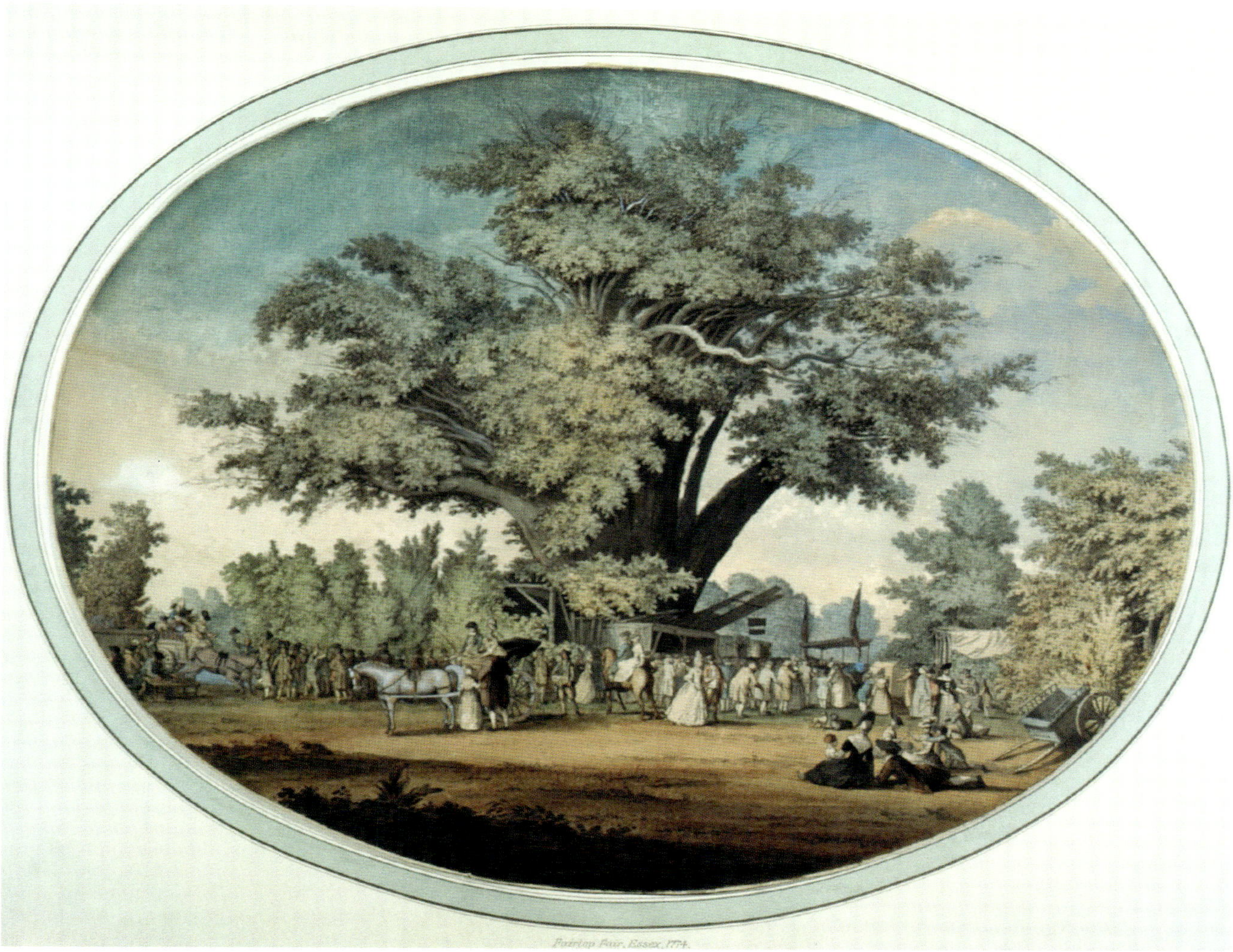

Fredville Oak, included in Strutt's *Sylva Britannica* under its name of Majesty (fig. 5). In William Hasted's *History and Topographical Survey of the County of Kent* (1778-99) the tree dominates a view of Fredville, the seat of John Plumptre. It almost conceals the house, and a group of figures are shown standing around it with hands linked, evidently trying to measure its girth. This is a tree which still stands, and is now regarded as the largest maiden oak in Britain.

Another oak which still stands is the Panshanger Oak, which was painted by Thomas Medland in 1814. This painting does not appear to have been exhibited, and it was almost certainly a commission from Lord Cowper, the owner of the tree. The painting, which measures 112 by 140 centimetres, remained in his house until it was demolished in the 1950s.[74] This was not, in 1814 at least, a particularly old tree. It is described by Strutt as an 'elegant tree' which

45 J. G. STRUTT
'Panshanger Oak'
Plate IV from J. G. Strutt, *Sylva Britannica; or, Portraits of Forest Trees, distinguished for their antiquity, magnitude, or beauty. Drawn from nature and etched by Jacob George Strutt* (London: J. G. Strutt and Colnaghi and Co, 1822). 19182 a.6.
The Bodleian Libraries, The University of Oxford

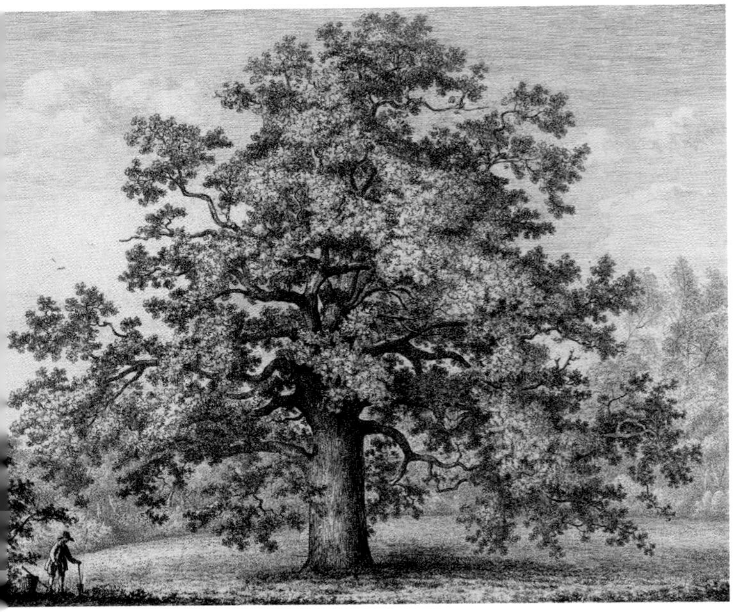

'appears … to have scarcely reached its prime … The waving lightness of its feathered branches … the straightness of its trunk, and the redundancy of its foliage, all give it a character opposite to that of antiquity, and fit it for the cultivated and sequestered pleasure grounds, belonging to the mansion of Earl Cowper.'[75] Medland published an aquatint of it in 1831, which was inscribed 'Drawn from Nature by T. Medland, 1814, when the Tree was at its greatest state of Beauty'.[76] Medland's view of the tree emphasizes its location in parkland, with well-dressed accompanying figures clearly involved in recreation and leisure. Strutt depicts it with a single gardener in the foreground (fig. 45): his view of the tree makes it look much shorter and stouter than the depiction by Medland, who probably exaggerated its proportions to flatter its owner.

Paintings of named trees were also exhibited at the Royal Academy. Strutt showed two paintings of celebrated trees, both of which are currently untraced: *A Scene in Savernake Forest, Wiltshire, with a View of the King Oak,* in 1824, and *The Great Ash at Carnock, Stirlingshire,* in 1826.[77] These were large paintings.[78] The *Scene in Savernake Forest* was shown again at the British Institution in 1825, when its measurements were recorded as 4 ft 4 in by 5 ft 2 in, or 132 by 158 cm (including the frame). Both trees were included in his *Sylva Britannica,* so the paintings acted as an advertisement for the publication. James Ward did many drawings of named trees, including the Beggar's Oak, but only exhibited one oil painting of this kind. This was *The Yeldham Oak*, shown at the RA in 1834 (fig. 46). The old tree, which stood on common land at a crossroads, is shown as one element in the rural social structure and economy, with church and gentry represented by Yeldham Hall and Yeldham Church in the distance, while a farmhouse, sportsmen with hounds, and a poor pedlar complete the harmonious vision.[79] The tree is clearly in the later stages of its life, 'stag-headed' and picturesque rather than beautiful. The Yeldham oak does not figure in any of the lists of ancient oaks given by Evelyn, Hunter, Gilpin or Burnett, nor in the plates of Strutt and Burgess, but it was clearly a source of regional pride. The *Essex Standard* was most enthusiastic about Ward's painting:

> … a very admirable picture of this most remarkable and very old tree. … the chief interest of the picture is the Old oak, and the fidelity with which its endless branches … are represented, is most extraordinary, and could only have been accomplished by such persevering assiduity, as Mr Ward is known to have devoted to the subject, during his visit into Essex last autumn. A prominent situation has been assigned to the picture at Somerset House, where it is greatly admired on account of the extraordinary antiquity and size of the tree, as well as a work of Art … It is emphatically an English scene: it is also one of the most striking objects in Essex.[80]

The critic of the *Athenaeum* was less fulsome in its praise, but also noted that 'the whole forms a scene elegant and English'.[81] This tree no longer survives: by 1859 it was reported that it was 'a monarch in ruins' with very little foliage to be seen.[82]

46 JAMES WARD

The Yeldham Oak at Great Yeldham, Essex

1834 | Oil on canvas | 129.5 x 199.4 cm

Private Collection, Photo © Christies Images/Bridgeman Images

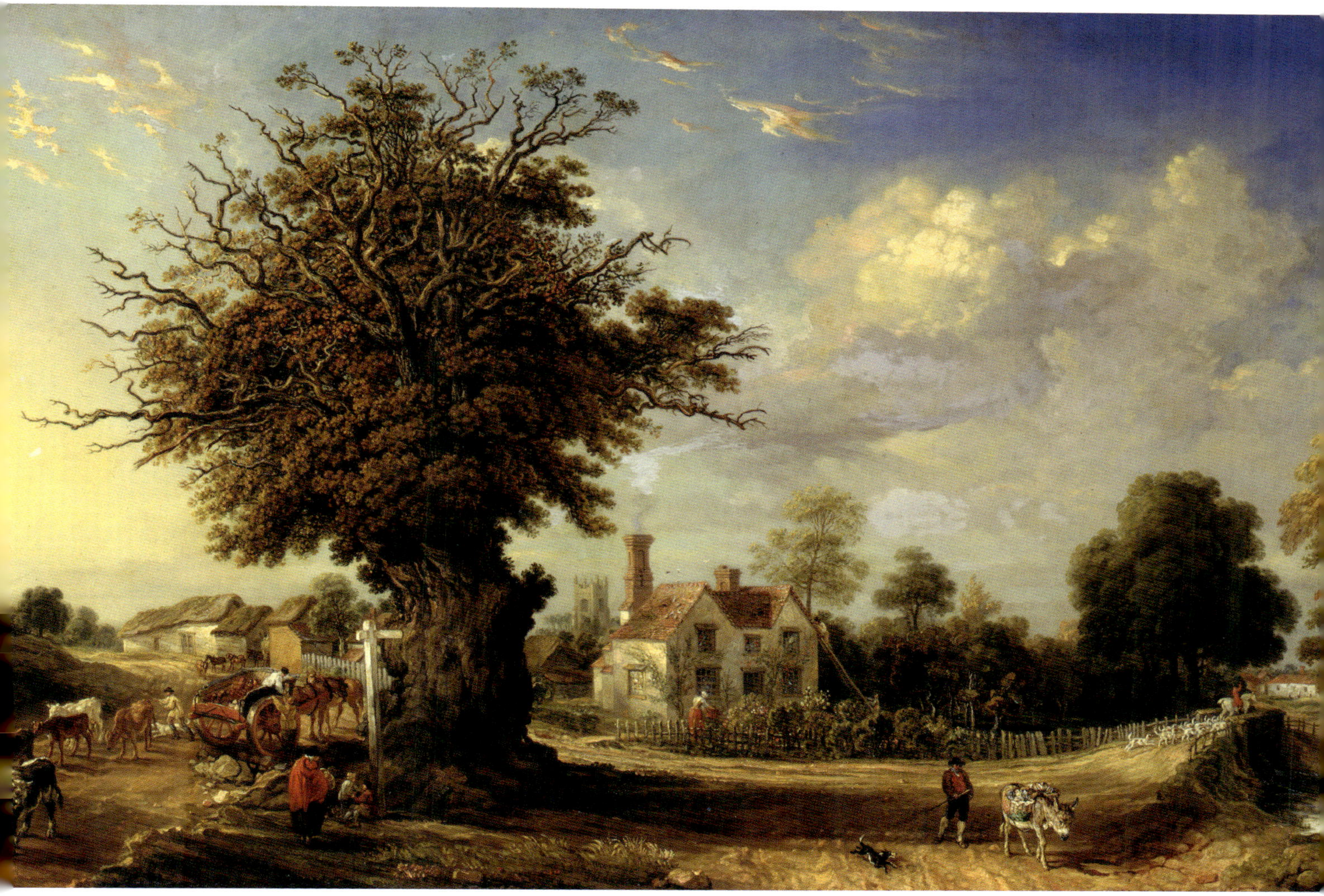

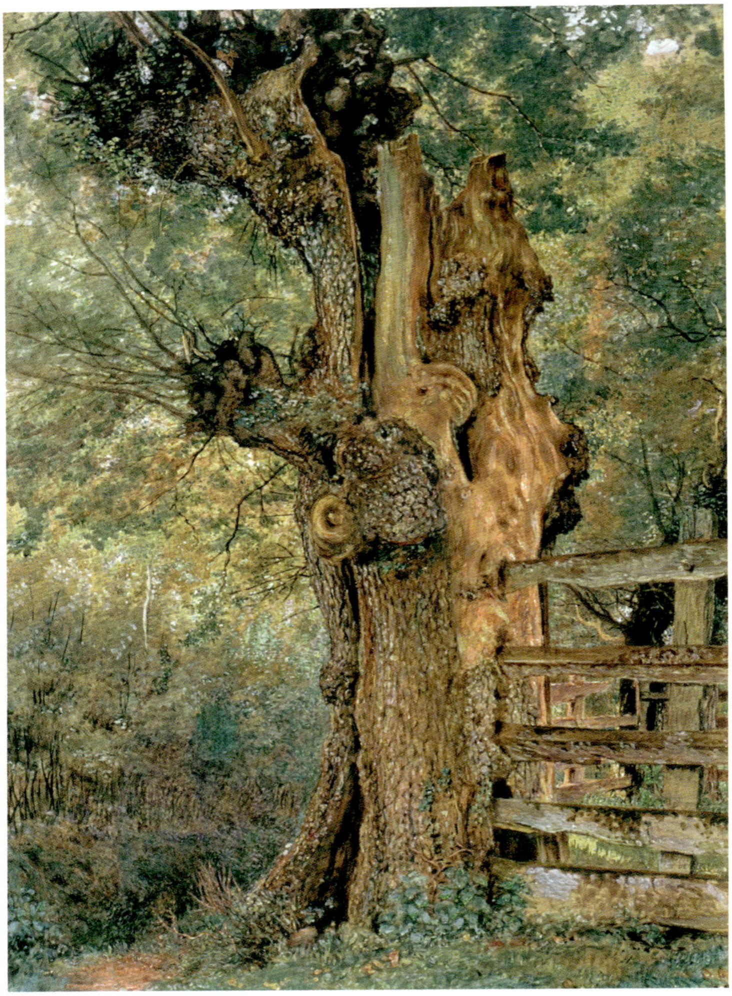

47 WILLIAM HENRY HUNT
Pollard Elm on the Edge of the Village Pound
1833 | Watercolour | 76.2 x 55.9 cm
Harris Museum and Art Gallery
Lancashire, UK/Bridgeman Images

48 SAMUEL PALMER
In a Shoreham Garden
c.1830 | Indian ink with watercolour and gouache on prepared board | 28.2 x 22.3 cm
© Victoria and Albert Museum, London

Even when they did not exhibit portraits of celebrated trees, several artists were demonstrably affected by the vogue for tree portraits, especially in the 1820s and early 1830s. John Crome's well-known painting, *The Poringland Oak* (fig. 3), which probably dates from 1818 and may have been shown at the British Institution in 1824, is contemporary with many other portrait studies of named trees. However, the oak tree is not particularly old, and it is not mentioned in any of the standard works on trees. Even more than the Yeldham oak, it seems to have been of purely local significance. In Crome's lifetime the painting was only described as 'Scene at Poringland'; it acquired its current title later on. The juxtaposition of an oak tree with boys bathing is rich in symbolic significance. This is a village tree, on common land, appreciated for its association with popular recreation. The pond which it shades is facilitating healthy exercise by young men who might grow up to join the navy and become 'hearts of oak' themselves.

William Henry Hunt's watercolour, dated 1833 and generally known as *Pollard Elm on the Edge of the Village Pound* (fig. 47) is also, evidently, a portrait of a particular tree, in very particular circumstances, with the ends of what looks like a fenced enclosure embedded in its trunk. The contrast between the rugged bark and the smooth surface of the exposed wood is lovingly delineated, probably reflecting Hunt's knowledge of a plate in Strutt's *Sylva Britannica* showing a chestnut tree at Cobham Park known as 'The Four Sisters.'[83] Hunt's elm tree is definitely

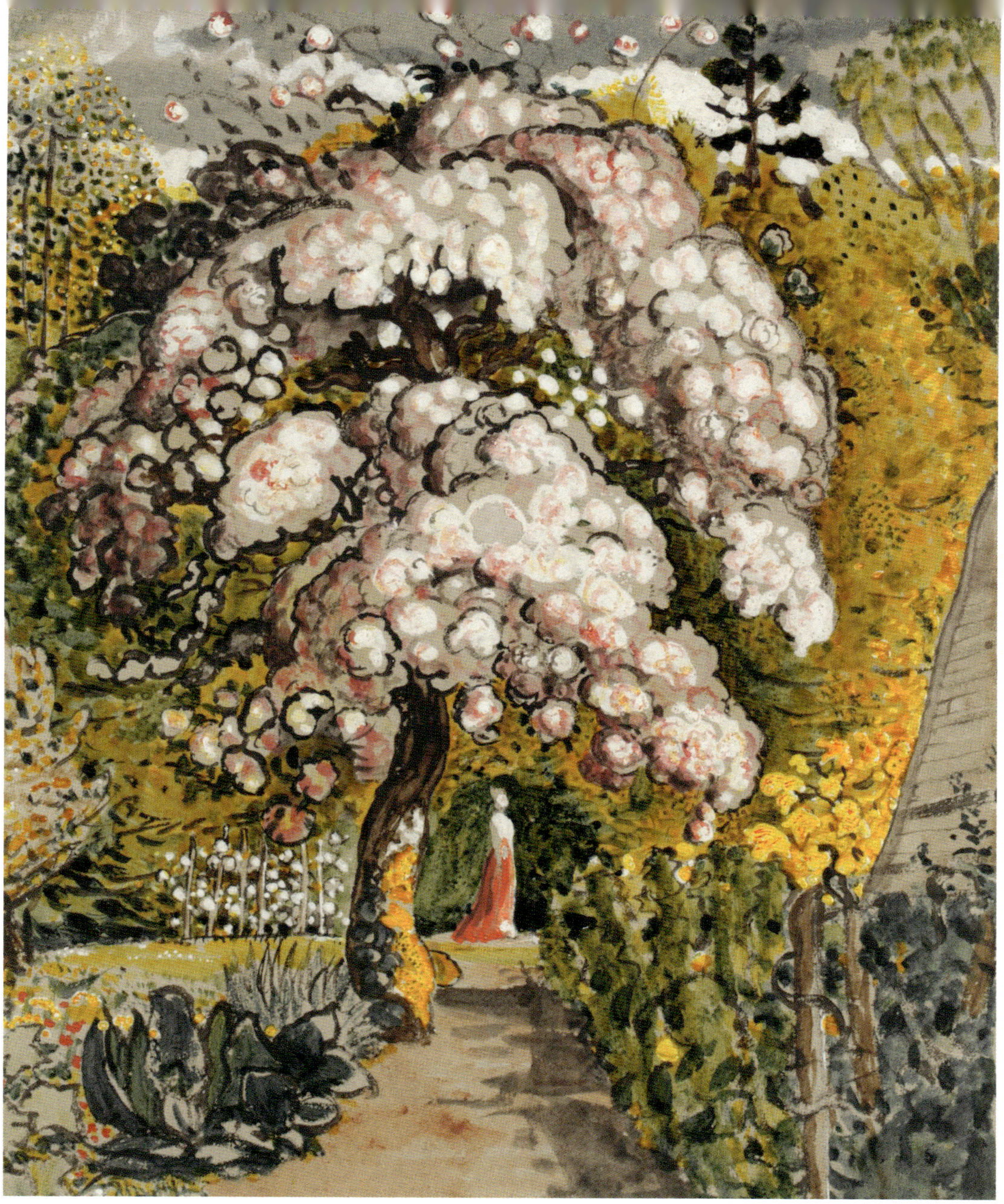

a village tree, subject to utilitarian exploitation rather than an easy life as the ornament of a gentleman's park. The title may be misleading: it is unlikely that the fenced enclosure is a village pound, which would be made of stone or brick so that the animals and birds kept in it could not escape.[84] It is uncertain whether Hunt chose to make such a lovingly detailed portrait of this tree because he felt it was particularly picturesque, or because he saw it as the victim of vandalism, its sides pierced by the fence which was accelerating its decay. Whatever the circumstances, the closeness of his attention to the details of the tree is remarkable.

John Linnell and Samuel Palmer were also affected by the fashion for tree portraits. Linnell made a very careful study of the King Beech at Knole, a tree which appears in both Burgess's and Strutt's publications. Linnell's study is, however, more accurate than either of their plates, comparing very well with a photograph of the tree taken by Francis Frith in 1905.[85] Palmer, as we have seen, made many tree studies in his sketchbook in 1824, and wrote at one point that he could see trees as men. Around 1830 he made watercolours of young, flowering trees – *In a Shoreham Garden* (fig. 48) and *Pastoral with Horse Chestnut* (fig. 10). While we cannot identify these trees, we may be pretty certain that they were studied from actual examples. They have much in common with the tree portraits of the time, in the way they fill the picture space and are accompanied by figures and animals, both to give a sense of scale and to suggest a wider role for the tree as shelter, in one case, or as ornament in the other.

49 JOHN CONSTABLE

Trees at Hampstead: The Path to Church

c.1822 | Oil on canvas | 91.4 x 72.4 cm

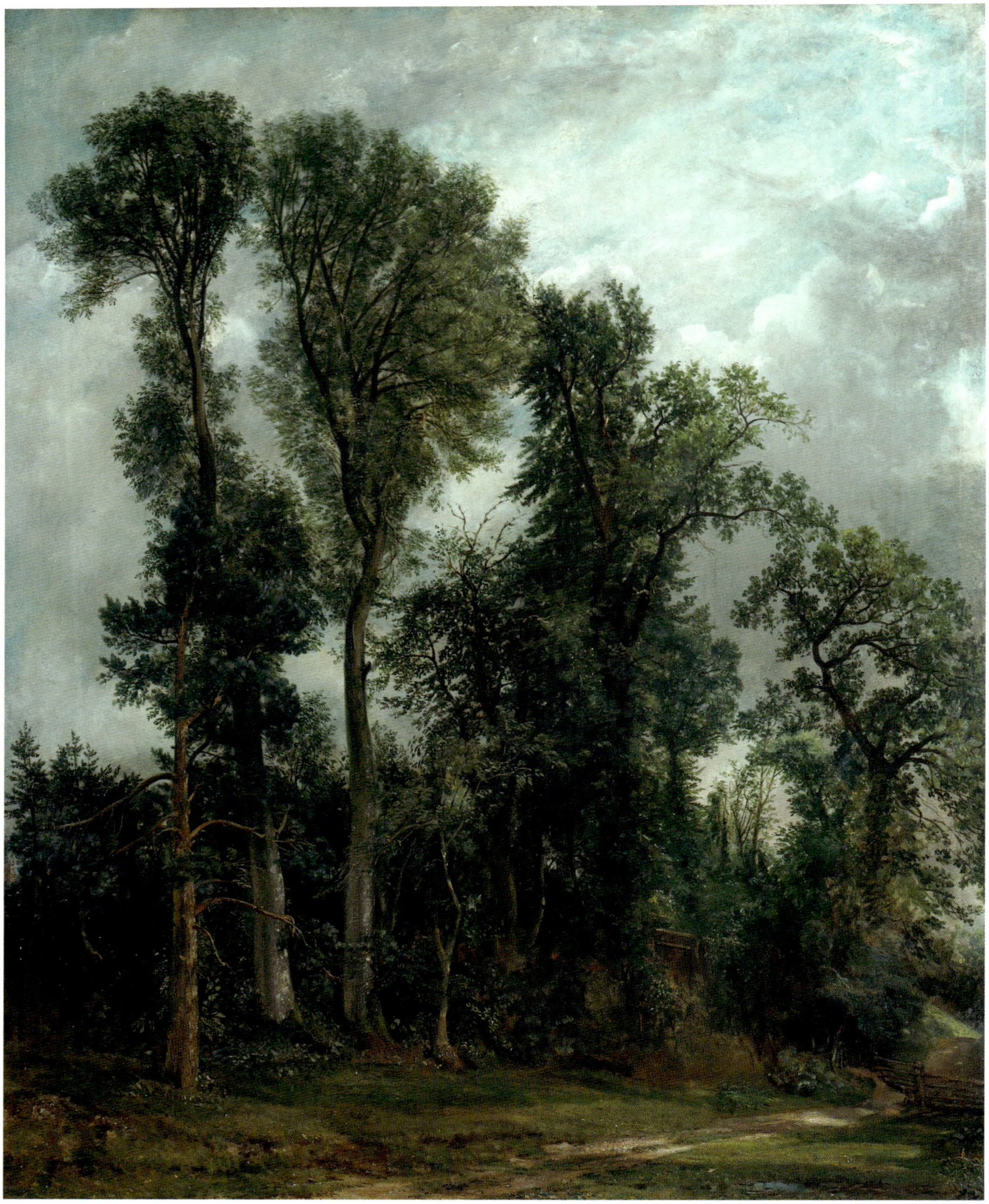

The most evocative portraits of trees in this period, however, are by John Constable. Constable and his wife were friendly with the Strutts and saw them regularly in the years between 1823 and 1826, just at the time when Strutt was turning his separate plates of the *Sylva Britannica* into a volume. Constable was a subscriber to the book, and no doubt he would have enjoyed discussing the depiction of trees with Strutt, although their friendship was sorely tested at the end of the decade when Strutt failed to repay a loan.[86] In the letter Strutt wrote to Constable to apologise for this failure, he declared: 'I consider the benefit of your society and conversation as a privilege and advantage, of no ordinary value.'[87]

Constable's portraits, like Palmer's, are generally of relatively young trees, which are slender and delicate, unlike the rugged old oaks favoured by Strutt and Burgess. A 'group portrait', *Trees at Hampstead: The Path to Church,* was shown at the Royal Academy in 1822 (fig. 49), and Constable clearly expected it to do well. He wrote to his friend John Fisher that he had painted 'a natural (but highly elegant) group of trees, ashes, elms, and oak &c – which will be of quite as much service as if I had bought the feild [sic] and hedge row, which contains them, and perhaps one time or another will fetch as much for my children.'[88] Like the near-contemporary *Salisbury Cathedral from the Bishop's Grounds* (fig. 6), with its framing Gothic arch of elms, this painting subtly implies that a love of nature can lead us to God. Constable was interested in trees as individuals, recording their growth and decay both before and after he drew or painted them. He added a note, for example, to his 1817 drawing of elm trees (fig. 32), to record that the main tree blew down in April 1835. A later drawing, *Study of trees made in the grounds of Charles Holford, Esq., at Hampstead,* exhibited in 1834 (fig. 50) contrasts a Scots pine and a larch, the one growing dead straight and the other curving and entwining with itself, and appearing to reach out towards the other tree, as if it were a human body engaged in a dance.

Constable's account, in his lecture notes, of the fate of a beautiful young ash tree has become very well known (fig. 51). Keith Thomas cited it as an example of the Romantic tendency to anthropomorphize trees as if they were pets. Constable showed a drawing of the tree in his lecture, and commented:

> Many of my Hampstead friends may remember this young lady at the entrance to the village. Her fate was distressing, for it is scarcely too much to say that she died of a broken heart. I made this drawing when she was in full health and beauty; on passing some time afterwards, I saw, to my grief, that a wretched board had been nailed to her side, on which was written in large letters, 'All vagrants and beggars will be dealt with according to law.' The tree seemed to have felt the disgrace, for even then some of the top branches had withered. Two long spike nails had been driven into her side. In another year one half became paralysed, and not long after the other shared the same fate, and this beautiful creature was cut down to a stump, just high enough to hold the board.[89]

In the drawing, a mother and child sit disconsolately at the foot of the tree. Constable would have been well aware of the contrast this presented to the well-known Beggar's Oak, which was allowed to spread its roots and foliage naturally so that beggars could shelter comfortably in its shade. Constable's comment on the fate of the Hampstead tree, therefore, was an indictment of a society which no longer cared for its poor, as well as an early example of an ecological approach to nature.

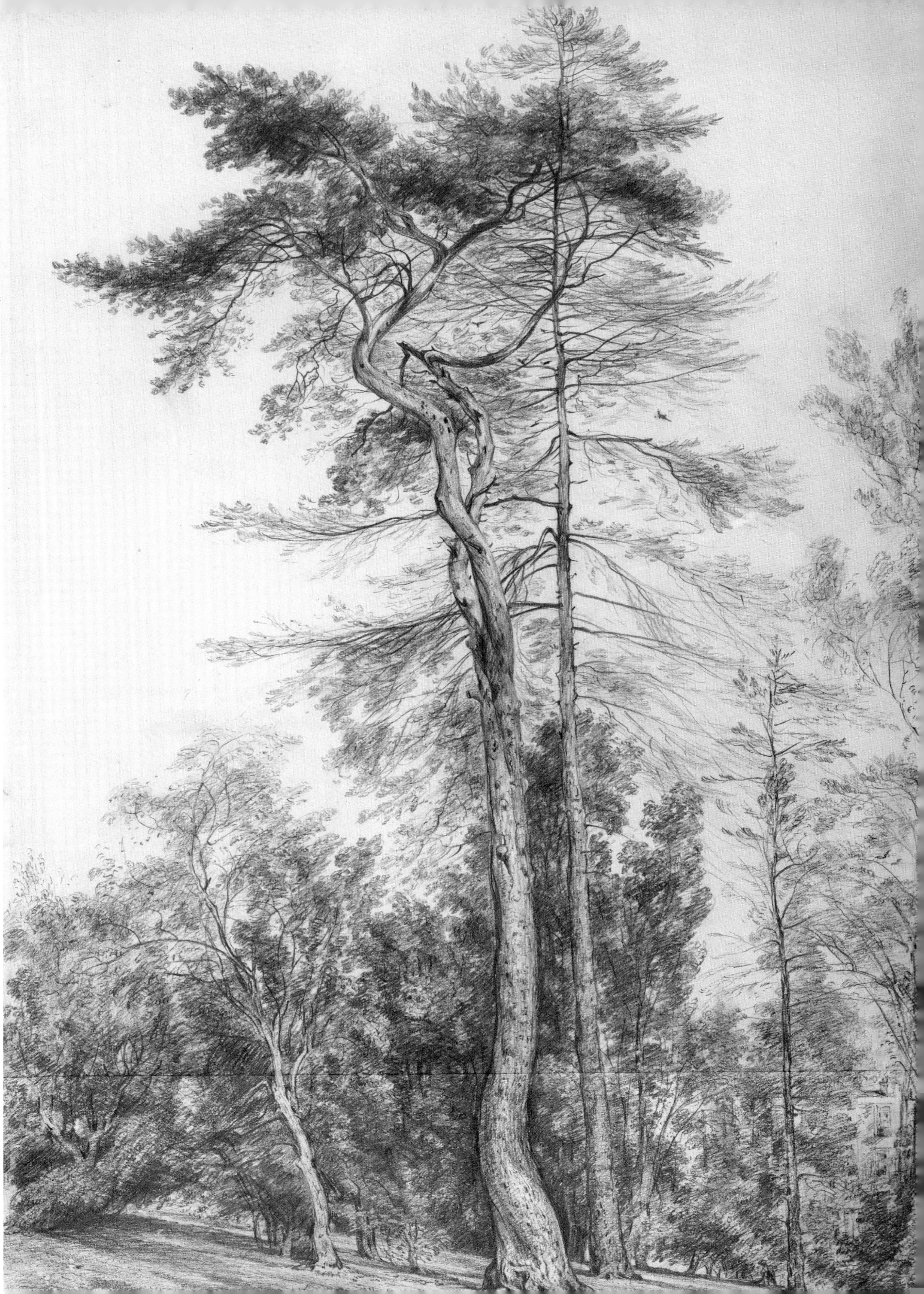

50 JOHN CONSTABLE
Study of trees made in the grounds of Charles Holford, Esq., at Hampstead | c.1833 | Graphite | 73.4 x 49.3 cm
Higgins Art Gallery and Museum, Bedford

51 JOHN CONSTABLE
An Ash tree
c.1835 | Graphite and watercolour | 99 x 68 cm

Portraits of trees, and especially ancient trees, flourished in the early decades of the nineteenth century, at a time when the landed aristocracy had good reason to feel threatened by social and political change. They depicted single trees as identifiable individuals, often marked by all the vicissitudes of a long life, and all the more worthy of respect if their foliage, trunks and branches had become damaged over time. Implicitly or explicitly, these images stress the relationship of trees to human beings, as the focus for various kinds of human behaviour, and as repositories of history. With this background, Loudon felt he had to define his use of the term 'portrait' for his illustrations of trees in his *Arboretum Britannicum*: he stated that his object was 'to give a faithful portrait of the species, neglecting such circumstances as may be peculiar to the individual' and leaving out trees that are mutilated, ill-balanced, or imperfectly clothed with tufts of foliage.[90] As with human beings, however, it is these deviations from the norm which give character to the individual, and make the tree portraits of the period before Loudon wrote both varied and appealing.

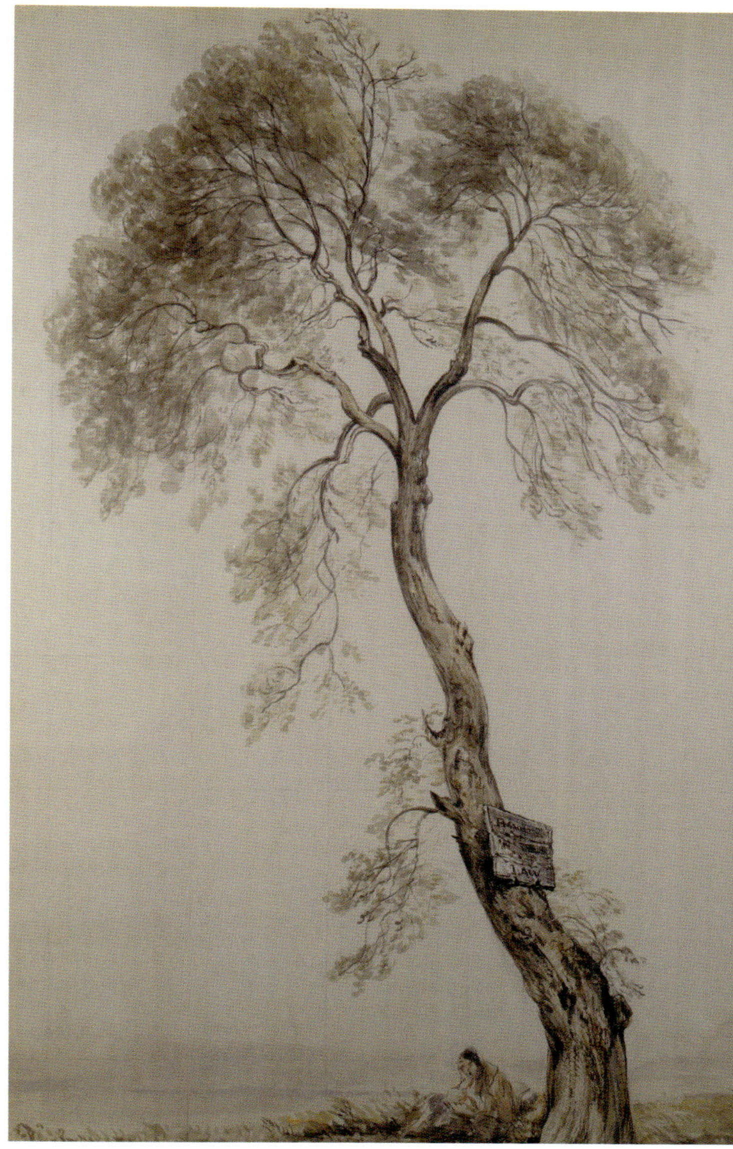

ENDNOTES

1 John Evelyn, *Silva: or a Discourse of Forest-Trees and the Propagation of Timber in his Majesty's Dominions ... with notes by A. Hunter* (York: J. Dodsley et al., 1776); William Gilpin, *Remarks on Forest Scenery, and other Woodland Views (relative chiefly to picturesque beauty) illustrated by the scenes of New-Forest in Hampshire* (London, 1791); John Claudius Loudon, *Arboretum et Fructitem Britannicum, or, the Trees and Shrubs of Britain* (London: Longman, Orme, Brown, Green, and Longmans, 1838); J. G. Strutt, *Sylva Britannica; or, Portraits of Forest Trees, distinguished for their Antiquity, Magnitude, or Beauty. Drawn from nature and etched by Jacob George Strutt* (London: J. G. Strutt and Colnaghi and Co, 1822); H. W. Burgess, *Eidodendron: Views of the general Character and Appearance of Trees Foreign & Indigenous as connected with Picturesque Scenery* (London: J. Dickinson, 1827).

2 William Cowper, *The Yardley Oak*, an unfinished poem, written c.1791 or 1792, first published posthumously in 1806; Keith Thomas, *Man and the Natural World. Changing Attitudes in England, 1500-1800* (London: Allen Lane, 1983), pp. 212-223.

3 Ronald Hutton, *Blood and Mistletoe: The History of the Druids in Britain* (New Haven and London: Yale University Press, 2009), p. 42.

4 Ibid, p. 111.

5 Ibid, pp. 129-5, 155-65. Charles James Fox, Anna Seward and William Blake have all been claimed as members of these Druidical lodges (see Ibid, pp. 134-5, 159, 193-8).

6 (Gilbert Burnett), 'Amoenitates Querneae', in Burgess, *Eidodendron*, p. 23.

7 Ibid, pp. 24-5.

8 Anon, *English Forests and Forest Trees, Historical, Legendary and Descriptive* (London: Ingram, Cooke & Co, 1853), p. 34.

9 Strutt, *Sylva Britannica*, p. 25.

10 (Burnett), 'Amoenitates Querneae', pp. 9-10.

11 Strutt, *Sylva Britannica*, p. 10.

12 Hayman Rooke, *Descriptions and Sketches of some Remarkable Oaks in the Park at Welbeck, in the County of Nottingham, a seat of His Grace the Duke of Portland* (London: J. Nichols, 1790), p. 12. But he says it is the 'common people' who give it that name – the Parliament was actually held at Clipstone palace nearby.

13 Strutt, *Sylva Britannica*, Plates 3, 12, 35, 36.

14 (Burnett), 'Amoenitates Querneae', p. 10.

15 *Howlett's Views in County of Lincoln*, 1800 (Witt Library).

16 *Burthorp Oak*, ll. 7-8.

17 Anon, *English Forests and Forest Trees*, p. 47.

18 (Francis Mundy), *Needwood Forest* (Lichfield: John Jackson, 1776), p. 42.

19 Ibid, p. 43.

20 Ibid, p. 44.

21 Ibid, p. 45.

22 John Nightingale, *A Topographical Description of the County of Stafford* (London, 1820).

23 *The Derby Mercury*, 30 September 1857, issue 3427.

24 John D. Baird and Charles Ryskamp, *The Poems of William Cowper*, vol III (Oxford: Clarendon Press, 1980-95), p. 314.

25 Ibid, ll. 8-11.

26 Ibid, ll. 62-68.

27 Ibid p. 315, citing *Victoria County History*.

28 (Burnett), 'Amoenitates Querneae', p. 17.

29 Evelyn, *Silva, with notes by A. Hunter*, p. 502.

30 Ibid, p. 502; Charles Watkins, ed., *European Woods and Forests: Studies in Cultural History* (Wallingford and New York: CAB International, 1998), p. 102.

31 Rooke, *Descriptions and Sketches* p. 11.

32 Beryl Hartley, 'The Artist as Naturalist and Experimenter: Landscape Painting and Science 1740-1850' (PhD thesis, Imperial College, University of London, 1995), p. 125.

33 Gilpin, *Forest Scenery*, p. 115.

34 Ibid, p. 116.

35 Ibid, p. 121.

36 Ibid, p. 139.

37 Ibid, pp. 165-70.

38 Ibid, p. 143.

39 Natural History Museum Library MSS BANKS COLL FAM.

40 It is difficult to establish the publication dates of these volumes. In library catalogues, *Sylva Britannica* is usually given a publication date of 1822, *Eidodendron* of 1827, since these are the dates on their respective title pages. However, it is clear that the title pages were completed several years before the books were actually published. Strutt's Frontispiece is dated 1826; Burnett's essay in Burgess's book mentions several dates in 1829, and the Introduction refers to William IV, who came to the throne in 1830.

41 For example, Strutt's Plate IX is 'The Salcey Forest Oak'. Burgess, in his plate 54, depicts the same tree, but entitles it 'An old oak', with a subtitle indicating that it is in Salcey Forest. In Burgess's lithograph, the battered and hollow trunk and branches of the tree make fantastic shapes. Strutt's etching is more detailed, more prosaic and, we

might suppose, more objective.

42 See the Strutt correspondence preserved in the Warwick County Record Office, CR 1709/116.

43 Strutt, *Sylva Britannica*, 1830 edition, p. 33.

44 Ibid, p. 33.

45 Strutt, *Sylva Britannica*, 1826, p. 38.

46 Strutt, *Sylva Britannica*, 1830, p. 71.

47 Strutt, *Sylva Britannica*, 1826, p. 35.

48 Ibid, p. 3.

49 Strutt, *Sylva Britannica,* 1830, p. 16.

50 All three drawings are in the Yale Center for British Art.

51 This painting is in the Clarendon Collection, the National Trust of Tasmania.

52 The 2nd Lord Bagot, *Memorials of the Bagot Family: compiled in 1823* (Blithfield: Wm Hodgetts, 1824), pp. 146, 158.

53 Ibid, pp. 159-162.

54 Strutt, *Sylva Britannica,* 1826, p. 3.

55 Lord Bagot, *Memorials* , p. 160. In the case of the Cliff, or King Oak the fall in value was drastic, from £293.10s.7d in 1812 to £156.7s.11d in 1823 (presumably because the tree had decayed, or lost branches, in the meantime).

56 Thomas, *Man and the Natural World*, p. 214, 217.

57 See Strutt, *Sylva Britannica,* 1826, pp. 5, 8, 10.

58 *Hampshire Advertiser*, Saturday 22 January 1831, issue 392.

59 Evelyn, *Silva, with notes by A. Hunter*, p. 500.

60 Julian Hight, *Britain's Tree Story: the History and Legends of Britain's Ancient Trees* (London: National Trust Books, 2011), p. 28.

61 *Illustrated London News*, Saturday 31 January 1857, Issue 842, p. 83.

62 Yorkshire 1 Sketchbook, 1816. TB CXLIV, Folio 10 verso and Folio 11 recto. Tate.

63 (Charles Empson), *The Cowthorpe Oak, from a painting by the late George William Fothergill, from accurate sketches made on the spot, expressly for this work … with a descriptive account, by Charles Empson* (London: Ackermann & Co, 1841), frontispiece.

64 Hight, *Britain's Tree Story*, pp. 28-9.

65 George Lipscombe, *History and Antiquities of the County of Buckingham* (London: J. and W. Robins, 1847), p. 587.

66 Meredith's arguments are recounted in Anand Chetan and Diana Brueton, *The Sacred Yew* (London: Arkana/ Penguin Books, 1996), pp. 99-104.

67 Strutt, *Sylva Britannica*, 1826, p. 8.

68 'Magna Carta and the Ankerwycke Yew', www-runnymede.unet.com/history/ magnacarta.htm – retrieved 4 August 2014.

69 Gilpin, *Forest Scenery,* pp. 141-2.

70 Anon, *Fairlop Oak and Fairlop Fair: Memorabilia* (Waddesdon: Kylin Press Ltd, 1982), p. 8.

71 Ibid, p. 16.

72 Ibid, pp. 20-22.

73 *The Times*, issue 16473, Thursday 20 July 1837, p. 7.

74 It was sold in the Panshanger Sale at Christie's, London, on 16 October 1953 (lot 91). Photo Witt Library.

75 Strutt, *Sylva Britannica,* 1826, p. 4.

76 British Museum.

77 1824, no. 247, and 1826, no. 411.

78 In a letter to William Bree (9 April 1826), Strutt writes: 'I have sent only one picture to Somerset House, viz, the Great Ash at Carnock, which I think is a very successful picture … I am now getting on with some smaller pictures …' (Warwick County Record Office, CR 1709/116).

79 These features are listed in a review in *The Farmer's Magazine*, Vol. I, 1834, p. 254.

80 *Essex Standard, and Colchester, Chelmsford, Maldon, Harwich, and General County Advertiser*. Sat, 24 May 24 1834, Issue 177.

81 *Athenaeum*, no. 341, 10 May 1834, p. 356.

82 *Bury and Norwich Post, and Suffolk Herald*, 28 June 1859. Issue 4018.

83 Strutt, *Sylva Britannica,* 1826, Plate XIII.

84 The watercolour has been identified with an item listed in Hunt's studio effects in 1864, 'A Study of a Pollard, near a Pond,' assuming that 'Pond' is a typographical error for 'Pound'. John Witt, *William Henry Hunt (1790-1864). Life and Work, with a Catalogue* (London: Barrie and Jenkins, 1982), p. 156.

85 Illustrated in Hight, *Britain's Tree Story*, p. 149. Linnell's drawing is illustrated in K. Crouan, *John Linnell: A Centennial Exhibition* (Cambridge: Fitzwilliam Museum, 1982), p. 80.

86 See R. B. Beckett, ed., *John Constable's Correspondence* (Ipswich: Suffolk Records Society, 1962- 9), II, pp. 304, 317, 323, 325, 358, 412, 420-1, 429; and R. B. Beckett et al, ed., *John Constable: Further Documents and Correspondence* (HMSO: Suffolk Records Society, 1970), pp. 299-301.

87 Beckett, ed., *John Constable's Correspondence,* II, p. 301 (letter dated 25 January 1830).

88 Beckett, ed., *John Constable's Correspondence,* VI, p. 73, letter dated 20 September 1821.

89 Beckett, ed., *Further Documents and Correspondence*, p. 71. Cited in Thomas, *Man and the Natural World*, pp. 222-3.

90 Loudon, *Arboretum*, Vol. I, p. 202.

52 EDMUND GEORGE WARREN

'Rest in the Cool and Shady Wood'

1861 | Watercolour | 77.7 x 120.3 cm

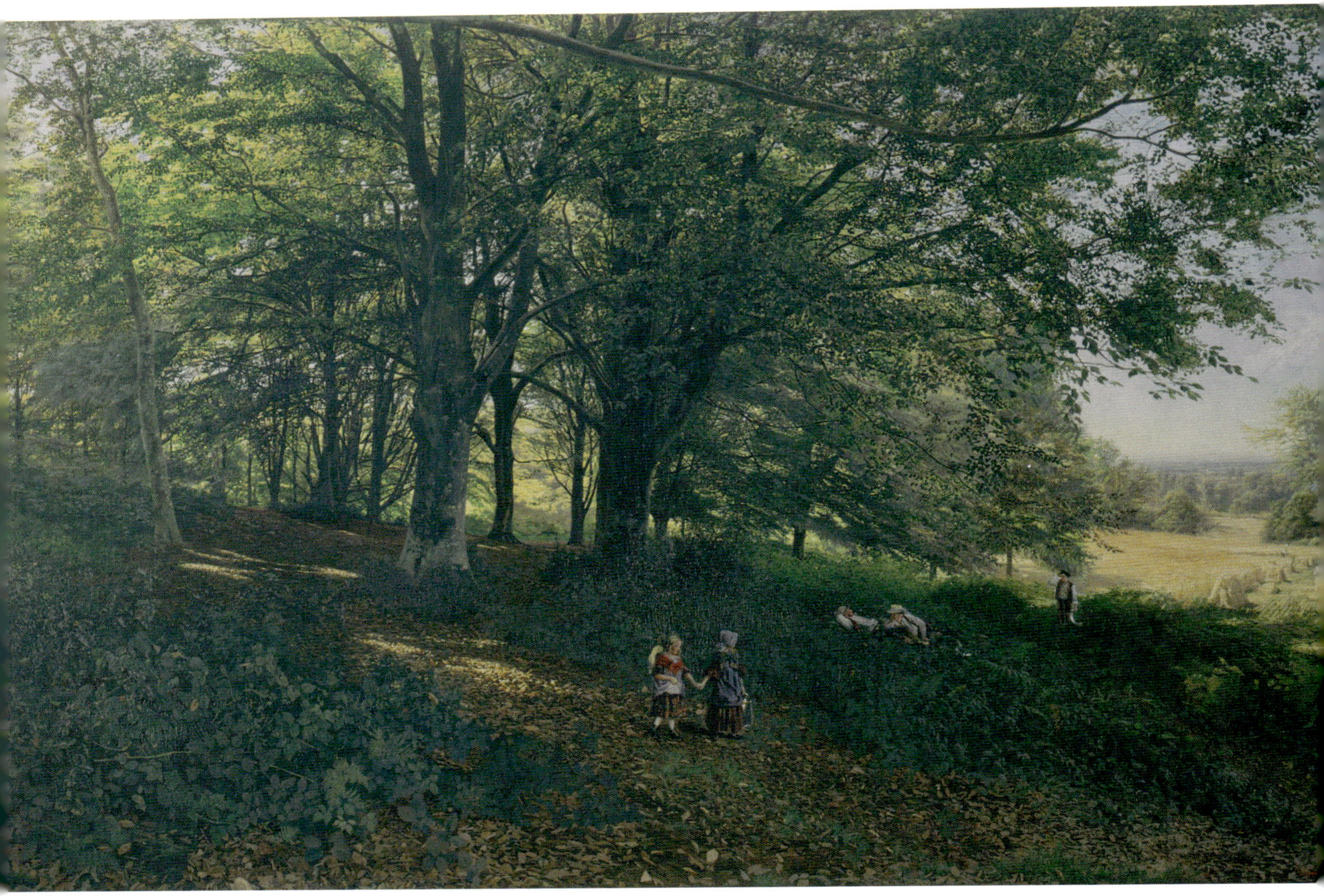

FIVE

The Pleasures of the Woods

THE LAST TWO chapters have focused on isolated trees, whether as models in drawing manuals or as individual portraits. As we have seen, when it came to tree portraits the oak was supreme; it was first also in the manuals which took care to differentiate between the different species. In woodland scenes, however, a different aesthetic came into play.[1] The cool recesses of the woods were seen as desirable retreats from the heat and crowds of the cities. In the past they had been primarily sources of timber and practical resources for commoners. Now they became increasingly important as recreational areas for the middle and eventually lower classes. Artists responded to these changes by producing appealing representations of forest glades, with sunlight shining through leaves and chequered shade on the ground. For these scenes the beech tree became the favoured species, casting a shade that was deep but not impenetrable, surrounded by carpets of dead leaves that were comfortable to sit on but also immensely tempting to the artist, with their varied russet tones (fig. 52).

The woods were also seen as places for reading and composing poetry. In eighteenth and nineteenth-century England there was a rich poetic tradition of finding contemplative tranquillity and visual beauty in woodland. Thomas Gray wrote to his friend Horace Walpole in 1737, describing how he would spend whole mornings reading Virgil and Horace at the foot of one of the 'most venerable beeches' of Burnham.[2] Poems were written in praise of particular forests: Alexander Pope's *Windsor Forest* (1713) and Francis Mundy's *Needwood Forest* (1776) being two of the best-known. William Cowper loved to walk in the woods, and in the first book of his very well-known poem, *The Task* (1785), he describes the beauties of 'the woodland scene/ Diversified with trees of ev'ry growth/ Alike yet various' – including 'the grey smooth trunks/ Of ash or lime or beech' which are contrasted with the darker forms of the elm and oak:

> Of deeper green the elm; and deeper still,
> Lord of the woods, the long-surviving oak.[3]

William Wordsworth and Samuel Taylor Coleridge regularly composed lines in the woods, and groves and bowers feature strongly in their work. In *The Tables Turned* (1798) Wordsworth advises his readers to leave their books and go into the woods:

> One impulse from a vernal wood
> May teach you more of man,
> Of moral evil and of good
> Than all the sages can.[4]

In *To my Sister*, written in the same year, he entreats Dorothy to put on her 'woodland dress,' leaving her book behind so that they can drink in 'the spirit of the season.'[5] Coleridge's famous *Lime-Tree Bower* (1797) was in his garden rather than in the woods, but in these lines he shows a sensitivity to the visual effects in the woods that can be paralleled in the work of the artists:

> … Pale beneath the blaze
> Hung the transparent foliage; and I watch'd
> Some broad and sunny leaf, and lov'd to see
> The shadow of the leaf and stem above
> Dappling its sunshine! …[6]

Such lines often acted as direct sources of inspiration to artists, and they also had an effect on the reception of the paintings, providing a range of poetic associations which could be invoked by visual representations of woodland scenes.

53 EDWARD VILLIERS RIPPINGILLE
Sketching Party in Leigh Woods
c.1828 | Graphite and brown wash | 17.5 x 27.5 cm
Bristol Museums and Art Gallery

54 JOHN SELL COTMAN
In Rokeby Park
c.1805 | Watercolour and graphite | 33 x 22.9 cm
Yale Center for British Art, Paul Mellon Collection

PARTIES IN THE WOODS

On the whole, the poets were solitary in the woods, or in the company of a single favoured friend. But artists might go in more convivial sketching parties, like the group drawn in the late 1820s by Edward Villiers Rippingille (fig. 53) in Leigh Woods, just across the River Avon from Bristol. Picnics in the woods became popular, as these locations became safer. There was a concomitant shift from private to public locations, from country estates owned by an individual to woodlands where access was more open. The distinction between the two was somewhat blurred, as owners of country estates often allowed public access (or access at least to the 'respectable' and well-dressed) at certain times of the week or year. Many woodland areas were common land, which meant that they could not be fenced off; on the other hand this might mean that the middle-class visitor would have to share them with such inconveniences as commoners' pigs, running riot and ploughing up turf in the autumn.[7] During the course of the nineteenth century, many areas of woodland were disafforested or enclosed: Windsor Forest was enclosed in 1815, with the remaining deer being driven into Green Park, and deer were excluded from the New Forest in 1851.[8] Enclosure acts meant that woodlands which had formerly been common land passed into private ownership, often in small parcels to compensate the holders of commoners' rights. But there were also repeated campaigns to keep such areas open to all, with the result that, by the later years of the century, there were substantial areas of woodland which were specifically designated as being for the use and enjoyment of all classes of the community, such as the New Forest, Richmond Park, Burnham Beeches and Epping Forest. These became popular haunts for artists, especially those that were within easy reach of London.

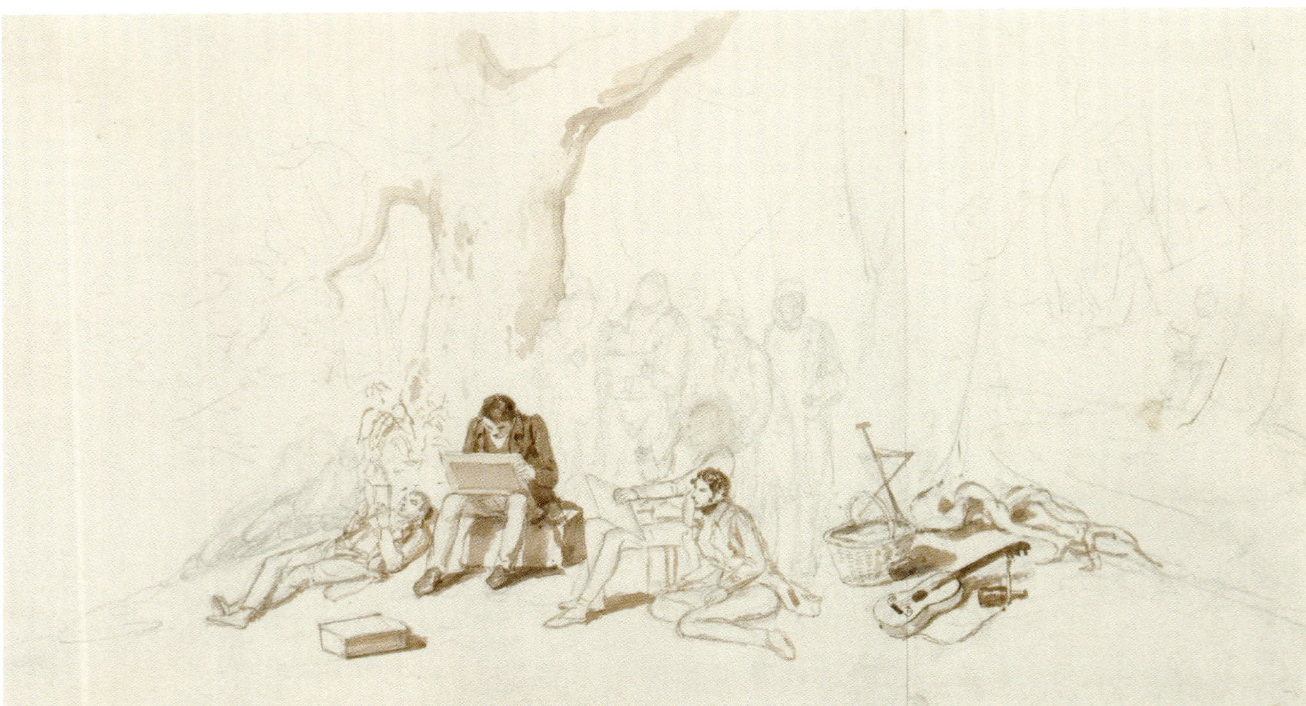

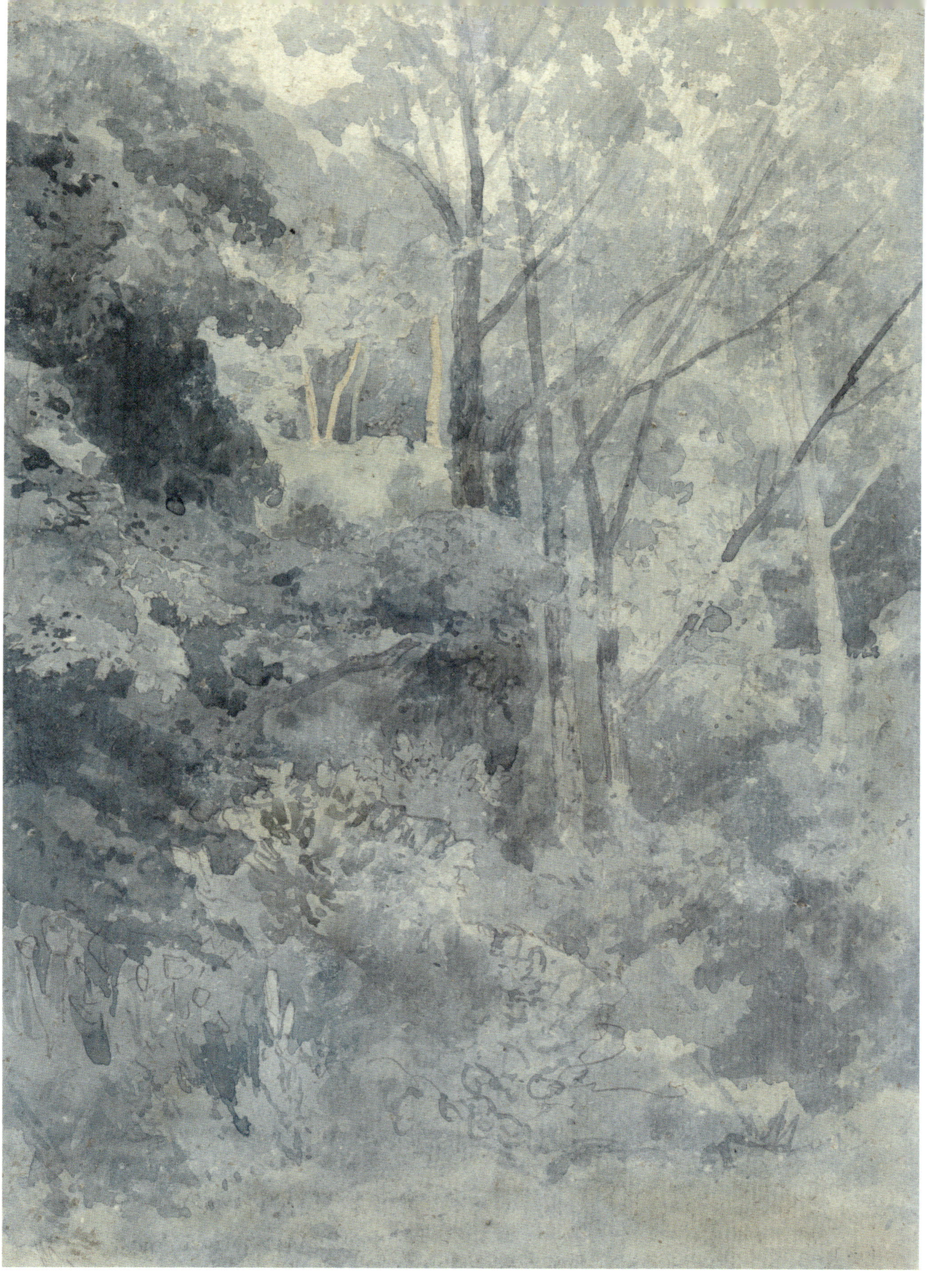

55 JOHN LINNELL
A Forest Scene
1818 | Oil on paper laid down on panel | 64.8 x 89.5 cm
Private Collection, Photo: Mike Fear

These changes in the use and ownership of the woods affected the way artists approached them. In the eighteenth century the most important woodland scenes were based on studies made on private country estates, such as Hearne's studies in Downton Vale, and this tradition continued in the early years of the nineteenth century. John Sell Cotman, for example, made drawings in the woodland around Brandsby Hall, Duncombe Park, and Rokeby Park in Yorkshire, the homes of his patrons (fig. 54).[9] In 1815, however, John Linnell went to Windsor Forest, then recently enclosed, to make studies of woodcutters (fig. 55), and in the 1820s Rippingille, Francis Danby and his friends took the ferry across the Avon from Bristol to Leigh Woods, an area that was freely accessible to any Bristol citizen. In an extension of woodland subject matter, paintings of shady avenues bordering public lanes, by artists such as Thomas Creswick and Frederick Richard Lee, became popular in the 1820s and 1830s. In the 1840s and 1850s John Martin exhibited paintings of Richmond Park, owned by the Crown but effectively open to the public at this period, a state of affairs that was made permanent in an Act of Parliament in 1872. Richard Redgrave, in the 1850s and 1860s, made studies in the woods around his home at Abinger, in Surrey: these were mostly privately-owned woods, to which he had access as a local resident. In the 1860s paintings of Burnham Beeches, then in their pre-enclosure state, were frequently seen in watercolour exhibitions.

Many of the artists were, therefore, exhibiting scenes their audiences could relate to directly, as they were representing woods and parks that were open to all and within easy reach of London, or, in the case of Leigh Woods, of Bristol. Sometimes the human element in their scenes consisted of conventional rustic figures such as woodcutters, milkmaids and the children of rural labourers, either at work or travelling from one place to another. In several instances, however, the figures were themselves middle-class visitors to the woods, wearing fashionable clothing and engaged in leisure pursuits, reading books, sketching, making conversation, admiring the view. The paintings thus reflected current social practices.

There was a rich artistic tradition of woodland scenes in art, from the work of Ruisdael and Hobbema in seventeenth-century Holland, through the etchings of the much-admired Antoine Waterloo, to the woodland scenes of Gainsborough and Morland in the eighteenth century. These works, however, had depicted the pre-enclosure economy, whereby holders of common rights could take fuel and sand from the woods and let their pigs feed on acorns and beech-mast.[10] In the nineteenth century, these rights were dying out or being commuted by enclosure acts, which often aroused popular indignation and resistance. The resulting protests routinely harked back to the classic example of the medieval woodland hero, Robin Hood: the association of the woods with popular freedom was deeply ingrained in the national consciousness.[11]

In addition to the indignation aroused by destruction of common rights, there were increasing fears that woodland, once it passed into private hands, would be lost forever to housing development, especially as some of the most favoured areas were close to cities and therefore prime building land. In 1828 Jacob George Strutt published a volume of etchings entitled *Deliciae Sylvarum* (the delights of the woods). This was a much more modest undertaking than his great *Sylva Britannica,* consisting of just 8 plates, including illustrations of Windsor Forest, Epping Forest, and Burnham Beeches. In the commentary Strutt expresses his fear that Epping Forest 'a few years hence, may be almost entirely merged in patrician villas or straight-lined inclosures.'[12] A similar fear haunts John Eagles, writing in 1856 of his relief that the Clifton Suspension Bridge had not been built on its proposed site adjoining Leigh Woods:

> These fine woods would certainly in the end be sacrificed to it, and be cut into small gardens for suburban villanous edifices, and lengthy lines of brick wall would be all we should have for this delightful free range.[13]

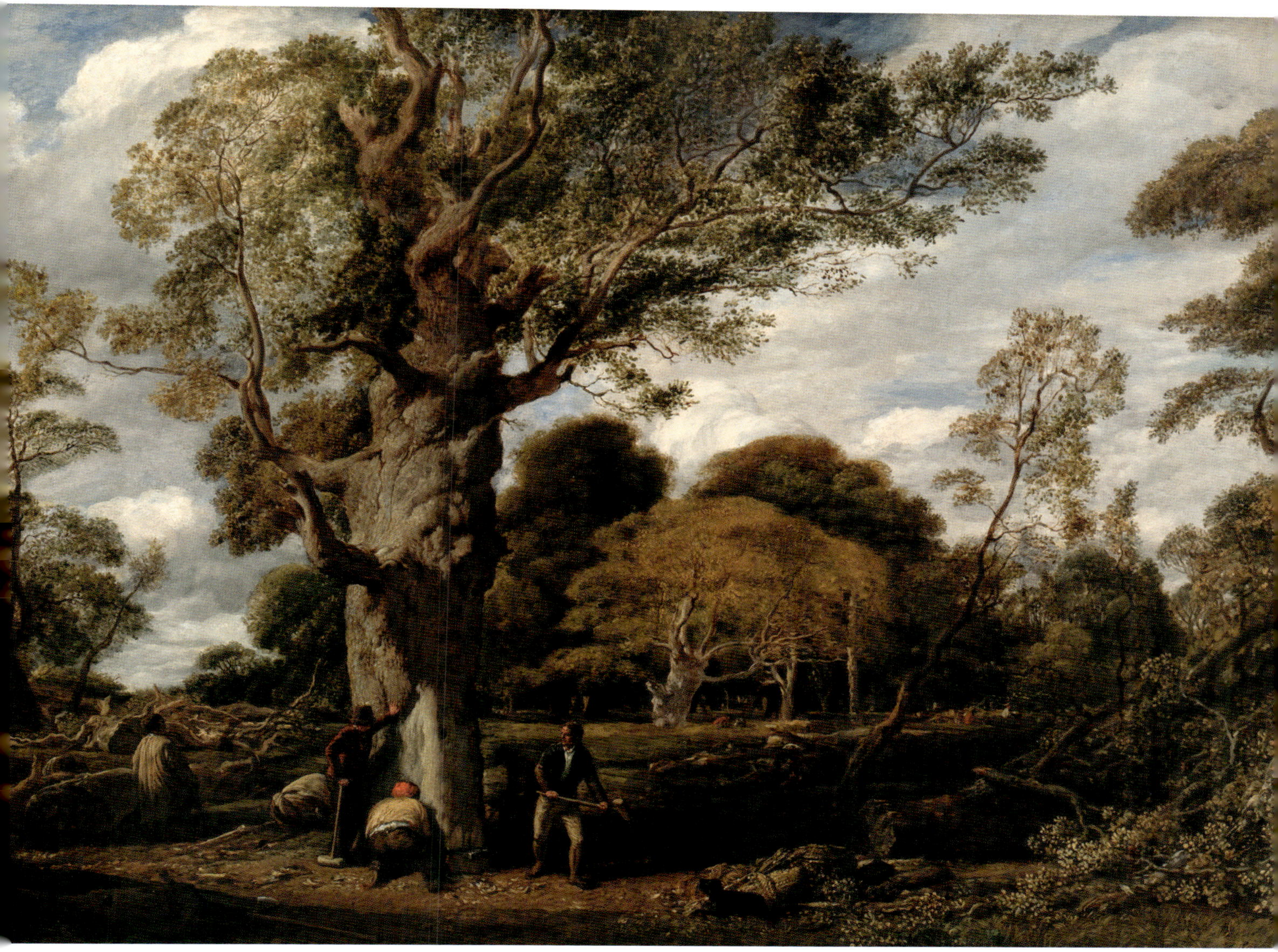

This was just a temporary reprieve, as the bridge was eventually erected in 1864. However, only the woodland south of the bridge was developed for housing, leaving the area to the north freely accessible for recreation, as it still is today, in the care of the National Trust.

It was not only the artists who wanted to preserve particular woodlands and keep them open to public access. The campaigns to save Burnham Beeches and Epping Forest from development involved influential writers and public figures and, in the case of Epping Forest, were both lengthy and dramatic. In Epping Forest, the lords of the manor tried to put up fences and end the right of the commoners to lop trees. The Commons Preservation Society, which had been founded in 1865, took up their case and fought a legal battle over three years between 1871 and 1874. The case was then taken up by the City of London Corporation, which had acquired common rights as a result of a land purchase in the Forest. Two Acts of Parliament, in 1871 and 1878, eventually ensured that the Forest, or at least that relatively small area of it that remained, was open to the public in perpetuity. However, even after 1878 protests continued when the Corporation in its turn tried to ban the lopping of trees, and a midnight meeting was held in November 1879, by torchlight, with some six thousand participants.[14] The preservation of Burnham Beeches was more straightforward. The land was put up for sale and would have gone to developers for the erection of 'superior residences', but the City of London Corporation bought it in 1880 to protect it as an open space and wildlife reserve.

56 FRANCIS DANBY
A Scene in Leigh Woods
1822 | Oil on panel | 35.2 x 50.4 cm
Bristol Museum and Art Gallery, UK Purchased, 1956, Bridgeman Images

In his book on Burnham Beeches, Francis George Heath, who spearheaded the campaign for its preservation, claimed in 1883 that artists and writers had helped to save the woods from building development because of their efforts over the preceding decades:

> Never before … has art done so much for our English landscapes as in the present day … by the force of sentiment, aided by the most perfect representations of Nature which Art can produce … [artists and writers have ensured that] sentiment has saved the New Forest, the Forest of Epping, and the Forest of Dean … Sentiment has been saving commons, parks and other open spaces everywhere, and its latest triumph is the preservation of Burnham Common and of Burnham Beeches. …[15]

Heath's description of the delights of a beech wood doubtless owes something to these paintings of the previous decades, as well as to his own experiences:

> From the burning midday heat of the open glade, it is delicious to plunge into the greenwood; and few forest trees offer such complete and refreshing shade as the delightful Beech. As we lean with luxurious ease against its spacious bole, soft with mossiness, how refreshing to look up into the heaven of leafiness above – how soothing to listen to the music of the leaves as they make merry in the sunshine![16]

Written descriptions of the woods in this period invariably stress the coolness of the woods in summer sunshine, and the aesthetic effects of the contrasts between light and shade this produces.

THE CHEQUERED SHADE

In paintings from the early nineteenth century onwards, there is a growing concern with the effects of sunlight in the woods: mid-nineteenth-century artists, especially Thomas Creswick, Richard Redgrave and Edmund George Warren, became proficient in representing patches of transparent, bright green leaves lit from behind, and the chequered patterns of shade on the ground beneath the branches. The concern with such effects reflects, on the one hand, the importance that was given to studying from nature in the open air, and on the other, the value placed on the woods as places of resort on the hottest summer days. Poetry helped to make such effects seem peculiarly English. Milton's lines in *L'Allegro* – '… many a youth and many a maid/ Dancing in the chequer'd shade' are occasionally quoted in titles of exhibited works,[17] and Milton's use of the phrase may itself derive from Shakespeare's description of a peaceful wooded glade in *Titus Andronicus*:

> The birds chant melody on every bush.
> The snake lies rolled in the cheerful sun,
> The green leaves quiver with the cooling wind
> And make a chequered shadow on the ground.[18]

The phrase also appears in Pope's *Windsor Forest*:

> Here waving groves a chequer'd scene display,
> And part admit, and part exclude the day;
> … There, interspers'd in lawns and opening glades,
> Thin trees arise that shun each other's shades.[19]

The summer months – June, July and August – were the usual times represented.

A popular book on forests, published in 1853, compares the different seasons and shows a clear preference for spring and summer. In spring, 'on every side, all objects seem awakening to new life, and are intensely enjoying its delights.' In springtime a man 'comes forth from the silent society of the forest a happier, a better, and a wiser man.'[20] The forest is beautiful in winter, under snow and frost,

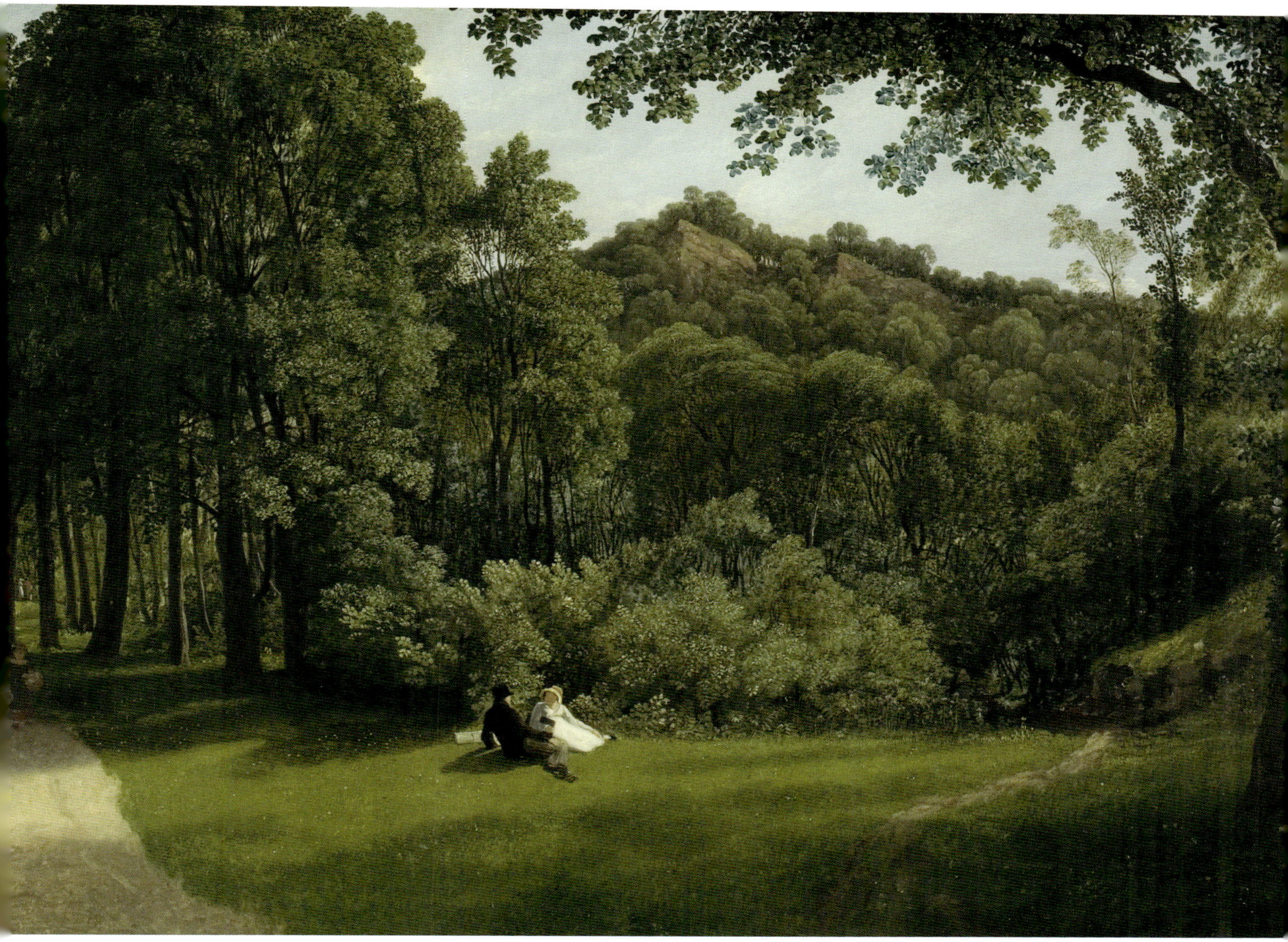

but the author has little time for autumn, with its appearance of 'dissolution and decay', while the wind moans in the half-leafless tress and the birds twitter in a melancholy state. Best of all is summer, a time for spending a day in the woods in company with others:

> Pleasant and merry are the parties who join together to spend a summer's day in the woods, whether it be in May or July, or still more delightful in 'the leafy month of June'. There is a freshness and a freedom about the forest that soon breaks down all the angularities of individual character and many of the conventional restraints of society … Every body is happy because every body is natural and free, and they are natural and free because they are in the midst of nature and freedom.[21]

In this period, artists, too, showed a preference for the woods in summer, when parties of pleasure-seekers would congregate in the glades and clearings, and especially in the oft-quoted 'leafy month' of June. This phrase occurs in Coleridge's *Rime of the Ancient Mariner*, as a brief glimpse of a sylvan paradise in the midst of a nightmarish tale:

> A noise like of a hidden brook
> In the leafy month of June,
> That to the sleeping woods all night
> Singeth a quiet tune.[22]

In a broadly similar way, paintings of woodland scenes provided respite from the discomforts of London in the exhibition season.

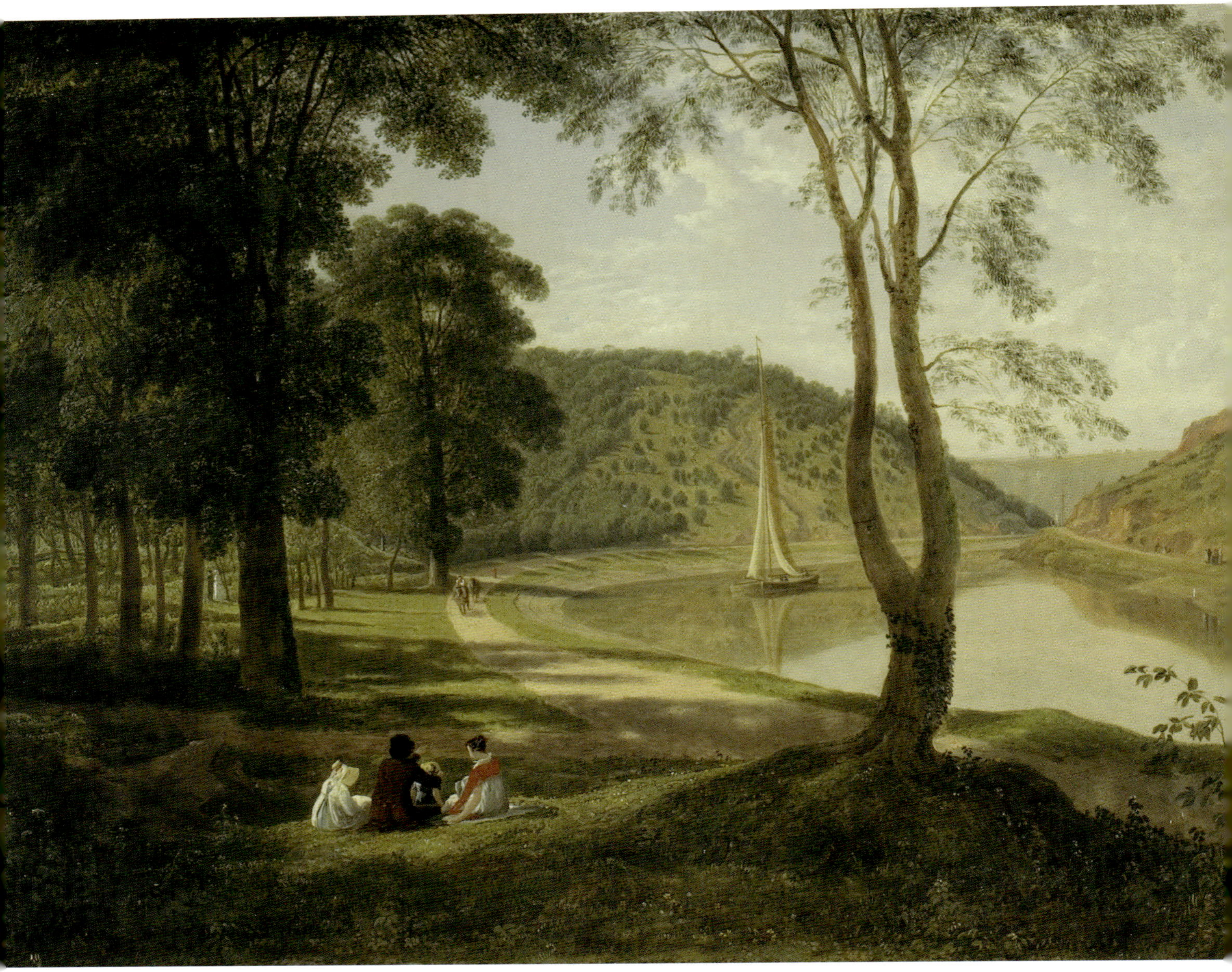

One of the first artists to immerse himself in the woods was John Sell Cotman. In the years between 1803 and 1805, Cotman made many drawings and watercolours in the woods around the houses of his patrons, Brandsby Hall and Rokeby Park in Yorkshire, the homes of the Cholmeley and Morritt familes respectively. In each case Cotman was employed to give drawing lessons to family members, and he was on unusually friendly terms with them, especially the Cholmeleys. They called him 'Cottey' and treated him almost as a member of the family, as surviving correspondence testifies. In an atmosphere of country house culture and visits to neighbouring families, an artistic interest in trees was encouraged. Cotman seems to have begun in 1803 with drawings of individual trees, many of which are now in an album in the British Museum (put together later for his pupils).[23] In her letters, Mrs Cholmeley compares Cotman's 'fine, bold, wild' drawings of trees to the 'very tame' drawings by the older artist Amos Green, and later expresses a wish that Cotman could see the trees by Edward Swinburne, the owner of a nearby estate at Capheaton.[24]

57 FRANCIS DANBY
View of the Avon Gorge
1822 | Oil on panel | 34.6 x 46.6 cm
Bristol Museum and Art Gallery, UK Purchased, 1956, Bridgeman Images

From pencil drawings of individual trees, Cotman progressed to the watercolours of woodland for which he is now best known. *In Rokeby Park* (fig. 54) dates from 1805. It is a close-up view of foliage with no figures and no distant view; there is very little space even in the foreground. As David Hill writes, 'at first sight it presents us with no more than a dappled confusion of trees, branches and leaves.'[25] However, Cotman carefully contrasts patches of light and dark: shadowed masses of leaves are placed against sunlit trees beyond, trunks and branches silhouetted dark against light, or light against dark backgrounds. The different species also provide contrasts, with oak or elm in the left foreground set against the lighter forms of ash in the background, in a process that is similar to the landscape gardening of Capability Brown and reminiscent of Cowper's description of woodland in *The Task*. Cotman went on to produce several other studies of trees in this fashion, but had difficulty finding buyers for them and so many, like this one, remained in his own collection.

The studies produced by John Linnell in Windsor Forest in 1815 are very different in character. Windsor Forest was in the process of being enclosed at the time when Linnell was there: the Act for its enclosure was passed in 1813 and the enclosure was completed in 1817. Linnell spent a month, from late May to the end of June, staying at Winkfield with his sister and his fiancée. His particular interest was not so much the play of light on the foliage, as the structure of the trees and the activities of the woodcutters. In this respect he was following in the footsteps of Paul Sandby and more especially of Benjamin West, whose oil painting, *Woodcutters in Windsor Park*, was executed in 1796 (now in the Indianapolis Museum of Art). Linnell's beautiful watercolour study of an old oak (fig. 34) became the basis for an exhibition picture, *A Forest Scene* (fig. 55), which was shown at the Society of Painters in Oil and Water-Colours in 1819. In this painting, woodcutters have removed the bark and placed wedges in the base of the tree. The man who wields the axe looks vigorous and well-dressed, a heroic worker like those in Linnell's painting of *Kensington Gravel Pits* (1813, Tate Britain). When the tree falls it will join a large number of other mature trees which lie around it, evidence of widespread clearance, presumably as a result of the enclosure. A sheet of studies in the British Museum shows that Linnell had studied the processes carefully from life.[26]

In contrast to Linnell's woodcutters, the figures in Francis Danby's paintings of Leigh Woods are enjoying leisure rather than working. The area known as Leigh Woods was privately owned by the Smyth family of Ashton Court, but citizens of Bristol were free to stroll in it.[27] *A Scene in Leigh Woods* (fig. 56) and *View of the Avon Gorge* (fig. 57) are a pair of modestly-sized panel paintings that were made in 1822, probably for a private patron in Bristol, and never exhibited in Danby's lifetime. The well-dressed groups in the foregrounds are clearly middle-class visitors to the woods, indulging in relaxation and conversation. Although they sit in the sun rather than the shade, perhaps placed there by the artist for aesthetic reasons, in other respects the paintings convey the popular idea of the woods as places of cool shade and escape from summer heat. In the *View of the Avon Gorge* a family group sits on the grass in the foreground and the long shadows cast by the trees indicate that it is afternoon, while the companion painting shows a young couple, the woman clutching a drawing portfolio under her arm. In both paintings, the shadows make variegated patterns on the ground, and additional figures can be seen strolling amongst the trees or walking along the paths.

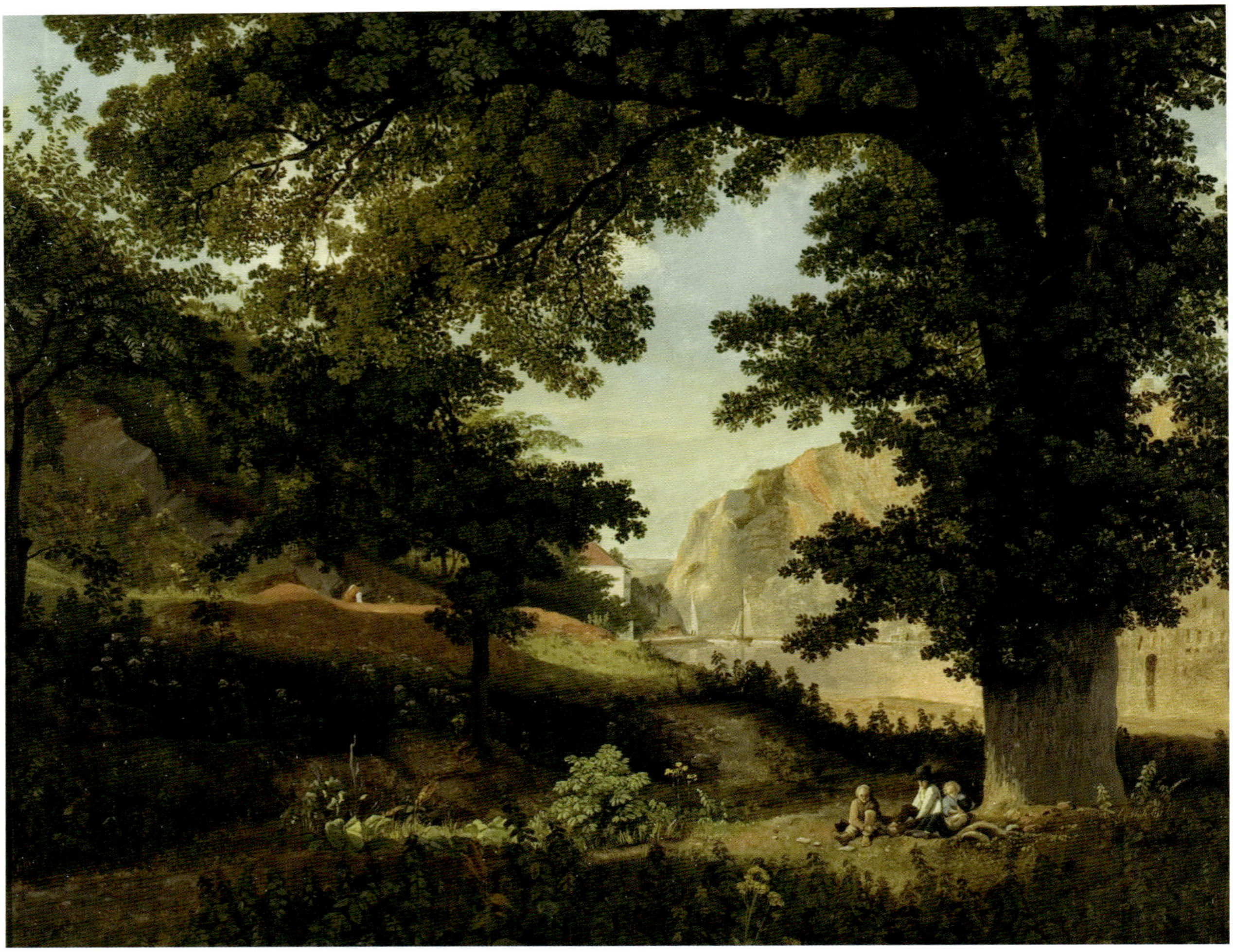

As Rippingille's drawing suggests, these woods were the site of convivial gatherings of artists and their friends in the 1810s and 1820s. In a letter to his son, the amateur artist George Cumberland writes of going alone to the woods in June 1818, starting early to avoid the heat, and sitting down at each shady tree to read his copy of Dante's *Paradiso*.[28] The artist and critic John Eagles, however, writes in his collection of essays, *The Sketcher*, that 'they are too beautiful for solitude, you long for someone to whom to express your admiration.' He says that he has often spent whole days in these woods – 'It is the very best artist's ground, not on a very extensive scale, and of a character unique' – sometimes alone 'and sometimes with a happy fraternity of the stainer's company, choice daubers and paper spoilers (i.e. painters).'[29] Danby himself writes of spending days in the woods with particular artists, and thus being enabled to form a judgment of them.[30] In Rippingille's drawing, which was probably the first idea for a group portrait, Danby may be the figure under the tree, working intently on a painting while his companions read poetry or examine each other's drawings. The picnic basket, empty bottle and guitar indicate the importance of relaxation and music in these gatherings.

Danby was working on a picture entitled *The Golden Age* in 1827, and he wrote a description of it which emphasizes the importance of specific varieties of trees and the contrasts of light and shade they create. 'A large chestnut tree in full blossom' occupied the centre of the design, 'light ashes' arched over a vista to the distance, there was a view 'in a dark wood over a small meadow on which are sporting some young people in sunshine, relieved brightly on the gloom behind', and the sun shone through high pine trees, 'touching rich colour'd bark with evening light.'[31] The prominence of the chestnut tree in blossom, and the idea of a very English depiction of the Golden Age, are both reminiscent of the work of Samuel Palmer and his friends at this period, although Danby eventually decided his conception was 'too local' and replaced the chestnut with

58 FRANCIS DANBY
Clifton Rocks from Rownham Fields
c.1821 | Oil on panel | 40 x 50.8 cm
Bristol Museum and Art Gallery
UK Purchased, 1927, Bridgeman Images

59 FRANCIS DANBY
Children by a Brook
c.1822 | Oil on panel | 74.9 x 62.2 cm
Yale Center for British Art
Paul Mellon Collection

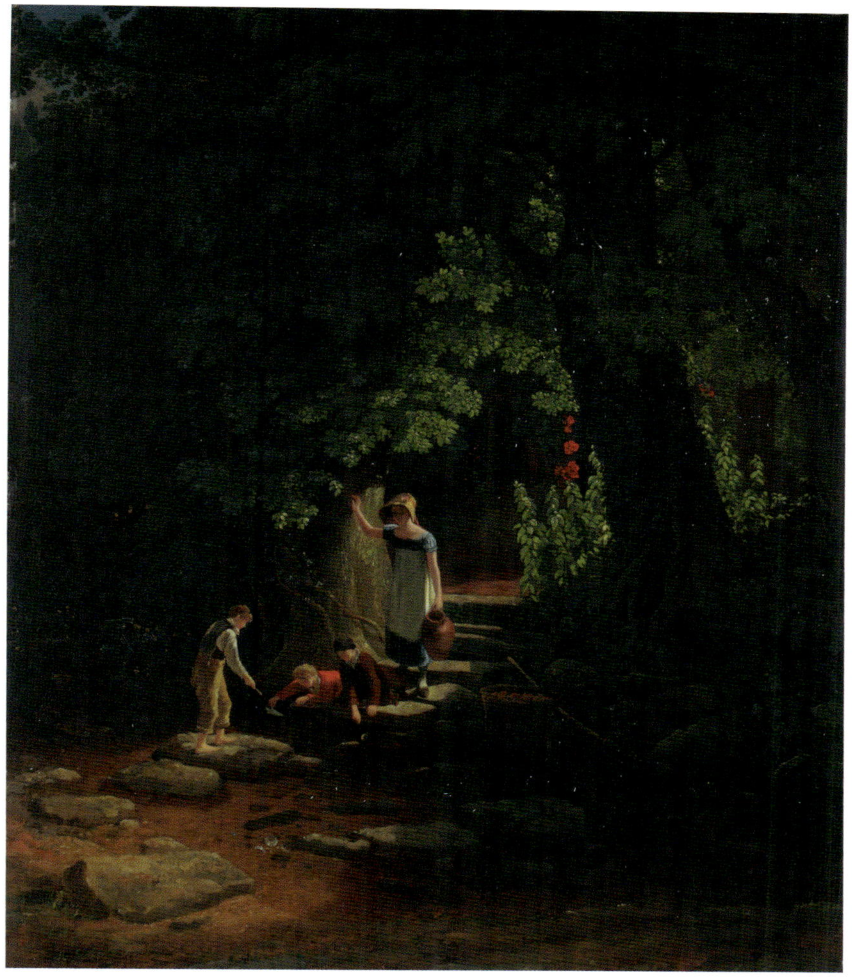

a palm tree. The sense of an English idyll is also present in *Clifton Rocks from Rownham Fields* (fig. 58), in which a mature oak spreads its foliage over the scene in a manner very similar to the composition of Hearne's *View from below Pool's Farm* (fig. 17). In Danby's painting, however, it is clear that this is not a private vale, but a pleasant place that is accessible to all: children relax in the patch of sunlight at the foot of the tree, men stroll along the path behind, and sailing boats travel along the river.

In other paintings of this period, such as *Children by a Brook* (fig. 59), Danby shows the dramatic effect of the sun shining through leaves, particularly sweet chestnut leaves, which are similar to beech leaves in their transparency, contrasted with the deep shade of a wood on a summer's day. His friend Rippingille wrote a letter to the poet John Clare, in the summer of 1824, which specifically mentions this effect. He encourages Clare to come and see the Bristol trees, water and woods in the sunshine: 'see branches of the most luxuriant foliage hanging over the river as bright as a diamond forming the darkest recesses and hollows of the richest colours, the brown earth mixing with the endless varieties of greens produced from reflections and from the sun shining through broad sheets of leaves …'[32] Eagles, too, writes of tree branches 'sweetly bending, and, as the sunbeams passed through the transparent leaves, apparently dropping emeralds upon the earth's bosom.'[33] Evidently, Danby's lost painting, *Clearing up after a Summer Shower*, which was exhibited at the Royal Academy in London in 1822, showed similar effects. It was subsequently much admired by Richard Redgrave, who wrote a long description of it in his *Century of Painters of the English School*, published in 1865, drawing attention to 'a group of chestnuts and other trees, their wetted leaves coming like emeralds off the dark cloud.'[34] The repeated references to precious stones in all three passages – to diamonds and emeralds – are an indication of how much artists and writers appreciated the brilliant light effects and dramatic contrasts visible in sunlit woods.

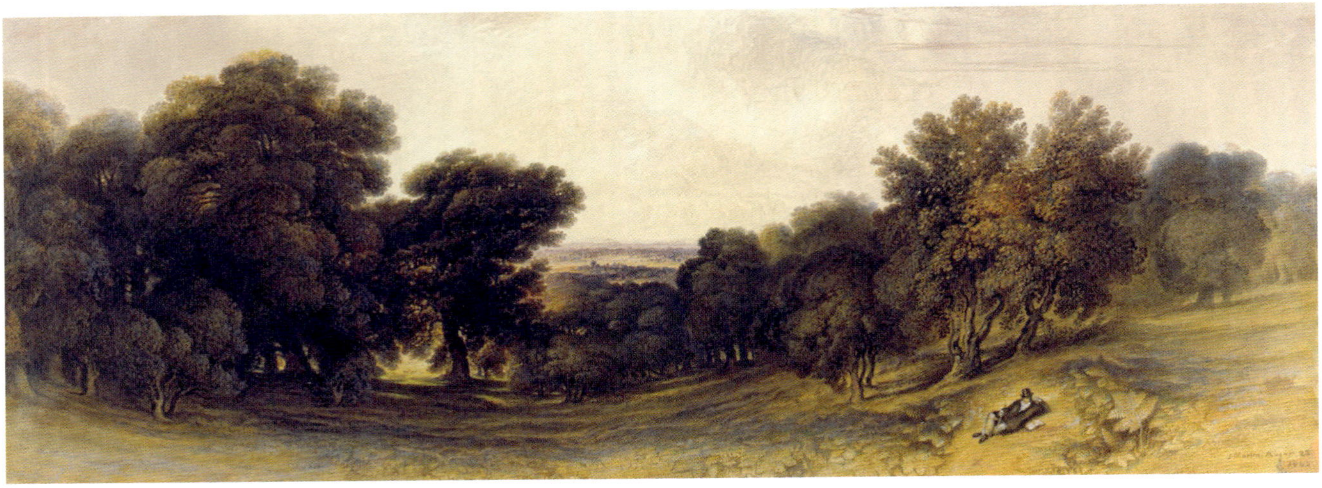

Danby's paintings of middle-class visitors relaxing in the woods are similar, in their subject matter, to a series of watercolours by John Martin. In the 1840s and 1850s he exhibited a total of seven views of Richmond Park at the Royal Academy. In all the surviving paintings from this series solitary figures, couples, or family groups walk along paths in the shade of the trees, or sit on the grass. In one watercolour, dated 1843 (fig. 60), the figure seems to be the artist himself, reclining on a sunny bank with a book. In a later watercolour, *Richmond Park* (fig. 61), the central tree is an ancient oak with a seat around it, which subsequently came to be known as 'Martin's Oak'.[35] A family strolls in the foreground, and sunlight coming through the trees to the right illuminates a patch of grass in front of them. Critics noted the effects of light in such scenes. In 1852 the *Morning Chronicle* reviewer wrote of a later view with a similar title, that it was 'noticeable from the merit of the perspective between the trees, and the happiness with which the slanting rays of the setting sun are imitated among the stems.'[36] Richmond Park was effectively open to the public in the mid-nineteenth century. Like Leigh Woods, therefore, it was a place where city-dwellers could escape the heat and noise of their usual surroundings. It was famous for the extensive views it afforded over the countryside, and Martin's woodland scenes typically show distant views, highlighted in the titles he gave to them in the Academy catalogues. Martin had published *Characters of Trees* in 1817 (fig. 28), and all his woodland scenes incorporate carefully-drawn trees, the outlines and structure of their trunks and ramification clearly visible. Usually, entire trees are shown, which means that they dwarf the figures beneath them.

In contrast to these paintings by Danby and Martin, Constable's woodland scenes are set in private estates, and

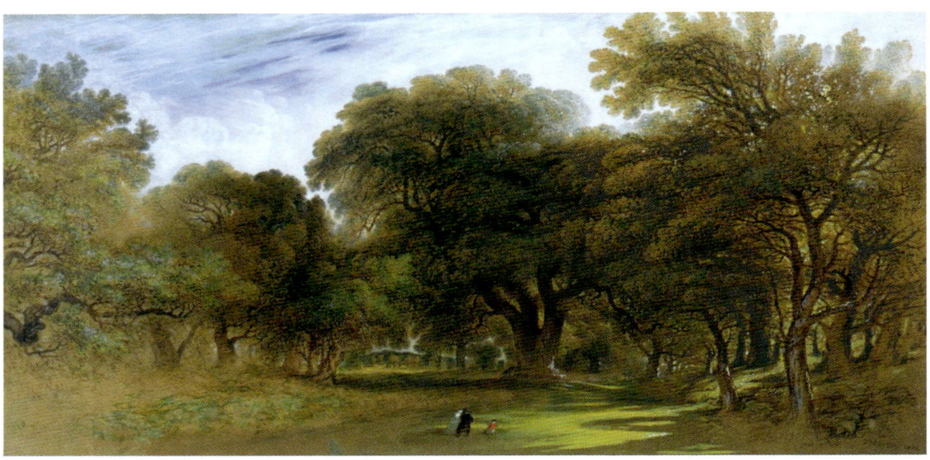

60 JOHN MARTIN
Richmond Park
1843 | Watercolour | 27.9 x 70.8 cm

61 JOHN MARTIN
Richmond Park
1850 | Watercolour | 29.6 x 59.4 cm

62 DAVID LUCAS *after* JOHN CONSTABLE
The Cornfield
1834 | Mezzotint | 56.8 x 49.1 cm

populated, if at all, by deer rather than middle-class visitors. In 1800 he made a large drawing of a very shady spot, a stream with a rickety footbridge surrounded by trees.[37] Constable returned to this drawing many years later and produced four oil paintings, of which one was exhibited at the Royal Academy in 1830 and another at the British Institution in 1833.[38] In the Royal Academy catalogue the painting was described as 'Dell Scene, in the park of the Rt Hon the Countess of Dysart, at Helmingham, Suffolk', making it quite clear that it was a private location and not a public one. *The Cenotaph* (1836; National Gallery, London) is also a scene studied on a private estate, that of Sir George Beaumont at Coleorton. Here the shadows are even deeper than in *Helmingham Dell*, and the trees are brown and wintry. There is a subtle suggestion of watery sunshine coming through the trees to the forest floor, but it is not a painting that would make the nineteenth-century viewer think of summer picnics in the woods, unlike the scenes by Danby and Martin. There is more sunshine in Constable's *Cornfield* of 1826 (National Gallery), but it is mainly in the distance rather than in the tree-shaded lane in the foreground. However, this painting seems to have been an important source of inspiration for later painters of woodland scenes. Its foreground light and shade could be seen as an example of 'chequered shade' and the contrasts between light and shade were emphasized in the mezzotint of it by David Lucas (fig. 62). It became very well-known, as it was the painting presented to the National Gallery by subscribers after Constable's death in 1837.

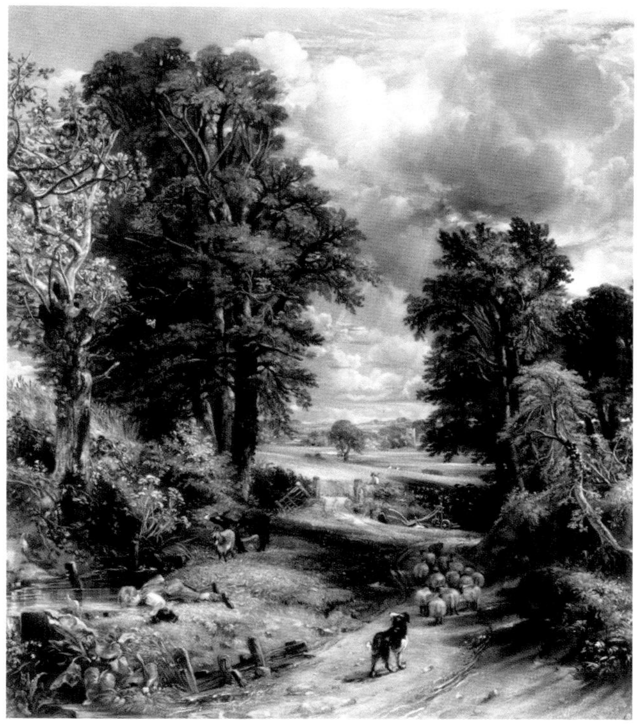

63 RICHARD REDGRAVE
An Hour with the Poets 'in the leafy month of June'
1853 | Oil on canvas | 78.5 x 104 cm
Private Collection, Photo © Christies Images/Bridgeman Images

THE MID-NINETEENTH CENTURY: CRESWICK, LEE AND REDGRAVE

One of Constable's admirers was Thomas Creswick, who consistently exhibited woodland scenes over a career spanning forty years. Creswick made a particular point of studying the structure of trees and the effects of light and shade in avenues, wooded lanes and glades. In 1846 he chose to add Shakespeare's lines 'The green leaves quiver with the cooling wind and make a chequered shadow on the ground' to the title of his painting, *The Pleasant Way Home*, when it was shown at the Royal Academy. The basic composition is similar to that of Constable's *Cornfield*, with dappled patches of light leading the eye into the distance past a fine ash tree. *The Times* critic wrote that Creswick 'patches [the avenue] with sunlight in his favourite manner' and the *Critic* declared that 'There are few landscapes in the Gallery more covetable or more admired than this.'[39] The artist returned to this theme in 1848 with a painting actually entitled *Chequered Shade* (untraced). This was described by the *Athenaeum* as 'one of the gems of the exhibition' but also as 'a hackneyed subject – an avenue of trees'.[40] In the following year Creswick produced a further depiction of an avenue in dappled shade, *The Shade of the Beech Trees*, in which the complex root structure of the beeches is reminiscent of Sandby's Luton Hoo drawings. This drew the comment that 'the foliage of the beech is caught with the eye of a botanist, and rendered with the feeling of a painter.'[41]

Frederick Lee was another artist whose representations of shady avenues elicited favourable critical responses. In 1846 a critic was finding the crowds, heat and smell (that is, the smell of oil from the paintings) of the Royal Academy oppressive. He wrote :

> We long to plunge into one of those charming avenues of Lee's, where the hot sun falls with such vigour on the summits of the trees, but does not reach the pleasant pathway by which we would sit, or at any rate only reveals its existence by those streaks of light upon the ground, whereat we could gaze pleasantly.[42]

This comment probably relates to Lee's *Woodland Ferry*, which was hung close to Creswick's *The Pleasant Way Home*, 'two beautiful landscapes' according to *The Times* reviewer.[43] Lee, like Creswick, later exhibited a painting with the title of *The Chequered Shade*. This was shown at the Royal Academy in 1854 and was a joint production with Thomas Sidney Cooper the animal painter: Lee painted the landscape, an avenue of trees, while Cooper contributed the sheep sitting in the shade on the road beneath them.[44] This painting, too, is reminiscent of Constable's *Cornfield*, but there are important differences. The fact that the sheep are resting, rather than walking along the lane, gives that element of 'repose' which was so highly valued by nineteenth-century commentators on landscape paintings. The same quality is hinted at in the reviewer's reference, above, to 'the pleasant pathway by which we would sit.' Secondly, the contrasting patches of light and shade are sharply distinguished from one another, so that the viewer may really feel that the sun is shining. If the reviewer's comment in 1846 is to be believed, this had already been a characteristic of Lee's woodland scenes for a decade or more.

Along with Creswick and Lee, Richard Redgrave attracted critical approval for his depictions of wooded landscapes in the 1840s and 1850s. In 1849 he exhibited *Sun and Shadow*, which may have been a woodland scene, and in this year a critic wrote of him in terms which suggest not just the subject matter of his landscapes but also the feelings they evoke:

> Redgrave goes into the wood; he sees the branches interlaced over him; the leaves dapple the vault of shade and ring the changes on sunny light and sombre dark … his heart is filled with pleasure and love.[45]

The titles of lost works from this period indicate that Redgrave had a strong sense of the historical and literary associations of English woodland. In 1850 he exhibited a painting with the following title, referring to the author of the famous *Sylva*: 'The woods planted by Evelyn, and still the property of his descendants. "As the days of a tree are the

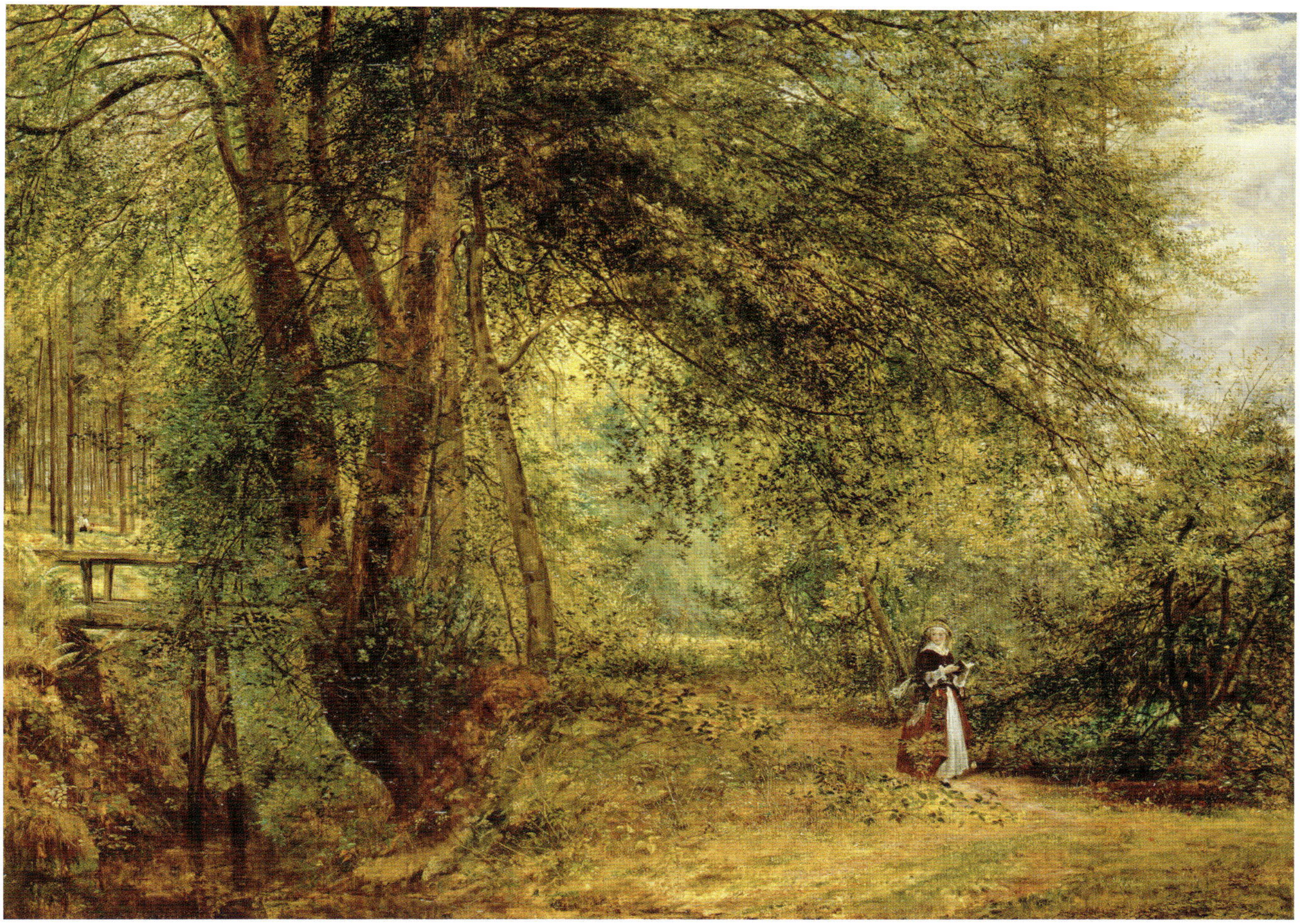

days of my people, etc." Isaiah, LXV, 22.'[46] In that summer he and his family took lodgings near Kilve, in Somerset, where they were joined by James Clarke Hook and his wife. The two couples 'used to paint together in a romantic and shady glen, once frequented by Coleridge and his brother poets', according to Redgrave's *Memoir*.[47] Wordsworth's death in April 1850 doubtless meant that the poet was much in their thoughts that summer. The result of these studies was 'a large upright picture' of 'a tree-shaded brook with sunbeams playing through the leaves, a "wizard stream" where any lover of nature would wish to spend the long summer day', a 'delicately beautiful piece of leafiness.'[48] This was *A Poet's Study* (untraced). In the Royal Academy catalogue of 1851 Redgrave added the explanation: 'Wordsworth is said to have sat for hours in this glen with Coleridge and Southey.'[49]

Two years later Redgrave again took up the theme of the connection between poetry and woodland scenery in *An Hour with the Poets. 'In the leafy month of June'* (fig. 63), one of several woodland landscapes that he exhibited at the Academy in 1853. The subtitle refers, once again, to Coleridge, to the lines from *The Ancient Mariner* that describe a 'hidden brook' singing to the woods. In Redgrave's painting, a well-dressed woman walks along a path through a beech wood, reading a book. Above and behind her, sunlight is filtered through the leaves, creating dappled effects of great complexity, and to the left there is a brook, crossed by a wooden footbridge. This painting, too, was widely admired. One critic wrote:

> Mr. Redgrave abounds in woodland scenery, touched with a lightness and an airiness which we look for in vain elsewhere. Of all these pieces … we prefer his 'Hour with the poets.' The leafiness of this picture is wonderful. The month of June was certainly never before so expressly presented on canvas.[50]

In addition to his large exhibition landscapes, Redgrave painted exquisite small works which remained in his collection and were donated to the Victoria and Albert Museum after his death. One of these is the watercolour, *Parkhurst Woods* (fig. 64), which demonstrates a highly sophisticated

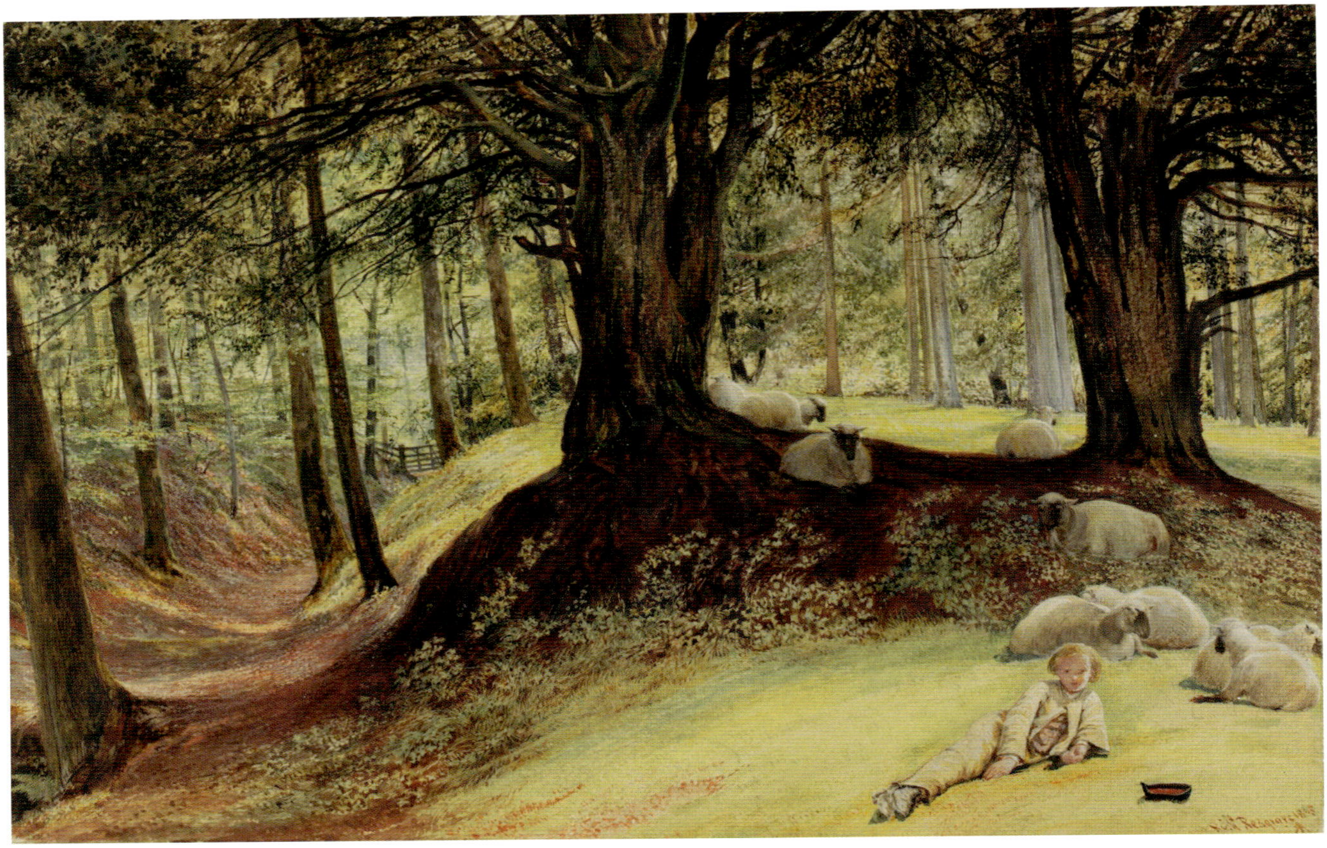

understanding of filtered, dappled and reflected light in a beech wood. Two mature yew trees, their roots clinging to exposed earth banks, provide a dark foreground feature, against which the sunlit grass and beech leaves look all the more dazzlingly bright. Sheep rest under the trees and a small boy, looking rather too well-dressed to be a shepherd, lies in the sunlight, gazing towards the observer. There is also a middle-class figure in the small oil painting, *Sweet Summer Time* (fig. 65), which contrasts a brilliantly sunlit field with the dark wood behind. Sheep occupy the foreground and, in the middle distance on the left, labourers pile up firewood or hurdles. On the extreme right of the painting, a figure, perhaps the artist, watches the activity going on. The deep shadows of the woods in these two paintings would undoubtedly have suggested delicious coolness and repose to any Victorian viewer.

A book published in 1851 shows that Creswick, Lee and Redgrave had already acquired reputations, by this early date, as painters of sunshine and shade in woodland. This was *Sketches after English Landscape Painters*, a lavish production consisting of engravings by the French artist Louis Marvy, with commentaries on the plates by William Makepeace Thackeray. Marvy had come to London to escape the 1848 French revolution, and while in England he was introduced by Thackeray to Sir Thomas Baring. The introduction explains that several of the works engraved were in Baring's collection. However, for the plate after Constable Marvy engraved *The Cornfield* from the National Gallery. Marvy's print exaggerates the contrast between light and shade in the foreground and Thackeray, in his commentary, admires 'the chequered light on the road' as well as 'the trees and their leafage.' Creswick is represented in the book by a study of an avenue with figures seated under the trees – possibly the *Chequered Shade* exhibited at the Academy in 1848 (fig. 66). Thackeray comments 'when one looks at these charming works of Mr. Creswick, one imagines the painter happy in his serene occupation … tracing the course of the river, the forms of rocks, *the play of the sunshine amidst the leaves*' (my italics). Redgrave's landscape, a view of figures seated on logs in front of oak trees, with sun shining through their leaves, was described by Thackeray as 'a quiet little piece of chequered shade and sun-shine, suggestive of repose and peaceful meditation.' The plate after Lee shows an open scene, a field with a ploughman, but Thackeray's

64 RICHARD REDGRAVE
Parkhurst Woods, Abinger, Surrey
1865 | Watercolour | 25.5 x 38.2 cm

65 RICHARD REDGRAVE
Sweet Summer Time – Sheep in Wotton Meadows
1869 | Oil on panel | 21.6 x 34.9 cm

commentary refers, nevertheless, to his 'avenues of English trees, bright with native air and sunshine … the eye gazes delighted in … the chequered shades and lights of those favourite lanes in which the artist loves to linger…'[51] The repetition of the word 'chequered' is remarkable, and shows how much it had become common currency amongst art critics when writing about woodland scenes in this period.

It may have been the bright fields and shady beech woods beloved of Richard Redgrave that inspired a younger painter, the watercolourist Edmund George Warren, to produce some of the most detailed woodland scenes ever painted. The appeal of this kind of subject matter is summed up in his most famous work, *'Rest in the Cool and Shady Wood'* (fig. 52), exhibited at the New Society of Painters in Watercolours in 1861. In this large watercolour, two children have just walked through a beech wood on a path. They turn to look at the adjoining shade, where two farm labourers lie stretched out on the grass, while a third man, holding a sickle, walks towards them. A bright, sunny harvest field is seen beyond, the stooks of wheat set up neatly in rows. As one reviewer commented, it 'is indeed cool and dewy in the shade, yet in the sunshine sparkling bright.'[52] Another critic praised the 'veracity' with which Warren had painted 'the delicate tracery of boughs in shade telling against the sunny green beyond, the holly, the brambles, and ground of dead leaves.'[53] Warren appears to have specialized in studies of beech trees. In 1858 he exhibited a large watercolour of a beech in the Forest of Dean, which was praised for its truthfulness: 'The rounded stem and arms of the noble tree, with all its accidents of moss, stain, and lichen, sunfleck and shadow, the multitudinous leafage … the thick carpet of last year's russet leaves that strew the ground, are rendered with marvellously patient and successful labour.'[54] A year later a reviewer noted the 'dead, thick strewn winter leaves coming out in every shade of red, brown and paler russet' in his *Avenue, Evelyn Woods*, a location also painted by Redgrave.[55]

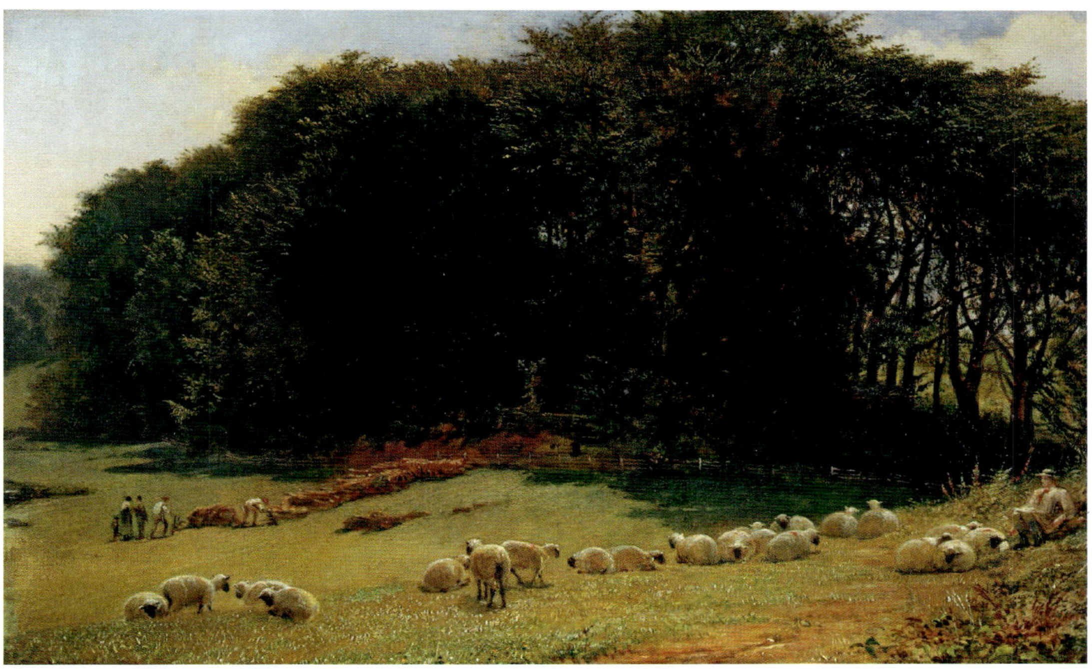

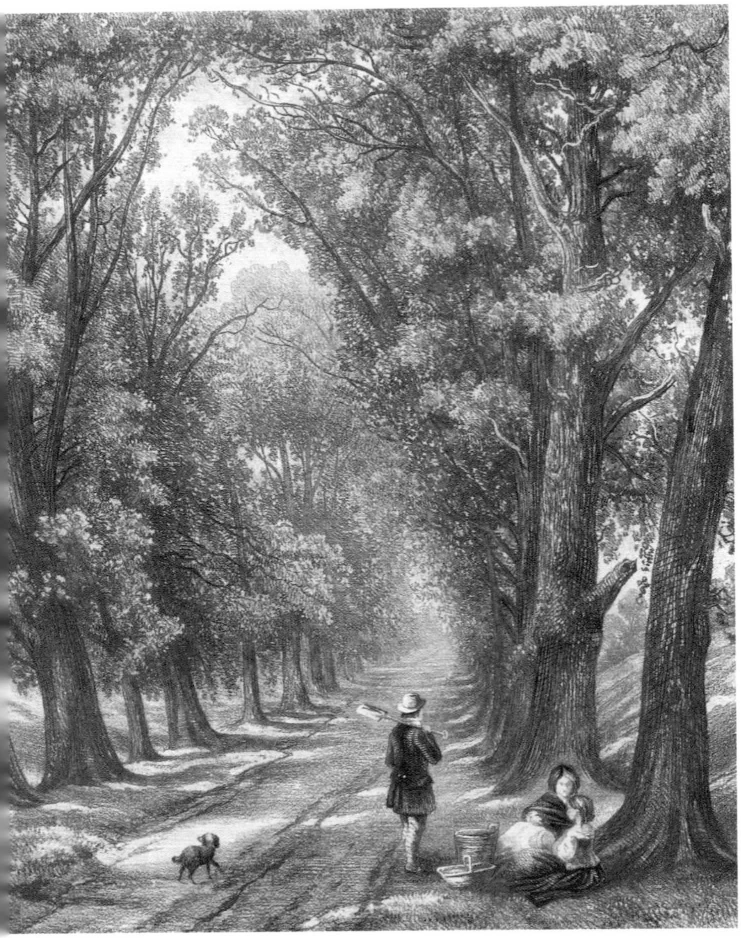

66 L. MARVY *after* THOMAS CRESWICK
plate from *Sketches after English Landscape Painters*, 1851, 2 Delta 675.
The Bodleian Libraries, The University of Oxford

Warren was criticized, however, for being too dependent on photography. *The Times* reviewer (presumably Tom Taylor) noted his use of photography in 1858, but simply stated that Warren had 'called the photograph to his aid as well as nature' in drawing his beech tree in the Forest of Dean. A year later Taylor was more disapproving:

> Mr. Warren is quite right in availing himself of the photograph, but he has not yet learnt how to use its help aright. He must become its master, and not submit to it like a slave …

Too slavish a dependency on photographs would, thought Taylor, result in work that was 'deficient in play and variety of colour', with leaves lacking life and suggesting fixedness rather than freedom of movement.[56]

The illustrations to this chapter demonstrate that paintings of woodland scenes become increasingly detailed and meticulously finished from around 1850 – just at the time when photographers were taking to the woods and producing many images that would be extremely useful to painters. As we shall see in Chapter Seven, the 1850s was also the decade when the Pre-Raphaelites were producing highly detailed tree paintings, and there is no doubt that Warren was influenced by their example, as were the artists of the older generation of Creswick and Redgrave. The Pre-Raphaelites, in their turn, learnt much from photography. Early photographs of trees usually focused on the effects that were relatively easy to reproduce, such as the textures of mature tree trunks or the ramification of bare branches in winter. It was much more difficult to show foliage in these early decades, since the patches of light on the leaves would expand during the developing process to look like snow.

Early landscape photographs are notoriously difficult to date, and it is hard to say who was influencing whom: were the photographers deliberately seeking out subjects and effects that they had seen in paintings, or were the landscape painters simply following the example of the photographers? It is certainly true that in the 1850s both painters and photographers were spending much time in the woods. In the report of the very first meeting of the Photographic Society, in February 1853, we find that 'After the reading of the Papers some specimens chiefly of wood scenery taken by Sir Wm. J. Newton were exhibited.'[57] In September of the same year, a correspondent praises 'the admirable stereoscopic views, particularly those of Burnham Beeches by Mr. Fenton, exhibited at a late meeting of the Photographic Society'.[58] William Newton and Roger Fenton exhibited many photographs of Burnham Beeches in the 1850s, drawn there, presumably, by the ancient pollards, some of which were many centuries old. This relatively small area of woodland, situated within easy reach of London and near to growing residential commuter areas such as Beaconsfield and Farnham, was already well known because of its connections with the poet Thomas Gray, and in the 1830s and 1840s the historian George Grote and his wife entertained musicians there, including Felix Mendelssohn.[59] An undated painting by Thomas Creswick (fig. 67) emphasizes the extraordinary shapes of

67 THOMAS CRESWICK
Burnham Beeches
Oil on canvas | 85.5 x 110 cm
Buckinghamshire County Museum

the 'monster' trees, seen from a low perspective against a background of sun-dappled leafage, with boys looking for rabbits in the earth bank below the nearest tree.

In the 1860s, Myles Birket Foster and Charles Davidson exhibited watercolours of Burnham Beeches at the Society of Painters in Watercolour (the Old Watercolour Society). Davidson's work, shown in 1868, was entitled *'In the Leafy Month of June' – Burnham Beeches*. It contains no human figures, only deer – as if the solitary walker has come quietly upon them in the depths of the wood, approaching on a path bordered with the gnarled roots of mature beeches.[60] Birket Foster's view of the old beeches by one of the ponds in the wood (fig. 2) is unusual in showing, not June, but autumn, with glorious russet tones in the foliage and in the leaves that carpet the ground. In the foreground, children with baskets are presumably gathering beech-nuts to feed to the family pig, a reminder that this used to be a place where holders of common rights could set free their pigs to graze on the beech-mast. Paintings such as these – and indeed the whole tradition of woodland scenes in the British art of this period – support F. G. Heath's claim that artists had changed public perceptions, ensuring that Burnham Beeches and other such places would be preserved from developers. As was the case with Leigh Woods, Bristol, the location of Burnham Beeches exposed it to the threat of development for housing, but at the same time made it more than ever imperative that such delightful spaces should be available to the inhabitants of growing cities, providing opportunities for spiritual refreshment and meditation.

Developments in the painting of woodland scenes in Britain are parallelled by the now better-known history of the Barbizon artists and the Forest of Fontainebleau. In the first half of the nineteenth century, the Forest of Fontainebleau, formerly a royal forest, became a popular haunt for artists, writers and pleasure seekers from Paris. The artists of the 'school of Barbizon', Théodore Rousseau, Jean-Baptiste-Camille Corot and Narcisse Virgile Diaz de la Peña made many studies of woodland there. Diaz, in

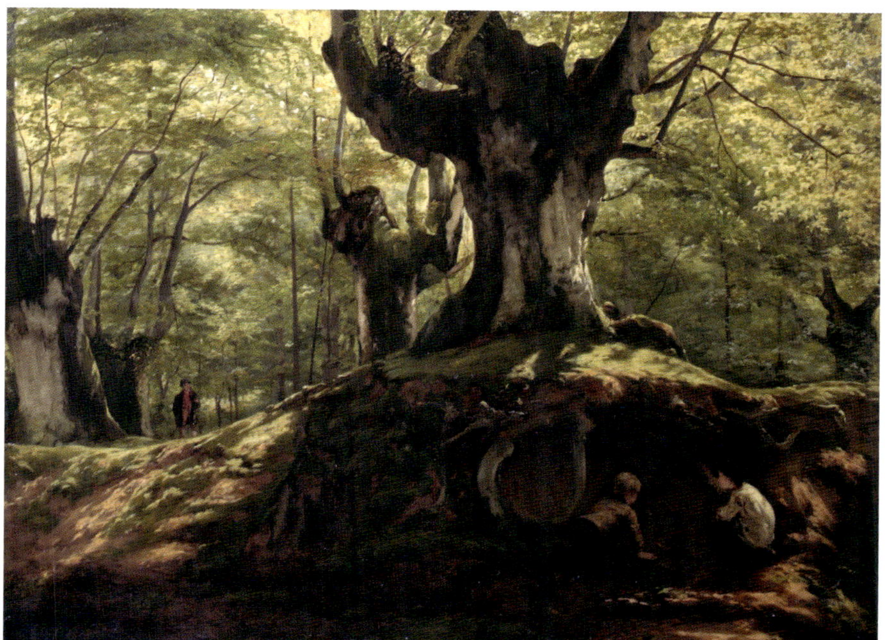

particular, made the idea of the 'sous-bois' – the undergrowth, the forest interior – one of his special objects of study.[61] However, in their works prior to 1850 the Barbizon painters, unlike their British contemporaries, rarely show a concern with the effects of sunlight filtered through leaves and casting patterns of chequered shade upon the ground. This effect is more obvious in the work of the photographers who went to the Forest in the 1850s and 1860s. Gustave Le Gray was one of the first of these, and he was able to capture the effects of sunlight shining through leaves and dappled shade on the ground as early as 1851-2.[62] Le Gray's photographs were exhibited, and much admired, in London as well as Paris, so his work, too, may well have influenced the British artists.

The campaigns to save Epping Forest and Burnham Beeches, in the 1870s and 1880s, demonstrated a strong public affection for the woods and a growing belief that they should be open to all. As this chapter has shown, artists, like writers, played their part in spreading an appreciation of the visual beauties of woodland, and especially of the play of light and shade under the canopy of the trees. Some of the scenes discussed in this chapter incorporate distant views, but these were by no means essential to their success. The woodland scenes were classic 'refuge' landscapes, in Jay Appleton's terms, offering a sense of security and shelter which was evidently welcome to their viewers and buyers.[63] They both responded to and encouraged the contemporary social practice of going to the woods to escape the summer heat. These paintings celebrated the native trees, particularly the beech, which was so common a feature of the woods in southern England. Much of their appeal arose from the fact that they represented the familiar, the landscape of the everyday. These scenes became all the more precious at a time when, as we shall see in the next chapter, exotic trees were becoming more common, both in the actual landscape and in representations of artists' travels.

ENDNOTES

1 In this chapter I use the words 'wood' and 'forest' as interchangeable terms, which is how they were used by nineteenth-century artists and critics when describing the kind of paintings covered here. However, as we saw in Chapter One, the term 'forest' also had a stricter legal definition, when it referred to a large area, not necessarily consisting entirely of woodland, such as the royal forests.

2 Houghton Towneley, *English Woodlands and their Story* (London: Methuen & Co Ltd, 1910), pp. 23-4.

3 William Cowper, *The Task* (1785), Book One, ll. 300-303 and 312-3.

4 William Wordsworth, *The Tables Turned* (1798), ll. 21-4.

5 William Wordsworth, *To My Sister* (1798), ll. 14, 27-8.

6 Samuel Taylor Coleridge, *This Lime-Tree Bower my Prison* (1797), ll. 47-51.

7 [Harriet Grote], *Some Account of the Hamlet of East Burnham, by a late resident* (London: Savill & Edwards, 1858), p. 29.

8 William Menzies, *The History of Windsor Great Park and Windsor Forest. Illustrated with photographs by the Earl of Caithness and Mr Bembridge, of Windsor* (London: Longman, Green, Longman, Roberts, and Green, 1864), pp. 37-8; Rose de Crespigny and Horace Hutchinson, *The New Forest: Its Traditions, Inhabitants and Customs* (London: John Murray, 1895), p. 65.

9 See David Hill, *Cotman in the North: Watercolours of Durham and Yorkshire* (New Haven and London: Yale University Press, 2005).

10 Michael Rosenthal, 'The Rough and the Smooth: Rural Subjects in Later Eighteenth-Century Art', in Michael Rosenthal, Christiana Payne and Scott Wilcox, eds., *Prospects for the Nation: Recent Essays in British Landscape, 1750-1880* (New Haven and London: Yale University Press, 1996), pp. 37-59.

11 See Simon Schama, *Landscape and Memory* (London: Fontana Press, 1996, first published HarperCollins, 1995), Part One Chapter Three, 'The Liberties of the Greenwood'.

12 Jacob George Strutt, *Deliciae Sylvarum: or, grand and romantic Forest Scenery in England and Scotland* (London: J. G. Strutt, 1828), p. 3.

13 John Eagles, *The Sketcher* (Edinburgh and London: William Blackwood & Sons, 1856), p. 150, footnote.

14 Towneley, *English Woodlands*, p. 187.

15 Francis George Heath, *Burnham Beeches*

(London: William Rider & Sons, 1883), pp. 19-20.

16 Ibid, p. 77.

17 For example, Samuel Palmer, *In the Chequered Shade* (watercolour, 1861, no. 586 in R. Lister, *Catalogue Raisonné of the Works of Samuel Palmer* (Cambridge: Cambridge University Press, 1998)) and John Linnell, *L'Allegro, 'Many a youth and many a maid, dancing in the chequered shade'* (oil on canvas, 1849, Harris Museum and Art Gallery, Preston). John Milton, *L'Allegro* (1645), ll. 95-6.

18 William Shakespeare, *Titus Andronicus* (c. 1590), Act II, Scene III, ll. 12-15.

19 Alexander Pope, *Windsor Forest* (1713), ll. 17-18, 21-22.

20 Anon., *English Forests and Forest Trees, Historical, Legendary, and Descriptive* (London: Ingram, Cooke, & Co, 1853), pp. 19-20.

21 Ibid, p. 22.

22 Samuel Taylor Coleridge, *The Rime of the Ancient Mariner* (1798), ll. 369-72.

23 For this album, which contains 46 pencil studies, see Hill, *Cotman in the North*, pp. 80-81.

24 Hill, *Cotman in the North*, pp. 70, 102. Letters dated 26 November 1803, and 7 August 1805.

25 Ibid, p. 125.

26 British Museum 1953,1215.8. Katharine Crouan, *John Linnell: A Centennial Exhibition* (Cambridge: Cambridge University Press,1982), pp. 14-15.

27 Long Ashton Local History Society, *Long Ashton and Leigh Woods* (Stroud: Chalford Publishing Co, 1997), p. 7.

28 Francis Greenacre, *Francis Danby. 1793-1861* (London: Tate Gallery in association with City of Bristol Museum and Art Gallery, 1983), p. 17.

29 Eagles, *The Sketcher*, p. 100.

30 Greenacre, *Francis Danby*, p. 17.

31 Letter from Danby to John Gibbons, 6 January 1827. Cited in Greenacre, *Francis Danby*, p. 107.

32 British Museum, Egerton MS 2246, f. 366, cited in Eric Adams, *Francis Danby: Varieties of Poetic Landscape* (New Haven and London: Yale University Press, 1973) p. 40.

33 Eagles, *The Sketcher*, p. 126 – written 1833.

34 R. and S. Redgrave, *A Century of Painters of the English School* (London: Smith, Elder & Co, 1865), Vol II, p. 442.

35 Martin Myrone, ed., *John Martin: Apocalypse* (London: Tate Publishing, 2011), p. 190.

36 *Morning Chronicle*, 2 June 1852, cited in Myrone, *John Martin*, p. 191.

37 See R. B. Beckett, 'Constable's "Helmingham Dell"', *Art Quarterly* (Spring 1961) pp. 2-14.

38 These paintings are now in the Nelson-Atkins Museum of Art, Kansas City, Missouri, and the John G. Johnson Collection, Philadelphia, respectively.

39 *The Times*, 18 May 1846, p. 6; *The Critic* 3.75, 6 June 1846, p. 653. *The Pleasant Way Home* was sold at Christie's, London, 5 June 1981 (Important Victorian Pictures, lot 5).

40 *Athenaeum*, 1073, 20 May 1848, p. 512.

41 *Illustrated London News*, supplement, 26 May 1849, p. 350. *The Shade of the Beech Trees* was sold at Christie's, London, 13 May 1977 (Fine Victorian Pictures, lot 105).

42 *New Monthly Magazine and Humorist*, 77.306, June 1846, p. 243.

43 *The Times*, 18 May 1846, p. 6.

44 *The Chequered Shade* was sold at Christie's, London, on 19 February 2003 (Sale 6747, The Forbes Collection of Victorian Pictures and Works of Art).

45 *The Spectator*, 23 June 1849, p. 591, cited in Susan P. Casteras and Ronald Parkinson, eds., *Richard Redgrave 1804-1888* (New Haven and London: Yale University Press, 1988) p. 72.

46 Royal Academy exhibition, no 534.

47 F. M. Redgrave, *Richard Redgrave, CB, RA. A Memoir, compiled from his Diary* (London: Cassell & Company Ltd, 1891), p. 71.

48 *Art Journal*, June 1851, p. 158; *Examiner*, 2262, 7 June 1851, p. 358.

49 The painting was shown at the Exposition Universelle in Paris in 1855 (no. 922), along with *The Woodland Mirror* (no. 923, RA 1852).

50 *Fraser's magazine for town and country*, 47.282, June 1853, p. 713.

51 *Sketches after English Landscape Painters*, by L. Marvy, with short notices by W. M. Thackeray (London: David Bogue, 1851), unpaginated.

52 *Blackwood's Edinburgh Magazine*, 90.550, August 1861, p. 206.

53 *Spectator*, 27 April 1861, p. 445, cited in Scott Wilcox and Christopher Newall, *Victorian Landscape Watercolors* (New York: Hudson Hills Press, in association with the Yale Center for British Art, 1992), p. 110.

54 *The Times*, 19 April 1858, p. 9.

55 *Sharpe's London magazine of entertainment and instruction for general reading*, 29, January 1859, p. 331.

56 *The Times*, 27 April 1859, p. 11.

57 *Journal of the Photographic Society*, No 1 (3 March 1853), p. 5.

58 *Journal of the Photographic Society*, No. 9 (September 1853), p. 115. The letter, from 'G. M. L.', is dated 23 August 1853.

59 Towneley, *English Woodlands*, pp. 35-42.

60 Charles Davidson, *'In the Leafy Month of June' – Burnham Beeches*. Watercolour and bodycolour, 44.7 x 67.22 cm. Walker Art Gallery, Liverpool.

61 See Kimberly Jones, *In the Forest of Fontainebleau: Painters and Photographers from Corot to Monet* (Washington: National Gallery of Art, 2008).

62 See, for example, *Bas-Breau, Forest of Fontainebleau* (Victoria and Albert Museum).

63 Jay Appleton, *The Experience of Landscape* (London: Wiley, 1975).

68 THOMAS DANIELL

Hindoo Temples at Agouree, on the River Soane, Bahar

1795 | Aquatint | 46.5 x 60.2 cm

69 JOHN MARTIN

Eve at the Fountain

1825 | Mezzotint | 19.8 x 26.8 cm

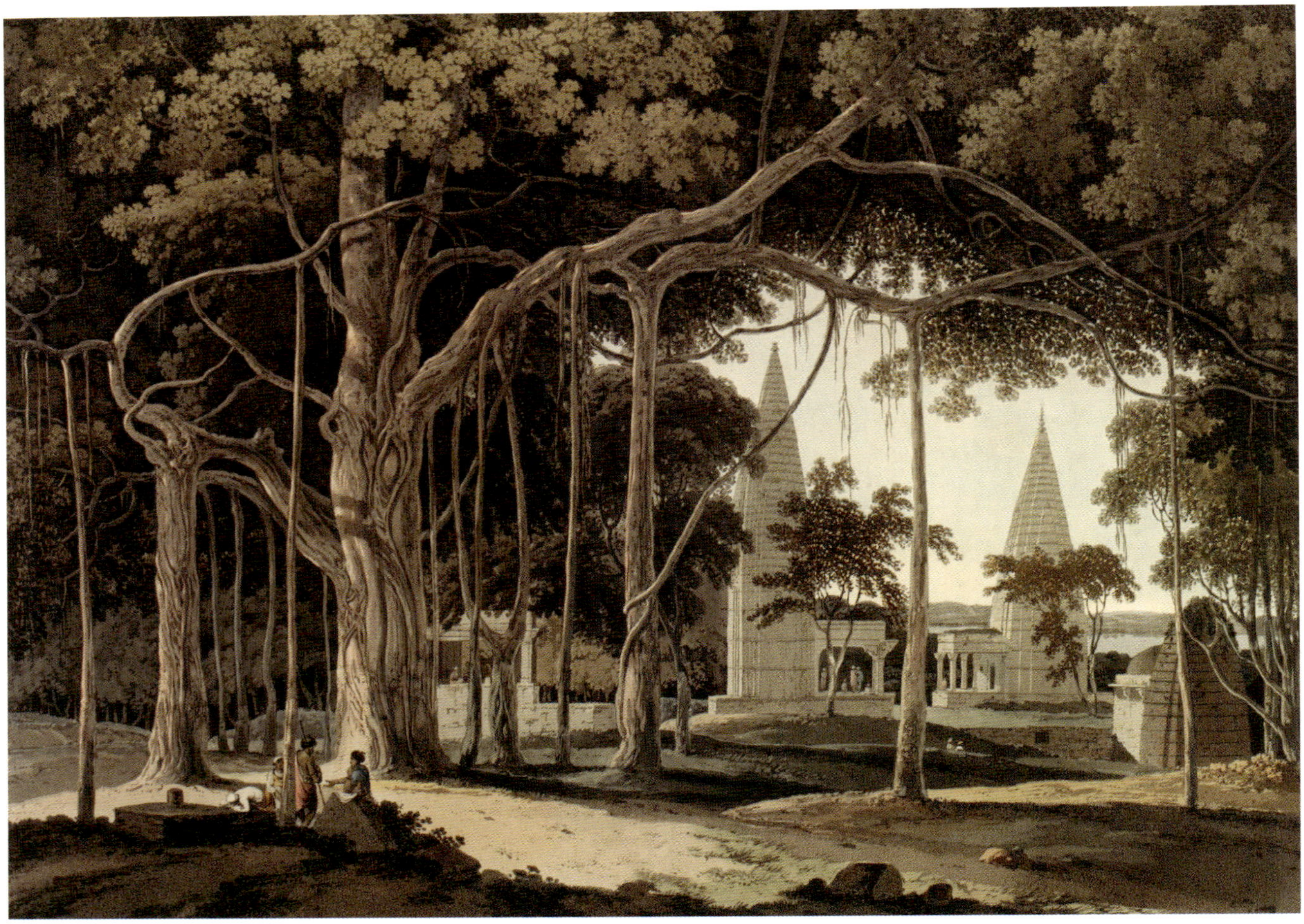

SIX

Exotic Trees: A Taste of Paradise

In a short but highly influential passage in his epic poem *Paradise Lost* (1667), John Milton lists the trees in the Garden of Eden:

> … overhead up grew
> Insuperable height of loftiest shade,
> Cedar, and pine, and fir, and branching palm[1]

Milton specifies that Eve first sees Adam under a 'platan' (a plane tree), and describes the tree from which Adam and Eve took the leaves to cover their nakedness as an Indian fig tree – that is, a banyan tree (fig. 68):

> The fig-tree, not that kind for fruit renowned,
> But such as at this day to Indians known
> In Malabar or Decca spreads her arms
> Branching so broad and long, that in the ground
> The bending twigs take root, and daughters grow
> About the mother tree, a pillared shade
> High overarched, and echoing walks between;[2]

The banyan tree could not be grown in the British climate, though it became a staple item in pictures of India. Cedars, pines, firs, palms and planes, however, were all amongst the new species being introduced into Britain from the late sixteenth century onwards. By the eighteenth century they were familiar features in landscaped parks and botanic gardens, where they might be seen as a recreation of Paradise. Artists such as J. M. W. Turner and John Martin would use these exotic trees to populate an imaginary landscape (fig. 69), and in the case of Turner Italian, or hybrid trees appear in scenes that are nominally English. They played an important role in the work of those artists who travelled abroad and wished to convey the flavour of such desirable locations as the countryside around Rome, the Holy Land, India or the Pacific. The favourite trees of the artists discussed in this chapter were the stone pine, the cypress, the olive; the European larch and the Norway spruce; the palm, the acacia; the cedar of Lebanon; and the banyan. These are trees which, in painting, clearly designated a 'foreign' or an imaginary scene; or else, in the living landscape, they indicated a sophisticated arboretum or landscape park.

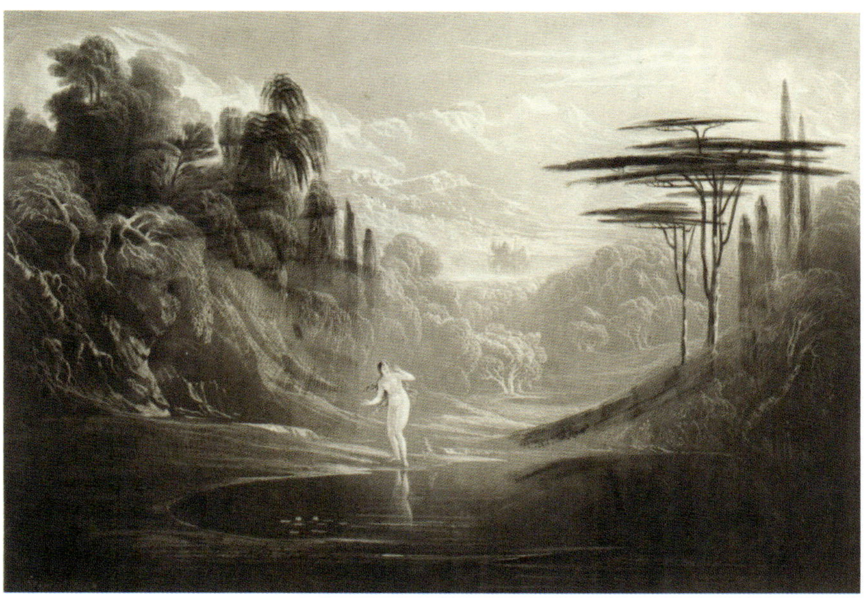

70 WILLIAM HODGES
A View in the Island of Otaheite
1773 | Pen and Indian ink wash, tinted with watercolour | 36.2 x 54 cm

The aesthetic interest in exotic trees had complex origins and justifications. The great variety of new trees being discovered and brought to Britain excited botanists and students of natural history, who recorded and classified them. The artists who travelled to uncharted locations, such as William Hodges (fig. 70), took pleasure in recording unfamiliar shapes and growth patterns. The origin of these trees in far-flung territories gratified national pride in the growth of the Empire, and catered to the desire both for tourism and for the vicarious delights of travel literature. As certain trees, notably the cedar of Lebanon, became common in gentlemen's parks, they also acquired social status and prestige. Those trees with their origins in Italy and the Middle East could be related to a knowledge of classical history and literature, and to scenes and prophecies in the Bible. For the landscape painter and the landscape gardener, imported trees offered new opportunities to contrast shapes, colours and textures. For the painter, stone pines, cypresses, cedars of Lebanon, palms, larches and spruces provided easily recognizable shapes and linear silhouettes, perhaps more satisfying – and easier – to draw than the abundant foliage of the British forest trees. And, in addition, the Italian trees would remind viewers and patrons of the works of the revered Old Masters, particularly Claude Lorrain. Artists and their patrons were relatively conservative, and most of the trees depicted were those already known, if not from art, then from literature. A newly-discovered tree was most exciting for the botanist, but for these trees to acquire resonance in art they needed, it seems, the associations and meanings developed over many centuries of human history. Hence, in this period, newly-discovered trees in Australia, South America or Africa made relatively little impact on British art, and this chapter will focus instead on the trees of Europe, the Middle East, India, and the Pacific.

Exotic trees were at first grown in botanical gardens such as the Physic Garden at Chelsea and Princess Augusta's garden at Kew (later to become the Royal Botanic Gardens), then in landscaped gardens and arboretums.[3] Capability Brown was so keen on the cedar of Lebanon, with its deep colour and graceful silhouette, that it became his signature tree.[4] Brown particularly appreciated the deep tones of foreign evergreens and of the larch tree, and planted American species, such as sumachs, which would produce brilliant reds and oranges in the autumn. This did not please everybody. William Chambers derided the sumachs as 'American weeds' and Humphrey Repton, on at least one occasion, suggested grubbing out Brown's larches and firs and replacing them with native birches and thorns.[5] Richard Payne Knight complained about the mixing of native and foreign trees, and called on 'Harmony' to banish the larch and the fir, preferring, in his own estate of Downton Vale, to use the deep tones of the native yew.[6] Nevertheless, Horace Walpole commented in 1770 that the introduction of foreign trees and plants had 'contributed essentially to the richness of colouring so peculiar to our modern landscape'. He singled out for particular approbation 'the mixture of various greens [and] the contrast of forms between our forest-trees and the northern and West-Indian firs and pines.'[7]

In the first half of the nineteenth century the taste for foreign trees gathered strength. In his treatise on *Useful and Ornamental Planting* (1832), George Sinclair, the head gardener of Woburn Abbey, describes some of the contrasts that could be achieved by mixing foreign and native species – the acacia with the oak, the black American walnut with the elm, the Spanish chestnut with the beech – and goes on to argue that the foreign species are also valuable because of the associations they invoke:

> … the interest arising from the adoption of foreign trees into domestic scenery is not confined to their picturesque effects. They remind us of the climes whence they come, or the scenes with which they were associated. In exploring a well-selected arboretum, the eternal snows of the Himalaya, the savannahs of the Missouri, the untrodden forests of Patagonia, the vallies [sic] of Lebanon, pass in review before us: we seem to wander in other climes, to converse with other nations.[8]

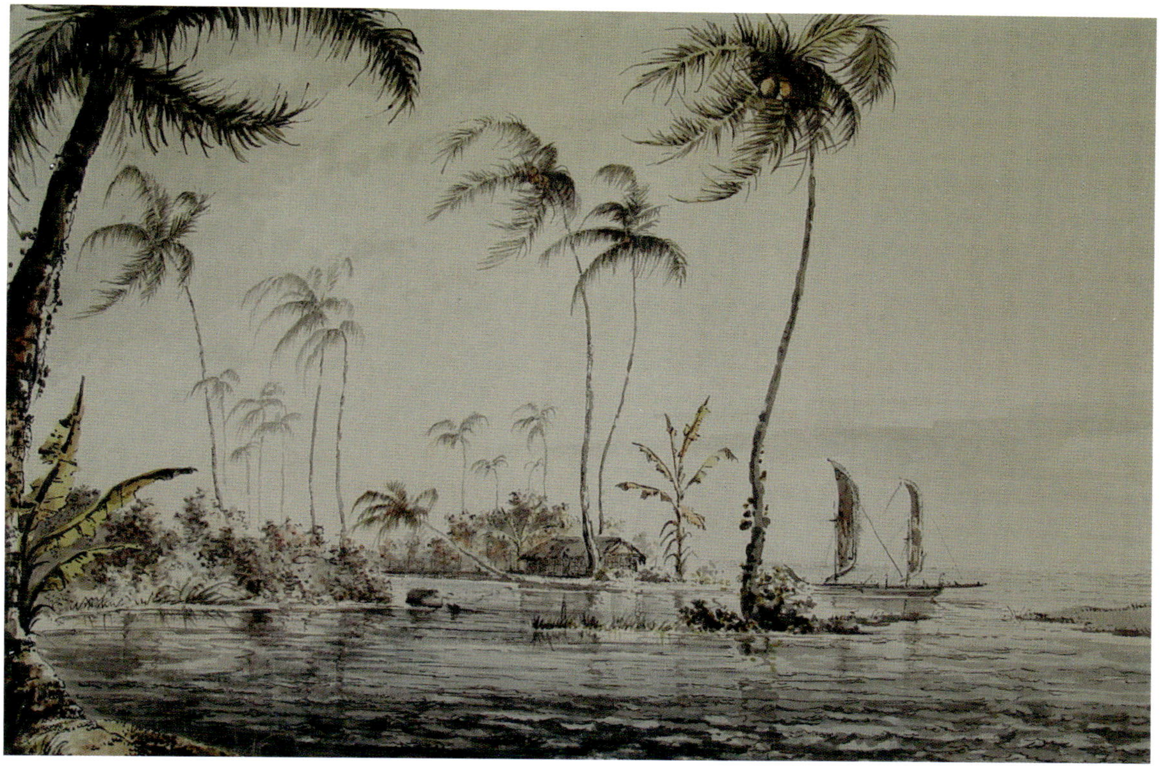

As we have seen, in 1838 Loudon, in his *Arboretum Britannicum*, argued that to plant foreign trees on a country estate was a sign of good taste.[9]

A rather extreme case of the preference for foreign trees was that of William Barron, head gardener at Elvaston Castle in Derbyshire, author of *The British Winter Garden* (1852). He admitted that he had always been 'passionately fond of evergreens' and he was contemptuous of the native deciduous trees, with their lack of shelter when it was most needed, their litter of decayed leaves, and their naked appearance in winter – 'an assemblage of leafless stems without either beauty of form or outline.' His attitude to some of the native species smacks of social snobbery, when he complains about other landowners, evidently regarding them as much less discerning than his own 'late noble employer', Charles Stanhope, the 4th Earl Harrington:

> What is so common as to see, even at the present day, close to our mansions, such commonplace things as elms, ashes, sycamores, poplars, or any other rubbish that the nearest provincial nursery may happen to be overstocked with …[10]

Barron writes eloquently of the aesthetic effects of evergreens, and the variety of shape, size and colour to be found amongst them. He praises, for example, the 'beauty of form or outline, from the formal Araucaria and fastigiated Junipers, to the wild grandeur of the pine, and even to the delicate, graceful, and flowing habits of the Cryptomeria Japonica, Funebral Cypress, Deodar Cedar, and Hemlock Spruce.'[11] Many of these foreign evergreens were planted in the new public arboretums and city parks that sprang up in the nineteenth century, with both aesthetics and practicality in mind. They provided colour and shelter all year round, and a minimum of litter in the autumn.[12] In this way an aesthetic originally propounded for an élite cascaded down to the general population.

Exotic trees also acquired prestige because of their literary and historical associations. The major books on trees – Evelyn's *Silva*, Gilpin's *Forest Scenery*, Strutt's *Sylva Britannica*, Loudon's *Arboretum Britannicum* – devote considerable amounts of space to the role of specific trees in biblical and classical history and literature. They quote from comments on trees, and accounts of famous specimens in Pliny's *Natural History* (79 CE), Virgil's *Georgics* (29 BCE) and Pausanius's *Description of Greece* (c.150 CE) – and, of course, from the Bible. Naturally, these accounts focused on trees that grew in the Middle East and the Mediterranean. Both Evelyn and Gilpin, for example, mention the great plane trees celebrated in Pliny's *Natural History*, in whose shade armies rested and emperors dined.[13] In praise of the

71 EDWARD LEAR
The Cedars of Lebanon
1861 | Oil on canvas | 68 x 113.5 cm
Private collection, Photo © Peter Nahum at The Leicester Galleries, London, Bridgeman Images

cedar of Lebanon (fig. 71), Gilpin cites Psalm 92 (verse 12): 'the righteous shall flourish like a palm-tree; and spread abroad like a cedar of Lebanon' and the prophet Ezekiel: 'the Assyrian was a cedar in Lebanon with fair branches, and a shadowing shroud, and of an high stature; and his top was among the thick boughs'.[14] Gilpin also mentions Milton's identification of the banyan as the tree in the Garden of Eden.[15] Strutt is mainly concerned with ancient oaks, and has only two exotics in his *Sylva Britannica*, the Enfield cedar and the plane tree at Lee Court. However, his commentary, too, mentions biblical and classical precedents: the sacred associations of the cedar and the stories of Socrates conversing in the shade of the plane.[16] Loudon is more interested in tracking the different species of trees, and he lists all those which are recorded in Theophrastus's *Historia Plantarum* (c.300 BCE), drawing on recent research to assign them their modern botanical names. This gives him a list of 170 species known to the ancient Greeks, of which he can say, with evident pride 'the whole ... with scarcely any exceptions, are in British gardens and hot-houses'.[17]

Most of the drawing manuals included exotics along with the native trees, though they usually placed the natives – especially the oak, beech, ash and elm – first. Alexander Cozens's *The Shape, Skeleton and Foliage of 32 Species of Trees* (1771) was particularly comprehensive. It included the cedar, cypress, larch-fir, spruce or Norway fir (that is, the Norway spruce, *picea abies*), palm, and 'Italian pine', but also the Spanish chestnut, horse chestnut, laburnum, laurel, walnut and weeping willow – 12 non-natives, of which we might say 6 were truly exotic. Other manuals included just a few non-native species, the larch being included in nearly all of them, often accompanied by the Norway spruce. The cedar of Lebanon and the acacia occur in most of the manuals, the stone pine and cypress less often. Kennion's *Essay on Trees in Landscape* (1815) includes the acacia, plane, cedar, spruce fir and larch in a total of 24 types. Harding's *The Park and the Forest* (1841) has a similar proportion, four exotics, the larch, cedar of Lebanon, plane and stone pine, out of a total of nineteen species. Barnard's *Trees from Nature* (1868) provides illustrations of 30 trees, of which eight are exotics: the larch, spruce fir, plane, acacia, stone pine, olive, cedar of Lebanon, and juniper. Burgess's *Eidodendron* (1827) specifically refers to foreign trees in its title, and accordingly includes a large number: the spruce fir, deciduous cypress, cedar of Lebanon, larch, red cedar, stone pine, Weymouth pine, silver fir, acacia, plane, ilex and cypress. All of these appear, however, to have been studied from specimens in Britain. By contrast, Barnard, in 1868, lists the places where he has studied his trees, including the coast of Genoa for four of them and Switzerland for five more, but he states that his series is 'almost entirely composed of those indigenous to our country', his definition of 'indigenous' perhaps accommodating any that were widely grown in Britain.[18] None of the manuals include the banyan tree, and hardly any the palm. Until we come to Barnard's publication, olive trees are also conspicuous by their absence.

INDIA AND THE PACIFIC: BANYANS AND PALMS

As we have seen, however, even when artists went to the Pacific and India, and depicted coconut palms and banyan trees, they could link these new types of tree with well-established prototypes that were hallowed by their biblical, or at least literary associations. This was true of William Hodges, who travelled to Polynesia with James Cook's second expedition, from 1772 and 1775. The Pacific islands were seen as an untouched Paradise, hence it was appropriate that their trees should include palm trees, even though these were tall, slender coconut palms (*cocos nucifera*), rather than the date palms of the Bible. The first sight of Tahiti, according to the botanical draughtsman on the expedition, George Forster, was of a plain covered with fertile bread-fruit trees 'over which rose innumerable palms, the princes of the grove'.[19] Hodges recorded their appearance in a fluent watercolour (fig. 70), which captures the curving silhouettes of the palm fronds in the wind,

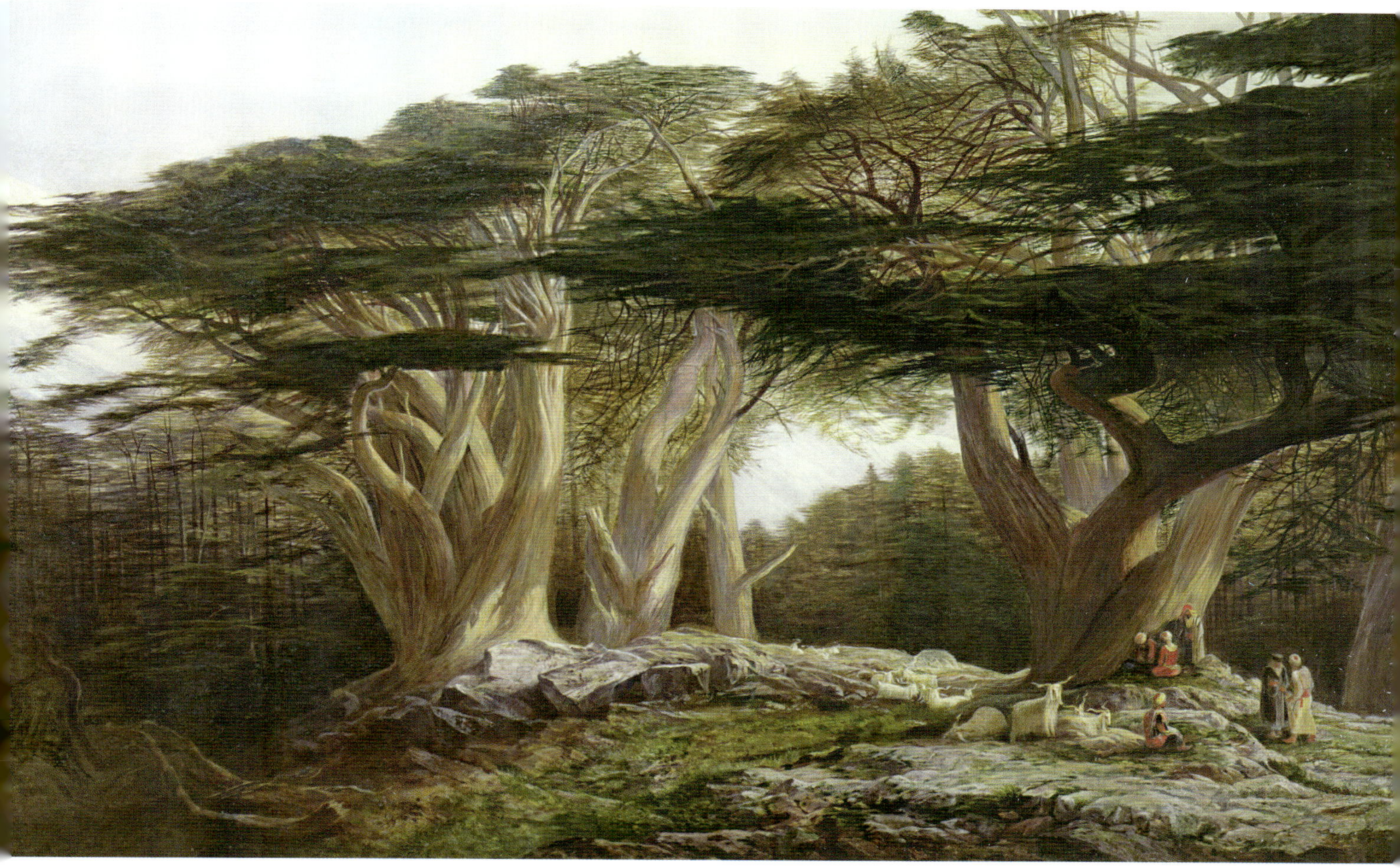

and the swaying motion and delicacy of their trunks. His inscription on the verso states that 'the plants ar[e] Coco Nut Tree & Plantain which are indigenous' and declares that they were 'Drawn from Nature.' These slender palms then became something of a trademark for Hodges's views of Tahiti, giving them an authentic air. Coconut palms also grow in India, where Hodges travelled under the patronage of the Governor-General, Warren Hastings, from 1780 to 1783. In one of his Indian views, *Tomb and distant View of the Rajmahal Hills* (c.1781, Tate Britain), a single coconut palm soars up into the sky, dwarfing the distant mountains and intensifying the impression of space on the plain below. This is also based on a study from nature, but in this case a comparison with the drawing shows that Hodges altered the line of the tree to make it even more fragile and serpentine.[20]

Hodges was followed to India by Thomas Daniell and his nephew William Daniell, who were there from 1786 till 1794. Amongst the large number of aquatints they produced, there are several views of banyan trees. One of the most impressive, *Hindoo Temples at Agouree, on the River Soane, Bahar* (fig. 68), frames the stone temples with a huge mature banyan tree whose aerial roots have descended to the ground to create the effect of a forest.[21] In the letterpress to their aquatints, the Daniells noted that temples were placed under banyans in the villages they visited, and that Hindu temples are 'exposed or half concealed among deep and solemn groves, no less holy in the popular opinion, than the edifices they shelter.'[22] The Daniells' positive attitude towards banyan trees was shared by Hodges, who linked them to the wise administration of his patron, Warren Hastings. Hodges wrote in his *Travels in India*, published in 1793:

> This is one of those curious productions in nature which cannot fail to excite the attention of the traveller. The branches of this tree having shoots depending from them, and taking root, again produce, and become the parents of others. These trees, in many instances, cover such an extent of ground, that hundreds of people may take shelter under them from the scorching rays

72 JOHN ROBERT COZENS
St Peter's from the Villa Borghese
1782–3 | Graphite and watercolour | 25.7 x 37 cm
Whitworth Art Gallery, The University of Manchester, Bridgeman Images

> of the sun. The care that was taken in the government, and the minute attention to the happiness of the people, rendered this district, at this time (1781) a perfect paradise. It was not uncommon to see the manufacturer at his loom, in the cool shade, attended by his friend softening his labour by the tender strains of music.[23]

William Gilpin, too, recognized the banyan as a sacred tree, now often inhabited by a Brahmin who 'spends his solitary hours in wandering among the verdant allies of his tree', praying for the inhabitants of the district who, in return, bring him 'the necessaries of life'.[24] The banyan tree benefited from associations with the Garden of Eden, and provided a parallel with the sacred groves of the Druids, or the trees which were thought to have given rise to the structures of Gothic cathedrals.

Thomas Daniell exhibited several paintings of banyan trees at the Royal Academy. In 1821 he showed a large picture, entitled 'The Sacred Tree of the Hindoos which contains an ancient temple and idol of Mahadan near Harduwar, on the river Ganges'.[25] This is a close-up view of an impressive tree, full of references to the strangeness of India. Monkeys perch on its branches, offerings hang above a central shrine in the trunk, Indians dance, play music or smoke hookahs on a platform beneath the tree, while sculptures of the sacred bull, Nandi, are visible in the foreground shade. The massive tree towers over the observer's low viewpoint. This painting was exhibited a year after Francis Danby's *Upas Tree* and provides a telling contrast to the barrenness and desolation of the earlier work. In contrast the painting of a banyan tree by Thomas's nephew William, exhibited in 1831 with the brief title of 'The Banyan Tree' is a much more scientific depiction, taken from a distance like Strutt's near-contemporary etchings of trees.[26] Here there are no signs of any shrine or temple, and the figures do not worship the tree but simply rest in its shade.

In addition to its appearance in Milton's *Paradise Lost*, the banyan tree was well known as a result of the description of it in Robert Southey's long epic poem, *The Curse of Kehama* (1810). This is often quoted in the books on trees. Rebecca Hey in 1837, for example, provides a long quotation from the poem, including these lines:

> T'was a fair scene wherein they stood,
> A green and sunny shade, amid the wood:
> And in the midst an aged banyan grew.
> It was a goodly sight to see
> That venerable tree, …
> So like a temple did it seem, that there
> A pious heart's first impulse would be prayer.[27]

Southey's lines recognize the sacred nature of the tree, and are similar to the way Strutt describes aged oaks in his *Sylva Britannica*. Hey, however, was writing two decades later, from a stance of Christian evangelicalism. She disparages the banyan as 'Idolatry's polluted shrine', and, in contrast to the positive views taken by Hodges and Gilpin, declares that 'Under the shadow of the banyan the Brahmins spend, or rather waste, much of their time in religious seclusion', praying to 'gods that cannot save'.[28] The changes in artists' representations of the tree would seem to parallel a decreasing tolerance towards the Hindu religion as British power in the region increased.

ITALY: STONE PINES AND CYPRESSES

More secular associations were stirred up by the classic trees of Italy: the stone pine (*pinus pinea*; also known as the umbrella pine) and the Italian cypress (*cupressus sempervirens*). These trees appear in the landscapes of Claude Lorrain and Richard Wilson. The stone pine, particularly, summed up the fragile beauty of the Italian landscape. Gilpin praised its aesthetic value:

> The foliage of the stone-pine is as beautiful as the stem. It's [sic] colour is a deep warm green; and it's [sic] form, instead of breaking into acute angles, like many of the pine-race, is moulded into a flowing line by an assemblage of small masses.[29]

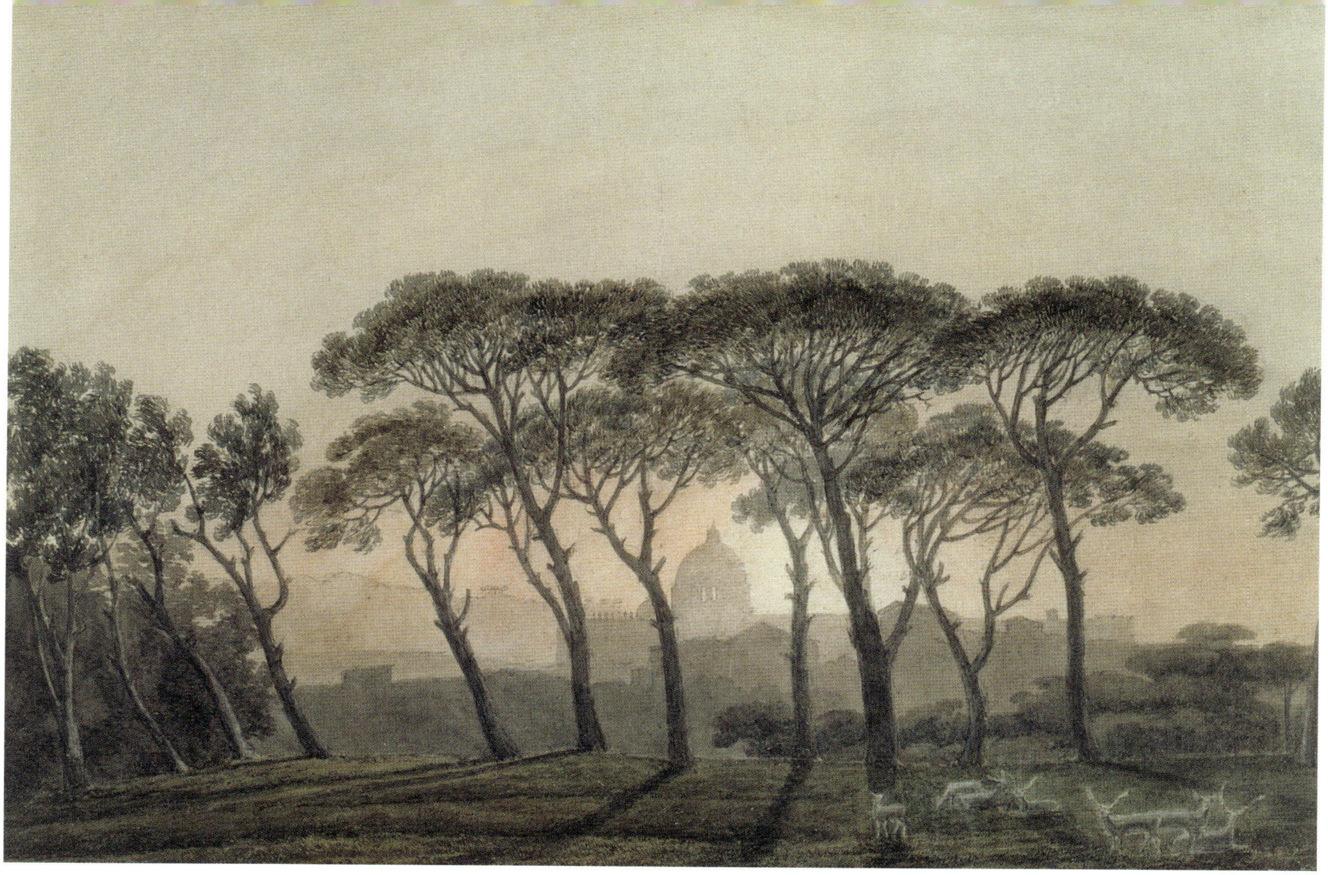

This 'flowing line' was particularly appreciated by artists. In 1832 George Sinclair described how its 'vast canopy, supported upon a naked column of great height, forms one of the chief and peculiar beauties in Italian scenery, and in the living landscapes of Claude.'[30] The cypress, in contrast to the stone pine, was appreciated for its compact form, its strong vertical emphasis and its very deep green, almost black colouring. The two trees were often combined in the gardens planted in the Renaissance, which had matured by the eighteenth century when they became popular sites for artists' sketching excursions. The contrasting shapes of the two trees were the basis for one of John Robert Cozens's series of etchings, published in 1789, based on a drawing he had done in the Villa Negroni in Rome. A similar group of trees in the same garden was sketched by the sculptor John Flaxman, who recorded in an inscription that they were 'planted by M. Angelo' [ie. Michelangelo].[31]

In the watercolours of the later eighteenth century, the role of trees in British country-house culture influenced artists' reaction to the Italian landscape, with an emphasis on those trees cultivated in gardens rather than growing in the wild or in agricultural areas. John Robert Cozens, the son of Alexander Cozens, travelled to Italy in the company, successively, of two English landowners who had a passionate interest in trees. Richard Payne Knight, who took him in 1776-8, was later to lay out his own estate, Downton Vale in Herefordshire, and write about trees in his poem *The Landscape*. William Beckford, the proprietor of Fonthill in Wiltshire, was the pupil and close friend of Alexander Cozens, who had taught him at Eton, and was already a positively pagan worshipper of trees on his 'Hill of Pan' before he travelled to Italy with J. R. Cozens in 1782.[32] It is hardly surprising, therefore, that Cozens's views of the Italian countryside, executed on these two trips, often feature sensitive drawings of trees. In a view of *Lake Albano*, from the first trip (Leeds City Art Gallery) a pair of slender stone pines occupies the foreground, their foliage filling the luminous sky like clouds. On the second trip he painted *St Peter's from the Villa Borghese* (fig. 72), in which the dome of the church is seen through a screen of stone pines against a softly glowing peach-coloured sky. The trees are generally more distinctive in shape on his second trip. In 1817 William Wordsworth, visiting Rome, saw a solitary pine tree on Monte Mario and was told that his friend Sir George Beaumont had bought it to save it from being felled. Wordsworth described it as 'one of the broad-topped pines, looking like a little cloud in the sky, with a slender stalk to connect it to its native earth', and wrote a poem about it, saying that it supplanted 'the whole majesty of Rome … /Crowned with St Peter's everlasting

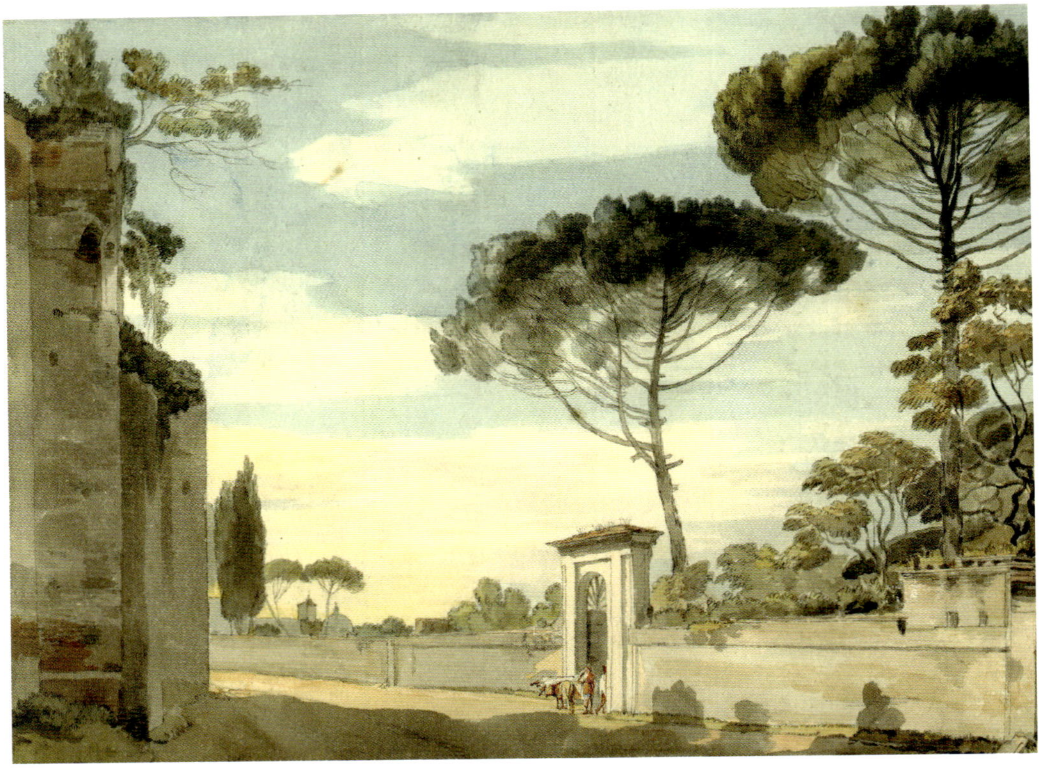

Dome.'[33] Sir George Beaumont, like Beckford, had been taught by Alexander Cozens at Eton and also owned several drawings by John Robert Cozens, which Wordsworth would have seen.

The stone pine also features in drawings by Thomas Jones and Francis Towne from the early 1780s. Towne's drawing of 1780, *Part of the Ancient Roman Wall between Porta Salaria and Porta Pinciana* (fig. 73) shows two large stone pines growing in a walled garden, their branches delicately brushed against the sky. Towne used this drawing as the basis for an oil painting of the same spot (now in Exeter, Royal Albert Memorial Museum), which he exhibited at the Royal Academy in 1800. Thomas Jones kept a journal while he was in Italy from 1776 to 1782, and his comments show that he had a good knowledge of trees, as well as of their depiction in paintings by the Old Masters Claude, Gaspard Poussin and Salvator Rosa. His sensitivity to trees can, perhaps, be linked to his background as a member of a landowning family, and in his comments on the trees of Italy he makes a clear distinction between the countryside and the gardens. In the Roman Campagna he noted 'Groves & Walks of the finest and most luxuriant forest Trees imaginable – The Ilex, Chesnut, Plane, Oak & Wallnut [sic] grow to an Amazing Size, to which we may add the Noble Pines & Cypresses which are planted in the Gardens & Vineyards.'[34] He contrasted this to Tivoli, where the olive trees were not large enough to provide the shaded foreground he was familiar with in Claude's paintings. He agreed that the scenery, which he thought had shaped Gaspard Poussin's approach to landscape, was beautiful:

> But here is wanting the large Umbrageous Tree – to deck the foreground – The Plantations being chiefly Olive, which growing thin & stragling [sic], cast not the Venerable Shade of the Forest – though, in the distance – they have a good Effect ...[35]

Jones took Francis Towne up to Santa Maria dei Monti, near Naples, which reminded him of Salvator Rosa's works:

> Here may visibly be traced the Scenery that Salvator Rosa formed himself upon – only taking away the Pinetrees [sic], which were, perhaps, planted since his time, and which indicate a State of Cultivation not suited to his gloomy mind ...[36]

Jones' watercolour, *In the Road to Santa Maria dei Monti, near Naples* (fig. 74), shows these stone pines in the middle distance, emerging from the rocky hillside like mushrooms, their forms echoed in the clouds above.

In his journal, Thomas Jones also noted 'a large *Plane* tree on the Edge of the Water call'd the *Arbor Santa*, which

73 FRANCIS TOWNE

Part of the Ancient Roman Wall between Porta Salaria and Porta Pinciana, Rome

1780 | Pen and grey ink with grey wash and watercolour

20.7 x 27.1 cm | © The Trustees of the British Museum

74 THOMAS JONES

In the Road to Santa Maria dei Monti, near Naples: Morning

1781 | Graphite and watercolour | 21.1 x 27.8 cm

© Tate, London 2017

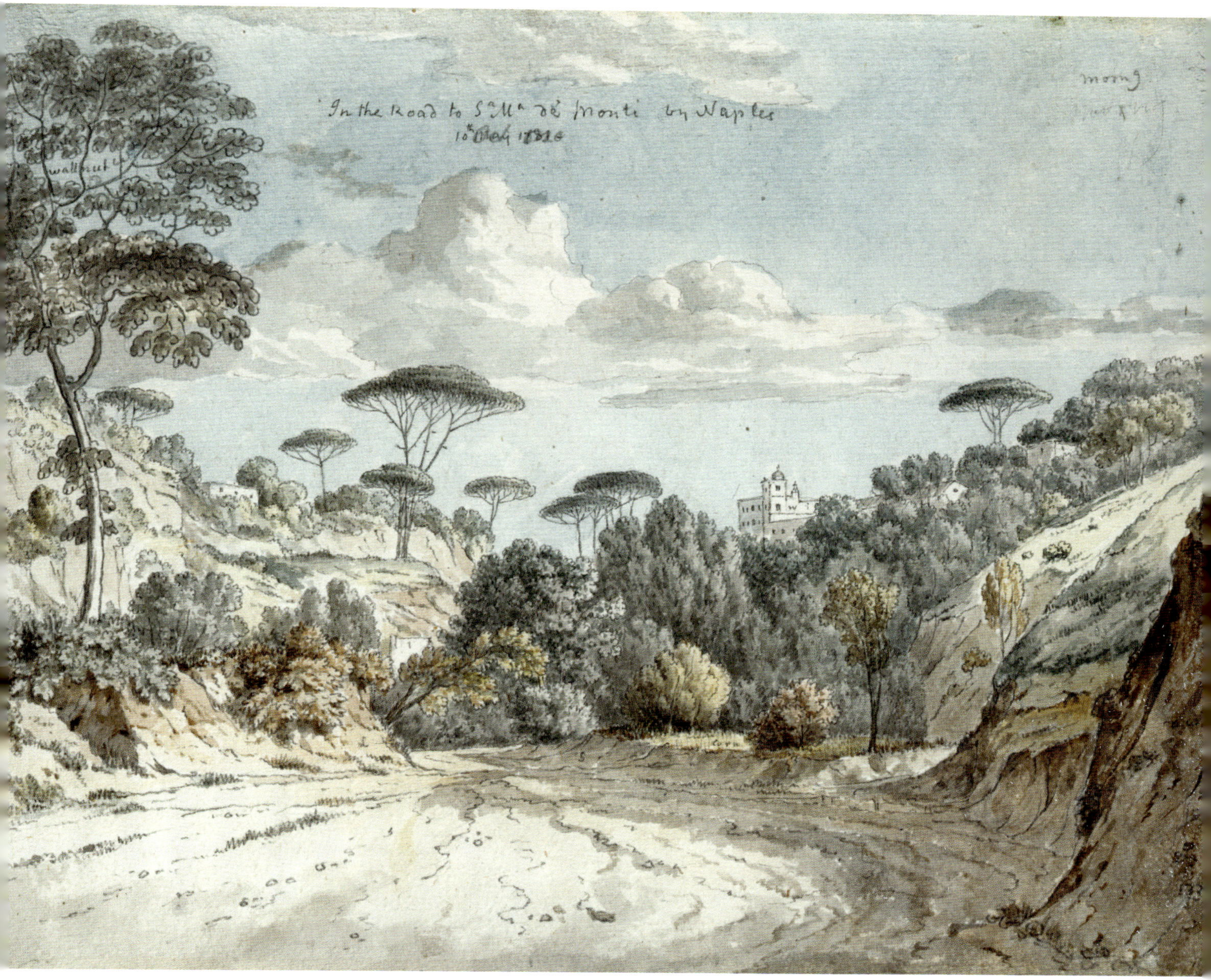

75 J. M. W. TURNER
Mer de Glace, in the Valley of Chamouni, Switzerland
1803 | Watercolour and graphite | 70.5 x 104.1 cm
Yale Center for British Art, Paul Mellon Collection

76 J. M. W. TURNER
Whalley Bridge and Abbey, Lancashire
c.1811 | Private Collection
Image © Ashmolean Museum, University of Oxford (LI197.5)

has a hollow within that I believe w'd contain a dozen persons & I was told here that my Old Master *Wilson* when in this country made use of it as a Study to paint in –'[37] A drawing of this tree by Richard Wilson, dating from 1754-6, is now in the Yale Center for British Art. It shows a large, rambling tree, with three subsidiary trunks joined at the base, where three hollow spaces could, indeed, serve as artists' studios. The drawing is similar to the portraits of ancient trees being produced in Britain in the eighteenth century, which record, and perhaps even exaggerate, the irregularity of the forms and the ravages of time. The result is, therefore, very different from the slender, elegant, ideal trees which populate the painted landscapes of Wilson and his pupils, and, indeed, of Claude himself. Another contrast to the focus on elegant Italian trees in this period is a drawing by Francis Towne of an olive tree, entitled *A Study on the Spot at Tivoli* (1781, Tate Britain). This concentrates on the gnarled trunk and roots of the mature tree, clinging to a rocky hillside: the rocks take up the larger part of the picture space and the tree is relegated to a small corner of the paper. It is indeed 'thin & stragling' in Jones's terms.

J. M. W. TURNER: TREES DOMESTIC AND FOREIGN

A different kind of contrast to the formal, garden-like beauty of Italy was provided by the trees of Switzerland. Here the predominant trees were the European larch (*larix decidua*) and the Norway spruce (*picea abies*), often called, in this period, the spruce fir: spiky, pointed trees which thrived in harsh conditions, and whose forms lent sublimity to a landscape painting. Sir Thomas Dick Lauder, in his edition of Gilpin, published in 1834, described the way their dark, distinctive shapes were set off by the bright whiteness of snow and the jagged forms of rocks and mountains:

> What can be more truly sublime than to behold … the glazed white summits of Mont Blanc, or the Jungfrau, rising over the interminable forests of spruce firs which clothe the bases of the mountains, whilst … gigantic specimens … rise in groups among the rocks before us, many of them shivered, broken, and maimed by tempests, their dark forms opposed to all the brilliant prismatic hues of some immense gorgeous glacier …[38]

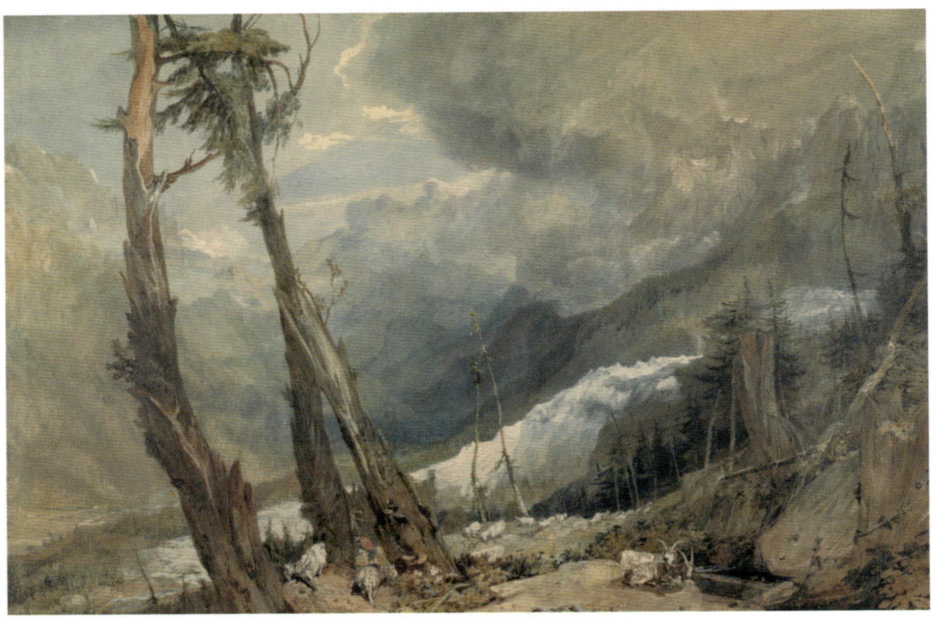

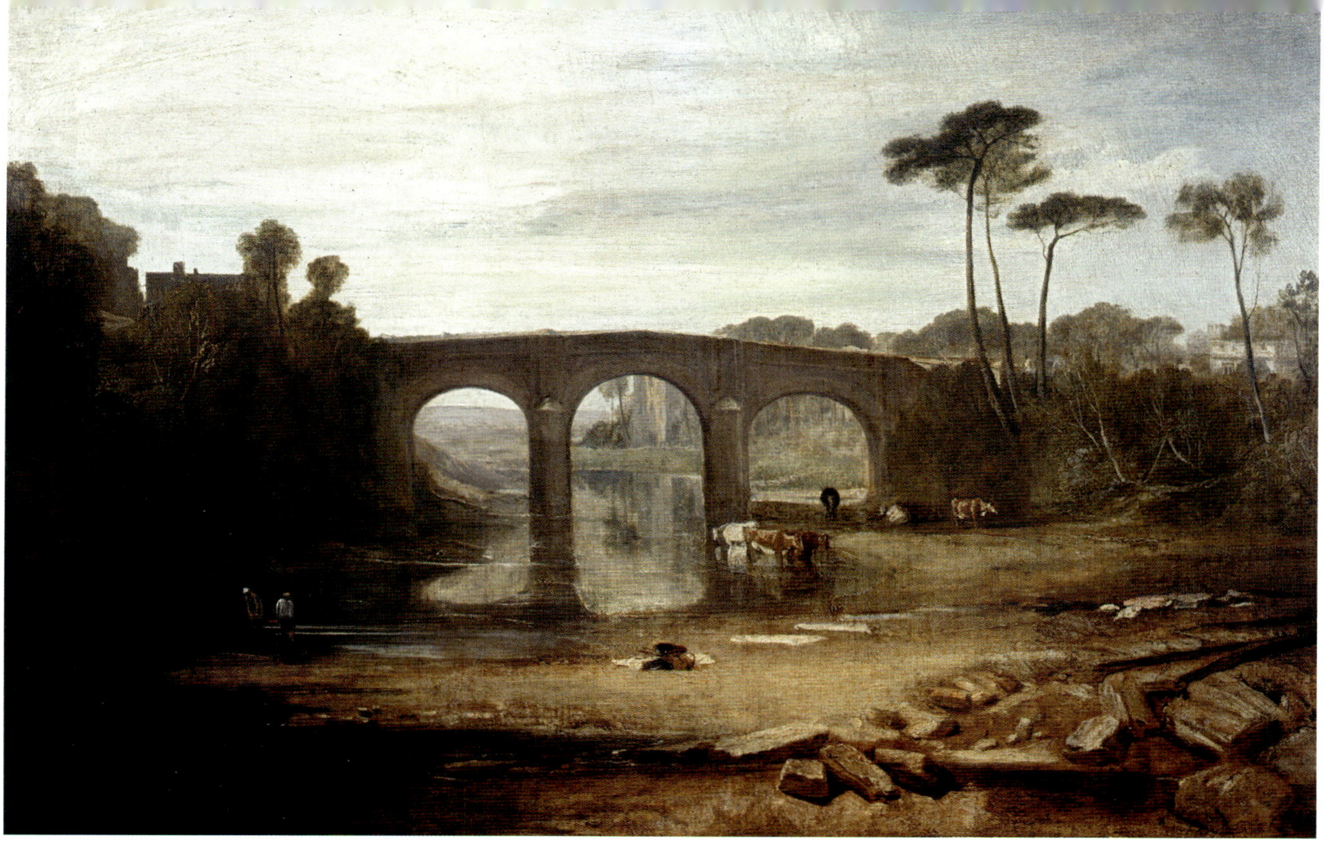

Trees like these cling precariously to the mountains in J. R. Cozens's *Entrance to the Grand Chartreuse* (Ashmolean Museum), where their diminutive size creates an impression of vast height. Seen in close up, their spindly forms are contrasted with a pillar of rock and a rushing torrent in Francis Towne's drawing, *Near Mount Splügen* (Tate Britain), of 1781. They are at their most sublime, however, in J. M. W. Turner's *Mer de Glace, in the Valley of Chamouni, Switzerland* (fig. 75), a watercolour based on studies made on his first trip abroad in 1802. Here, huge irregular trees and shattered stumps in the foreground demonstrated the force of the Alpine storms, while the repeated triangular forms of further trees diminish rapidly in scale to suggest great distances. It may well have been this watercolour, or another one like it, that prompted Lauder's comment above.

J. M. W. Turner was exposed to the works of the earlier generation of travellers to Italy and Switzerland, and especially to J. R. Cozens, whose watercolours he copied in his unofficial 'training' with Dr Thomas Monro in the 1790s. As a result, he seems to have formed his taste in trees largely from these eighteenth-century exemplars, as much as from Claude. In his British landscapes, Turner shows a preference for slender trees, such as Scots pines and willows, rather than the major forest trees, oak, ash, beech and elm, and sometimes his supposedly British trees look remarkably Italianate. Turner made detailed studies of forest trees at an early stage in his career. Watercolours of parkland trees – beeches at Norbury Park, Leatherhead and an oak tree at Hampton Court, Herefordshire – have been dated c.1796, and demonstrate a careful study of the branching and foliage.[39] On 30 October 1799 the diarist Joseph Farington records that Turner has been 'in Kent painting from beech trees.'[40] A group of oil sketches of woodland scenes from around that time concentrate on the trunks and the light between beech trees, with the odd occasional sweep of autumn foliage.[41] In two early oils, *Newark Abbey* (c.1807, Yale Center for British Art) and *The Forest of Bere* (1808, Petworth House) the forms of the trees, pollarded willows and chestnuts respectively, are skilfully delineated. In both these paintings, the trees are relatively small and transparent, with visible branching in the foreground examples, while those behind have their forms softened by mist. The trees look authentically English, but the paintings hardly do justice to the variety and massiveness of trees in the countryside.

In contrast to Turner's early English trees, the stone pines in *Whalley Bridge and Abbey, Lancashire* (fig. 76) are as delicate as anything in J. R. Cozens, even though Turner, at this stage in his career, had not visited Italy. Their beautifully-shaped heads act like clouds in the sky, while their slender trunks seem to sway slightly in the breeze. In other paintings, Turner seems deliberately to

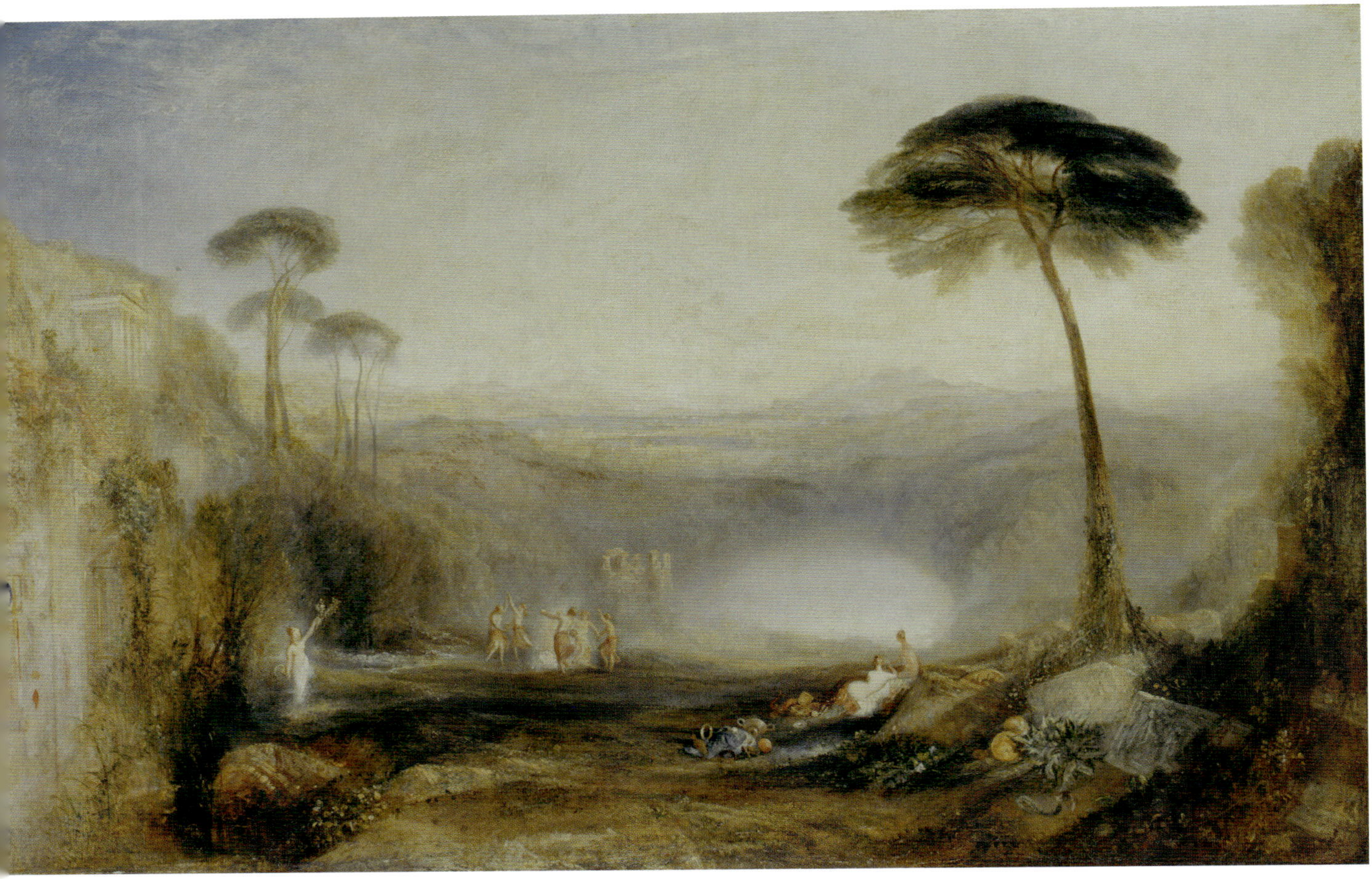

have adopted Italianate tree forms in an attempt to raise the status of his landscapes. Their grand scale and composition certainly suggest that he was setting out to challenge Claude. *Thomson's Aeolian Harp* (1809, Manchester Art Gallery) and *Richmond Hill, on the Prince Regent's Birthday* (1819, Tate Britain) are both views of the Thames, but the trees, especially in the latter, are tall and slender, and of indeterminate species. They could possibly be Scots pines, but they look rather more like Italian stone pines. The same could be said of the foreground trees in *Crossing the Brook* (fig. 11). It is a Devonshire landscape, but there are no trees like this in any of the preliminary sketches or drawings. Yet the main tree is remarkably detailed, with crooked angles and stumps on the branches which suggest that it is a portrait of an actual tree. John Ruskin had a high opinion of Turner's tree-drawing. He made a careful study of part of this group, in a neutral tint, 'to show its complexities of light and shade', and donated it to the Ruskin School of Drawing in Oxford, for the use of the art students of the future.[42] In his commentary on the drawing, he specified that the trees were 'a group of Scotch firs', that is Scots pines, but their feathery foliage has confused modern commentators, who have sometimes identified them as ash trees.[43]

By the time Turner finally got to Italy in 1819, then, he had already painted many Italianate trees. He rarely made studies of trees on his travels. In the Italian landscapes of his maturity, such as *Childe Harold's Pilgrimage* (1832, Tate Britain), there is often only a single tree, a tall stone pine with a slender trunk and a compact head of foliage, which became a kind of signature tree for him. Although the general effect of such landscapes is usually characterized as 'Claudian', Turner's use of trees is actually very different from Claude's. When stone pines occur in Claude's work, they are usually much wilder-looking and less symmetrical, and they are accompanied by other kinds of tree, beeches or chestnuts, the 'Umbrageous tree' to 'deck the foreground' and to provide his famous sidescreens of framing trees and foreground shade. In Turner's painting, *The Golden Bough* of 1834 (fig. 77) one of these symmetrical stone pines on the right is answered on the left by a group of six, but they are even more frail in appearance, more like clouds than trees.

77 J. M. W. TURNER
The Golden Bough
1834 | Oil on canvas | 104.1 x 163.8 cm
© Tate, London 2017

IDEAL LANDSCAPE: JOHN MARTIN AND SAMUEL PALMER

Turner's trees made an impact on John Martin, whose *Characters of Trees* (1817) includes a very tall pine, its foliage delineated in a way similar to Turner's trees, with dark masses in the foreground and lighter foliage behind. Martin never travelled abroad; yet he produced designs of foreign trees – pines, firs, cedars and palms – in scenes representing Paradise, which became very influential through their reproduction in the form of prints. He would have seen some of these exotic trees in landscaped parks, such as Sezincote House, Gloucestershire, where he made studies for a set of aquatints in 1817.[44] The gardens at Sezincote were designed by Humphrey Repton in an 'oriental' style with assistance from the painter Thomas Daniell, epitomizing the reciprocal influence between painting and landscape gardening in this period. Martin's series of mezzotints to illustrate Milton's *Paradise Lost* (1824-5) required him to give visual form to the trees specified in the poem, and he used his imagination to make these trees look at once familiar and outlandish. *Eve at the Fountain* (fig. 69), for example, includes a pair of strange trees with horizontal layers of foliage: presumably they are meant to be cedars of Lebanon, but they are much taller than any specimens Martin could have seen. Their trunks are slender and delicate, their foliage cloud-like. Very tall cypresses rise up behind them. In other plates Martin depicts palm trees, which, again, are very tall and slender, more like the coconut palms of the Pacific than the date palms of the Middle East. In this emphasis on the soaring height of the exotic trees, Martin was, of course, being faithful to Milton's original text with its mention of 'Insuperable height of loftiest shade'. Trees like these appear also in Martin's exhibited oil paintings, such as *The Eve of the Deluge* (1840, Royal Collection) and *The Plains of Heaven* (1854, Tate Britain).

Another painter of ideal landscape was Samuel Palmer; unlike Martin, he did travel to Italy and the exotic trees in his paintings are based on careful studies from nature. In the 1846 edition of *Modern Painters*, Ruskin wrote of Palmer 'I have never seen a stone pine or a cypress drawn except by him' – an astonishing tribute from the great champion of Turner.[45] Most modern commentators would agree that it is well deserved. Palmer, as we have seen, was already very skilled at tree drawing before he went to Italy on his long honeymoon from 1837 to 1839. The most famous drawing he did there (and the one that Ruskin may have seen) is *The Cypresses at the Villa d'Este* (fig. 78). These trees were widely celebrated and many artists had drawn them before, including William Collins, who had shown his study of them to Palmer.[46] Palmer's watercolour is inscribed 'drawn on the spot' and as far as one can tell, he has made no attempt to idealize the trees, transcribing all their oddities and imperfections such as broken branches and asymmetrical foliage. The use of watercolour, touched with pale green and white in the highlights, especially in the trees on the left, gives a real sense of volume. As a result, the trees seem alive and individual. Many years later, Palmer wrote to a young friend and pupil 'One might draw the cypresses in the Villa d'Este for a year and not exhaust them.'[47] Palmer's fondness for the cypresses means that, more often than not, his Italian landscapes focus on cypresses rather than stone pines. Stone pines, if included, are often subordinate. In *A Dream in the Appenine* (1864, fig. 79) the screen of trees on the right, which mask the sunset, is composed mostly of cypresses with just one stone pine. However, in a late watercolour, *The Golden City: Rome from the Janiculum* (1873, National Gallery of Victoria, Melbourne), three majestic, finely detailed stone pines rise above a vision of Rome bathed in a sunset glow, while a row of cypresses on the right leads the eye down the hill towards the city. Palmer never visited Italy again after 1839, so the trees in his later landscapes are based on the studies he had made there, transformed by the effects of memory and imagination.

78 SAMUEL PALMER

The Cypresses at the Villa d'Este

1838 | Watercolour, gouache and graphite on blue paper | 31.4 x 23.2 cm

Yale Center for British Art, Paul Mellon Collection

79 SAMUEL PALMER

A Dream in the Appenine

1864 | Watercolour and gouache | 66 x 101.6 cm

© Tate, London 2017

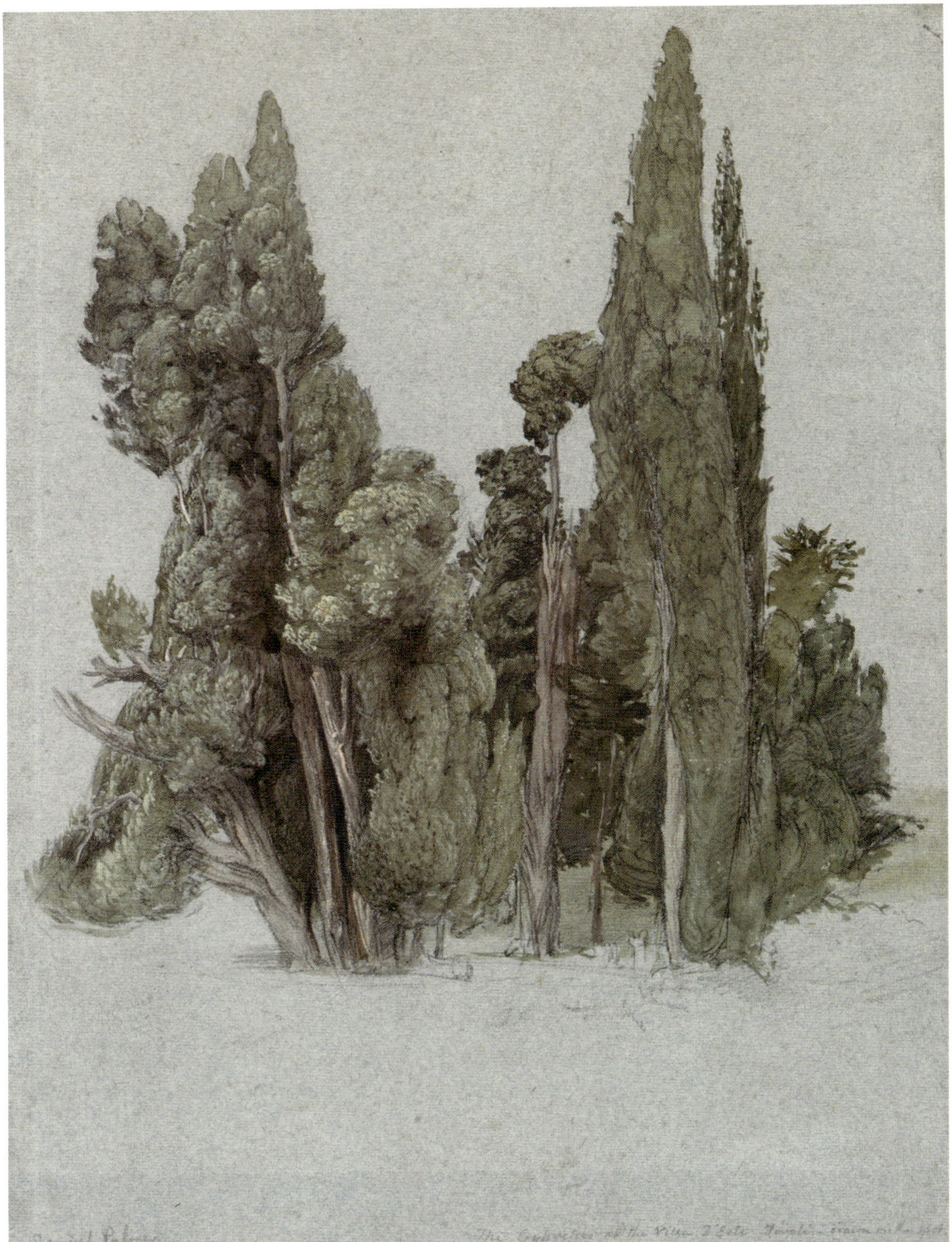

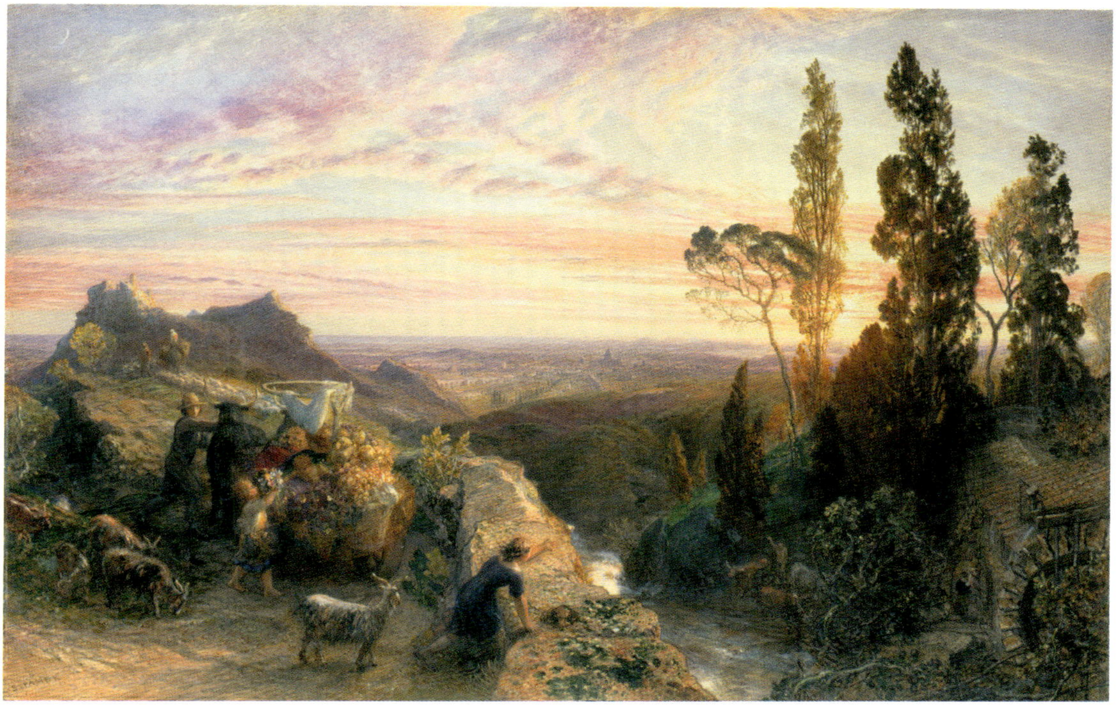

EDWARD LEAR: A LIFE OF TRAVEL

Palmer's enthusiasm for trees is matched by that of Edward Lear – but in Lear's case, the study of exotic trees covered a much wider geographical spread and occupied him over a lengthy career of travelling and living abroad. Lear's knowledge of trees was prodigious, he wrote extensively about them, and he was constantly prepared to be open to new experiences. On his first visit to Italy he fell in love with the olive trees which earlier travellers had ignored or disparaged; in the 1850s and later he was in Egypt, equally delighted with palms growing near age-old temples or newly-planted acacias; in 1868 he recorded his changing reactions to the pine forests of Corsica; in 1873-4, by then in his sixties, he was amazed by the variety of trees in India. He was particularly sensitive to the contrasts between the natural, curving, irregular growth patterns of trees and the more geometric lines of architectural or rock formations: one of his most successful oil paintings was a view of the Temple of Bassae in Greece, framed by luxuriant oak trees whose massive trunks had once provided the prototype for earlier wooden versions of such buildings. Lear's private letters and journals, and his published accounts of his travels, provide ample evidence of the attraction he felt towards trees. Most of his studies of trees are watercolours or drawings, but his most ambitious tree subject was a large oil painting, nine feet wide, of the famous cedars of Lebanon. His writings show that he admired the trees of Turner and Martin, but, unlike these earlier artists, his practice depended heavily on study on the spot. His enthusiasm for the variety of species of trees seems to have been based, not exclusively on a religious world-view (despite the attention he lavished on the Lebanon cedars) but rather on a scientific appreciation of the diversity apparent in natural history. A liberal and a rationalist in matters of religion, Lear was apparently stimulated, rather than challenged, by the ideas of Darwin.[48] At the same time, this scientific approach was combined with a warm emotional response to his subject matter.

When Lear first travelled to Italy in 1837, he was well prepared for drawing trees. His work on ornithology had trained him to make accurate observations, and introduced him to the classification of species. As we saw in Chapter Three, he had also undergone a self-imposed course of study of trees, using drawing manuals by J. D. Harding and others. He saw his first olive trees at Lecco, on his way to Rome, and wrote to his sister Ann 'I think them very beautiful, more like a huge lavender bush, or a fine grey willow than anything else, and all over green olives.'[49] When he made drawings of Tivoli, he placed the olives that Thomas Jones had described as 'thin & stragling [sic]' in the foreground,

80 EDWARD LEAR
Tivoli
28 September 1838 | Black chalk and Chinese white on tan paper
30.5 x 45 cm | Ms Typ 55.26, no. 123
Houghton Library, Harvard University

81 EDWARD LEAR
The Temple of Apollo at Bassae
c.1854–5 | Oil on canvas | 146.4 x 229.5 cm

lavishing attention on their twisting trunks and branches (fig. 80), with the villa at Tivoli and its famous waterfalls visible only in the distance, in a gap between the trees. Lear also travelled extensively in Greece and Albania, and his favourite place was Corfu, of which he wrote 'The extreme gardeny verdure – the fine olives, cypresses, almonds, and oranges, make the landscape so rich.'[50] Lear preferred the countryside, where the trees grew in a semi-wild state, to the formal gardens that had impressed his eighteenth-century predecessors, and he also seems to have had a fondness for trees useful to mankind, such as fruit or nut trees. Later in life, on seeing Corfu again, he made this note in his diary: 'the loved olive ... No wonder the Olive is undrawn – unknown: so inaccessible = poetical = difficult are its belongings.'[51] In an oil painting, *Corfu From Ascension* (c. 1860, Yale Center for British Art) he juxtaposes an olive grove with snow-capped mountains in the distance and ruins in the foreground. There are some goats near the ruins, but the olive trees seem even more alive than the animals, their trunks swaying like the movements of graceful dancers.

The contrast between trees and buildings is developed further in Lear's large oil painting, originally entitled *The Temple of Bassae or Phigaleia, in Arcadia, from the Oakwoods of Mt Cotylium* (fig. 81). This was a view of a monument in a remote location, the temple of Apollo Epicurius, which the architect C. R. Cockerell had excavated in the early years of the century, and which was well known in Britain because the frieze was removed and placed in the British Museum in 1815. Lear devoted much more attention to the oak trees in the painting than to the temple, which he represents inaccurately, without

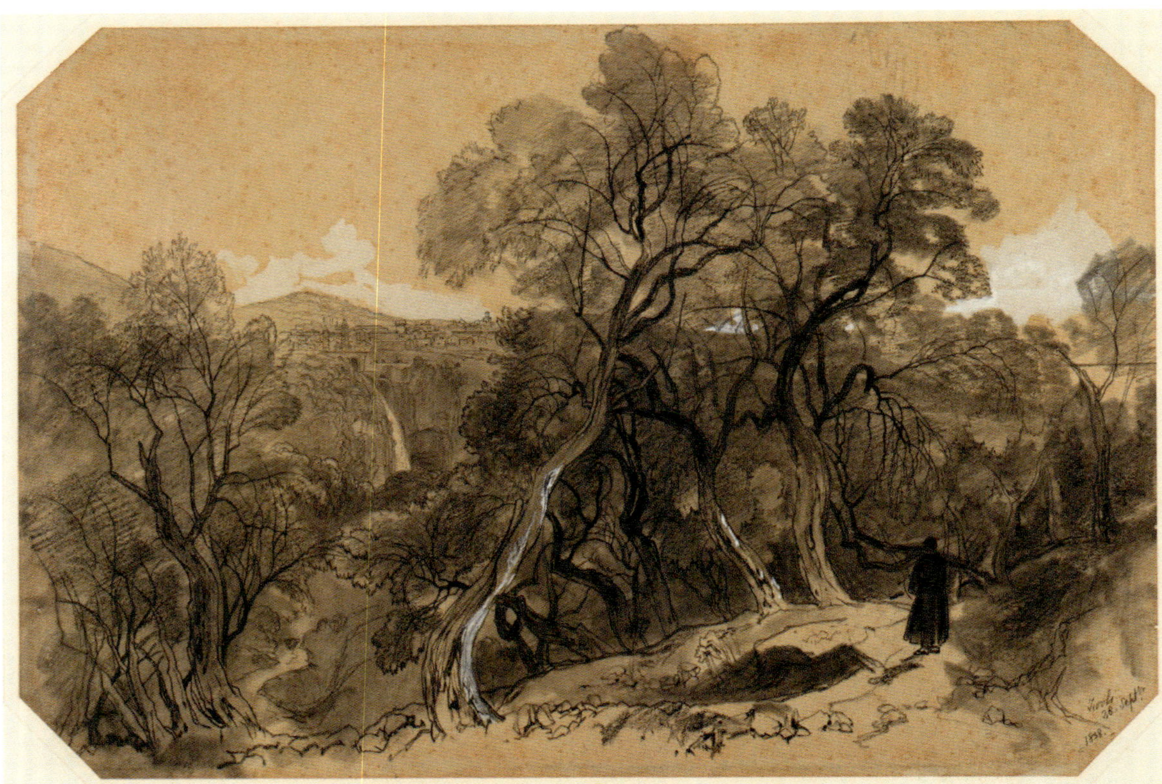

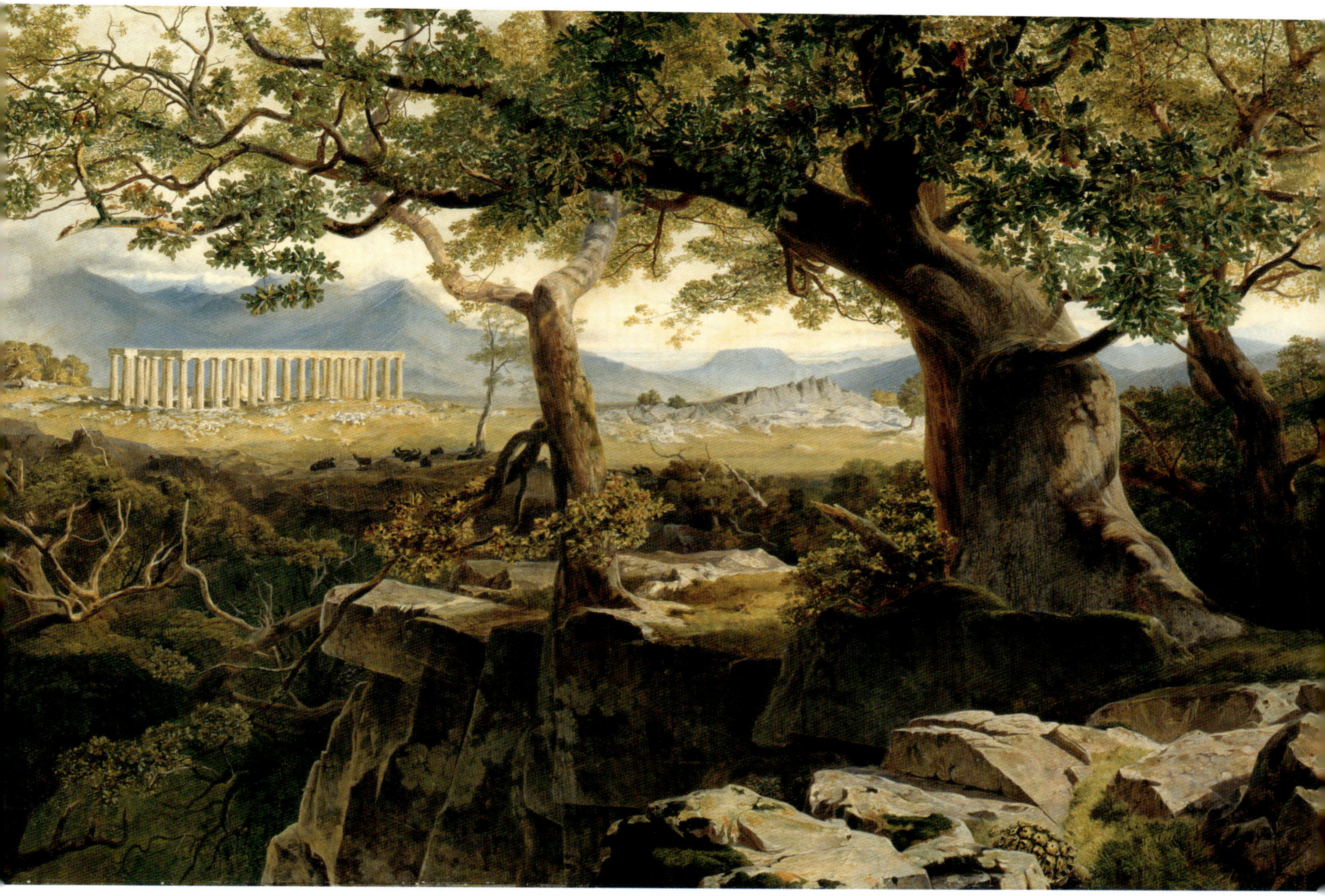

its internal cella. The trees are of the same species as the English oak (*quercus robur*) – and therefore exotic only in their setting and accompaniments. They are shown growing out of the rock, inviting reflections on the relationship of architecture to natural materials and forms. The idea is similar to that of Constable's *Salisbury Cathedral from the Bishop's Grounds* (fig. 6), in which the framing arch of the elm trees suggests the origins of Gothic architecture. Lear made watercolour studies on the spot in March 1849, and in these, too, he devoted more attention to the trees, and the overall setting, than to the temple itself.[52] The painting of the oil version was, however, done in England, in the autumn of 1853, when Lear was trying to follow Pre-Raphaelite principles under the direction of Holman Hunt. Presumably he felt justified in doing this as the oaks were of the same kind, although in Greece they would have grown faster and produced less dense timber. He found oil painting out of doors a frustrating experience, as he wrote to Hunt:

> I got oak boughs indoors, but did no good by so doing … if I could only get the leaves done, and one little bit of fern, I could get the branches and rocks easily. But the leaves are falling fast …[53]

Lear exhibited the painting in 1855 at the Royal Academy, where it was generally well received, though one critic found that 'the foliage of the trees betrays an excessive amount of labour' and another wrote 'We cannot quite account for that oak-tree rising from the solid rock; but still believe in some secret marble cleft in which its roots burrow … the oak trunks are serpentine and bossy.'[54] The painting was bought by a group of subscribers and presented to the Fitzwilliam Museum, Cambridge, in 1860.

Lear travelled widely in Greece, Albania and Egypt in the late 1840s and early 1850s. Wherever he went, he was particularly attracted by the lushness and variety of the vegetation. Vivien Noakes describes him arriving in Cairo

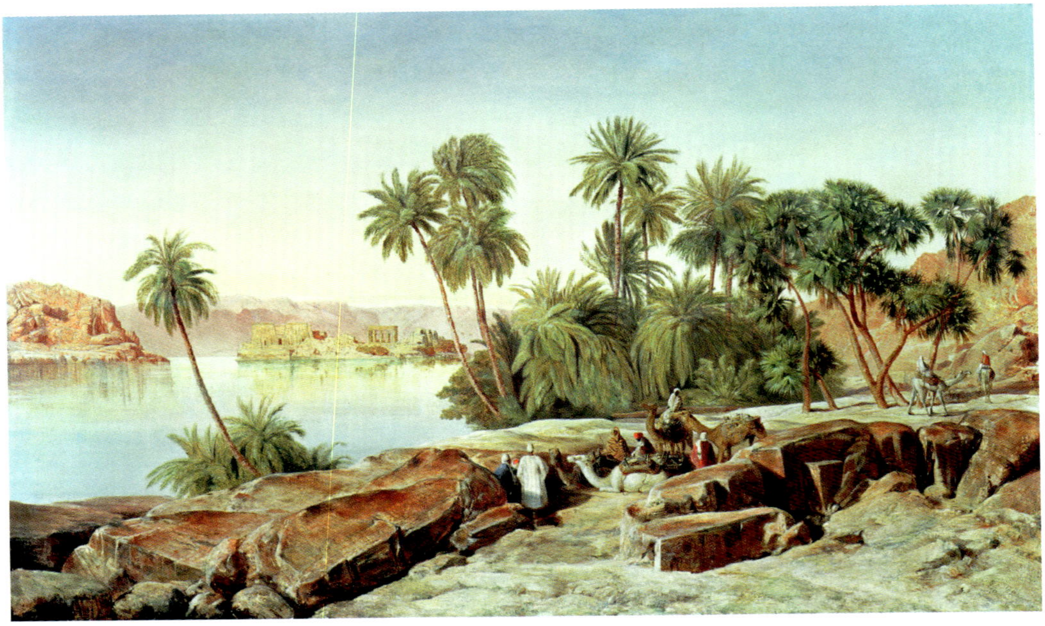

in December 1853, where his hotel room looked out over a garden of high palms and green acacia trees, filled with doves, kites and crested hoopoes – all the rich, colourful beauty he had missed in a dark, damp London winter.[55] John Frederick Lewis's painting, *Study for The Courtyard of the Coptic Patriarch's House in Cairo* (c.1864, Tate Britain), with its doves in a green acacia tree in a sunlit courtyard, provides a visual parallel to Lear's description. Lear painted innumerable watercolours, and at least 20 oils of the temple of Philae on the Nile, usually accompanied by the date palms growing nearby.[56] In one painting, Philae is viewed, like the temple of Apollo at Bassae, through a screen of trees, in this case palm trees (fig. 82). On the back of the canvas, Lear inscribed lines from a poem by his friend Alfred Tennyson, 'You ask me why, tho' ill at ease'. This is a poem which praises England as the land of freedom but expresses a longing for warmer climes, ending 'And I will see before I die/ The palms and temples of the South'.[57] Lear himself was similarly torn by the competing attractions of England and the Mediterranean. On a later visit to Egypt in 1873, he saw the acacia avenue that had been planted only five years earlier by the Empress Eugénie of France along a new road leading to the Pyramids. His oil painting, *The Pyramids Road, Gizeh* (private collection) shows extremely lush trees, their foliage filling more than half the picture space, shading a broad causeway 'in the middle of wide waters' with the pyramids visible on the horizon in the misty distance.[58]

The tree which impressed Lear most in the Middle East, however, was the fabled cedar of Lebanon. The famous writers on trees had cited travellers' accounts suggesting that only a very few trees were left on Mount Libanus. Alexander Hunter, in his commentary on Evelyn's *Silva*, said that they were 'preserved with a religious strictness' and the focus of celebrations involving thousands of priests and monks.[59] By this time (1776) cedars of Lebanon were, of course, well known from English botanic gardens and country estates. Gilpin, however, claimed that they grew perfectly only in Lebanon. In England they were strong or beautiful – never both together: 'in its youth we have some idea of its beauty without its strength; and in its advanced age we have some idea of its strength without its beauty'.[60] Lear had every reason to suppose, therefore, that a large oil painting of the cedars, based on sketches he had made on the spot, would arouse interest and sales. His first thought when he saw the cedars, in May 1858, was of John Martin's paintings. He wrote to his sister:

> So fine a view I suppose can hardly be imagined – more perhaps like one of Martin's ideal pictures … I cannot tell you how delighted I was with those cedars! – those enormous old trees – a great dark grove – utterly silent, except the singing of birds in numbers'.[61]

The parallel horizontal strokes he uses for the foliage, particularly in his sketches, are similar to the shapes in Martin's print, *Eve at the Fountain*, but Lear's drawing of the trunks and branches is quite different. The trees are chunky yet elegant, uniting beauty with strength, as Gilpin (who had not been there) said they would. Lear's oil painting, entitled

82 EDWARD LEAR
Temple of Philae
1855 | Oil on canvas | 91 x 145 cm
Martin Davies Collection, Bridgeman Images

The Cedars of Lebanon, was the largest he ever produced, at nine feet wide (274 cm.). The original painting is untraced, and is now known only from a reduced replica (fig. 71). Following his earlier practice with *The Temple of Bassae*, Lear painted the large oil in an English winter, working in 1860-1 from the cedars in the gardens of the Oatlands Park Hotel in Walton-on-Thames, on the site of a royal residence, which were believed to have been planted by the eldest son of Charles I. He wrote with obvious pride to his young friend Marianne North (later to become an important painter of trees herself) that even the local sparrows admired the painting:

> The cedars are so advanced that millions of sparrows are said to sit – (I never saw them myself,) on the window ledges, pining with hopeless despair at not being able to get inside.[62]

Lear must have been aware that this was a familiar trope from Pliny's stories of the ancient Greek painters – Zeuxis's painting of grapes, which was so lifelike that birds came to peck at them – and it would hold particular appeal for him as he was always conscious of the trees as habitats for birds.

The first version of *The Cedars of Lebanon* was exhibited in Liverpool in the summer of 1861, where it attracted favourable comment. Lear was highly amused when a reviewer declared that 'Mr Lear has in this great picture not only achieved a professional success, but he has also conferred an obligation of the highest order on the whole Christian world.'[63] Another local reviewer pointed out, however, that it was too large for most private homes, even though it was 'a most effective and gigantic work, one which does great credit to the English school of art in landscape'.[64] It was also noticed by the London *Art Journal*, which described it as a 'marvellous work'.[65] In the following year, it was exhibited in London. It was shown in the crowded International Exhibition of 1862, and was hung very high up.[66] Lear must have been encouraged by the comments he received, however, since he decided to ask an equally high price for it. Having heard that John Everett Millais had sold *Spring (Apple Blossoms)* for 450 guineas, Lear fixed a price of 700 guineas.[67] This was a bad miscalculation. Millais was well known, and an ARA, and his painting, although it was a picture of trees, also featured several pretty young women, depicted on a large scale, rather than the few nondescript Arabs and goats in Lear's *Cedars*. 700 guineas was much more than any buyer was willing to pay, and Lear finally sold it for only £200 in 1867.[68] As a result of his experience with *The Cedars of Lebanon*, Lear moved away from large-scale oil painting, and put more effort into his travelogues, watercolours and small oil paintings.

His descriptions of the pine forests of Corsica, written in 1868 and published as *The Journal of a Landscape Painter in Corsica* (1870), show a willingness to be moved by new experiences, combined with strong preferences for particular trees. At first, he was not impressed by the 'gloomy' world of the pines:

> Gladly would I exchange all the magnificent monotony of these tall straight mountain trees for one glimpse of the beautiful Pinus maritima bending over the rocks by the sea at Kakiskali or Mount Athos.[69]

Just a few days later, however, Lear finds the pines 'exquisitely beautiful, and unlike any I have ever seen; perfectly bare and straight to a great height, they seem to rise like giant needles from the 'deep blue gloom' of the abyss below'.[70] His watercolours, and the illustrations to his published journal, dramatize the contrast between the dark pines and the sunlit mountains, with the tall, straight pine trunks set against sharp, irregular rock formations (fig. 83). Once more he thinks of John Martin:

> Generally speaking, the Corsican pine has but little lateral foliage, but sometimes on the outskirts of the forest you meet with trees that have broad arms and dark lines of flat spreading leafage, exactly resembling some in Martin's pictures.[71]

Nevertheless, even after this, he confesses 'I would rather live amongst palms than pines.'[72]

83 EDWARD LEAR

Forest of Bavella

29 April 1868 | Watercolour and sepia ink over graphite on tan paper | 37.4 x 53.3 cm | MS Typ 55.26, no. 1267

Houghton Library, Harvard University

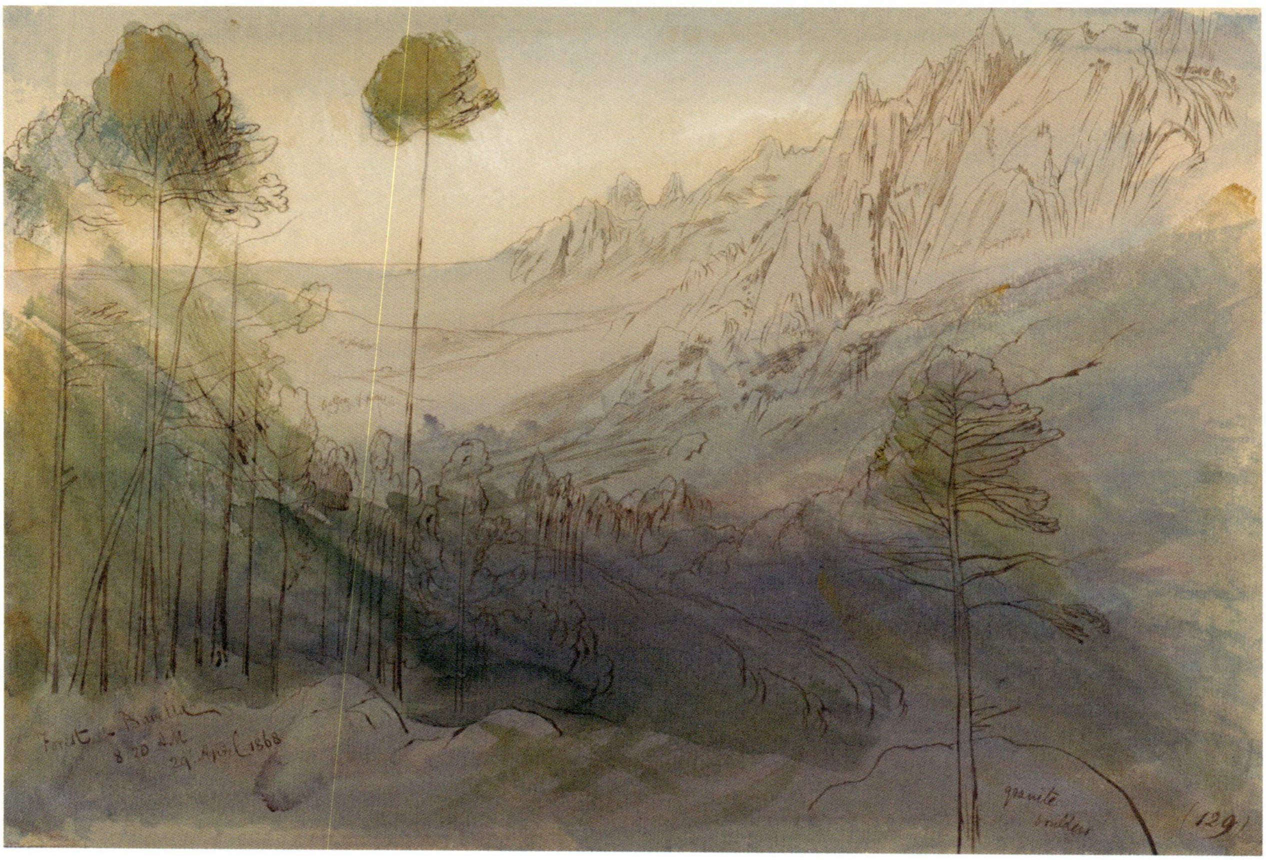

In 1872, the year he turned sixty, Lear was invited to travel to India with Lord Northbrook, the Viceroy, and his journals show that he was overwhelmed by the trees, spending hours drawing them even when he barely knew their names.[73] Sketches made at Darjeeling are inscribed 'strangle tree' and 'jungle-bungle/tangle jangle'; in others he calls the trees 'Vulgar or Pumptious tree' and 'Semi-genteel or Squamble tree'.[74] Like Hodges and the Daniells, he particularly appreciated the banyan trees. In March 1874 he breakfasted in the immense roots of a banyan tree, and observed pilgrims in their bright clothes against the backdrop of the 6,000-year-old tree from which Krishna jumped and killed the big snake Kali.[75] He made a drawing of a banyan tree at Barrackpore on 28 December of the same year (fig. 84), recording that he painted it between 11 and 1, and again between 7 and 8 am the following day. Here there are no shrines or worshippers, just a curious natural phenomenon: abundant golden foliage as in his acacia avenue, clustered trunks, and a figure leaning against the tree, suggesting welcome shade. Lear's interest in trees, and his ability to discriminate between different varieties of the same species is amply demonstrated by the letter he wrote to Northbrook in June 1876, offering advice on the different kinds of palm Northbrook might consider for a heraldic device: Lear draws, and describes, nine different types, specifying the regions in which they are found, and

 EDWARD LEAR

Barrackpore

28/29 December 1873 | Watercolour and sepia ink over graphite on white paper | 30.2 x 45.4 cm | MS Typ 55.26, no. 1563
Houghton Library, Harvard University

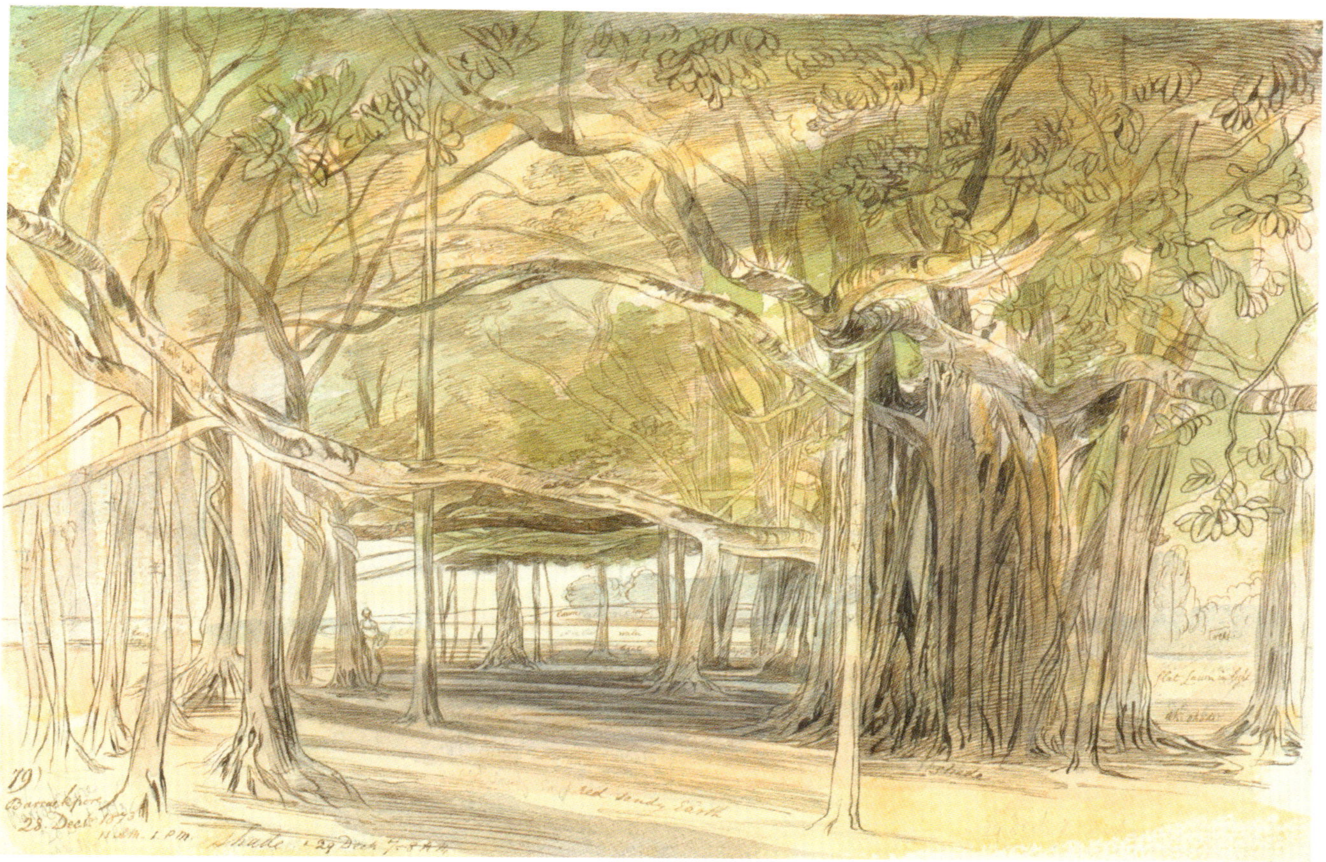

indicating the qualities, such as straight stems, which make them more or less suitable for heraldry.[76]

Lear was unusual in his passion for trees, which he took further than most artists of his time. Nevertheless, the examples discussed in this chapter show how important a study of the shapes and growth patterns of trees was to those British artists who wished to convey the flavour of a different country. Exotic species suggested an idyll or a paradise, whether it was in the imagination, in gardens and arboretums, or in the countries being opened up to travel and tourism. They provided a counterbalance to the equally strong appreciation of the native species, the oaks, beeches, ashes and elms of the woods and hedgerows. The approaches to foreign trees changed over time and according to the temperament of individual artists. Artist visitors to Italy in the eighteenth century, and Turner, gave the highest value to the stone pine: Palmer preferred the cypress, and Lear the olive. The banyan, appreciated as a sacred tree in the late eighteenth and early nineteenth centuries, was stripped of its Hindu associations in later works, and became merely a scientific curiosity. We can discern the influence of country-house culture in the eighteenth century, when the preference was for trees that would be suited to a garden, but in the nineteenth century there is a growing appreciation of trees in the countryside, available to all travellers, and not just a narrow elite.

ENDNOTES

1 Book IV, ll. 7-9.

2 Book IV, l. 478; Book IX, ll. 1101-1107. Karen L. Edwards, *Milton and the Natural World: Science and Poetry in Paradise Lost* (Cambridge University Press, 1999), pp. 143-154.

3 See Paul A. Elliott, Charles Watkins and Stephen Daniels, *The British Arboretum: Trees, Science and Culture in the Nineteenth Century* (London: Pickering and Chatto, 2011), for the development of arboretums in the late eighteenth and nineteenth centuries.

4 Jane Brown, *The Omnipotent Magician: Lancelot 'Capability' Brown, 1716-1783* (London: Chatto and Windus, 2011), p. 79.

5 Dorothy Stroud, *Capability Brown* (London: Faber and Faber, new edition, 1975 (first published 1950)), p. 165; Stephen Daniels, *Humphrey Repton: Landscape Gardening and the Geography of Georgian England* (New Haven and London: Yale University Press, 1999), p. 136.

6 Richard Payne Knight, *The Landscape, A Didactic Poem* (London: W. Bulmer & Co, 1794), ll. 55-63.

7 Horace Walpole, *On Modern Gardening* (London: Brentham Press, 1975), p. 24.

8 George Sinclair, *Useful and Ornamental Planting* (London: Baldwin and Cradock, 1832), p. 129.

9 Elliott, Watkins and Daniels, *British Arboretum*, p. 17.

10 William Barron, *The British Winter Garden, being a Practical Treatise on Evergreens* (London: Bradbury and Evans, 1852), pp. 5, 11.

11 Ibid, p. 13.

12 Elliott, Watkins and Daniels, *British Arboretum*, p. 32-5.

13 John Evelyn, *Silva: or a Discourse of Forest-Trees and the Propagation of Timber in his Majesty's Dominions … with notes by A. Hunter* (York: J. Dodsley et al., 1776), pp. 349-50; William Gilpin, *Remarks on Forest Scenery, and other Woodland Views (relative chiefly to picturesque beauty) illustrated by the scenes of New-Forest in Hampshire* (London, 1791), Vol. I, pp. 122-5.

14 Ezekiel 31:3.

15 Gilpin, *Forest Scenery*, Vol I, pp. 73-6.

16 J. G. Strutt, *Sylva Britannica; or, Portraits of Forest Trees, distinguished for their Antiquity, Magnitude, or Beauty. Drawn from nature and etched by Jacob George Strutt* (London: J. G. Strutt and Colnaghi and Co, 1822), pp. 7, 31.

17 John Claudius Loudon, *Arboretum et Fructitem Britannicum, or, the Trees and Shrubs of Britain* (London: Longman, Orme, Brown, Green, and Longmans, 1838), Vol. I, p. 16 ff.

18 George Barnard, *Trees from Nature* (London: Winsor and Newton, 1868), commentary to plate XXX.

19 Opening of his book, *A Voyage around the World*, 1777, cited in Geoff Quilley and John Bonehill, eds., *William Hodges 1744-1797: The Art of Exploration* (New Haven and London: Yale University Press, 2004), p. 23.

20 Quilley and Bonehill, *William Hodges*, p. 148.

21 Mildred Archer, *Early Views of India: The Picturesque Journeys of Thomas and William Daniell 1786-1794. The Complete Aquatints* (London: Thames and Hudson, 1980), no. 74 and plate XIV.

22 Archer, *Early Views of India*, commentary to no. 18.

23 William Hodges, *Travels in India, during the years 1780, 1781, 1782, and 1783* (London: printed for the author and sold by J. Edwards, 1793), p. 27.

24 Gilpin, *Forest Scenery*, Vol. I, p. 156.

25 Private collection. Illustrated in Maurice Shellim, *Oil Paintings of India and the East by Thomas Daniell RA (1749-1840) and William Daniell RA (1769-1837)* (London: Inchcape & Co Ltd in conjunction with Spink & Son Ltd, 1979), TD 103, p. 92.

26 Private collection. Illustrated in Shellim, *Oil Paintings of India*, WD 28, p. 118.

27 Rebecca Hey, *The Spirit of the Woods* (London: Longman, Rees, Orme, Brown, Green and Longman, 1837), p. 184.

28 Ibid, pp. 188, 185.

29 Gilpin, *Forest Scenery*, Vol. I, p. 80.

30 Sinclair, *Useful and Ornamental*, p. 144.

31 Kim Sloan, *Alexander and John Robert Cozens: The Poetry of Landscape* (Yale University Press/ Art Gallery of Ontario, 1986), p. 158; the Flaxman drawing is in the Yale Center for British Art.

32 Beckford in letter to Alexander Cozens, 19 May 1780: 'I ran across the Lawn, mounted the Hill of Pan and addressed myself to the Sylvan Deities in the midst of their consecrated Foliage', Lewis Melville, *The Life and Letters of William Beckford of Fonthill* (London: William Heinemann, 1910), p. 85.

33 Frederick A. Whiting, 'The Pine Tree of Monte Mario', *Country Life*, 2 April 1976, p. 1055-6.

34 A. P. Oppé, ed., 'Memoirs of Thomas

Jones', *Walpole Society* XXXII, 1946-48, pub. 1951, p. 66, entry for 16 November 1777.

35 Ibid, p. 67.

36 Ibid. p. 104, entry for 2 June 1781.

37 Ibid, p. 58, entry for 30 April 1777.

38 *Remarks on Forest Scenery, and other woodland views, by the late William Gilpin, A. M. edited by Sir Thomas Dick Lauder, Bart* (Edinburgh: Fraser & Co; London: Smith, Elder & Co; Dublin: W. Curry, jun. & Co, 1834), Vol I, p. 178.

39 A. Wilton, *The Life and Work of J. M. W. Turner* (London: Academy Editions, 1979), nos. 155, 157, 184.

40 K. Garlick and A. Macintyre, eds., *The Diary of Joseph Farington, Vol. IV, January 1799 – July 1801* (New Haven and London: Yale University Press, 1979), p. 1292.

41 M. Butlin and E. Joll, *The Paintings of J. M. W. Turner* (New Haven and London: Yale University Press, rev. ed., 1984), nos. 35 a-h.

42 Ruskin's revision to the Rudimentary series (1878), retrieved from The Elements of Drawing website, ruskin.ashmolean.org, 26 July 2016.

43 Italianate ash trees, admittedly. Alastair Smart in *The Telegraph*, 22 March 2012.

44 See Michael J. Campbell, *John Martin, 1789-1884, Creation of Light. Prints and Drawings from the Campbell Collection* (Valencia, Madrid and Bilbao: Bancaja, 2006), nos. 22, 23 and 26.

45 John Ruskin, *Modern Painters I*, 1846 ed, E. T. Cook and A. Wedderburn, eds., *The Works of John Ruskin* (London: George Allen, 1903-12), Vol. 3, p. 578.

46 See Matthew Hargraves, *Varieties of Romantic Experience: British, Danish, Dutch, French and German Drawings from the Collection of Charles Ryskamp* (New Haven: Yale Center for British Art, 2010), pp. 93-4.

47 R. Lister, *The Letters of Samuel Palmer* (Oxford: Clarendon Press, 1974), May 1858, p. 540.

48 Peter Levi, *Edward Lear: A Biography* (London: I. B. Tauris, 1995), p. 230.

49 October 1837, cited in Levi, *Edward Lear*, pp. 72-3.

50 Letter to Ann, 19 April 1848, cited in Vivien Noakes, *Edward Lear: The Life of a Wanderer*, rev. ed., (Stroud: Sutton Publishing, 2006), p. 73.

51 Diary, 18 April 1866, cited in Noakes, *Edward Lear: The Life*, p. 177.

52 Some of these are now in the Ashmolean Museum, Oxford.

53 Vivien Noakes, *Edward Lear 1812-1888* (London: Royal Academy, 1985) p. 103, letter dated 12 October 1853.

54 *The Critic*, 14.340 (1 June 1855) p. 266; *Athenaeum*, 1439 (26 May 1855), p. 623.

55 Noakes, *Edward Lear: The Life*, p. 105.

56 Noakes, *Edward Lear 1812-1888*, p. 146.

57 Ibid.

58 Noakes, *Edward Lear 1812-1888*, p. 154.

59 Evelyn, *Silva*, p. 313.

60 Gilpin, *Forest Scenery*, Vol I, p. 77.

61 11 May 1858, Noakes, *Edward Lear 1812-1888*, p. 112.

62 Noakes, *Edward Lear 1812-1888*, p. 112.

63 Lear wrote to Chichester Fortescue on 5 September 1861 that a Liverpool paper (as yet untraced) had described the *Cedars* as 'the great Lion' of the exhibition and 'praised it to the skies,' concluding with the paragraph quoted here. Lady Strachey, ed., *Letters of Edward Lear to Chichester Fortescue, Lord Carlingford and Frances Countess Waldegrave* (London: T. Fisher Unwin, 1907), p. 194.

64 *Liverpool Mercury*, 30 August 1861, issue 4228.

65 *Art Journal*, 82, October 1861, p. 317.

66 *The Times*, 11 June 1862, p. 6. Issue 24269.

67 Noakes, *Edward Lear 1812-1888*, p. 10.

68 Ibid.

69 *Edward Lear in Corsica: The Journal of a Landscape Painter* (London: William Kimber & Co Ltd, 1966), pp. 84-5.

70 Ibid., p. 102.

71 Ibid., pp. 107-8.

72 Ibid., p. 108.

73 In June 1878 Lear wrote to Sir Joseph Hooker to ask for his help in identifying Indian trees. He was making a set of drawings for Alfred Seymour: 'I cannot get at the Botanical names of the trees, – & in one instance, am not sure of the Ordinary English one' (Letter dated 3 June 1878, Vivien Noakes, ed., *Edward Lear, Selected Letters* (Oxford: Oxford University Press, 1990), p. 252).

74 Scott Wilcox, *Edward Lear and the Art of Travel* (New Haven: Yale Center for British Art, 2000), p. 111; Ray Murphy, ed., *Edward Lear's Indian Journal: watercolours and extracts from the diary of Edward Lear (1873-1875)* (London: Jarrolds Publishers Ltd, 1953), facing p. 92.

75 Ibid., p. 94.

76 Hofer Collection, Houghton Library. Letter dated 19 June 1876.

85 J. M. W. TURNER

Bolton Abbey

c.1825 | Watercolour | 28.1 x 40 cm

Lady Lever Art Gallery, National Museums Liverpool, Bridgeman Images

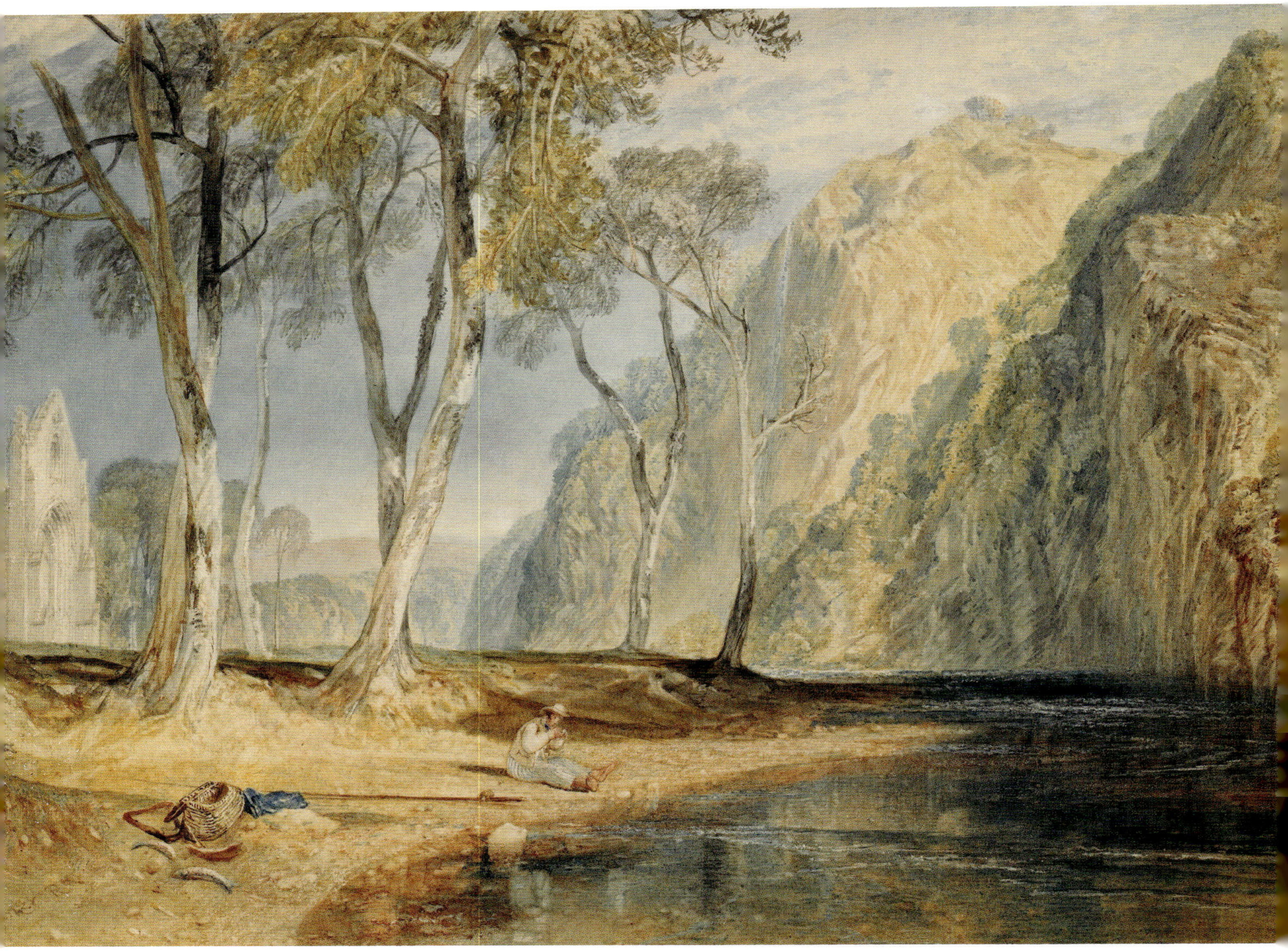

SEVEN

John Ruskin and the Pre-Raphaelite Tree: 1840–1870

As we have seen in previous chapters, one of the major issues involved in the painting and drawing of trees was the tension between the general and the particular. Sir Joshua Reynolds and Joseph Holden Pott in the later eighteenth century, and John Claudius Loudon and J. D. Harding in the 1830s, all cautioned against trying to show individual leaves and their distinctive shapes. On the other hand, there was a strong movement in favour of discriminating between the characters of different species of trees. The vogue for portraits of named trees also encouraged artists to pay attention to the individual rather than the generic tree. In 1846 Henry Twining wrote that the 'landscape portrait' was now the most acceptable form and 'requires that the various kinds of trees and plants should be indicated with much more precision.'[1] The Pre-Raphaelites and their associates took up this challenge, producing full-colour paintings of trees in remarkable detail, including the textures of bark and the shapes of individual leaves.

From 1849, William Holman Hunt, John Everett Millais and their followers brought about a revolution in landscape painting, working directly from nature in the open air. In their paintings, the sun shines through separately outlined leaves and picks up details of ivy growing up trunks; the trunks and branches are depicted with meticulous attention to the finest gradations of texture. Each species of tree is carefully discriminated. These paintings are the natural culmination of a half-century of tree portraits and drawing manuals. However, they differ from this tradition in their emphasis on painting (with a few exceptions) without preliminary drawing: the drawing was done directly on the canvas. They also differ in their refusal to accept the rules laid down by the drawing manuals, that separate leaves should not be indicated. Indeed, the Pre-Raphaelites gloried in the 'minutiae' that earlier theorists had seen as the fault of primitive art.

Their champion John Ruskin famously claimed in 1851 that the Pre-Raphaelites had followed his own advice in *Modern Painters* Volume One (1843) to 'go to nature in all singleness of heart ... rejecting nothing, selecting nothing and scorning nothing.'[2] He wrote extensively and eloquently on trees throughout his career. He was proud of his own drawings of trees, and gave them – especially his drawings of branches and leaves – pride of place in his own manual, *The Elements of Drawing*, published in 1857. However, his published remarks on tree drawing and painting before 1849 do not suggest that Ruskin's ideas were primarily responsible for the Pre-Raphaelites' initial move to botanical exactitude. As a critic, he doggedly continued to maintain that Turner was a great painter of trees, and his references to the Pre-Raphaelites' trees are marked by ambivalence. In the process of defending Turner and (to a much lesser extent) the Pre-Raphaelites, he denigrates – in addition to most of the landscape painters of the seventeenth century – some of the best tree-painters of the first half of the nineteenth century, including Thomas Creswick, Richard Redgrave, William Henry Hunt, and, most consistently and unforgivably, John Constable.

However, the achievements of the Pre-Raphaelites were built on those of this earlier generation. In the naturalistic landscape paintings of the early nineteenth century, such as Constable's *Flatford Mill* of 1817 (fig. 1) or Francis Danby's *Children by a Brook* (fig. 59), the different species are recognizable, and careful attention is paid to the light and shade of a particular moment. Both Constable and William Henry Hunt made detailed studies of the textures and accidental features of tree trunks (figs. 8, 47). As we have seen in Chapter Five, in the exhibitions of the 1840s paintings of English beech woodlands by Thomas Creswick and Richard Redgrave were attracting critical approval for their depiction of the 'chequered shade'. The development of photography also laid strong foundations for the tree-painting of the 1850s. Early photographers were able to produce detailed transcriptions of particular aspects of trees, especially the textures of bark and the ramification of trees in winter, both of which became prominent effects in Pre-Raphaelite landscape painting.

86 JOHN RUSKIN
Stone Pines at Sestri, Gulf of Genoa
30 April 1845 | Graphite and pen with wash and white bodycolour | 44.2 x 33.4 cm
Image © Ashmolean Museum, University of Oxford (WA.RS.ED.022)

JOHN RUSKIN: PRAETERITA *AND* MODERN PAINTERS *I*

Ruskin tells a story in his autobiography, *Praeterita*, about a moment of epiphany that came about when he was drawing an aspen tree from nature at Fontainebleau in May 1842, as a result of which he abandoned conventionalism and copying and resolved to study from nature alone:

> The branches against the blue sky began to interest me, motionless as the branches of a tree of Jesse on a painted window. ... Languidly, but not idly, I began to draw it; and as I drew, the languor passed away: the beautiful lines insisted on being traced, – without weariness. More and more beautiful they became, as each one rose out of the rest, and took its place in the air. With wonder increasing every instant, I saw that they 'composed' themselves, by finer laws than any known of men. At last, the tree was there, and everything that I had thought before about trees, nowhere.[3]

It is significant that what Ruskin was focusing on here was the ramification of the tree – 'the branches against the blue sky'. This is also a feature of his surviving tree drawings, which mainly date from the 1840s. As Christopher Newall has pointed out, Ruskin's style of drawing is based on J. M. W. Turner's *Liber Studiorum* engravings, relying on a carefully defined outline in pen and ink or the point of the brush, with washes of warm and earthy browns.[4] He had access to original watercolours by Turner in his father's collection, including *Bolton Abbey* (fig. 85), whose slender ash trees he particularly admired. Ruskin's formal instruction in tree-drawing came from J. D. Harding, the author of influential drawing manuals, who not only taught Ruskin but also travelled in Italy with him in 1845. Ruskin also knew John Claudius Loudon, who told his father that Ruskin was a 'natural genius' and commissioned him to write articles in his *Architectural Magazine* in 1837 and 1838.[5] He would certainly have known, therefore, about Loudon's *Arboretum Britannicum.*

Ruskin was particularly proud of his own drawing of *Stone Pines at Sestri* (fig. 86), executed on 30 April 1845. The slender branches of the stone pine are traced with great delicacy. This drawing hung in Ruskin's father's bedroom, and Ruskin later donated it to the Ruskin Drawing School at Oxford, as an example for students to study and copy. In his notes to the collection, written in 1878, he describes it as having been done 'with the utmost possible speed consistent with care'. By this time, however, he had covered the top of the drawing with a mount, so that the crown of the most complex of the trees, which he now regarded as less successful, could not be seen.[6] Ramification is also the main focus in a copy Ruskin made of part of the trees in Turner's large oil painting, *Crossing the Brook*, 'to show its complexities of light and shade'.[7] This, too, was donated to the Ruskin Drawing School. The foliage in both these drawings is suggested, rather than defined; but in another fine drawing, *Trees in a Lane, perhaps at Ambleside*, dated 1847 (Ruskin Library, University of Lancaster), Ruskin outlines the young leaves of oak and ash trees in springtime. Even in this drawing, however, the emphasis is on ramification, as the young leaves do not obscure the trunks and branches of the trees. In February 1852 his father suggested that Ruskin was better than Turner at drawing trees, but Ruskin vehemently denied this, referring to the watercolour of *Bolton Abbey*:

> All the practice I have had in tree drawing would not enable me even to copy the little jutting branch of the tree next the river on the right hand: His is a power essentially above mine, of a different and totally unattainable class.[8]

This was a strong reaction to well-meant praise, indicative of Ruskin's almost pathological fear that anyone should be considered better than Turner in any area of landscape painting.

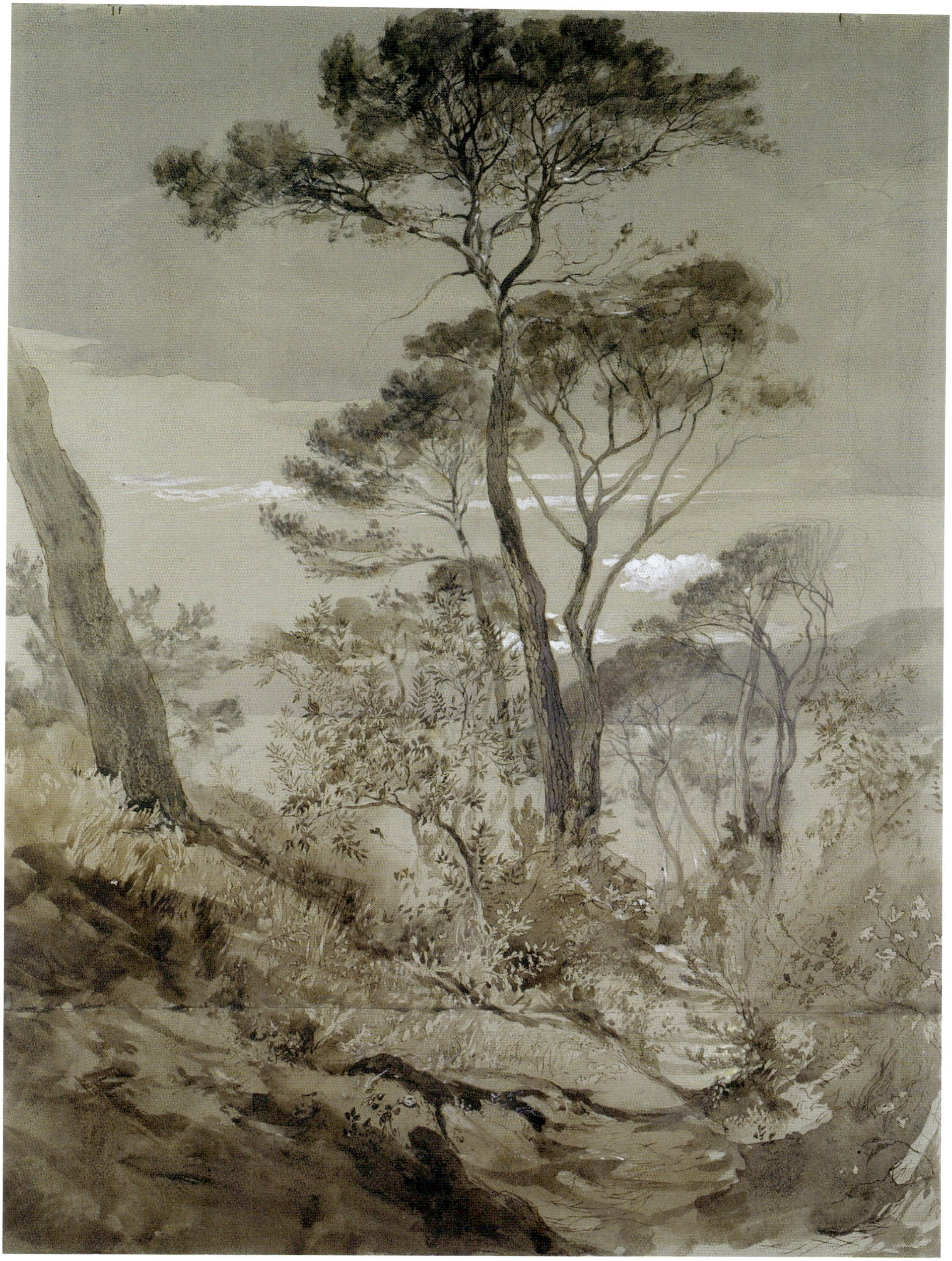

Many of Ruskin's surviving drawings are of parts of trees – leaves, buds, sprays of foliage – rather than of entire trees. In *Praeterita* he writes about the regular drawing exercise he undertook every day in his youth, while his father read to Ruskin and his mother for half an hour after breakfast:

> I always had a fresh-gathered outer spray of a tree before me, of which the mode of growth, with a single leaf full-size, had to be done at that sitting in fine pen outline, filled with the simple colour of the leaf at one wash.[9]

In the catalogue of his drawings compiled by Cook and Wedderburn for the *Works of John Ruskin*, fifteen drawings of oak trees are included, but they are all of buds, sprays, leaves, shoots and twigs. Despite his training with J. D. Harding, and his obvious love of trees, Ruskin seems to have shied away from making studies of trees in their entirety or in colour. He worked only in watercolour, never in oil, in any case. When he drew the trees in the field behind his house at Denmark Hill in 1860, in another drawing that was reproduced in *Praeterita*, he chose to represent them in winter, without foliage, when their trunks and branches were fully visible.[10]

In Ruskin's first book, *Modern Painters* I (1843) the remarks on tree-painting suggest that he is still very much under the influence of his teacher, J. D. Harding, whom he designates as, next to Turner, 'unquestionably the greatest master of foliage in Europe'.[11] Ruskin writes that it is 'more important to give the appearance of energy and elasticity in the limbs which is indicative of growth and life, than any particular character of leaf, or texture of bough'.[12] This goes against the whole tenor of the drawing manuals (except Harding's) with their emphasis on the characters of the different species. A long section in *Modern Painters* I entitled 'Of Truth of Vegetation' is largely about branching. Since the express purpose of the book was to show that Turner was superior to the Old Masters, the ramification of Claude Lorrain, Gaspard Poussin and Salvator Rosa is severely criticised as false, and contrasted with the truthful ramification of Turner's trees. Ruskin declares in this volume that Turner is 'the only painter who ever drew the stem of a tree' while Titian came closest before him, surpassing Turner in the muscular development of the larger trunks, but 'missing the grace and character of the ramifications'.[13] Ruskin recognised the importance of tree anatomy in his remark that, because of the muscular qualities of the tree trunk, it is done best by men who can draw the human figure.[14] Ruskin declares that the Old Masters also failed to represent leaves correctly. He advises his readers to take a three-foot elm branch, put it on a table and try to draw it, leaf by leaf; then to look at a painting by Gaspard Poussin in which the leaves are all the same, tied on in bunches.[15] On the other hand, the seventeenth-century Dutch painters, Meindert Hobbema and Jan Both, are criticized for excessive detail in their painting of leaves:

> They can paint oak leafage faithfully, but do not know where to stop, and by doing too much, lose the truth of all, lose the very truth of detail at which they aim, for all their minute work only gives two leaves to nature's twenty.[16]

In putting in so much detail, Ruskin argued, they lost the harmony and repose of nature. Turner's trees, however, are, in his view, just right, showing evidence of careful study from nature but not spoiling its harmony and mystery through excessive detail.

By the time he produced the third edition of *Modern Painters*, Volume I in 1846, Ruskin was more critical of his drawing master. He complained that Harding's foliage was never sufficiently finished, and that in his manual, *The Park and the Forest*, 'no single branch or spray is faithfully copied'.[17] Travelling with Harding in 1845, Ruskin had written to his parents that Harding's drawings 'are all for impression – mine all for information'.[18] Nevertheless, Ruskin was still dismissive of those who depicted trees with excessive detail. William Henry Hunt, he says, is the only man who can paint real leaf-green under sunlight, but he fails in foliage, as the daguerrotype does, from over-fidelity – 'for foliage will *not* be imitated, it must be reasoned out and suggested'.[19] Ruskin praises the forest studies of

87 JOHN EVERETT MILLAIS
The Woodman's Daughter
1850–1 | Oil on canvas | 88.9 x 64.8 cm
Guildhall Art Gallery, City of London, Bridgeman Images

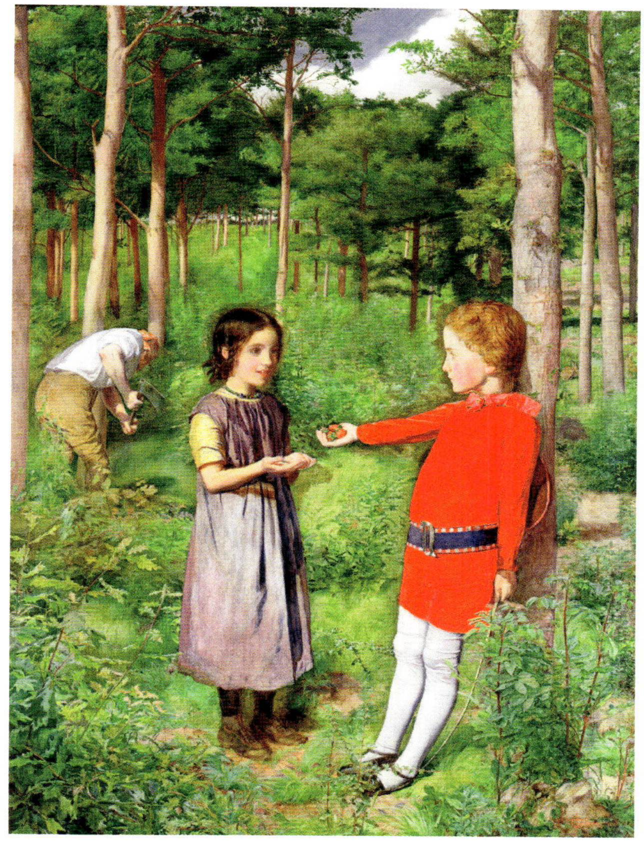

John Linnell, but Linnell, too, is criticized for 'over fulness of detail and a want of generalization in the effect'. Ruskin is more complimentary about Samuel Palmer, whose detailed studies of cypresses foreshadowed some of the tree-painting of the Pre-Raphaelites.[20] The revisions to this volume also include a dismissive reference to Constable, who, says Ruskin, is 'unable to draw even a log of wood, much more the trunk of a tree.'[21]

HUNT AND MILLAIS IN THE WOODS, 1850-1852

There would have been rather mixed encouragement in Ruskin's first volume, then, for William Holman Hunt and John Everett Millais as they began to make careful studies of trunks and foliage, painting every detail they could see, direct onto the canvas, in full sunlight. The pioneer in this endeavour seems to have been Millais, whose *Ferdinand lured by Ariel* (Makins Collection), painted in the summer of 1849 and exhibited in 1850, includes very detailed study of horse chestnut leaves. The careful study of leaves was taken up in October of the same year by James Collinson. William Michael Rossetti's *Journal* of the Pre-Raphaelite Brotherhood records that Collinson was 'finishing up the trees outside to a pitch of the extremest minuteness' in the view through the window in his painting of *The Emigrant's Letter* (Manchester Art Gallery). The next day Collinson reports that 'he has done about twenty leaves to the ash-tree in his picture.'[22] This is a tiny part of the picture, which is an indoor cottage scene. It is evidence of an interest in landscape that would later find full expression in Collinson's painting of *A Mother and Child in a Landscape* (c.1855, Yale Center for British Art), a painting executed in the Isle of Wight, with figures framed by tree trunks and branches, with ash and oak foliage silhouetted against the sky. The painting Holman Hunt was working on in 1849, *A Converted British Family Sheltering a Christian Missionary from the Persecution of the Druids* (Ashmolean Museum, Oxford), also includes some beautiful leaf-painting, but these are vine leaves, growing on the family's hut and symbolic of the wine of communion, rather than the leaves of a tree.

In the summer of 1850, Holman Hunt and Millais progressed from leaves to trees, with a particular emphasis on tree trunks. Millais was painting in Wytham Woods, near Oxford, while Hunt worked at Knole Park, near Sevenoaks. Both artists were painting literary subjects in forest settings. Millais's painting, *The Woodman's Daughter* (fig. 87), was based on a poem by Coventry Patmore. The perspective effect of slender oak trees receding into the distance has been linked to an early Renaissance source, Paolo Uccello's *Hunt in the Forest*, which had been donated to the University Galleries in Oxford in the same year.[23] The background to Hunt's picture, *Valentine Rescuing Sylvia from Proteus* (Birmingham Museum and Art Gallery), seems, rather, to look to contemporary British painting, the beechwood scenes by Creswick and Redgrave with their dappled shade. The surface textures and excrescences of Millais's trees, especially the one in the right foreground, have little to do with fifteenth-century painting, being studied with a scientific

88 WILLIAM HENRY MILLAIS
Hayes Common
1852–3 | Oil on canvas | 55.9 x 86 cm
Yale Center for British Art, Paul Mellon Collection

exactitude that recalls Constable and William Henry Hunt, or perhaps contemporary photography. Holman Hunt was also taking the painting of his tree trunks very seriously, as is evident from the letter he wrote to his friend John Lucas Tupper: 'the trunks of the trees are yellow and red but appear to be purple and green to the unscientific'.[24] The two artists seem to have striven to outdo one another in the depiction of leaves, Millais's foreground oak leaves being matched by the heap of dead beech leaves in Hunt's painting. Both, however, chose compositions and viewpoints that left little room for the portrayal of the branching of the trees, so if they had been influenced by Ruskin's advice on drawing an elm branch, leaf by leaf, in *Modern Painters* I, they had ignored the overriding emphasis he put on the accuracy of ramification.

When they were exhibited at the Royal Academy in 1851, the paintings by Hunt and Millais attracted some qualified praise from the critics. The *Literary Gazette* complimented Millais on his 'devoted study of nature' in 'the drawing of the young shoots of the ash and the oak trees, in the bark of the trunks, and in other minutiae of detail' and appreciated Hunt's 'surprising labour bestowed upon the dead leaves'.[25] But the young painters were warned that, to make a picture look like nature, something more than mere copying was required. Too much detail would destroy the aerial perspective and the harmony of effect. Other reviews, notably the one in *The Times*, took a different line, subjecting the Pre-Raphaelites to savage criticism. It was at this point that Ruskin stepped into the critical debate. Urged on by Coventry Patmore, Ruskin wrote to *The Times* and defended the artists against their critics. However, his two letters made no mention of their tree-painting. Instead of the landscapes by Millais and Hunt, Ruskin chose to praise Charles Alston Collins's painting of a nun in a flower-filled garden, *Convent Thoughts* (Ashmolean Museum), for its botanical accuracy in the representation of water-lilies.[26] Soon afterwards, Ruskin met Hunt and Millais, and became a personal friend to the group as well as their prominent champion.

Ruskin seems to have shared some of the reservations of the critics as far as the painting of trees by Hunt and Millais was concerned. In September 1851 he added a footnote to his Fifth Edition of *Modern Painters* I, on the Pre-Raphaelites:

> Their foliage, like the rest of the accessaries [sic] in their paintings, is inimitable in its parts, but as yet imperfectly generalized.[27]

In the summer and autumn of 1851, Millais and Hunt were painting side by side at Ewell, Surrey, on *The Hireling Shepherd* (Manchester Art Gallery) and *Ophelia* (Tate Britain). If they knew Ruskin's comment, they studiously ignored it: increasingly, these are portraits of specific trees, not 'generalized' at all. Moreover, the trees they chose to paint were pollarded willows, contrary to Ruskin's published advice in a footnote to the second edition of *Modern Painters* (1846) that artists should choose 'real nature' – not 'cicatrized to the pollard'.[28] Pollarded willows appear in Constable's landscapes, and the composition of Hunt's *Hireling Shepherd* suggests that he may have been looking at Constable's painting, *Flatford Mill*. At this period Hunt and Millais were close to Charles Robert Leslie, Constable's biographer, who would have told them about Constable's work.[29]

THE MILLAIS BROTHERS ON HAYES COMMON, 1852

Millais's brother, William Henry Millais, also spent time with Hunt and John Everett Millais in Surrey in the summer of 1851, painting a small picture entitled *The Rookeries*, which was shown at the Royal Academy in 1852. This is now lost, but its probable subject is described by Holman Hunt, writing of Worcester Park Farm: 'There a glorious avenue of elms still flourished, seen for many miles as the dispersing and attracting point of a noisy brood of rooks, who wended their long flights to and fro in the drowsy morning and evening.'[30] It seems likely from the title that this was a painting in which trees were the main focus.

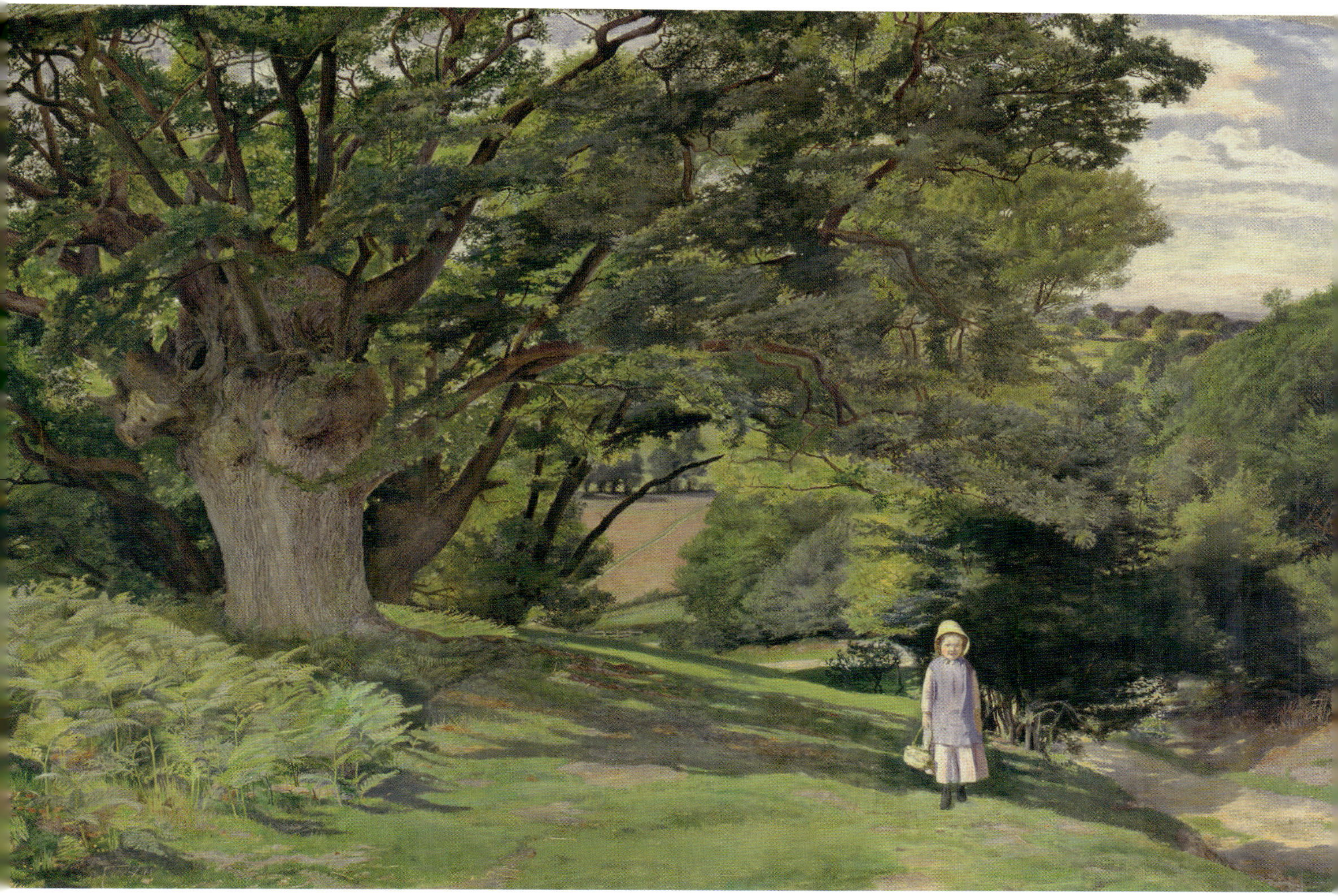

In March 1852 John Everett Millais (and probably his brother too) attended a lecture by Leslie, in which Leslie talked about Constable living in the country and painting out of doors. According to George Price Boyce's account of this lecture, Leslie told how Constable

> Gave names to the trees about him, and used to speak of a graceful ash called by him 'the young lady who died of a broken heart', having had an ugly board nailed to its side with the warning 'Trespassers Beware'.[31]

This was Leslie's fifth lecture on landscape painting; Hunt and Millais may well have attended the earlier lectures in the series, which began in 1848. Leslie's account of the ash tree is taken from his record of Constable's lectures at Hampstead in the 1830s (fig. 51).

In the summer of 1852 John Everett Millais was painting in the open air again, this time lodging with his brother, William Henry, at the George Inn in Bromley, Kent. The two brothers painted ancient oak trees on Hayes Common. John Everett's painting was *The Proscribed Royalist* (Lloyd Webber Collection), in which a hollow oak shelters the male protagonist. The old tree's textured bark and mossy roots are lovingly delineated, although exhibition-goers might have been more impressed by the soulful expressions of the star-crossed lovers and the smooth silk of the woman's dress. The oak tree was apparently called the Millais oak in later years.[32] In William Henry's painting, *Hayes Common* (fig. 88), however, a fine pollarded oak tree is the main actor. It stretches its branches across the whole picture surface, in an ambitious composition which incorporates distant views

89 WILLIAM HENRY MILLAIS
Hayes Common
1852 | Watercolour | National Art Library
© Victoria and Albert Museum, London

of fields and hedgerows. Separate oak leaves are visible, in varying degrees of light or shade, and the complex ramification of the ancient tree is clearly legible. The tree trunk, with its hollows and its bosses, and its ridged bark, is also the product of careful study. The little girl in the foreground, supplied, according to family tradition, by John Everett, looks like something of an afterthought. In this painting, too, the dappled light suggests the influence of Creswick and Redgrave.

Hayes Common was rejected by the Royal Academy. Edward Lear wrote to William Henry Millais (whom he called 'Uncle William') to commiserate:

> If all the landscapes at the Exhibition are better than that of my Uncle William which they have rejected – all I can say is – it must be a good exhibition indeed. I suppose it was because the tree was green and not asphaltum colour that they turned it out … Your own idea – and that of Daddy Hunt, Anthony and others – that grass is of a rich green colour is most ridiculous and reprehensible – and you should leave it off as soon as you can.[33]

Lear groups William Henry with Holman Hunt and Mark Anthony as artists who are challenging the academic convention of the 'brown tree' in favour of the colours they actually see when painting from nature. As a result of its rejection, we have no critical reaction to *Hayes Common*, and in the literature on John Everett Millais it has been overshadowed by his brother's more famous painting.

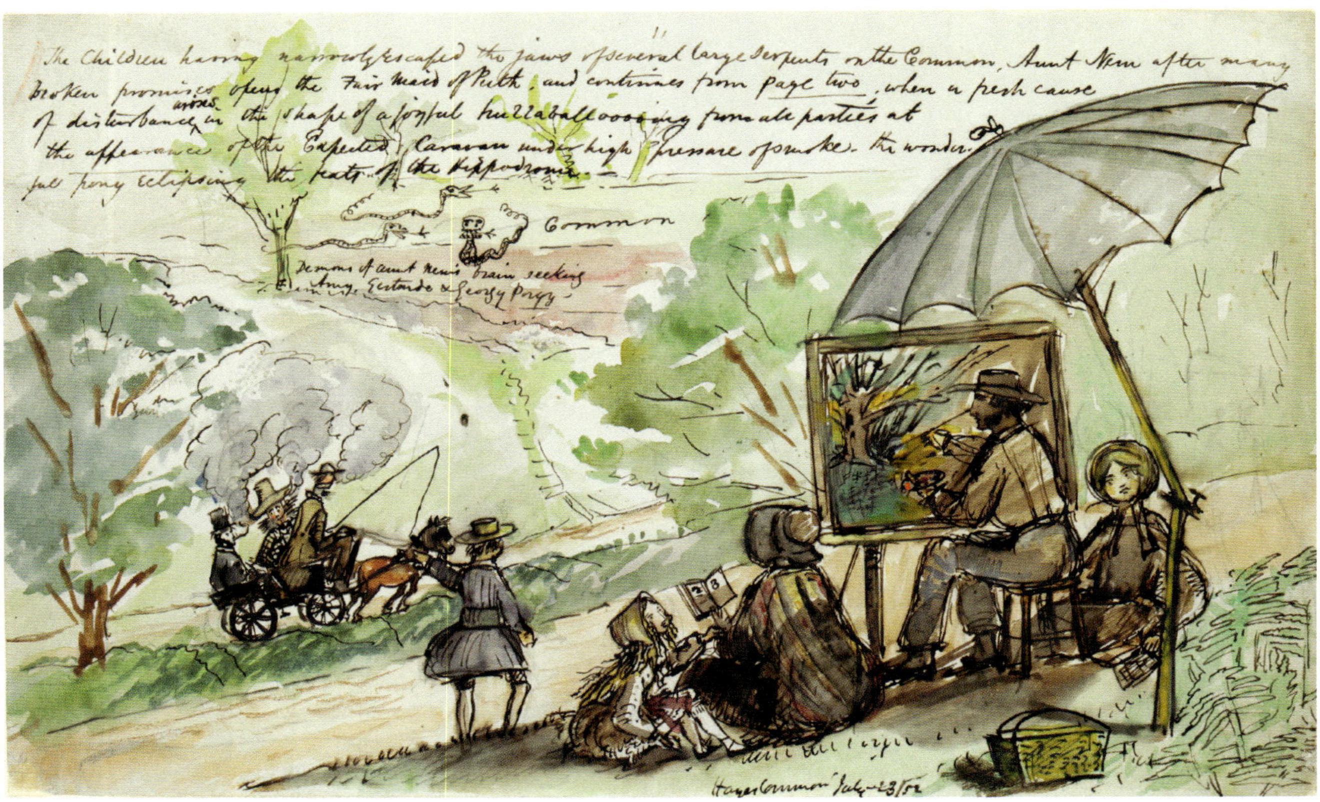

90 *After* MARK ANTHONY
'The Monarch Oak'
from *The Illustrated London News*, 14 May 1853, p. 384.
The Bodleian Libraries, The University of Oxford

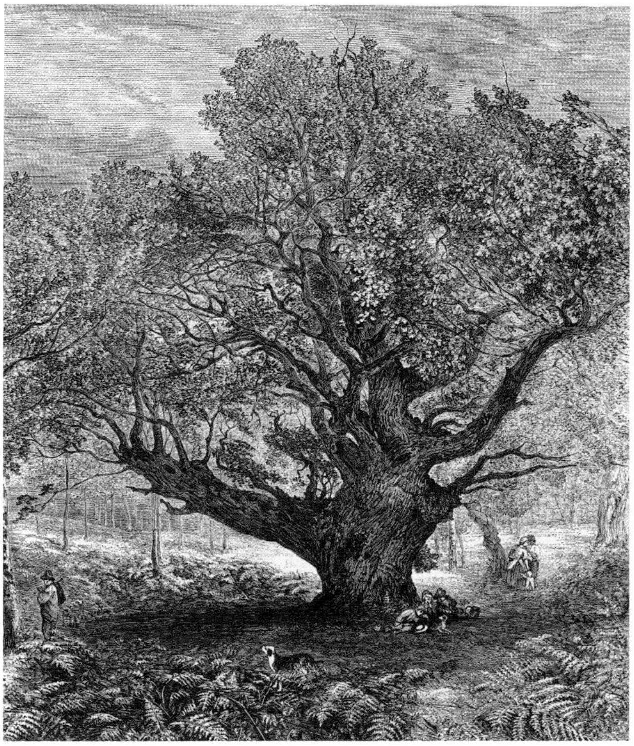

In the *Life and Letters* compiled by John Everett Millais's son, a drawing by William Henry of himself painting the picture (fig. 89) has even been miscaptioned as a sketch of John Everett painting the background of 'The Royalist'.

INCHBOLD, ANTHONY, HUGHES AND BOWLER, 1852-5

In that same summer, John William Inchbold was painting *The Chapel, Bolton* (Northampton Museum and Art Gallery). This was a noted picturesque ruin, the subject of Ruskin's favourite watercolour by Turner (fig. 85) and of many other images that capitalized on its dramatic setting and its fine windows and Gothic mouldings. Inchbold, however, chose a deliberately unpicturesque view, in which trees predominate. The bright leaves of the ash tree in the foreground, depicted in various degrees of sunlight and shadow, are set against the dark masses of ivy growing against the chapel wall. Inchbold's painting was hung in the West Room at the RA in 1853, along with John Everett Millais's *Proscribed Royalist.* In the same room was Mark Anthony's massive *The Monarch Oak*, presumably also a product of that summer of 1852 (fig. 90). The Pre-Raphaelites were admirers of Anthony's work: in the *Pre-Raphaelite Journal* William Michael Rossetti records that his brother Dante Gabriel Rossetti, John Everett Millais and Ford Madox Brown went in February 1850 to see Anthony's pictures, some of which 'delighted them greatly' and in April 1850 William Michael Rossetti himself noted 'astounding Anthonys' at the British Artists' exhibition in Suffolk Street.[34]

Mark Anthony had studied in France and knew the forest scenes of the Barbizon group, including Théodore Rousseau, whose paintings of old oak trees were a parallel development to the British tree portraits. Anthony's huge picture, *The Monarch Oak*, was exhibited at the Royal Academy in 1853. Visitors to the Academy could hardly miss it, since it measured around 16 by 10 feet.[35] It was engraved for the *Illustrated London News*, and the reviewer was evidently briefed by Anthony, as he or she was able to identify the area where the tree was situated:

> The subject matter of this picture ... was taken in the old portion of Windsor Forest, which lies north-west from the town and castle, beyond St Leonard's Hill ... It abounds in ancient trees – trees coeval with the Norman William (tradition assigns one not far distant from this spot to him); some, perhaps, even more ancient ... A curious incident is related in connexion with this 'monarch oak'. For some years it was the abode of a fox, which was skilful enough to baffle his pursuers. In the centre, where the branches fork out, there is a hole some four feet deep, in which he lodged.[36]

The story gives the tree a definite character as a nurturing and protective presence, reminiscent of records of people taking refuge in trees.

91 HENRY ALEXANDER BOWLER
The Doubt: 'Can these Dry Bones Live?'
1855 | Oil on canvas | 61 x 50.8 cm
© Tate, London 2017

The summers of 1853 and 1854 saw further notable paintings of trees by the Pre-Raphaelites and their followers. Arthur Hughes began *Orlando in the Forest of Arden*, later to be revised and renamed *The Long Engagement* (Tate Britain), in April 1853. The foreground beech tree trunk is described in great detail, with moss, leaf shadows and ivy growing up it, brilliantly lit by the sun. Hughes found his tree at Burnham Beeches, and his correspondence with the poet William Allingham in the following year suggests a shared interest in trees and an ongoing conversation about the qualities of the different species. Allingham writes to Hughes from New Ross, Ireland, in August 1854:

> Do you intend 'Orlando' for the Academy Exhibition next year? This is a woodland country and I often see a treebole with moss and ivy that brings your picture and self into my head. Sycamores are already turning sere. But they are shabby trees at any time – except just in early spring. I never saw an oak I cared for. The elm is rather fuzzy and ill-mannered looking. I like ash and birch and chestnut and thorns – but beech best of all – it is so cheerful, unaffected and friendly.[37]

Allingham's preference for the beech is significant, in view of the popularity of woodland scenes, usually depicting the beech woods of southern England, in the 1840s and 1850s. Hughes had to choose a beech for his painting since its narrative centred around the carving of the beloved's name on the smooth trunk. In its juxtaposition of young lovers with an ancient tree, it clearly shows the influence of Millais's *Proscribed Royalist*. Two years later Hughes showed that he also appreciated the beauty of the elm tree, castigated by Allingham as 'rather fuzzy and ill-mannered looking'. The foreground of his painting of a boy who returns home to find his mother's grave, *Home from Sea* (Ashmolean Museum), begun in 1856, has a carefully-painted elm trunk on the right-hand side and a bough with leaves (complete with spider's web) above the figures. In September 1854 Ford Madox Brown was also painting in woodland, working on his painting of *The Brent at Hendon* (Tate Britain), in which the exposed tree-roots are a remarkable feature, and the scene as a whole is reminiscent of the woodland interiors of Richard Redgrave.

Hughes's *Orlando in the Forest of Arden* was rejected by the Royal Academy in 1855, perhaps because it was unfinished. Nevertheless, the exhibition of 1855 included two important Pre-Raphaelite tree paintings, Henry Alexander Bowler's *The Doubt: 'Can these Dry Bones Live?'* (fig. 91) and John William Inchbold's *A Study, in March*, also known as *In Early Spring* (fig. 92).[38] Bowler's painting is remarkable on several counts. It is possibly the first detailed portrayal of a horse chestnut in British art since the Shoreham work of Samuel Palmer. The leaves are shown in extraordinary detail, not as repeated shapes but with great variety. They range in colour and size from small, fresh green leaves to larger, browner and coarser specimens. There is enormous variety, too, in the ways they are affected by the sunlight: some are in shadow, some in reflected light, and others have the sun shining through them. The painting is also remarkable because the tree is used allegorically. The germinating chestnut on the gravestone, with its inscription 'Resurgam' (I will rise again) suggests natural regeneration, either as an alternative to, or as proof of, spiritual resurrection. This is a subtext of many paintings and drawings in the period, but it is rare for the symbolism to be expressed so explicitly. Inchbold's painting is notable for showing the beauty of trees in winter. Photographers had been taking photographs of winter trees for some time – because it was easier to photograph bare branches than foliage – but until this time paintings of bare trees had been rare in British art. *A Study, in March* portrays a crisp cool day, with the sun

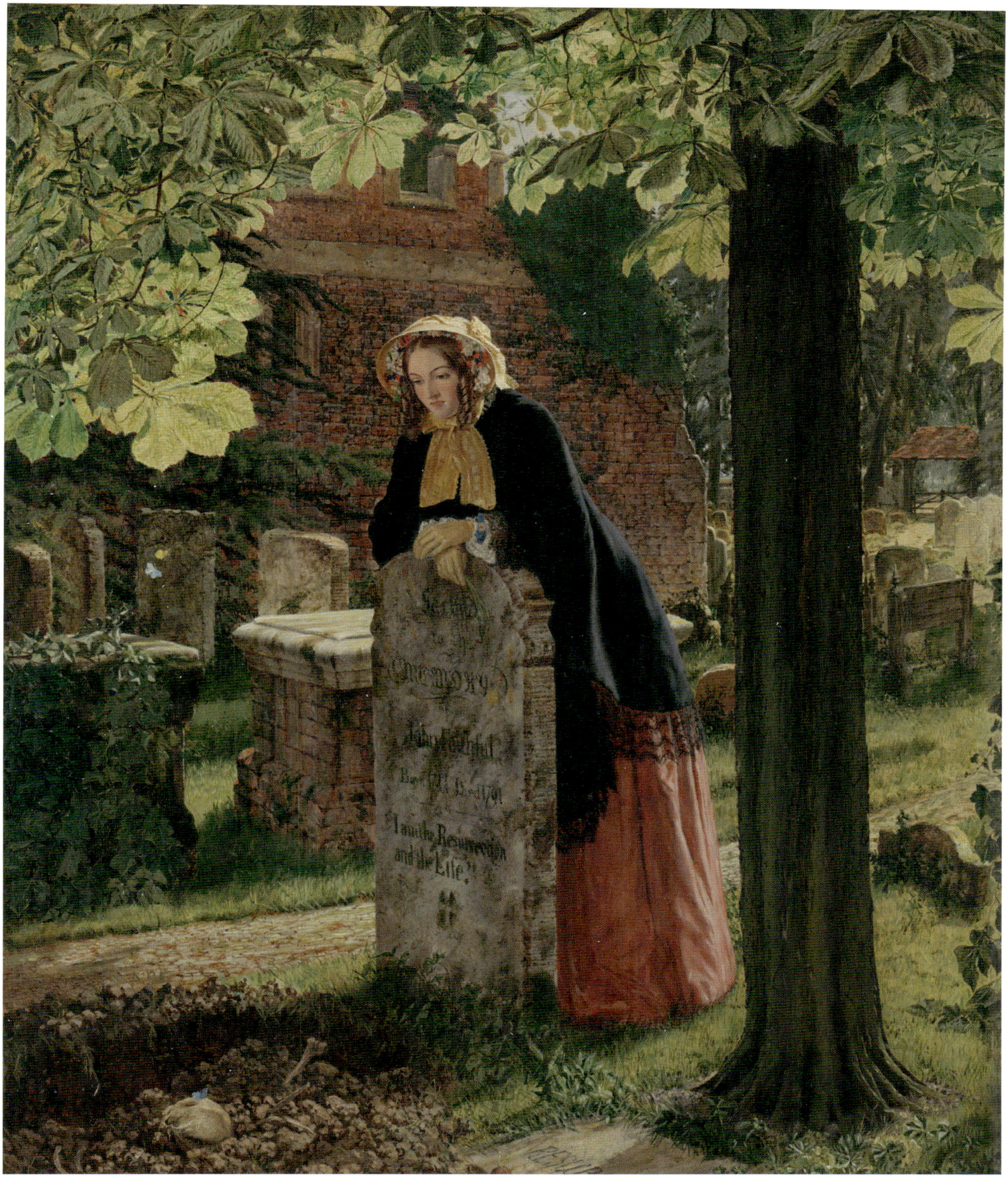

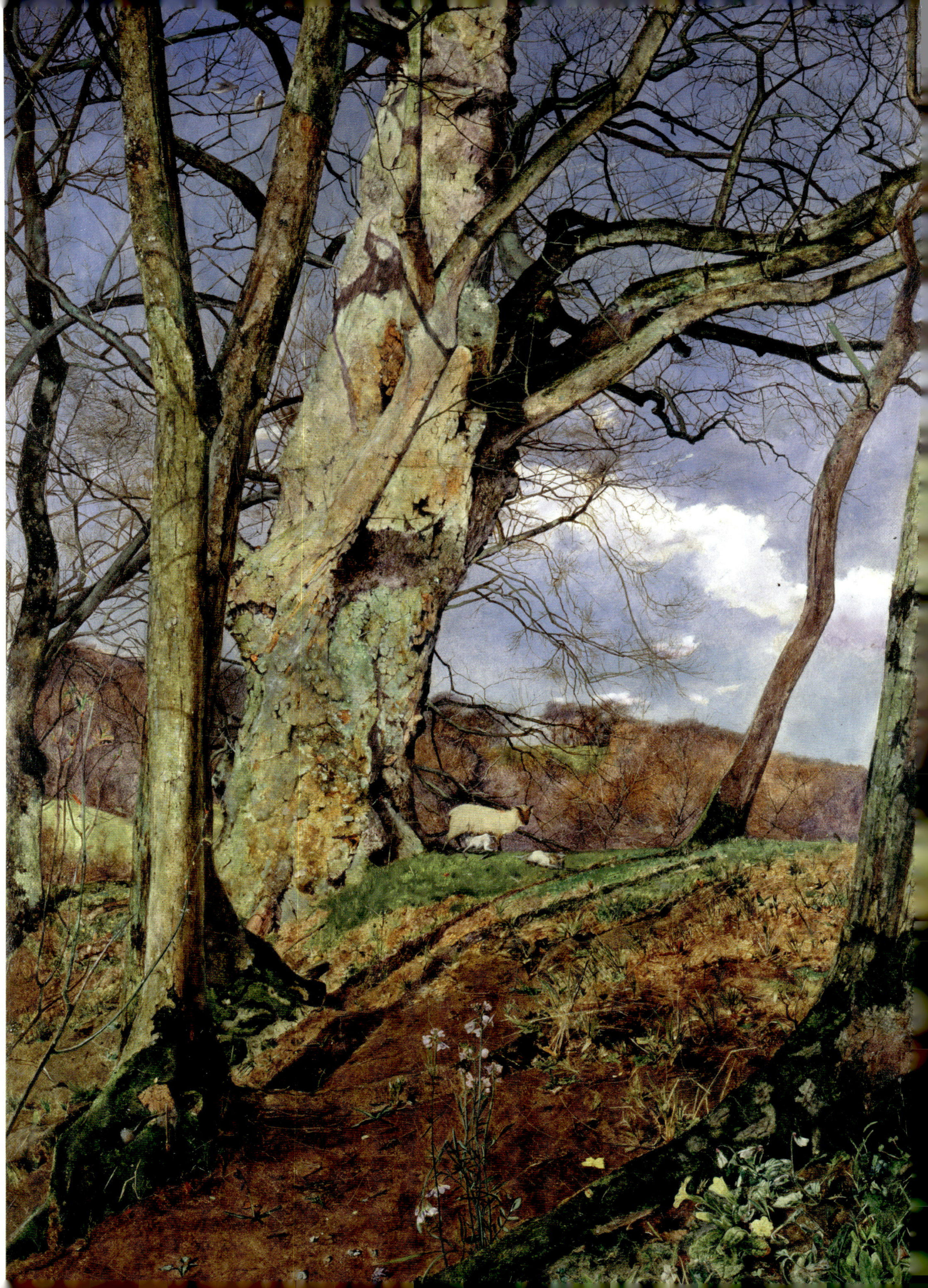

92 JOHN WILLIAM INCHBOLD
A Study, in March
Exhibited 1855 | Oil on canvas | 53 x 35 cm
Image © Ashmolean Museum
University of Oxford (WA1962.4.2)

beginning to warm up the earth and the wildflowers and lambs giving promise of the summer to come. Its central motif is a mature sycamore tree, its bark lovingly detailed. Because it is winter, the ramification of the trees is clearly shown, in a tour de force of naturalistic observation that should have pleased Ruskin. Inchbold followed up this painting with *Mid-Spring* (private collection), shown in 1856, a view of a similar area of woodland when the trees are in leaf and the flowers in profusion.[39]

By this time the reviews suggest that the critics were becoming used to Pre-Raphaelite precision. The proliferation of photographs of trees and woodland had accustomed people to seeing fine detail in images, and the older conventional, shorthand means of notation now seemed less convincing. In 1855 the critic of the *Athenaeum* criticized Lee for his 'indecipherable foliage, where spiky touches serve for willow, fan-work for chestnut, jags for oak, dots for elm, and spots for beech.'[40] Inchbold's paintings, by contrast, were commended as 'the work of a young but evidently gifted observer, though hung out of reach … full of the minute poetry that lurks under every lichen and in the heart of every bud'.[41] In the following year the same journal found Inchbold's *Mid-Spring* to be 'wonderful, with an execution which would bear a fairy's eye. His knowledge of nature would set up a gallery of mere manufacturing landscapers'.[42] The *Art Journal* praised Bowler's *The Doubt* for its 'most perfect imitation' of natural and artificial objects, including 'the overhanging leafy canopy'.[43]

JOHN RUSKIN: ACADEMY NOTES, MODERN PAINTERS *3, 4 AND 5,* THE ELEMENTS OF DRAWING, *1855-1860*

In 1855 Ruskin began publishing his *Academy Notes*. He had been friends with the artists since publishing his letters to *The Times* in 1851, but *Academy Notes* gave him the opportunity to praise, or criticize, their work publicly. However, in the intervening period Ruskin's friendship with Millais had foundered after the notorious holiday in Scotland in 1853, when Millais fell in love with Ruskin's wife Effie. By 1855 Ruskin's marriage had been annulled and Millais was soon to marry Effie. This scandal inevitably affected his relationship with the rest of the group. In the 1855 *Academy Notes*, Ruskin noted only that Inchbold's *Study, in March* was 'exceedingly beautiful' but he was roundly critical of the leaf-painting of Redgrave and Creswick: 'that which pretends to Pre-Raphaelite distinction of detail; but is in all detail industriously wrong'. Redgrave, wrote Ruskin, was guilty of 'perpetual error, assuming that all leaves of trees may be represented by oval, sharp-pointed touches of yellow and green – as if leaves had not their perspective, shadows, and changes of hue like everything else!'[44] To demonstrate the correct way to paint leaves, Ruskin referred not to a landscape painting, but to the leaves in Collinson's *The Writing Lesson*, a genre painting with geraniums on a windowsill, and to the leaves around the heads of the main characters in Titian's *Bacchus and Ariadne* in the National Gallery.[45]

This was hardly fair, of course. Painting a few leaves on a pot plant, or on a wreath, is very different from painting a whole tree, or a mass of foliage in a woodland scene. However, on this occasion Ruskin seems to have come down on the side of the Pre-Raphaelites, using them (rather than Turner) as the criterion of excellence in tree-painting.

It was also in 1855 that Charles Robert Leslie published his lectures on landscape in his book, *A Hand-book for Young Painters*. He took issue with Ruskin's praise of Turner's trees in the first volume of *Modern Painters*:

> I have read with attention Mr Ruskin's remarks on Turner's trees and foliage, but without being convinced that he was so great a painter of these as of other features of Nature. With the exception of here and there a willow, and, in his Italian views, the frequent pine and cypress, I look in vain for a specific discrimination in his trees, or in the vegetation of his foregrounds, in which there is little that is English. I cannot remember an oak, an elm, an ash, or a beech, in any picture by him (only a fine decayed oak in one of his vignettes), nor do I remember anything much like the beauty of an English hedge. Neither has he expressed the deep verdure of his own country; and hence he is the most unfaithful (among great painters) to the essential and most beautiful characteristics of English midland scenery.[46]

Leslie had touched on a weak point, Turner's preference for foreign trees, even in supposedly English scenes, and his neglect of the four forest trees, oak, elm, ash and beech – the trees on which, coincidentally, the Pre-Raphaelites had also concentrated. In contrast to Turner, Leslie praised Constable for his faithful tree-painting.

Ruskin responded to this in *Modern Painters* 3, published in 1856. The trees in his watercolour by Turner, *Bolton Abbey*, were compared to plates from Leslie's *Life* of Constable to show that Constable's drawing of trees was 'barbarous'.[47] Again, this was hardly fair, since the plates were mezzotints by Lucas, not original works by Constable himself. Ruskin had a thorough knowledge of Turner's works, but to judge from *Modern Painters* one would think that he only knew Constable's from the illustrations to his copy of Leslie's *Life*. Ruskin followed this up in the fourth volume, also published in 1856, with illustrations of an aspen drawn under different degrees of idealization, including the Turneresque, the Hardingesque and the Constablesque, the last of these representing 'total worthlessness' and 'wholly false in ramification'. For an unidealized view he uses his own drawing of an aspen without leaves, presumably the drawing of May 1842 referred to in the story in *Praeterita*.[48] The Pre-Raphaelites do not get a mention at all. This is, to some extent, unsurprising, since Ruskin's main concern in this section is ramification, and the Pre-Raphaelites would have provided few examples for him to draw on. Nevertheless, it is telling that he can write in so much detail on the representation of trees without any reference to their works. There is also a long passage on tree trunks in *Modern Painters* 3 which does not mention them at all.[49]

Ruskin's remarks on the relative characteristics of different species suggest that he would have liked Bowler's *The Doubt* (though he never refers to it by name). Writing of leaf growth in *Modern Painters* 3, he compares the horse chestnut and the elm:

> ... if it be meant for one of the crowned and lovely trees of the earth, it will separate into stars, and each ray of the leaf will form a ray of light in the crown ...: and if it be a commonplace tree, rather prudent and practical than imaginative, it will not expand all at once, but throw out its ribs every now and then along a central rib, like a merchant taking his occasional and restricted holiday.[50]

Himself a merchant's son, Ruskin had a keen sense of the social hierarchy and often applied it to landscape. There is an echo here of the snobbery that led William Barron, in 1852, to write of elms as 'commonplace ... rubbish', not suitable for the surroundings of a mansion.[51]

Ruskin's strongest published praise of Pre-Raphaelite tree-painting is not about Millais, or Hunt, or Hughes, or Inchbold, but about William Dyce. This is his critique of

93 WILLIAM DYCE

Titian Preparing to Make his First Essay in Colouring

1856–7 | Oil on canvas | 91.4 x 70.5 cm

Aberdeen Art Gallery and Museums Collections

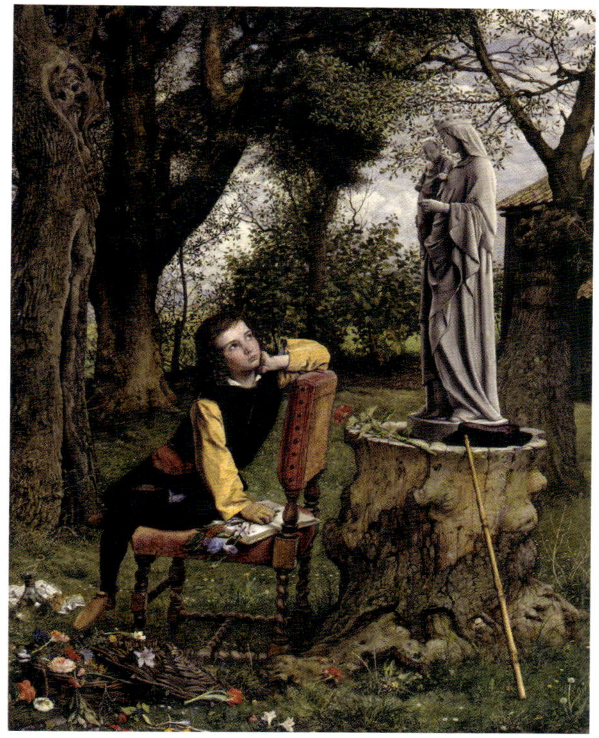

Dyce's painting, *Titian Preparing to Make his First Essay in Colouring*, shown at the Royal Academy in 1857 (fig. 93). To modern eyes it is chiefly remarkable for its precise delineation of four ancient trees, including a stump, a pollard and a hollow specimen. It is reminiscent of contemporary photographs in its focus on the accidents of age and the contrasting textures of bark and bare wood. Ruskin, however, chose to focus upon the treatment of oak leaves, which actually takes up only a small area of the picture. Dyce, he said, 'has rendered more of the finished grace and lovely composition of line in that oak foliage than has yet been seen in oak.'[52] It is fitting – and may not be coincidental – that a painting about the life of Titian should include finely drawn trees, since Ruskin had consistently praised Titian's tree-drawing.

Ruskin's commentary reflects his teaching practice at the Working Men's College, where he was bringing tree branches in for drawing lessons. His own drawing manual, *The Elements of Drawing* (published in 1857) gives a prominent role to the drawing of trees and bits of trees. The first part consists of a series of basic exercises, starting with the drawing and shading of squares. The first exercise to incorporate drawing from nature is number six: the student should choose a tree, nearly bare of leaves, seen against the sky or a pale wall, and, considering the boughs as rivers on a map, 'map them all out in flat shade' considering the tree 'nothing but a flat ramification on a white ground'.[53] This is basically the exercise Ruskin himself undertook when he made his drawing of an aspen tree in May 1842. The student can then progress to drawing boughs of trees fully rounded, and a spray of twelve to eighteen inches long. Ruskin prescribes two careful studies of a bough of every common tree – 'oak, ash, elm, birch, beech, etc' from different angles.[54] In *The Elements of Drawing* Ruskin also recommends studying tree trunks encircled by ivy: 'a not very thick trunk, say nine inches or a foot in diameter, with the ivy running up it sparingly, is an easy, and always a rewarding subject'.[55]

94 GEORGE PRICE BOYCE
A Girl by a Beech Tree in a Landscape
1857 | Oil on board | 29.8 x 47.9 cm
© Tate, London 2017

The Elements of Drawing had a direct influence on young artists. John Brett underwent a course of self-imposed study based on the exercises in the book.[56] Albert Moore's watercolour, *Study of an Ash Trunk* (Ashmolean Museum) may have been stimulated by Ruskin's prescriptions in *The Elements of Drawing*. It is a *tour de force* of accurate observation of the undergrowth around a tree trunk, which was shown at the RA in 1858. Another small work painted in 1857, which may also have been in the 1858 exhibition, was George Price Boyce's *A Girl by a Beech Tree in a Landscape* (fig. 94). This echoes the general composition of William Henry Millais's *Hayes Common*, with a portrait-like study of a beech tree on the left and a girl walking along a path on the right. It is now Boyce's only known oil painting. Albert Moore was only sixteen when he made his drawing; he later gave up landscape and took to painting women in classical dress, but Boyce had a long-standing interest in trees. In 1851 he recorded his admiration for 'the earnest and persevering study of Millais and Hunt, who have been for several months together in a retired part of the country painting mainly from nature the backgrounds to their pictures' – that is, the pollarded willows in *Ophelia* and *The Hireling Shepherd*.[57] In 1854 Ruskin and his father visited Boyce's studio and admired his drawings, including a (now lost) 'study of the twisted birch tree'.[58]

In his *Academy Notes* of 1858, Ruskin issued a very direct appeal to artists to paint the flowering trees and young leaves of an English spring. 'How strange' he wrote '... that no Pre-Raphaelite has painted a cherry-tree in blossom, dark-white against the twilight of April; nor an almond-tree rosy on the blue sky; nor the flush of the apple-blossom ... nor even so much as the first springing leaves of any tree in their pale, dispersed, delicate sharpness of shape'.[59] The artists rose to the challenge. In the Royal Academy exhibition of 1859, there were, evidently, many paintings of apple blossom.[60] The most prominent of these was Millais's *Spring (Apple Blossoms)* (Lady Lever Art Gallery, Liverpool) with its carefully painted orchard: this, however, had been under way since 1856, and was a natural development from Millais's *Autumn Leaves* (1856, Manchester Art Gallery) with its pile of dead leaves. Ruskin was not impressed: he described it as 'this fierce and rigid orchard – this angry blooming (petals, as it were, of japanned brass)'.[61] In 1859 he wrote: 'We cannot learn to paint leaves by painting trees-full, nor grass by painting fields-full. Learning to paint one leaf rightly is better than constructing a whole forest of leaf definitions.'[62] Ruskin seems to have come to the conclusion that the Pre-Raphaelite technique was not suitable for large masses of foliage – or at least that those artists who practised it had not mastered its basic skills.

Ruskin's most extended discussion of trees and tree-painting comes in volume 5 of *Modern Painters*, published in 1860. A long section – over a hundred pages in the *Complete Works* – is entitled 'Of Leaf Beauty.' It is here that he writes, as we have seen, of trees (and plants in general) as 'strange intermediate beings' who deserve 'boundless affection' from us.[63] Ruskin finds in trees lessons for political organisation, comparing trees to communities of men, to nations, to colonies and to families.[64] Ruskin divides them into two types – builders with the shield (mainly the deciduous trees) and builders with the sword (the pines and firs). Earlier, as we have seen, Ruskin contrasted the horse chestnut 'one of the crowned and lovely trees of the earth' with the 'commonplace' elm. He now says the willow is the most graceful of English trees.[65] He declares, however, that his favourite tree is the black spruce, by which he means the Norway spruce, *picea abies*.[66] He writes at length about its influence on human character in Switzerland, a country which was acquiring increasing importance for him. As an analogy to England, he chooses, not the oak or the beech, as one might expect, but the aspen: 'strong-trunked enough when put to proof, and very good for making cartwheels of, but shaking pale with epidemic panic at every breeze'.[67]

The Pre-Raphaelites painted quintessentially English trees – even John Brett, when painting his *Val d'Aosta* (Lloyd Webber collection) in the Alps in 1858, depicts chestnuts and birches in the foreground and middle ground, not Norway spruces. The other artists painted the four forest

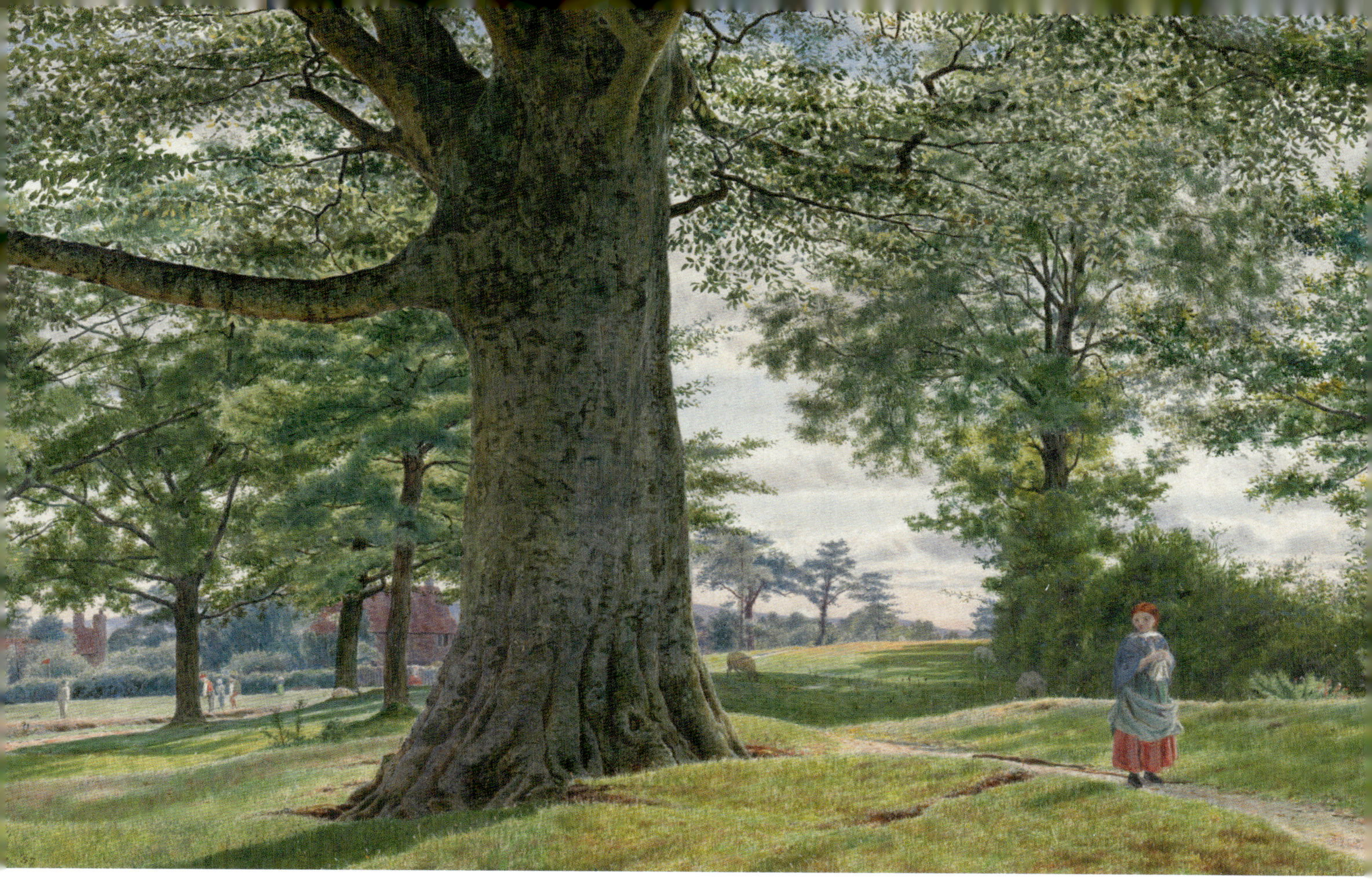

trees: oak, beech, elm and ash. Ruskin's comments in this last volume of *Modern Painters* imply that he is disappointed by Pre-Raphaelite tree-painting. When the Pre-Raphaelites, he says 'began to lead our wandering artists back into the eternal paths of all great Art, and showed that whatever men drew at all, ought to be drawn accurately and knowingly; not blunderingly nor by guess (leaves of trees, among other things), feeble young students said to themselves that they only had to paint leaves of trees as they grow, and they would produce beautiful landscapes directly'. Alas, says Ruskin, they were wrong. If you can paint one leaf you can paint the world, and few painters can do it. Ruskin names only sixteenth-century figure painters, starting with Titian – no Pre-Raphaelites at all.[68] He defends himself against the charge of inconsistency, setting a drawing of his own next to details from Hobbema in the hope that the comparison will help the reader to understand 'why, never having ceased to rate the Dutch painters for their meanness or minuteness, I yet accepted the leaf-painting of the Pre-Raphaelites with reverence and hope'.[69] He repeats his claim, first made in volume I of *Modern Painters*, that only Turner ever drew the stem of a tree.[70]

There is a sad postscript to Ruskin's discussion of tree-painting in a remark he made in *Proserpina*, published in the 1870s:

> My simple artist readers of long ago, when I told them to draw leaves, thought they could do them by the bough-full, whenever they liked. Alas, except by old William Hunt, and Burne-Jones, I've not seen a leaf painted, since those burdocks of Turner's ...[71]

Ruskin suffered from depression and mental illness in later life, which explains some of the inconsistencies in his writings. Nevertheless, his ambivalence towards Pre-Raphaelite tree-painting occurs throughout. Although they followed, or in the early years anticipated, his teaching, Ruskin could never quite accept the Pre-Raphaelites' meticulously-studied trees as the equal of those of his great hero, Turner. He was enthusiastic about Frederic Leighton's extraordinary study of a lemon tree (fig. 12); but this was a drawing rather than a painting, like Ruskin's own studies of trees.[72]

95 GEORGE PRICE BOYCE

At Binsey, near Oxford

1862 | Watercolour and ink | 31.1 x 53.7 cm

Higgins Art Gallery and Museum, Bedford

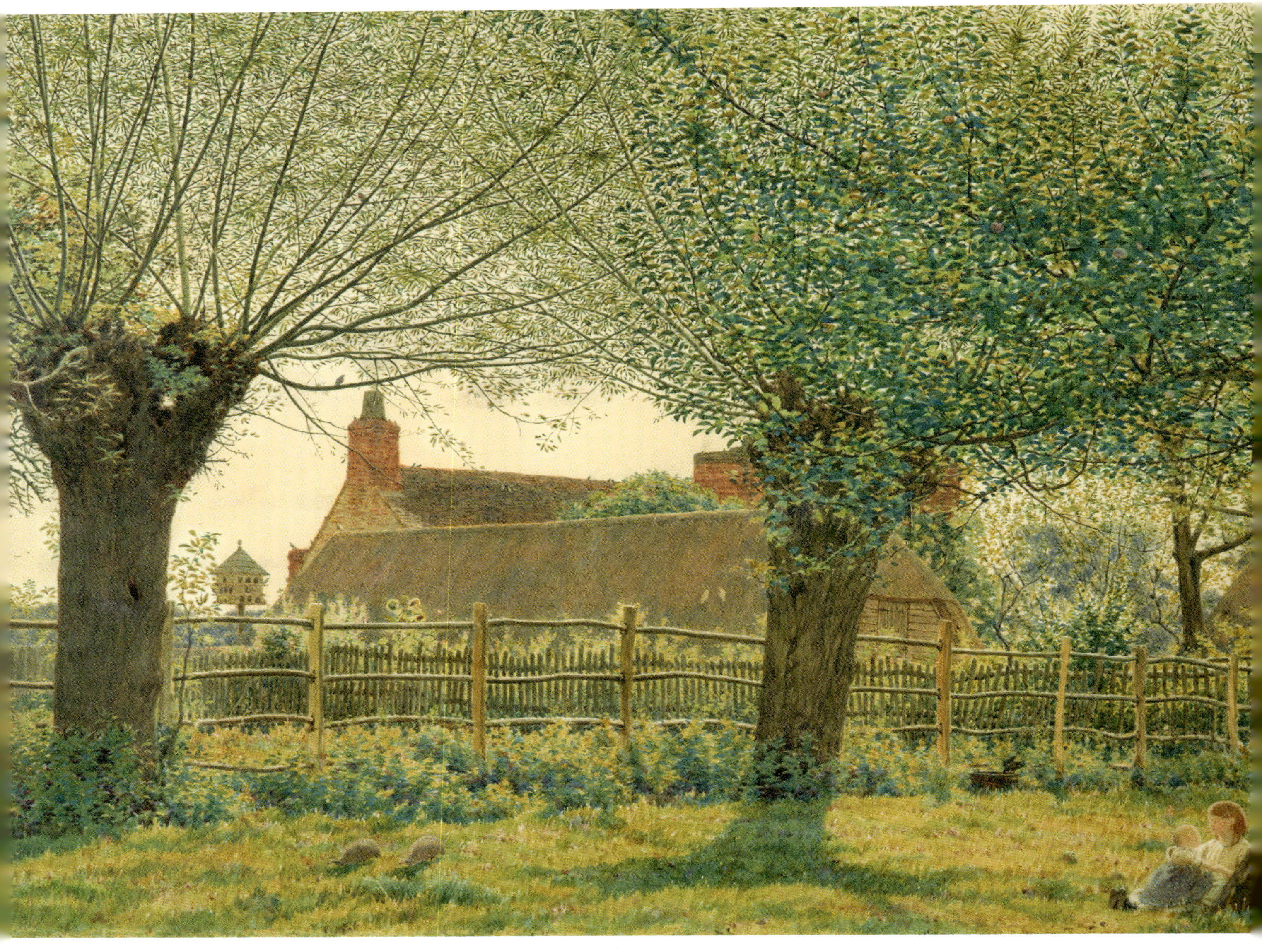

96 JOHN BRETT
The Hedger
1859–60 | Oil on canvas | 90 x 70 cm
Private Collection, Bridgeman Images

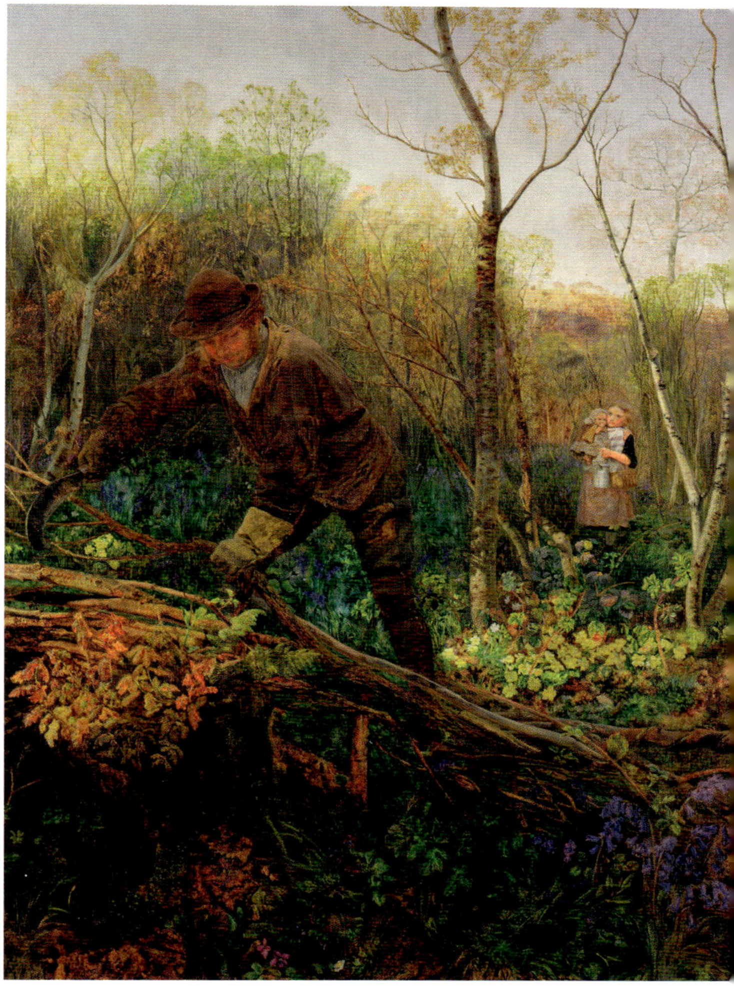

THE YOUNGER GENERATION: GEORGE PRICE BOYCE AND THE BRETTS

Despite Ruskin's disappointment, a younger generation of artists was building on the bold naturalism of the Pre-Raphaelite tree paintings of the 1850s. George Price Boyce painted no more oils, as far as we know, but he developed a very effective use of screens of trees in his watercolours. *At Binsey, near Oxford*, 1862 (fig. 95) is a particularly beautiful example of this device. The sun shines through the leaves of the pollarded willows and apple tree, creating delicate patterns which are counterpoised to the lushness of the grass beneath them. The human elements of the scene – farmhouse and barn, dovecot and fence, and the mother and child tucked away unobtrusively in the corner – are subordinate to the exuberance of the trees. John Brett also devoted careful attention to the trees in his paintings in the late 1850s and 1860s. An ancient twisted tree trunk with a single frail branch growing out of it provides an eloquent comment on the stunted life of the young boy in *The Stonebreaker* (1857-8; Walker, Liverpool). Two years later, *The Hedger* of 1859-60 (fig. 96) was a response to Ruskin's challenge that Pre-Raphaelite painters had not yet painted 'the first springing leaves of any tree in their pale, dispersed, delicate sharpness of shape'. Oliver Rackham, visiting the 1984 Pre-Raphaelite exhibition at the Tate Gallery, singled out this painting as an effective representation of oak and ash stools in early spring.[73] It seems that Ruskin was not impressed, since he advised Thomas Plint not to buy the work, despite its 'beautiful qualities, the subject being totally uninteresting'.[74] To modern eyes it is extremely interesting, as one of the few representations in nineteenth-century painting of the work that went on in the woods every year: hedging in the foreground, with a background of coppiced trees, hence the slender trunks rising together from a single stool.[75]

97 JOHN BRETT

February in the Isle of Wight

1866 | Watercolour and bodycolour | 46 x 35.4 cm

Birmingham Museums and Art Gallery, Bridgeman Images

98 ROSA BRETT

In the Artist's Garden

c.1859 | Oil on board | 15.6 x 14 cm

Private Collection

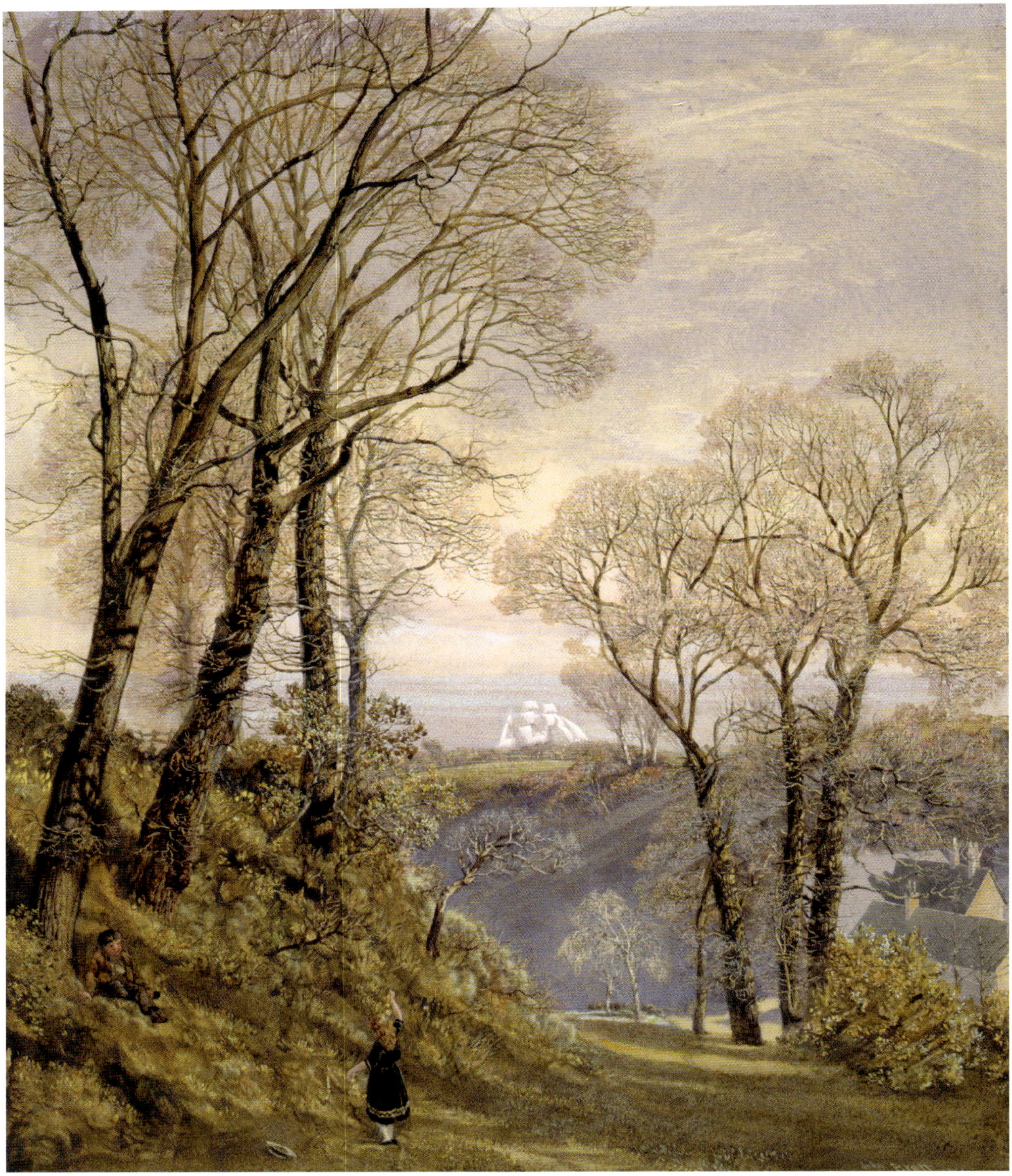

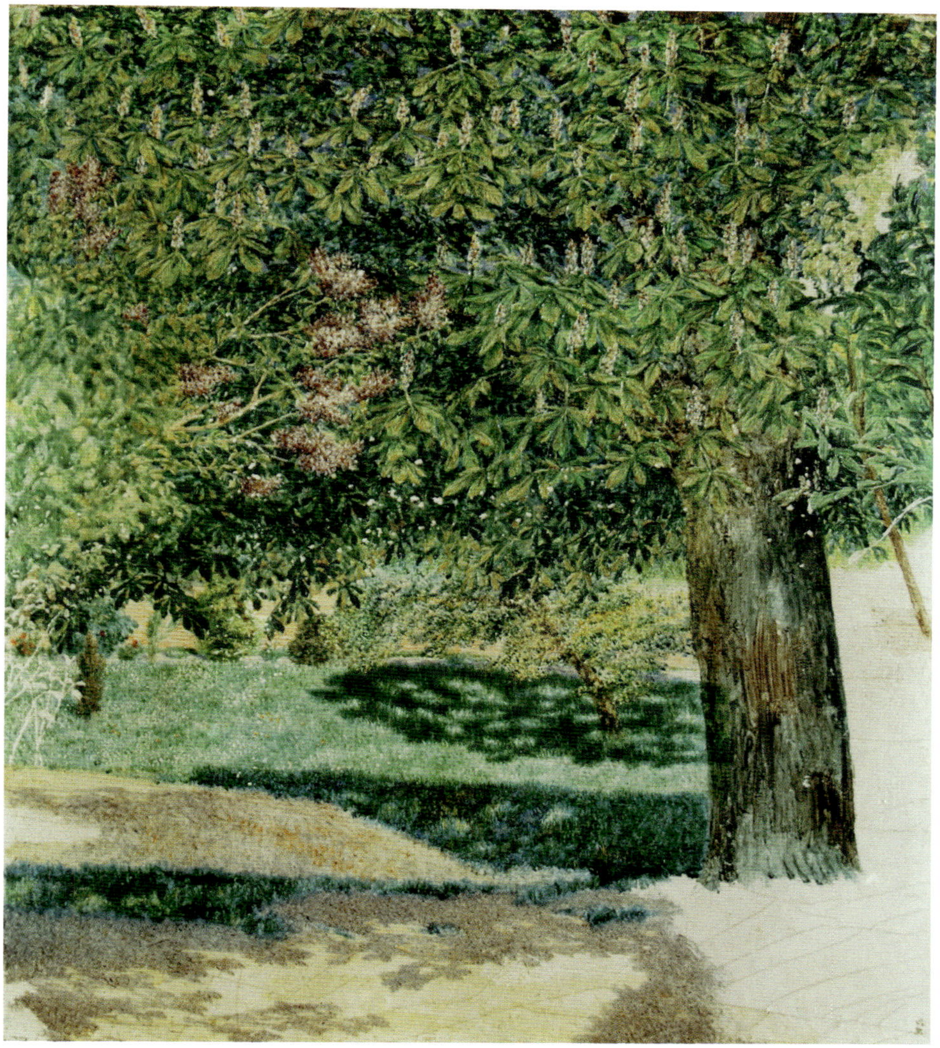

Ruskin's emphasis on the ramification of trees may have been in Brett's mind when he painted his watercolour, *February in the Isle of Wight* (fig. 97) in 1867. This is a virtuoso study of elegant ash trees in winter, their branches and twigs traced painstakingly against a bright sky. Brett painted further ravishing studies of trees before deciding to concentrate on sea and coastal painting for the rest of his life.[76] In contrast to the wintry scene portrayed in *February in the Isle of Wight*, there is a profusion of leaves and flowers in his sister Rosa Brett's tiny, delicate study now known as *In the Artist's Garden* (fig. 98). This is equalled only by Samuel Palmer's studies of trees in blossom in its magical intensity, and takes up one of his favourite subjects, the horse chestnut in flower. The painting was never exhibited or even finished, but it is justly admired today, perhaps showing the Pre-Raphaelite attention to the detailed beauty of trees in its most concentrated form.

In the paintings of the 1850s and 1860s, the close attention that had been paid to trees in the drawing manuals, illustrated books and portraits blossomed into a full-colour celebration of the details of oaks, elms, beeches, ashes and horse chestnuts – of their trunks and leaves in particular. The writings and drawings of John Ruskin did much to encourage this development, though he cannot be held wholly responsible. His love for Turner, and his attention to ramification, meant that he was repeatedly out of step with the artists of this period, and in some cases he lagged behind them. A patriotic love for the native trees and woods, and an awareness of the detail that could be captured by photography, were at least equally important in creating the conditions for this extraordinary body of work.

ENDNOTES

1 Henry Twining, Esq., *On the Elements of Picturesque Scenery, considered with reference to landscape painting* (London: printed for private distribution by George Barclay, 1846), p. 88.

2 John Ruskin, *Pre-Raphaelitism*, 1851, E. T. Cook and A. Wedderburn, eds, *The Works of John Ruskin* (London: George Allen, 1903-12) Vol. 12, p. 339.

3 John Ruskin, *Praeterita*, 1885-9, Cook and Wedderburn, eds., *Works*, Vol. 35, p. 313.

4 Christopher Newall et al, *John Ruskin, Artist and Observer* (Ottawa: National Gallery of Canada and London: Paul Holberton Publishing, 2014), p. 15.

5 Cook and Wedderburn, eds., *Works*, Vol. 1, pp. xxxvi-xxxviii. The remark about Ruskin being a natural genius is in a letter to John James Ruskin dated 30 November 1838.

6 '... there is another Stone-pine concealed by the Mount more elaborate, but less satisfactory than those below, which, therefore, are alone shown.' Ruskin's revision to the Rudimentary series (1878), retrieved from The Elements of Drawing website, ruskin.ashmolean.org, 26 July 2016.

7 Ibid.

8 John L. Bradley, ed., *Ruskin's Letters from Venice, 1851-2* (New Haven: Yale University Press, 1955), p. 199, cited in Robert Hewison, Ian Warrell and Stephen Wildman, *Ruskin, Turner and the Pre-Raphaelites* (London: Tate Gallery Publishing, 2000), p. 83.

9 Ruskin, *Praeterita*, Cook and Wedderburn, eds., *Works*, Vol. 35, p. 429.

10 Ibid, facing p. 402.

11 Ruskin, *Modern Painters* I, Cook and Wedderburn, eds., *Works*, Vol. 3, p. 578.

12 Ibid, p. 163.

13 Ibid, p. 252.

14 Ibid, p. 585.

15 Ibid, p. 588.

16 Ibid, p. 592.

17 Ibid, pp. 599-600.

18 Harold I. Shapiro, ed., *Ruskin in Italy: Letters to his Parents, 1845* (Oxford: Clarendon Press, 1972), p. 189, cited in Hewison et al, *Ruskin, Turner and the Pre-Raphaelites*, p. 153.

19 Ruskin, *Modern Painters* I, Cook and Wedderburn, eds., *Works*, Vol. 3, p. 603.

20 Ibid, pp. 604-5.

21 Ibid, p. 603.

22 William E. Fredeman, ed., *The P. R. B. Journal. William Michael Rossetti's Diary of the Pre-Raphaelite Brotherhood 1849-1853* (Oxford: Clarendon Press, 1975), p. 18. 8 and 9 October 1849.

23 Allen Staley, *The Pre-Raphaelite Landscape*, 2nd edition (New Haven and London: Yale University Press, 2001), p. 15.

24 27 Oct 1850, James H. Coombs et al, *A Pre-Raphaelite Friendship: The Correspondence of William Henry Hunt and John Lucas Tupper* (Michigan: Ann Arbor, 1986), p. 33.

25 *Literary Gazette: A Weekly Journal of Literature, Science and the Arts*, no. 1794 (7 June 1851), p. 396. See also *Bentley's Miscellany*, no. 29 (June 1851), p. 624.

26 John Ruskin, Letter to the Editor, *The Times*, 13 May 1851.

27 Ruskin, *Modern Painters* 1, Cook and Wedderburn, eds., *Works*, Vol. 3, p. 599.

28 Ibid, p. 627.

29 See Christiana Payne, 'John Constable, John Ruskin, and the Pre-Raphaelites', *British Art Journal*, Vol. XVI no 1 (Summer 2015), pp. 78-87.

30 William Holman Hunt, *Pre-Raphaelitism and the Pre-Raphaelite Brotherhood*, 2nd ed. (London: Chapman and Hall Ltd, 1913), Vol. I p. 191. Hunt says elsewhere that 'William Millais came and stayed, painting a small landscape.' (Ibid, pp. 218-20)

31 Virginia Surtees, ed., *The Diaries of George Price Boyce* (London, Old Water Colour Society, 1980), p. 7, entry for 25 March 1852. Boyce records that there was a 'crowded audience' and that he 'came across J. E. Millais, only knowing him by sight.'

32 See Jason Rosenfeld and Alison Smith, *Millais* (London: Tate Publishing, 2007), p. 96.

33 Undated letter to William Henry Millais from Edward Lear, in Admiral Sir William James, ed., *The Order of Release: The Story of John Ruskin, Effie Gray and John Everett Millais told for the first time in their unpublished letters* (London: John Murray, 1947), p. 177.

34 Fredeman, ed., *The P. R. B. Journal*, p. 68.

35 See records of hanging scheme of exhibition of 1853, Royal Academy Library, RA/SEC/23/1.
36 *Illustrated London News*, 14 May 1853, p. 382.
37 H. Allingham and E. B. Williams, eds, *Letters to William Allingham* (New York, Bombay and Calcutta: Longmans, Green and Co, 1911), p. 51. Letter dated 15/16 August 1854. See also Leonard Roberts with Stephen Wildman, *Arthur Hughes: His Life and Works* (London: Antique Collectors' Club, 1997), pp. 126-9.
38 Its modern title is *In Early Spring*, and it is presumed to be the painting exhibited in 1855 as *A Study, in March*. This identification is not certain, however.
39 Reproduced in Staley, *Pre-Raphaelite Landscape*, p. 155.
40 *Athenaeum* no. 1439 (26 May 1855), p. 623.
41 Ibid.
42 *Athenaeum* no. 1490 (17 May 1856), p. 621.
43 *Art Journal*, June 1855, p. 182.
44 Ruskin, *Academy Notes*, 1855, Cook and Wedderburn, eds., *Works*, Vol. 14, pp. 22, 20.
45 Ibid, p. 21.
46 Charles Robert Leslie, RA, *A Handbook for Young Painters* (London: John Murray, 1855), pp. 271-2.
47 Ruskin, *Modern Painters* 3, 1856. Cook and Wedderburn, eds., *Works*, Vol. 5, p. 162.
48 Ruskin, *Modern Painters* 4, 1856, Cook and Wedderburn, eds., *Works,* Vol. 6, pp. 97-101.
49 Ruskin, *Modern Painters* 3, 1856, Cook and Wedderburn, eds., *Works*, Vol. 5, pp. 156-165.
50 Ibid, p. 265.
51 Cited in Chapter Six, p. 137.
52 Ruskin, *Academy Notes*, 1857, Cook and Wedderburn, eds., *Works*, Vol. 14, p. 98.
53 Ruskin, *The Elements of Drawing*, 1857, Cook and Wedderburn, eds., *Works*, Vol. 15, p. 40.
54 Ibid, pp. 67, 71.
55 Ibid, p. 109.
56 See Charles Brett, 'John Brett and Ruskin's "The Elements of Drawing"', *Burlington Magazine*, CXLVII (September 2005), p. 613-16.
57 Surtees, ed., *Diaries*, p. 4 (18 November 1851).
58 Ibid, p. 13 (21 April 1854).
59 Ruskin, *Academy Notes*, 1858, Cook and Wedderburn, eds., *Works,* Vol. 14, p. 154.
60 Ruskin, *Academy Notes*, 1859, Cook and Wedderburn, eds., *Works*, Vol. 14, p. 233. Ruskin writes of Hughes's *The King's Orchard* that 'the apple-blossom, among all its ruddy rivals on the walls this year, is tenderly, but triumphantly, victorious'.
61 Ibid, p. 215.
62 Ibid, p. 233.
63 Ruskin, *Modern Painters* 5, 1860, Cook and Wedderburn, eds., *Works*, Vol. 7, pp. 14-16.
64 Ibid, pp. 41-2, 73.
65 Ibid, p. 90.
66 Ibid, pp. 102-3.
67 Ibid, p. 41.
68 Ibid, pp. 51-2.
69 Ibid, p. 54.
70 Ibid, p. 95.
71 Ruskin, *Proserpina. Studies of Wayside Flowers, while the air was yet pure, among the Alps, and in the Scotland and England which my father knew*, 1879 (published in parts, 1875-1886), Cook and Wedderburn, eds., *Works,* Vol. 25, p. 304.
72 See Mrs Russell Barrington, *The Life, Letters and Work of Frederic Leighton* (London: George Allen, 1906), Vol. I, p. 202 and Vol. II, pp. 42, 373.
73 Oliver Rackham, *Trees and Woodland in the British Landscape: The Complete History of Britain's Trees, Woodland, and Hedgerows*, (first published 1976; London: Phoenix Press, 4th Impression, 2004), p. 109.
74 Letter from John Ruskin to Thomas Plint, undated, John Rylands Library, University of Manchester, 1254 letter 15.
75 Allen Staley, Christopher Newall, et al, *Pre-Raphaelite Vision: Truth to Nature* (London: Tate Publishing, 2004), p. 186.
76 See *The River Dart* (1866) and *Oaks in May, Haslemere* (1868), illustrated in Christiana Payne, *John Brett, Pre-Raphaelite Landscape Painter* (New Haven and London: Yale University Press, 2010), pp. 93, 100.

Conclusion

THIS BOOK HAS surveyed the role of trees in British art over a crucial century in the country's history. This was a period when parkland and woodland, once the reserve of the very rich, for leisure, and the very poor, for subsistence, became accepted amenities for all the population. We can follow this transformation through the work of the artists. Paul Sandby, Thomas Hearne and John Sell Cotman studied trees in private parkland, and worked for patrons who were landowners; but Richard Redgrave, Myles Birket Foster and William Henry Millais, amongst others, went to areas of accessible woodland, catering for a public who enjoyed the opportunity to picnic in the woods in summertime. In the early part of the period, trees were associated with paternalism, sheltering beggars and providing support for squatters' cottages. Ancient trees were cherished, and valued as a 'natural' justification for the role of the landed aristocracy. By the mid-century, such ideas had become more or less obsolete, as the appreciation of trees came to be regarded as relevant to the entire population.

It was also a time when many new varieties came in to the country, and species of trees once known only in poetry or fable became realities. Haunting images of stone pines and cypresses in Italy, of banyans in India and palms in the Pacific, gave substance to literary evocations of Paradise. Yet the interest in new trees was balanced by a growing fondness for the natives, just as British conquests abroad and the resulting growth of the Empire produced a deep affection for the Home Counties and the countryside of southern England. This was particularly strong in the Pre-Raphaelites, who resisted John Ruskin's attempt to interest them in foreign trees. Oak, elm, beech and ash, the four 'forest trees' or 'timber trees', continued to provide staple fare for artists, joined occasionally by the horse chestnut and more often by the pollarded willow.

Throughout the period, artists loved trees and studied them closely. The contrasting characters of the different species were known and observed, following the example of the drawing manuals, which laid out their peculiarities in shape, texture and 'touch'. Individual artists had their preferences for particular types of tree: Paul Sandby for the beech, John Constable for the ash, Samuel Palmer for the horse chestnut and cypress, John Robert Cozens and J. M. W. Turner for the stone pine, Edward Lear for the olive. Where ancient trees were concerned, the overriding favourite was the oak, which dominates Jacob George Strutt's impressive series of tree portraits in *Sylva Britannica*. Writers, following William Gilpin, often named the oak as the most picturesque of all trees, and others stressed its symbolism as the support of Britain's naval strength. However, the beech also attracted many admirers: regarded in the eighteenth century as Claude Lorrain's favourite tree, in the nineteenth century it came into its own as the cheerful, convivial tree of woodland parties. The deep colour and commanding silhouette of the elm, and the graceful airiness of the ash, similarly, inspired many beautiful drawings and paintings.

Histories of landscape painting often focus mainly on painting in oil and watercolour, but where trees were concerned, the art of drawing was of vital importance. This is particularly clear in the case of Constable, whose painted trees rest on a foundation of repeated painstaking study in pencil. Trees in his landscapes were the equivalent of human figures in history paintings, and the study required to express them competently was analogous to the drawing from sculpture and the life model that went on in the Royal Academy. The many drawing manuals that catered for amateurs and professional artists, similarly, emphasize the importance of the 'anatomy' of trees. In this period, many of the most impressive images of trees are in black and white:

the etched plates of Strutt's *Sylva Britannica*, the lithographs of Henry William Burgess's *Eidodendron*, Constable's tree studies, and Palmer's drawing of the Lullingstone oaks. Others are in watercolour, with strong outlines, and colour added sparingly: Lear's drawings of olive trees at Tivoli and the banyan at Barrackpore, for example.

Utility and scientific interest went hand in hand with the aesthetic appreciation of trees. This is particularly evident in Loudon's *Arboretum Britannicum*, with its 600 tree portraits, all drawn by artists. Ironically, it was published in 1838, just a year before the invention of the daguerreotype. In subsequent years the new processes made possible by photography provided artists with a great range of images to which they could refer. Initially, this development seems to have influenced the tree-painting of the Pre-Raphaelites and their followers, with its emphasis on the texture of tree trunks, an effect that is also prevalent in early photographs. At the same time the advent of photography encouraged them to lavish attention on effects the early photograph could not manage, such as the true colour of foliage and the precise shapes of leaves.

This book has concentrated on British art, but the interest in trees that it documents was a feature of the period across the western world. Théodore Rousseau and the artists of Barbizon in France, Caspar David Friedrich in Germany, and the Hudson River School painters in the United States, all transcribed the features of their native trees, and all saw their trees as cause for patriotic pride. Oak trees were regarded in all three countries, as they were in Britain, as symbols of national identity. Fir trees provided symbols of enduring hope in Friedrich's famous *Cross in the Mountains (the Tetschen Altar)* (1807; Gemäldegalerie, Dresden). Rousseau's painting of *The Oaks of Apremont* (1852, Musée d'Orsay, Paris) was exhibited at the Exposition Universelle in 1855, and has since become an icon of his concern to preserve the Forest of Fontainebleau and its native species. In the eastern United States, artists such as Thomas Cole and Jasper Cropsey loved maple trees for the characteristic colours they gave to the New England autumn. The discovery of the redwood trees of California, however, was seen as marking out America as a providential land, because their great age made them witnesses of the life of Christ. Albert Bierstadt's huge portrait of one of these trees, *The Great Trees, Mariposa Grove* (1876; private collection) was exhibited in London in 1879.

The 1860s have provided a convenient terminus for this study, with the writings of Ruskin on trees and the paintings of the younger generation of Pre-Raphaelites. Needless to say, the story does not end there. Painters and photographers continued to be active in popular woodlands such as Burnham Beeches, and paintings of trees continued to feature in Royal Academy exhibitions. In 1916 Rex Vicat Cole continued the drawing manual tradition with his influential publication, *The Artistic Anatomy of Trees*. In the first half of the twentieth century, the Nash brothers, Paul and John, produced many haunting images of trees, drawing partly on the precedent of Samuel Palmer to see trees 'as men' and to invest them with a powerful symbolism. At the present time, many British artists take trees as their theme. Kurt Jackson both plants and paints trees in Cornwall. David Hockney has displayed paintings and photographs of them on a vast scale at Royal Academy exhibitions. Tacita Dean has continued the tree portrait tradition of Jacob George Strutt by making huge photographs of named trees, including Strutt's Majesty in Fredwell Park. A new group of artists, the Arborealists, have recently combined forces in exhibitions at home and abroad. The appeal of the tree is stronger than ever today, as we recognize its importance in promoting human wellbeing and combating climate change.

Bibliography

UNPUBLISHED WORKS

Beryl Hartley, 'The Artist as Naturalist and Experimenter: Landscape Painting and Science 1740-1850' (PhD thesis, Imperial College, University of London, 1995)

John Linnell, MS Autobiography, written in 1863, now in the Fitzwilliam Museum, Cambridge

Royal Academy records of hanging schemes of exhibitions, Royal Academy Library, RA/SEC/23/1

Strutt correspondence preserved in the Warwick County Record Office, CR 1709/116

PUBLISHED WORKS

Anon, *English Forests and Forest Trees, Historical, Legendary and Descriptive* (London: Ingram, Cooke & Co, 1853)

Anon, *Fairlop Oak and Fairlop Fair: Memorabilia* (Waddesdon: Kylin Press Ltd, 1982)

Adams, Eric, *Francis Danby: Varieties of Poetic Landscape* (New Haven and London: Yale University Press, 1973)

Aikin, John, *The Woodland Companion, or, a brief Description of British Trees, with some account of their uses* (London: Baldwin, Cradock and Joy, 1815)

Allingham, H., and E. B. Williams, eds, *Letters to William Allingham* (New York, Bombay and Calcutta: Longmans, Green and Co, 1911)

Anderson, Anne, et al, *Under the Greenwood: Picturing the British Tree from Constable to Kurt Jackson* (Bristol: Sansom and Company, 2013)

Appleton, Jay, *The Experience of Landscape* (London: Wiley, 1975)

Archer, Mildred, *Early Views of India: The Picturesque Journeys of Thomas and William Daniell 1786-1794. The Complete Aquatints* (London: Thames and Hudson, 1980)

Bagot, 2nd Lord, *Memorials of the Bagot Family: compiled in 1823* (Blithfield: Wm Hodgetts, 1824)

Ball, Johnson, *Paul and Thomas Sandby, Royal Academicians: An Anglo-Danish saga of Art, Love and War in Georgian England* (Cheddar, Somerset: Charles Skilton Ltd, 1985)

Baird, John D., and Charles Ryskamp, *The Poems of William Cowper* (Oxford: Clarendon Press, 1980-95)

Barbier, Carl Paul, *William Gilpin: His Drawings, Teaching, and Theory of the Picturesque* (Oxford: Clarendon Press, 1963)

Barnard, George, *Handbook of Foliage and Foreground Drawing* (London: Ingram, Cooke & Co, 1853)

Barnard, George, *Handbook of Foliage and Foreground Drawing* (2nd ed., London: Griffith and Farran, 1870)

Barnard, George, *Trees from Nature* (London: Winsor and Newton, 1868)

Barron, William, *The British Winter Garden, being a Practical Treatise on Evergreens* (London: Bradbury and Evans, 1852)

R. B. Beckett, ed., *John Constable's Correspondence* (Ipswich: Suffolk Records Society, 1962-69)

Beckett, R. B., ed., *John Constable's Discourses* (Ipswich: Suffolk Records Society, 1970)

Beckett, R. B. et al, eds., *John Constable: Further Documents and Correspondence* (Tate Gallery and Suffolk Records Society, 1975)

Bermingham, Ann, *Learning to Draw. Studies in the Cultural History of a Polite and Useful Art* (New Haven and London: Yale University Press, 2000)

Bermingham, Ann, ed., *Sensation and Sensibility. Viewing Gainsborough's Cottage Door* (New Haven and London: Yale University Press, 2005)

Bicknell, Peter, and Jane Munro, *Gilpin to Ruskin: Drawing Masters and their Manuals, 1800-1860* (Cambridge: Fitzwilliam Museum, 1987)

Bonehill, John, and Stephen Daniels, eds., *Paul Sandby: Picturing Britain* (London: Royal Academy, 2009)

Brett, Charles, 'John Brett and Ruskin's "The Elements of Drawing"', *Burlington Magazine*, CXLVII (September 2005), pp. 613-16

Brown, Jane, *The Omnipotent Magician: Lancelot 'Capability' Brown, 1716-1783* (London: Chatto and Windus, 2011)

Bryant, Joshua, *Progressive Lessons on the Art of Drawing Landscapes* (London: Rudolph Ackermann, 1807)

Burgess, H. W., *Eidodendron: Views of the general Character and Appearance of Trees Foreign & Indigenous as connected with Picturesque Scenery* (London: J. Dickinson, 1827)

Butlin, M., *Samuel Palmer's Sketchbook, 1824* (Clairvaux: Trianon Press, 1962)

Butlin, M., and E. Joll, *The Paintings of J. M. W. Turner* (New Haven and London: Yale University Press, rev. ed., 1984)

Campbell, Michael J., *John Martin, 1789-1884, Creation of Light. Prints and Drawings from the Campbell Collection* (Valencia, Madrid and Bilbao: Bancaja, 2006)

Casteras, Susan P., and Ronald Parkinson, eds., *Richard Redgrave 1804-1888* (New Haven and London: Yale University Press, 1988)
Chetan, Anand, and Diana Brueton, *The Sacred Yew* (London: Arkana/Penguin Books, 1996)
Cook, E. T., and A. Wedderburn, eds., *The Works of John Ruskin* (London: George Allen, 1903-12)
Cozens, Alexander, *The Shape, Skeleton and Foliage of 32 Species of Trees* (1786)
Craig, William Marshall, *An Essay upon the Study of Nature in Drawing Landscape* (London, 1793)
Crouan, Katharine, *John Linnell: A Centennial Exhibition* (Cambridge: Fitzwilliam Museum, 1982)
Daniels, Stephen, 'The political iconography of woodland in later Georgian England', in Denis Cosgrove and Stephen Daniels, eds., *The Iconography of Landscape. Essays on the symbolic representation, design and use of past environments* (Cambridge: Cambridge University Press, 1988), pp. 43-82
Daniels, Stephen, *Humphrey Repton: Landscape Gardening and the Geography of Georgian England* (New Haven and London: Yale University Press, 1999)
Davy, Charles, *Letters addressed chiefly to a young Gentleman upon subjects of Literature* (Bury St Edmunds: J. Rackham, 1787)
Dawe, George, *The Life of George Morland, with Remarks on his Works*, (London: Vernor, Hood and Sharpe, 1807)
Deakin, Roger, *Wildwood: A Journey through Trees* (London: Hamish Hamilton, 2007)
Coombs, James H., et al, *A Pre-Raphaelite Friendship: The Correspondence of William Henry Hunt and John Lucas Tupper* (Michigan: Ann Arbor, 1986)
de Crespigny, Rose, and Horace Hutchinson, *The New Forest: Its Traditions, Inhabitants and Customs* (London: John Murray, 1895)
Deutsche Historische Museum, *Unter Bäumen: Die Deutschen und der Wald* (Berlin: Sandstein Verlag, 2012)
Eagles, John, *The Sketcher* (Edinburgh and London: William Blackwood & Sons, 1856)
Edward Lear in Corsica: The Journal of a Landscape Painter (London: William Kimber & Co Ltd, 1966, first published in 1870 as *Journal of a Landscape Painter in Corsica*)
Edwards, Karen L., *Milton and the Natural World: Science and Poetry in Paradise Lost* (Cambridge University Press, 1999)
Elliott, Paul A., Charles Watkins and Stephen Daniels, *The British Arboretum: Trees, Science and Culture in the Nineteenth Century* (London: Pickering and Chatto, 2011)
Empson, Charles, *The Cowthorpe Oak, from a painting by the late George William Fothergill, from accurate sketches made on the spot, expressly for this work* , 2nd ed. (London: Ackermann and Co, 1842)
Evelyn, John, *Silva: or a Discourse of Forest-Trees and the Propagation of Timber in his Majesty's Dominions… with notes by A. Hunter* (York: J. Dodsley et al., 1776)
Fisher, Roger, *Heart of Oak, the British Bulwark* (London: J. Johnson, 1763)
Fleming-Williams, Ian, *Constable and his Drawings* (London: Philip Wilson Publishers Ltd, 1990)
Fleming-Williams, Ian, et al., *Constable: A Master Draughtsman* (London: Dulwich Picture Gallery, 1994)
Francia, Louis, *Progressive Lessons tending to elucidate the characters of trees, with the process of sketching, and painting them in Water Colours* (London: T. Clay, 1813)
Fredeman, William E., ed., *The P. R. B. Journal. William Michael Rossetti's Diary of the Pre-Raphaelite Brotherhood 1849-1853* (Oxford: Clarendon Press, 1975)
Fulford, Tim, 'Cowper, Wordsworth, Clare: The Politics of Trees', *John Clare Journal*, no 14, July 1995, pp 47-59
Fulford, Tim, *Landscape, Liberty and Authority: Poetry, Criticism and Politics from Thomson to Wordsworth* (Cambridge: Cambridge University Press, 1996)
Gilpin, William, *Remarks on Forest Scenery, and other Woodland Views (relative chiefly to picturesque beauty) illustrated by the scenes of New-Forest in Hampshire* (London: R. Blamire, 1791)
Gray, Thomas, *Elegy written in a Country Churchyard* (London: R. Dodsley, 1751)
Greenacre, Francis, *Francis Danby. 1793-1861* (London: Tate Gallery in association with City of Bristol Museum and Art Gallery, 1983)
[Grote, Harriet], *Some Account of the Hamlet of East Burnham, by a late resident* (London: Savill & Edwards, 1858)
Hardie, Martin, and James Laver, with notes and introduction by A. H. Palmer, *Catalogue of an Exhibition of Drawings, Etchings and Woodcuts by Samuel Palmer and other Disciples of William Blake* (London: Victoria and Albert Museum, 1926)

Hargraves, Matthew, *Varieties of Romantic Experience: British, Danish, Dutch, French and German Drawings from the Collection of Charles Ryskamp* (New Haven: Yale Center for British Art, 2010)

Harris, Esmond, Jeanette Harris and N. D. G. James, *Oak: A British History* (Macclesfield: Windgather Press Ltd, 2003)

Harding, James Duffield, *Elementary Art, or, the Use of the Lead Pencil, advocated and explained* (London: Charles Tilt, 1834)

Harding, Paul T., and Tom Wall, eds., *Moccas: An English Deer Park. The history, wildlife and management of the first parkland National Nature Reserve* (Peterborough: English Nature, 2000)

Harley, George, *Lessons on Drawing Trees* (London: R. Ackermann, 1829)

Hartley, Beryl, 'The Living Academies of Nature: Scientific Experiments in Learning and Communicating the New Skills of Early Nineteenth-century Landscape Painting', *Studies in History and Philosophy of Science*, 27 (June 1996), pp. 149-80

Hassell, J., *Memoirs of the life of George Morland* (London: James Cundee, 1806)

Hayes, John, *The Landscape Paintings of Thomas Gainsborough* (London: Philip Wilson, 1982)

Heath, Francis George, *Burnham Beeches* (London: William Rider & Sons, 1883)

Hewison, Robert, Ian Warrell and Stephen Wildman, *Ruskin, Turner and the Pre-Raphaelites* (London: Tate Gallery Publishing, 2000)

Hey, Rebecca, *The Spirit of the Woods, illustrated by coloured engravings* (London: Longmans, Rees, Orme, Green and Longman, 1837)

Hight, Julian, *Britain's Tree Story: the History and Legends of Britain's Ancient Trees* (London: National Trust Books, 2011)

Hill, David, *Cotman in the North: Watercolours of Durham and Yorkshire* (New Haven and London: Yale University Press, 2005)

Hodges, William, *Travels in India, during the years 1780, 1781, 1782, and 1783* (London: printed for the author and sold by J. Edwards, 1793)

Howard, Frank, *Frank Howard's Science of Drawing, being a Progressive Series of the Characteristic Forms of Nature. Part One: Trees* (London: William Pickering, 1839)

Hüet-Villiers, François, *Rudiments and Characters of Trees, Drawn and Engraved* (London: R. Ackermann, 1806)

Hunt, William Holman, *Pre-Raphaelitism and the Pre-Raphaelite Brotherhood*, (London: Chapman and Hall Ltd, 1913, 2nd ed.)

Hutton, Ronald, *Blood and Mistletoe: The History of the Druids in Britain* (New Haven and London: Yale University Press, 2009)

James, N. D. G., *A History of English Forestry* (Oxford: Basil Blackwell, 1981, 1990)

James, Admiral Sir William , ed., *The Order of Release: The Story of John Ruskin, Effie Gray and John Everett Millais told for the first time in their unpublished letters* (London: John Murray, 1947)

Jones, Kimberly, *In the Forest of Fontainebleau: Painters and Photographers from Corot to Monet* (Washington: National Gallery of Art, 2008)

Kennion, Edward, *An Essay on Trees in Landscape; or, an attempt to shew the propriety and importance of characteristic expression in this art, and the means of producing it: with examples* (London: T. Bensley, 1815)

Knight, Richard Payne, *The Landscape, a didactic poem* (London: W. Bulmer & Co, 1794)

Laporte, J., *Characters of Trees, drawn and engraved by J. Laporte* (London: John P. Thompson, 1800)

Lauder, Sir Thomas Dick, Bart, ed., *Remarks on Forest Scenery, and other woodland views, by the late William Gilpin, A. M. edited by Sir Thomas Dick Lauder, Bart* (Edinburgh: Fraser & Co; London: Smith, Elder & Co; Dublin: W. Curry, jun. & Co, 1834)

Law, Ernest, *The Chesnut Avenue, Bushy Park, Hampton Court, historically described and illustrated* (London: G. Bell and Sons Ltd, 1919)

Leach, Stephen, 'Good Melancholy Monsieur: Joseph Wright's Portrait of Sir Brooke Boothby', *British Art Journal,* Vol. 15, issue 1 (Autumn 2014), pp. 110-112

Leslie, Charles Robert, *Memoirs of the Life of John Constable, Esq., R. A., composed chiefly of his letters* (London: Longman, Brown, Green, and Longmans, 2nd ed., 1845)

Leslie, Charles Robert, RA, *A Hand-book for Young Painters* (London: John Murray, 1855)

Levi, Peter, *Edward Lear: A Biography* (London: Macmillan, 1995)

Lister, R., ed., *The Letters of Samuel Palmer* (Oxford: Clarendon Press, 1974)

Lister, R., *Catalogue Raisonné of the Works of Samuel Palmer* (Cambridge: Cambridge University Press, 1998)

Loudon, J. C., 'Directions for drawing Trees and Botanical Specimens from Nature, to any given scale, and more especially to the Scales adapted to the "Arboretum Britannicum"', *Gardener's Magazine*, XI, (1835), p. 401

Loudon, John Claudius, *Arboretum et Fructitem Britannicum, or, the Trees and Shrubs of Britain* (London: Longman, Orme, Brown, Green, and Longmans, 1838)

Lyles, Anne, ed., *Constable: The Great Landscapes* (London: Tate Publishing, 2006)

[M'Kewan, David Hall], *Lessons on Trees, in Water Colours, by M'Kewan* (Westminster: W. Dufour, 1860)

Mabey, Richard, *Flora Britannica* (London: Sinclair-Stevenson, 1996)

Mason, William, *The English Garden* (London: R. Horsfield, 1772)

Melville, Lewis, *The Life and Letters of William Beckford of Fonthill* (London: William Heinemann, 1910)

Menzies, William, *The History of Windsor Great Park and Windsor Forest. Illustrated with photographs by the Earl of Caithness and Mr Bembridge, of Windsor* (London: Longman, Green, Longman, Roberts, and Green, 1864)

Morris, David, *Thomas Hearne and his Landscape* (London: Reaktion Books, 1989)

Murphy, Ray, ed., *Edward Lear's Indian Journal: watercolours and extracts from the diary of Edward Lear (1873-1875)* (London: Jarrolds Publishers Ltd, 1953)

Myrone, Martin .ed., *John Martin: Apocalypse* (London: Tate Publishing, 2011)

[Mundy, Francis], *Needwood Forest* (Lichfield: John Jackson, 1776)

Newall, Christopher, et al, *John Ruskin, Artist and Observer* (Ottawa: National Gallery of Canada and London: Paul Holberton Publishing, 2014)

Noakes, Vivien, *Edward Lear 1812-1888* (London: Royal Academy, 1985)

Noakes, Vivien, ed., *Edward Lear, Selected Letters* (Oxford: Oxford University Press, 1990)

Noakes, Vivien, *Edward Lear: The Life of a Wanderer*, rev. ed., (Stroud: Sutton Publishing, 2006)

Oppé, A. P., ed., 'Memoirs of Thomas Jones', *Walpole Society* XXXII, 1946-48, pub. 1951, pp 1-143

Oppé, A. P., *Alexander and John Robert Cozens* (London: Adam and Charles Black, 1952)

Payne, Christiana, *John Brett, Pre-Raphaelite Landscape Painter* (New Haven and London: Yale University Press, 2010)

Payne, Christiana, 'John Constable, John Ruskin, and the Pre-Raphaelites', *British Art Journal*, Vol. XVI no 1 (Summer 2015), pp. 78-87

Postle, Martin, ed., *Johann Zoffany, RA: Society Observed* (New Haven and London: Yale University Press, 2011)

[Pott, Joseph Holden], An *Essay on Landscape Painting, with remarks general and critical, on the different schools and masters, ancient or modern* (London: J. Johnson, 1782)

Price, Uvedale, *Essays on the Picturesque* (London, J. Mawman, 1810)

Quilley, Geoff, and John Bonehill, eds., *William Hodges 1744–1797: The Art of Exploration* (New Haven and London: Yale University Press, 2004)

Rackham, Oliver, *Trees and Woodland in the British Landscape: The Complete History of Britain's Trees, Woodlands and Hedgerows* (first published 1976; London: Phoenix Press, 4th impression, 2004)

Rackham, Oliver, *Ancient Woodland: Its History, Vegetation and Use in England* (London: Edward Arnold Ltd, 1980)

Redgrave, R. and S., *A Century of Painters of the English School* (London: Smith, Elder & Co, 1865)

Reynolds, Graham, *The Later Paintings and Drawings of John Constable* (New Haven and London: Yale University Press, 1984)

Reynolds, Graham, *The Early Paintings and Drawings of John Constable* (New Haven and London: Yale University Press, 1996)

Roberts, Leonard, with Stephen Wildman, *Arthur Hughes: His Life and Works* (London: Antique Collectors' Club, 1997)

Rooke, Hayman, Esq., F.S.A., *Descriptions and Sketches of some Remarkable Oaks in the Park at Welbeck, in the County of Nottingham, a Seat of His Grace the Duke of Portland* (London: J. Nichols, 1790)

Rosenfeld, Jason, and Alison Smith, *Millais* (London: Tate Publishing, 2007)

Rosenthal, Michael, Christiana Payne and Scott Wilcox, eds., *Prospects for the Nation: Recent Essays in British Landscape, 1750-1880* (New Haven and London: Yale University Press, 1996)

Rosenthal, Michael, and Martin Myrone, eds., *Gainsborough* (London: Tate Publishing, 2002)

Sandby, William, *Thomas and Paul Sandby, Royal Academicians* (London: Seeley & Co Ltd, 1892)

Schama, Simon, *Landscape and Memory* (London: Fontana Press, 1996)

Shellim, Maurice, *Oil Paintings of India and the East by Thomas Daniell RA (1749-1840) and William Daniell RA (1769-1837)* (London: Inchcape & Co Ltd in conjunction with Spink & Son Ltd, 1979)

Sinclair, George, *Useful and Ornamental Planting* (London: Baldwin and Cradock, 1832)

Sketches after English Landscape Painters, by L. Marvy, with short notices by W. M. Thackeray (London: David Bogue, 1851)

Sloan, Kim, *Alexander and John Robert Cozens: The Poetry of Landscape* (Yale University Press/ Art Gallery of Ontario, 1986)

Sloman, Susan, *Gainsborough in Bath* (New Haven and London: Yale University Press, 2002)

Smith, Elise, '"The Aged Pollard's Shade": Gainsborough's *Landscape with Woodcutter and Milkmaid*', *Eighteenth-century Studies*, vol 41, no 1 (2007), pp. 17-39

Smith, John Thomas, *Nollekens and his Times* (London: Henry Colburn, 1828)

Smith, John Thomas, *A Book for a Rainy Day, or, Recollections of the events of the last sixty-six years* (London: Richard Bentley, 1845)

Stafford, Fiona, *The Long, Long Life of Trees* (New Haven and London: Yale University Press, 2016)

Staley, Allen, *The Pre-Raphaelite Landscape*, 2nd edition (New Haven and London: Yale University Press, 2001)

Staley, Allen, and Christopher Newall, *Pre-Raphaelite Vision: Truth to Nature* (London: Tate Publishing, 2004)

Stroud, Dorothy, *Capability Brown* (London: Faber & Faber, 1975)

Strutt, Jacob George, *Sylva Britannica; or, Portraits of Forest Trees, distinguished for their Antiquity, Magnitude, or Beauty. Drawn from nature and etched by Jacob George Strutt* (London: J. G. Strutt and Colnaghi and Co, 1822)

Strutt, Jacob George, 'The principal Forest Trees of Europe, considered as Elements of Landscape', *Magazine of Natural History*, Vol I (1829), Part II, September 1828, pp. 244-5

Strutt, Jacob George, *Deliciae Sylvarum: or, grand and romantic Forest Scenery in England and Scotland* (London: 1828)

Surtees, Virginia, ed., *The Diaries of George Price Boyce* (London: Old Water Colour Society, 1980)

Thomas, Keith, *Man and the Natural World. Changing Attitudes in England, 1500-1800* (London: Allen Lane, 1983)

Towneley, Houghton, *English Woodlands and their Story* (London: Methuen & Co Ltd, 1910)

Twining, Henry, Esq., *On the Elements of Picturesque Scenery, considered with reference to landscape painting* (London: printed for private distribution by George Barclay, 1846)

von Erffa, Helmut, and Allen Staley, *The Paintings of Benjamin West* (New Haven and London: Yale University Press, 1986)

Vaughan, William, et al, *Samuel Palmer 1805-1881: Vision and Landscape* (London: British Museum, 2005)

Vaughan, William, *Samuel Palmer. Shadows on the Wall* (New Haven and London, 2015)

Walpole, Horace, *On Modern Gardening* (London: Brentham Press, 1975)

Ward, Colin, *Cotters and Squatters: Housing's Hidden History* (Nottingham: Five Leaves, 2002)

Watkins, Charles, ed., *European Woods and Forests: Studies in Cultural History* (Wallingford and New York: CAB International, 1998)

Wheeler, Michael, *Heaven, Hell and the Victorians* (London: Cambridge University Press, 1994)

Whiting, Frederick A., 'The Pine Tree of Monte Mario', *Country Life*, 2 April 1976, pp. 1055-6

Wilcox, Scott, and Christopher Newall, *Victorian Landscape Watercolors* (New York: Hudson Hills Press, in association with the Yale Center for British Art, 1992)

Wilcox, Scott , *Edward Lear and the Art of Travel* (New Haven: Yale Center for British Art, 2000)

Wilton, Andrew, *The Life and Work of J. M. W. Turner* (London: Academy Editions, 1979)

Witt, John, *William Henry Hunt (1790-1864). Life and Work, with a Catalogue* (London: Barrie and Jenkins, 1982)

Wohlleben, Peter, *The Hidden Life of Trees: What they Feel, How they Communicate* (Vancouver: Greystone Books Ltd, 2016)

Woodall, Mary, ed., *The Letters of Thomas Gainsborough*, rev. ed. (Bradford: Cupid Press, 1963)

Young, Miss S. A., *Studies of Trees, with and without Foliage* (Edinburgh: Abram Thomson; London: Longman & Co; Glasgow: John Reid & Co; Dublin: John Cumming, 1834)

Index